# EURIPIDES

Little is known of the life of Euripides. He was born about 485 B.C. on the island of Salamis and may have begun his career as a painter before turning to writing. In the drama competitions of 455 B.C. he won his first chorus (a preliminary event) but lost the final competition for tragedies. During his lifetime his plays were often produced, but he won the Athenian drama prize only four times. He died in 406 B.C.; some (rather dubious) sources reported that he was accidentally attacked and killed by the king's hunting dogs while walking in the woods in Macedonia.

Euripides was a prolific writer, the author of some eighty-eight or more plays, of which nineteen have survived under his name. He was criticized by the conservatives of his time for introducing shabby heroes and immoral women into his plays, a practice that they considered degrading to the noble form of tragedy. However, audiences to whom his predecessors were cold and remote found Euripides direct and appealing. And he must have rnade a strong impression upon his fellow playwrights; such comic writers as Aristophanes went to great lengths to parody and ridicule his works and character. It is written in Greek accounts that Socrates rarely went to the theater but always attended a new play by Euripides. Upon hearing of his death, Sophocles, the aging genius of the stage in Euripides' day, paid his younger contemporary the honor of dressing his chorus in mourning.

Euripides became immensely popular after he died, and his influence altered drama forever. Considered by George Bernard Shaw to be the greatest of the Greek dramatists, Euripides is now regarded by many as the originator of the dramatic sensibility that developed into what we call "modern" European drama.

# Ten Plays
# by Euripides

Translated by Moses Hadas and
John McLean, with an Introduction by
Moses Hadas

BANTAM BOOKS
TORONTO · NEW YORK · LONDON · SYDNEY · AUCKLAND

EURIPIDES TEN PLAYS
*A Bantam Book*

PRINTING HISTORY
First Bantam publication October 1960
Bantam Classic edition / October 1981
2nd printing . . . August 1982
3rd printing . . January 1984
4th printing . . October 1985

ISBN 0-553-21219-2

Published simultaneously in the United States and Canada

Bantam Books are published by Bantam Books, Inc. Its
trademark, consisting of the words "Bantam Books" and
the portrayal of a rooster, is Registered in U.S. Patent and
Trademark Office and in other countries. Marca Registrada.
Bantam Books, Inc., 666 Fifth Avenue, New York, New York
10103.

PRINTED IN THE UNITED STATES OF AMERICA

O    12  11  10  9  8  7  6  5  4

# CONTENTS

———◆———

# Introduction

———◆———

## 1

EURIPIDES (approximately 485-406 B.C.) was the youngest of the great triad of Greek tragic poets; but so rapid was the efflorescence of tragedy that he was adult when Aeschylus was producing his greatest plays, and was himself survived by the nonagenarian Sophocles. Because the three were so close in time, because Greek literary art like Greek architecture tended to preserve forms once perfected, and most of all because the religious origins and associations of tragedy dictated at least formal adherence to traditional usages, there is a superficial sameness about the productions of all three. Their themes are drawn from the same body of myth, their dramatis personae are often identical, their stage conventions of actors and chorus, costume and scenery, are the same, and there is the same pattern of *episodes* of dialogue in iambic meter separated from one another by elaborate choral *stasima* in lyric meters. A near-sighted reader leafing through a volume of collected plays could not quickly identify their authors.

But the superficial similarities make the essential differences the more striking. Aeschylus and Sophocles have the remoteness as well as the grandeur of the classic; what they have to tell us is profound and momentous, but it belongs in an abstract realm not immediately relevant to ordinary experience. And in keeping with this remoteness their language too, in its stateliness as well as its lyricism, is at a far remove from the usual speech of ordinary men. Euripides, by contrast, is nearer our own end of the spectrum; once we acclimate ourselves to the special conventions which his theater demanded we can recognize that his premises and objectives and even his modes of expression are nearer our own world 'than are the Elizabethans. In his program and outlooks he is actually quite close to Ibsen and Shaw.

Even in his life and career Euripides stands apart from his environment. Aeschylus had been a soldier; the epitaph which he wrote for himself boasts of his prowess against the long-haired Persians and says nothing of his poetry. Sophocles held important public offices and was celebrated for his social gifts. Euripides seems to have remained isolated from his community. He is represented to us as a brooding and bookish recluse, born of a mother who peddled vegetables, unfortunate in two marriages, a misogynist, a misfit who moved to barbarian Macedonia at the end of his life and who was eventually torn to pieces by Molossian hounds for his general subversiveness.

That he was brooding and bookish is quite likely, and he may even have isolated himself in an underground library as he is alleged to have done. His unpopularity is indicated by his lack of success in the tragic competitions. Where Sophocles won many prizes Euripides is credited with only four, and some of these may have been for posthumous revivals. Even a masterpiece like the *Medea* took only a third. He was denigrated by the comic poets; several of Aristophanes' plays contain uncomplimentary allusions to Euripides' life and works and he is the principal butt of the *Frogs* and the *Thesmophoriazusae*. The removal to Macedonia is indeed an indication of discomfort in Athens; it is inconceivable that a Sophocles would take such a step.

But the gossip concerning his domestic life is clearly the product of calumny and is in part proven to be such by fragments of the third-century B.C. biography of Satyrus, recovered from papyri. The alleged misogyny, as anyone who reads the plays can see, is the reverse of the truth. In his sympathy for all the victims of society, including womankind, Euripides is unique not only among the tragic poets but among all the writers of Athens. If Euripides did not participate in the public life of Athens he was at least aware, on the evidence of his plays, not only of the intellectual but also of the political currents of his time. The *Andromache,* written early in the

Peloponnesian War, shows a loathing of Spartan arrogance and cruelty and deviousness. *The Trojan Women*, presented while the Syracusan expedition was in preparation and Athenian claims to moral superiority had been proven hollow, shows his utter disillusionment The retributive death is a palpable fiction Actually when news of Euripides' death reached Athens Sophocles dressed his chorus in mourning to pay homage to his insufficiently appreciated rival

Fuller vindication came in the generations following His plays continued to be applauded when those of Aeschylus and Sophocles had come to seem remote and irrelevant. It is no accident that whereas only seven each of the plays of these two have come down to us we have eighteen of Euripides, or if we count the doubtful *Rhesus* nineteen More important than the ampler survival of his own work is the fact that he, not Aristophanes, is the ancestor of New Comedy and hence of the main stream of European drama.

2

What makes it possible for us to regard Euripides as the ancestor of New Comedy, what makes his theater more accessible to us than Aeschylus' or Sophocles', is his descent from the heroic ideal to what may by contrast fairly be called the bourgeois. Dante justified calling his serious poem a comedy, in a letter to Can Grande della Scala, on the grounds that it moved from darkness to light and that, written in the vernacular, it was accessible even to the kind of people who congregate at the town pump. On these grounds many of Euripides' plays may similarly be called comedies. His language too approaches the colloquial; his plays tend to move from darkness to light. But most important, his personages do not invite tragedy in order to illustrate the operation of some grand ethical abstraction and to achieve heroism; theirs is the humbler aim of surviving as tolerably as may be amid conventional constraints which make tolerable existence difficult—not to die gloriously but to live happy ever after.

For achieving his end Euripides' regular strategy is a very simple one: retaining the old stories and the great names, as his theater required, he imagines his people as contemporaries subjected to contemporary kinds of pressures, and examines their motivations, conduct, and fate in the light of contemporary problems, usages and ideals. An incidental product of this approach is a critical deflation of the heroic outlook by something like a parody of the personages who are its vehicles. In the *Iphigenia at Aulis*, for example, Agamemnon and Menelaus are plainly pompous, ambitious, ineffectual politicians, Achilles a braggart soldier, Clytemnestra a middle class matron. The true heroine, whose selfless virtue makes the rest of the cast look tarnished and vulgar, is the simple Iphigenia.

But the main object of the new approach is to criticize the antiquated conventions of a constricting social order which hamper and oppress contemporary life. Plays like *Alcestis*, *Medea*, *Hippolytus* justify themselves amply as drama; but they acquire a new dimension of meaning if the reader is aware that in each the victim suffers from, and by implication criticizes, disabilities enjoined by current Athenian usages. The laws under which the audiences of these plays lived and which they presumably accepted without question denied basic human rights to women and foreigners and bastards, and the plays show the tragic consequences of this denial.

It is Euripides' *Electra* which affords our best illustration of the process and effects of subjecting a traditional myth to examination by contemporary rather than heroic norms, because in this one instance we have parallel versions of the story in the *Electra* of Sophocles and the *Choephoroe* of Aeschylus with which to compare it. The simple directness of Euripides' language and the relative realism of his action is an implicit criticism of the idealization of his predecessors, and the criticism becomes overt in the parody of Aeschylus' implausible recognition scene. But Euripides' object is not merely to offer a more realistic version of the well-worn myth. The great names are only a masquerade: what Euripides wishes to show is how the heroic deeds of legend look when carried out by contemporaries, what the people involved in such a story must be like, what the relevance of the story may be in terms of ordinary attitudes and behavior.

A startling innovation in decor announces these intentions at once. Instead of the customary temple or palace facade which tragedy regularly employed for its backdrop, we are shown a ramshackle hovel; and the first speaker is a tattered peasant. Electra is a self-pitying slattern obsessed with sex: it is a new thing for tragedy to be concerned with lack of proper cosmetics and a party dress. Orestes is a timorous young ruffian who acts and talks like the vagabond he is and who has come skulking into Argos by a back way. Clytemnestra is a well-meaning but wholly unimaginative suburban housewife. Aegisthus seems a decent sort whom it is hard to imagine as a villain or even a sinner. The murders are stripped of any heroic dignity and are merely sickening. Aegisthus is hewn down from behind while stooping for a religious ritual, by a man he had courteously invited to share in the ceremony and whom he had supplied with the cleaver. Clytemnestra is lured to her death by mother love: Electra had pretended she required her assistance with a newborn baby.

In the older versions the murders are softened by stylization and theology; they are part of the working out of a universal moral scheme and had been enjoined by irresistible divine authority. For Euripides the matricide is a completely unmitigated evil, and even the less heinous murder of Aegisthus is inexcusable, for the Argives are quite reconciled to the *coup d'état* which brought him to the throne and willing to let sleeping dogs lie. But Orestes is not so much a villain as a pitiful victim of a code long antiquated and now meaningless. To put the blame on Apollo is to make of him a monster too horrible to contemplate, and many critics have thought that it was part of Euripides' purpose to discredit belief in Apollo. Apollo does exist and his power cannot be questioned, but it is not a beneficent power and it is not responsible for the kinds of conduct for which men assume its authority. What Euripides discredits is not belief in the gods but the kind of belief which promotes such horrors as the *Electra* exhibits.

Other of Euripides' plays, and particularly those in which the Argive royal household—Agamemnon and Menelaus, Clytemnestra and Helen, Electra and Orestes—are involved, employ the technique which the *Electra* illustrates. What gives the family its distinction is of course the central role it played in the Trojan war, and at every possible turn Euripides underscores the monumental folly of that war. The most outspoken criticism of the war and of its frivolous cause is the *Trojan Women*. Here we see not only the utter ruin with which war afflicts the vanquished, but the utter demoralization which it visits upon the victors. When both have been demonstrated to the full we are shown the cause: in the midst of the scarred victims blackened by the smoke of their burned city and of the frightened victors there steps forth a bedizened and sensuous and indifferent Helen.

**3**

Because of his social criticism Euripides has been called a liberal and because of his attitude to the gods a rationalist. If by rationalist we mean disbeliever the term cannot apply to Euripides. In plays like *Hippolytus* or *Bacchants* the gods may be cruel and vindictive but they surely exist and they surely possess terrifying power. Nor is liberal the right label unless by liberal we mean one who is generally opposed to injustice and suffering. Actually Euripides' views on religion and society alike are expressions of a consistent philosophic outlook which the teachers called sophists maintained and promulgated and which brought upon them the hostility of such conservatives as Aristophanes and Plato.

The principle at issue rests upon a distinction drawn between *physis* ("nature") and *nomos* ("law" or "convention"). Those aspects of the world and society which are such by *nature* cannot be altered; man can only accommodate himself to them and make the best of them. But those aspects which are the product of *convention* were created by man for expediency's sake; when they are no longer expedient they not only may but should be altered. The gods belong to the same category as gravity or the weather; to attempt to explain their impingements upon the life of man is futile, for they operate by no human rationale. All that man can do is to be aware of the possibility of their impingement and take whatever precautionary measures are feasible. Even when he has done his best he may still be tripped up by forces beyond his control or calculation—and then we have tragedy.

But man himself needlessly adds to the tragic burden by treating aspects of his life which are in fact determined by convention as if they were determined by nature. Once upon a time the social code of the heroic age was useful and appropriate; to be controlled by it when it is no longer so results in such distortions of human values as we see in the *Electra*. Is the different value attached to man and woman, to Greek and barbarian, to freeman and slave, to the legitimate and the bastard, due to a difference in *physis* or in *nomos*? If it is due to a difference in physis then such tragedies as those of Alcestis and Medea, of Andromache and Hippolytus, are inevitable; but if these wrenchings of humanity are due only to convention they might have been avoided.

For the proper appreciation of these plays it is important

to realize that the conduct which they suggest may be reprehensible is the conduct which their audiences accepted as the correct norm. Admetus is not only a decent but an admirable man by conventional standards, as his punctilious insistence on entertaining Heracles shows. If his willingness to let his wife die for him seems to us monstrous, it would not have seemed so to his predominantly masculine Athenian audience. But a thoughtful spectator could hardly leave the theater without having his mind opened to the possibility that the assumption of masculine superiority is based mainly on smugness. The children of an alien mother were not, in Athenian law, entitled to privileges of citizenship; hence, Jason's repudiation of his barbarian wife and marriage with a Greek princess to ensure the future of Medea's children would seem correct and prudent behavior. It seems less so when Jason puts the masculine and Athenian justification of his behavior into words. He owes Medea no gratitude, he says, because women always must serve men. Moreover he gave more than he received because he brought Medea from lawless barbary to the superior atmosphere of law-abiding Greece. Only a very stupid audience could miss the irony. Medea's horrible murders are not condoned; but she would never have been driven to commit them if her rights as a human being had been recognized in the first place. Hippolytus, except for his abnormal loathing for love, is an admirable young man. He loathes love because that was the power which made him a bastard. If convention had not put bastards (who are in nature not different from other men) under disabilities, Hippolytus' mind need never have been twisted, and the tragedy need never have happened.

And so it is with other plays also. Tragedy is implicit in the nature of man as the sparks fly upward, but there is no reason why man should compound the sorrow by regarding his own conventions as laws of nature.

4

Nor is Euripides properly speaking a realist, though as compared with his predecessors he goes farther along the path towards realism than towards rationalism. Not only are the heroic figures of legend reduced to ordinary humanity plagued by the ills of contemporary society and sometimes dressed in tatters, but peasants and servants and even children appear on his stage. Yet his plays are not transcripts of life but artistic distillations in highly conventionalized forms. Verse was mandatory for all ancient drama, even for the more relaxed New Comedy of the next century and even for the Roman adaptations of it in the centuries following. Euripides accepts the convention not only of verse but of the equally artificial line-for-line dialogue (*stichomythia*) and formal long speeches (*rhesis*). But for his dramatis personae and their problems the richly embroidered grandeur of Aeschylus would be ludicrous, and Euripides' vocabulary and syntax as well as his imagery are virtually colloquial. He is the first Greek classic the student learns to read with confidence; Aeschylus is as difficult as Shakespeare is for a foreigner learning English.

But it is only the dialogue which is simple and straightforward; the choral portions use all the resources of lyric and their music and choreography appear to have required highly trained performers. Because of their different mode, Euripides' choral odes are more sharply set off from their contexts than his predecessors' and tend to become interludes to fill the intervals between acts. Sometimes their connection with the body of the play is tenuous and forced. In the *Electra*, for example, an elaborate description of the arms of Achilles is justified on the ground that it is wicked to murder a general who had a soldier so handsomely equipped in his army. In plays involving familiar characters and intrigue the chorus is indeed an awkward anachronism. It is hard to imagine fifteen women standing by while a mother murders her children. Frequently the chorus is begged to abet some deed of horror by keeping silent—which only underscores the implausibility. Once Euripides shows his irritation at the incubus: when the chorus of the *Orestes* explain that they have come to inquire after Orestes' health, they are told to go elsewhere to sing and dance and not disturb the invalid.

But Euripides makes skilful use of the incubus for providing a particular social background for characterization and action, and for receiving lessons on behalf of the community at large. Most plausible and most serviceable are the choruses of ordinary women attached to a heroine who report gossip they have overheard while washing clothes (as in *Medea*), or accompany their mistress on a pilgrimage and enjoy and describe the sights (as in *Ion*), or share their mistress' exile and nostalgia (as in *Iphigenia Among the Taurians*), or show their sympathy for a member of their sex in deep misfortune (as in *Andromache*). But even these typically "choric" functions tend to be transferred to the more economical Nurse and confidante, of whom Euripides makes such excellent use. The chorus whose odes are at once the most beautiful and the most essential to the play is that of the devotees of Dionysus in the *Bacchant*. Perhaps it was because this play was composed in Macedonia, where virtuosi choristers were not available, that Euripides here reverted to older modes.

## 5

The personages and the main outline of Euripides' plays were doubtless familiar to his audiences, for like his predecessors' they were for the most part concerned with

> *Presenting Thebes' or Pelops' line,*
> *Or the tale of Troy divine.*

But in the process of giving them greater contemporary relevance and interest, Euripides introduced and often mortised into the old stories intrigues involving love-stories, recognitions, adventurous travels, hair-breadth escapes, mostly drawn from folk motifs. To follow the novel and more complicated plots the audience would need to be apprised of locale, antecedent factors, and direction; this information Euripides supplies in his so-called "prologues." Actually all plays have prologues, for the term is properly defined as "that portion of a tragedy which precedes the entry of the chorus." What is peculiar to Euripides is his opening with a lengthy monologue which sets the stage for the action. Sometimes the monologue is delivered by a minor character, as in the brilliant example of *Medea*; sometimes it is "protatic," which is to say, delivered by a personage, frequently a deity, who has no direct part in the play.

More significant than Euripides' mode of opening a play is his characteristic mode of concluding it. Frequently a god appears "out of the machine" (a kind of crane which hoisted the actor representing the god to a point above the level and frequently out of the sight of the other actors), solves the complications left by the preceding action and supplies a happy ending. It was once the fashion to condemn this practice, for only a botcher could get his plot so involved as to require so illogical a solution.

But the botching was surely intentional, and meant to be disbelieved by at least the intelligent part of the audience.

In almost every case where some deity imposes a happy ending, the normal consequences of the action would be disaster. In *Iphigenia Among the Taurians* we are told that Thoas' troops control the narrow passage through which Orestes' boat must pass, and that a strong wind is blowing the wrong way. In *Medea* an angry mob bent on lynching Medea is at her door. In *Ion* Creusa can never escape the Delphian mob, and even if she should get safe back to Athens Ion would always hate and fear her. And in all these cases we are given grounds for doubting the miraculous solution. In *Ion* the freshness of the tokens allegedly exposed in Ion's infancy, particularly the verdant olive branch, is remarked upon. Medea's earlier appeal to King Aegeus of Athens for protection would make reasonable men doubt that she could command a chariot drawn by dragons. In *Iphigenia* it is doubtful whether Thoas would heed the Greek goddess, and as in the other plays the whole story has cast doubt on the benevolence of the gods.

It is not that Euripides means to ridicule the gods or even question their power. If they are measured by the norms of humanity, as the unenlightened in the audience would tend to measure them, they would indeed appear to be authors of evil. With other thinkers of the fifth-century enlightenment, Euripides conceived of gods and men as following disparate modes of behavior. What the gods do is beyond human control or even understanding; man must follow his own modes. The people in Euripides do and suffer as they do because they are the sort of people they are. If the palpably improbable endings of the plays are disregarded they would be not only more credible but more tragic and more meaningful. And if Euripides had been forced so to manipulate the action as to make the traditional or the happy ending its natural conclusion, he could not have made the human issues so clear-cut or the passions so violent.

It would appear, then, that Euripides is intentionally moving on two levels. It is no sop to conservatism when the gods out of the machine provide explanations (called "etiologies") for some traditional usage or institution. So much Euripides could accept; what he objects to is making the gods responsible for the motivations of men confronted by human crises. If you insist on the traditional or happy ending, he seems to be saying, here it is; but I shall make it as hard as I can for you to accept and I hope you will not. For a Medea to escape punishment is not truly a happy ending,

however much we may condemn society for warping her
character and making her violence inevitable.

6

If at his own conjuncture in the history of social and
religious thought Euripides exploited the god out of the
machine so effectively, his doing so made it impossible for
any successor to use the device except as a piece of archaism
or a jest. And so with the chorus, and so particularly with the
dramatis personae inherited from the heroic age. No serious
artist could again cultivate the old form, and the pensioners
of the Ptolemies who attempted it found no audiences. What
they and their successors produced were nothing more than
imitations, to be exhibited like specimens in a museum of
antiquities.

But the essential Euripides did have a progeny. Freed
from the constraints of the heroic names with their massive
and rigid associations, playwrights could create frankly contemporary characters and consequently invent plots to illustrate their interaction. So far New Comedy is the heir of
Old, for Old Comedy too (represented by Aristophanes)
was free to invent character and plot. But in its serious ob-
jective of examining the problems and motivations of
ordinary humanity, New Comedy, and all of European
drama which derived from it, descends not from Aristophanes'
farces but from the drama of Euripides.

Euripides' central innovation, which is reducing the heroic
to the contemporary, brings in its train other innovations
which connect him with New Comedy and modern drama.
There is, for example, a new concern with sexual passion,
which the older poets did not consider a sufficient motiva-
tion for tragedy. There is a new concern with intrigue and
suspense, surprise encounters and recognitions, and these
elements must have verisimilitude according to contemporary
standards. Most of all, there is concern for psychological understanding.

The images of the tragic personages which are accepted
as symbols in European literature were fixed by Euripides.
This is true not only of a Medea or Hippolytus, who do not
appear in the surviving work of Euripides' predecessors, but
even and especially of Electra and Orestes, who do. It is
through Euripides' lenses that we see these figures even in

Aeschylus and Sophocles. And even for these, Euripides' lenses may well be right; the point is that he was concerned with accurate psychological perception. His predecessors were not. Their personages tend to be types, almost mathematical symbols, to illustrate the operation of some universal principle, and the spectator sees them only frontally, at the point of conflict. Euripides shows us his characters in the round. We learn enough of their general attitudes and antecedents to see why they behave as they do, and they are firmly enough established as real persons for us to surmise how they might act in other encounters.

When psychological analysis is in question it is to be expected that a dramatist would show special interest in abnormal personalities; and here Euripides' delineations are true and illuminating. Often he provides a gauge for deviation by means of a foil who is normal—a nurse or a Pylades no longer mute. But it is in his treatment of abused and thwarted women that Euripides shows his keenest insights. It was his understanding of women, paradoxically, that gave him the reputation of being a misogynist.

7

For the modern reader whose access to Euripides must be through translations it is more natural, as it may be more profitable, to regard him as a pamphleteer rather than a poet. But he was a great poet and should be read as such; to present a poet in prose is to offer an inanimate instead of a pulsing organism. There are indeed fine verse translations of Euripides, but their merit depends on the individual poetic endowments of their translators, and a good translator does not and should not efface his own masterful personality. Verse translations therefore tend to be either grotesque or, if they are good poems, independent of Euripides. To study them may be illuminating, but it is not the study of a great poet working in a highly conventionalized and essentially alien tradition. To study poetic techniques, obviously, we must have before us the poet's own words.

But the substance of what he says we can apprehend in our own idiom. In the realm of human relationships, ideas, aspirations, the mature modern reader stands on the same ground as the ancient and is therefore competent to admire or deplore, to accept or reject, and most of all to have his own experience and perceptions enriched. To receive the enrichment which Euripides (not his interpreters) can offer, the glass through which we must look at him should be level and colorless—with no amber or purple tints of its own. Accordingly the present translators have aimed to make their version accurate and unadorned. Lyric passages, where language and imagery are more ornate, have been indicated as such by the use of italic type. Passages printed in italics are either choral odes or occasionally monodies to express some intense emotion; ordinary type represents the ordinary iambic meters used for the "spoken" portions. Within the choral passages, a long dash at the beginning of a line indicates a change of speaker. Square brackets indicate that competent editors have regarded the passage they enclose as an interpolation. Proper names supplied by the translators where the text refers to a personage by allusion are usually enclosed in parentheses.

# Alcestis

◆

ALCESTIS is our oldest surviving play of Euripides, but it is a mature work, for when it was produced (438 B.C.) he had already been writing for some seventeen years. We are told that Alcestis was the fourth play in a tetralogy, that is, it took the place of the usually ribald satyr play which customarily followed a series of three tragedies. This may explain the slightly burlesque tone of Heracles' drunken speech to the butler and his teasing Admetus at the end. But Alcestis is valid drama and characteristically Euripidean in its witty treatment of a sober theme.

Is it right for a man to let his wife die for him? Admetus, who is not only a decent but a superior man, as the approval of Apollo and his extraordinary courtesy to Heracles show, assumes without question that it is. We must remember that the audience was neither romantic nor feminist and shared Admetus' view. Actually Admetus' egotism is precisely like his father's, and his father's frankness shows the hollowness of Admetus' self-pity and indignation—as Admetus himself recognizes when he returns from the funeral. The audience too might realize that their assumptions need to be examined. The ending is happy only for those determined to have it so. Sensible people know, and Apollo has shown, that no one, and least of all the glutton we have seen, can wrest his victim from Death.

To appreciate the equivocations in Admetus' first conversa-

tion with Heracles the English reader should know that the
Greek words for "woman" and "wife" are identical, and
that the word "stranger," which Admetus applies to Alcestis,
means "unrelated by blood."

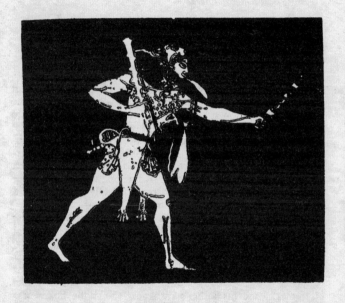

# ALCESTIS

## CHARACTERS

APOLLO
DEATH
CHORUS, *elders of Pherae*
HANDMAID
ALCESTIS, *wife of Admetus*
ADMETUS, *King of Pherae*

EUMELUS, *son of Admetus*
*and Alcestis*
HERACLES
PHERES, *father of Admetus*
BUTLER

*Guards, attendants, mourners*

The scene represents the palace of Admetus at Pherae.

Alcestis was acted in 438 B.C.

———◆———

[*Enter Apollo, gorgeously dressed, with bow and quiver.*]

APOLLO. House of Admetus, in which I condescended to put up with a slave's table, I a god! Zeus was the cause: he killed my son Asclepius by hurling the lightning into his breast, and I in my anger slew the Cyclopes who fashion Zeus' fire; for this has the father constrained me to do bond service to a mortal man.

I came to this land and tended cattle for my host, and I preserved his house to this day. In the son of Pheres I found a pious man, as I myself am pious, and I rescued him from death by tricking the Fates. These deities agreed that Admetus could escape Hades for the present by offering in exchange another body to the spirits below. He canvassed and solicited all his friends, his aged father and the mother who bore him, but he found no one except his wife willing for his sake to die and to forgo the light of day.

His wife is now moving about the house supported in his arms and is gasping her last, for upon this day it is fated for her to die and quit this life. I am leaving the friendly shelter of these halls lest the pollution of death come upon me within doors. Already I perceive Death hard by, the priest

of the dead who is ready to lead her down to the house of
Hades. Punctually does he arrive; he has been watching for
this day upon which she must die.

[*Enter Death, in a fearful and gloomy dress, with a
bare sword.*]

DEATH. Ha! Ha! What are you up to outside the palace,
why are you prowling about here, Phoebus? Are you at your
tricks again? Appropriating the dues of the powers below and
ending our perquisites? Was it not enough for you to prevent the death of Admetus by beguiling the Fates with a sly
trick? Now you have armed your hand with a bow to keep
guard also over this woman, this daughter of Pelias, who
saved her husband by undertaking to die for him herself.

APOLLO. Never fear. Justice and fair arguments are on my
side.

DEATH. What need of a bow if justice is on your side?

APOLLO. It is my habit to wear it always.

DEATH. Yes, and to give illegal aid to this house.

APOLLO. I am weighed down by the predicament of a
man that is my friend.

DEATH. Will you deprive me of this second body too?

APOLLO. I did not take that other from you by force.

DEATH. Why then is he upon the earth, and not below
ground?

APOLLO. Because he gave his wife as ransom, for whom
you are now come.

DEATH. Yes, and I shall drag her below, underneath the
earth.

APOLLO. Take her and go; I doubt if I can persuade
you——

DEATH. To kill whom I must? Why, that is my office.

APOLLO. Not so, but to cast death upon those that are ripe
for it.

DEATH. I understand your logic—and your zeal!

APOLLO. Is there any way, then, that Alcestis may reach
old age?

DEATH. There is not. Consider that I too take pleasure in
my prerogatives.

APOLLO. You would not be getting more than a single life.

DEATH. When the young die I gain the greater prize.

APOLLO. But if she die old she will be buried magnifi-
cently.

DEATH. Phoebus! You lay down your law in favor of the rich.

APOLLO. How do you mean? You a sophist too? Who would have thought it?

DEATH. Those who could, would buy the privilege of dying old.

APOLLO. Then you will not grant me this favor?

DEATH. No. You know my ways.

APOLLO. Yes, hateful to men and loathed by the gods.

DEATH. You cannot have everything which is not your due.

APOLLO. Yet will you forbear, exceedingly cruel though you are. A man will come to the house of Pheres, sent by Eurystheus to fetch a team of horses from the wintry regions of Thrace. He will be entertained in the house of Admetus, and will wrest this woman from you by force. Nor will you have any thanks from me; you will do this thing notwithstanding, and you will have my hate.

[*Exit Apollo.*]

DEATH. Talk on; it will do you no good. This woman shall descend to the house of Hades. I am advancing upon her to initiate my rites with the sword. Devoted to the nether gods is the head whose hair this weapon consecrates.

[*Exit Death into the palace. Enter Chorus.*]

CHORUS [*the mark at the beginning of a line indicates a change of speaker*].—What means this quiet before the halls?

—Why is the house of Admetus silent?

—No friend is near, none who might tell us whether we must mourn our queen as dead, or whether Pelias' child yet lives and looks upon this light, Alcestis, who has proven to us and to everyone that she is the noblest of wives.

—Does anyone hear a moaning, or a beating of hands in the house, or a wailing as if all were over?

—And yet none of the domestics stands before the house. Show thyself, O Healer, amid the billows of disaster!

—I'm sure they would not be silent if she were dead.

—She is already a corpse.

—At any rate, she is not yet gone forth from the house.

—How do you know? I am not sure. What gives you hope?

—How would Admetus have denied a cortege to his noble wife?

*—I do not see before the doors the pitcher of fountain water which is customary at the doors of the departed.*

*—Nor is there shorn hair in the vestibule such as falls in sorrow for the dead, nor the noise of the hands of young women.*

*—Yet this is the fated day—*

*—What is this you say?*

*—On which she is doomed to go below the earth.*

*—You have touched my soul, you have touched my heart.*

*—When the noble are afflicted, loyalty tried and true must grieve.*

*—No spot on earth is there, neither in Lycia nor in the waterless seats of Ammon, where a pilgrim's voyage might redeem this hapless life. Sheer fate is nigh, and I know not to whom I should go of them that sacrifice sheep at the altars of the gods.*

*—If only Phoebus' son (Asclepius) were alive and looked upon this light, then could she leave the shrouded abode and the gates of Hades and come to us; for he used to quicken even the dead before the Zeus-hurled bolt of lightning fire destroyed him. But now what hope of her life can I yet hold?*

*—All the rites have been accomplished by the king, upon the altars of all the gods do blood-dripping sacrifices abound. There is no remedy for these evils.*

[*Enter Handmaid, weeping.*]

LEADER. But here comes one of the attendants, all in tears. What fortune shall I hear? [*To Handmaid*] To grieve if anything befalls our masters is pardonable. But we should like to know whether the lady is still in life or whether she has perished.

HANDMAID. You may call her both living and dead.

LEADER. How can the same person be dead and still see the light?

HANDMAID. She is already drooping and breathing her last.

LEADER. Ah, unfortunate! Such a man, to lose such a wife!

HANDMAID. My master does not realize this; he has not yet felt it.

LEADER. Is there no longer hope of saving her life?

HANDMAID. No, for this is the day, and destiny is strong.

LEADER. Is everything requisite being done for her?

HANDMAID. The adornments with which her husband will bury her are ready.

LEADER. Let her know that she dies glorious, the best woman under the sun by far.

HANDMAID. Certainly the best. Who would gainsay it? What must the woman be who would surpass her? How could any woman demonstrate greater regard for her husband than by consenting to die for him? But this all the city knows, You will marvel when you hear what she did within the house. When she realized that the destined day had come she washed her white body with river water, and chose garments and ornaments from her cedar chests and adorned herself becomingly, and then she stood before the hearth and prayed: "Lady, I am going below earth, and for the last time I kneel before you. I beseech you, care for my orphan children: join to my son a loving wife, to my daughter a noble husband. Let not my children perish untimely like their mother, but with good fortune let them round out a happy life in their own country."

All the altars in the house of Admetus did she approach, and she crowned them and offered prayer, plucking sprigs of myrtle from the branches; she uttered no cry or groan, and the approaching evil did not alter the comely appearance of her person. Then she flew into her chamber and up to her bed. There she wept and spoke as follows: "O couch where I loosed my maiden zone by the hand of him for whom I die, farewell. I do not hate you. You have destroyed me alone. It is because I dread to betray you and my husband that I die. Some other woman will possess you, no more chaste, perhaps more fortunate."

She fell upon it and kissed it, and all the bedding was moistened with the tears that suffused her eyes. And when she has had her fill of weeping she flings herself forth from the bed and departs downcast. Often she makes to quit the chamber, and often she turns back, and again throws herself upon the bed.

Her children were hanging from their mother's dress and weeping, and she took them into her arms and fondled first one and then the other, as being on the point of death. All the servants throughout the house wept in pity for their mistress. But she extended her right hand to each one, and there was none so humble but that she addressed him and heard his reply.

Such are Admetus' evils within the house. If he had died he would have perished, but now that he has escaped he has such anguish as he will never forget.

LEADER. Admetus is surely groaning at this trouble, at having to lose his noble wife?

HANDMAID. Yes, he holds his dear wife in his arms and weeps, and beseeches her not to forsake him, asking what is impossible; for she is wasting away and sinking in her malady. Feeble as she is, a sad burden in his hand, still with the little breath that she has she desires to look upon the rays of the sun, for she never again will see it. This is the last time.

But I shall go and announce your presence. Not everyone is so well disposed to his lords as to stand by them in their troubles. But you have been friendly to my master from of old.

[*Exit Handmaid.*]

CHORUS. *O Zeus can there be any deliverance at all from these evils, any solution for the fortune which hovers over our lords?*

*—Ah me! Ah me! Is there any? Or shall I shear my hair and clothe me now in a habit of black raiment?*

*—Plain it is, my friends, too plain. Yet let us pray to the gods, for very great is their power.*

*—O Lord Healer, contrive some device for Admetus' evils!*

*—Grant it, yea grant it! Aforetime did you contrive it: be now too a deliverer from death; hold back bloody Hades!*

*—Alas! How you have suffered, O son of Pheres, bereft of your wife!*

*—Alack! This is enough to provoke self slaughter, more than enough to put one's neck in a hanging noose.*

*—Not a dear wife, nay, but the dearest wife will you see dead this day.*

*—Look, look! She comes forth from the house, and her husband with her.*

*—Cry out, O land of Pheres, and groan, for the noblest of women; disease is wasting her down to Hades below earth.*

LEADER. *Never shall I declare that marriage brings more happiness than sorrow. My evidence is past experience and the observation of the present misfortunes of the king, who is bereft of his excellent wife and will henceforward live a life unlivable.*

[*The palace doors open; enter Alcestis supported in the arms of Admetus, Eumelus and his sister clinging to their mother, and servants who proceed to arrange a couch.*]

ALCESTIS. *Sun and light of day, heavenly eddies of fleeting clouds——*

ADMETUS. Look upon you and me, two unhappy creatures who have done nothing to the gods for which you should die.

ALCESTIS. *Earth and that high-roofed palace in my native Iolcus, with its bridal bed!*

ADMETUS. Rouse yourself, poor woman, do not desert me. Pray to the gods who are powerful to pity.

ALCESTIS. *I see the two-oared boat, I see it upon the lake. The ferryman of the dead has his hand upon the pole, Charon is already calling me: "Why do you linger? Hasten! You are delaying us." So is he hurrying me, brusquely.*

ADMETUS. Alas! This is a bitter voyage for me that you speak of. Ah, unhappy! What sufferings are ours!

ALCESTIS. *He is dragging me, someone is dragging me—do you not see?—to the court of the dead. Under his dark brows he is gazing at me; he has wings. It is Hades. What will you do? Let go of me! What a road, what a luckless road I am entering upon!*

ADMETUS. A pitiful road for your friends, but most of all for me and the children who share this sorrow.

ALCESTIS. *Let me go, let me go now, lay me down: my feet have no strength. Hades is near. Dark night is creeping over my eyes. Children, my children, your mother is dying, dying. Farewell, my children, and look long upon the light.*

ADMETUS. Ah me! It is a bitter word I hear, worse than any death to me. For heaven's sake, do not have the heart to abandon me, for the sake of these children whom you are making orphans, be brave! If you should die I would no longer exist: I am in your power, to live or not, for your love I adore.

ALCESTIS. Admetus, you see how it is with me. I want to declare my wishes before I die. I have honored you, and at the price of my life I have caused you to look upon this light. For your sake I die, though I could have survived and married any Thessalian I wished and lived in a house happy with kingship. But I was not willing to live separated from you, with my children orphaned, and I did not begrudge my youth, which I possessed and enjoyed. And yet he that begot you and she that bore you betrayed you, though they had come to a time of

life fitting for death, fitting to save their son and die glorious.
You were their only child, and they had no hope of getting
other children if you were dead. Then I should have lived, and
you too, the rest of our time, and you would not be groaning
at the loss of your wife, and would not have to bring up your
children motherless. But some god has caused these things to
work out this way. So be it. But do you remember to render
me gratitude for these things. I do not seek an equal return.
That is impossible, for nothing is so precious as life. What I
ask is only fair, as you yourself will admit.

These children you love no less than I, if you are right-
minded. Let them be masters of my house. Do not marry a
step-mother over these children, a woman who will love them
less than I, who will, out of envy, lay hands upon your children and mine. Do not do such a thing, I implore you. For a
step-mother that comes later hates the children that were
there before she came; she is no gentler than a viper. A boy
has his father as a tower of strength; but how, my daughter,
can you have a happy girlhood? How will you find your
father's wife? May she utter no disgraceful slander about you
and ruin your marriage hopes in the flower of your youth!
You will have no mother to deck you for your marriage, nor
be present to hearten you in your child-bearing, dear child,
when nothing is so kindly as a mother. I must die. This evil
is coming upon me, not to-morrow or the next day, but in a
moment they will be speaking of me as dead. Farewell and
be happy. For you, my husband, there remains the boast
that you have married a noble wife; and for you, my children, that you are sprung from a noble mother.

LEADER. Rest assured. I do not hesitate to speak on his behalf. He will do these things if he is in his right mind.

ADMETUS. These things shall be as you say; they shall, never
fear. Alive you were my only wife, and dead you alone will be
called mine. No Thessalian bride shall ever call me husband
in your place; there is no woman noble enough in birth or excellent enough in beauty. Of children I have enough. I pray
the gods that I may have some joy of them; of you I have
had little enough of joy. This grief I will carry not for a year
but as long as my life endures, dear wife, and I shall loathe
her who bore me, and I shall hate my father, for their love was
in words, not deeds, whereas you sacrificed what you loved
most as ransom for my life, and so saved me. Shall I not groan
when I lose such a partner as you are?

I shall put a stop to the revels and the convivial parties, to the garlands and song which used to fill my house. Never again shall I touch the lyre, nor will I raise my spirits to chant to the Libyan flute. You have taken away the delight of my life. Your figure's likeness counterfeited by a craftsman's cunning fingers shall be stretched out upon my bed. I shall fall upon it and clasp it in my arms and call your name and imagine that I hold my dear wife in my arms when I do not—a cold pleasure no doubt, yet so may I bale out the heavy load of my soul. Visit me in my dreams and gladden me. It is sweet to look upon friends even by night, even for the moment they are there.

If I possessed the tongue and the melody of Orpheus, to charm Demeter's Maid or her husband by my songs and deliver you from Hades, I would go down, and neither Pluto's hound nor spirit-guider Charon at his oar would stop me before I had set your life in the light above. But there wait for me till I die, and make ready our home, to dwell with me. In the same cedar coffin with you I shall bid these children to place me, to lay my body side by side with yours. Not even dead would I be apart from you, my only faithful love.

LEADER. Yea, and I too will share this bitter grief for her with you as friend with friend, for she is worthy of it.

ALCESTIS. Children, you have heard your father say that he would not marry another woman after me, that he would not dishonor me.

ADMETUS. Yes, and I say it now again, and I shall abide by it.

ALCESTIS. Upon these conditions then receive these children from my hand.

ADMETUS. I do receive them, a precious gift from a precious hand.

ALCESTIS. Be you now a mother to these children in my stead.

ADMETUS. That I must be, now they are bereft of you.

ALCESTIS. Children, I go below when I ought to live.

ADMETUS. Alas, what shall I do when I am left without you?

ALCESTIS. Time will soften your grief. The dead are nothing.

ADMETUS. Take me with you, by the gods, take me down below.

ALCESTIS. I am enough who die for you.

ADMETUS. O fate, what a wife you are robbing me of!

ALCESTIS. My eyes are dimmed and grow heavy.

ADMETUS. I am undone then, if you will really leave me, dear wife.

ALCESTIS. You may speak of me as dead, dead and gone.

ADMETUS. Lift up your face, do not forsake your children.

ALCESTIS. Not willingly, to be sure; but farewell, my children!

ADMETUS. Look at them, look!

ALCESTIS. I die.

ADMETUS. What are you doing? Are you leaving us?

ALCESTIS. Farewell.

ADMETUS. I am ruined, poor wretch.

LEADER. She is departed; the wife of Admetus is no more.

EUMELUS. *Ah me, for my lot. Mamma has gone below. She is no longer, father, under the sun. She has left me, poor mother, and orphaned my life. Look, look at her eyelids, at her arms stretched out. Hear me, O hear me, mother, I beg you. It is I, it is I, mother, that call you, your little bird falling upon your lips.*

ADMETUS. She doesn't hear, doesn't see. I and you two are smitten with a heavy calamity.

EUMELUS. *I am young, father, and all alone; I am forsaken by my dear mother. Woeful things have I suffered, and you, my own sister, have suffered with me. Profitless, father, profitless was your marriage; you did not attain the goal of old age with her, for she has perished before. Now you have gone, mother, our house is ruined.*

LEADER. Admetus, this calamity must be borne. You are not the first nor yet the last of mortals to lose a noble wife. Know that death is a debt we all must pay.

ADMETUS. I understand, and this trouble did not swoop down upon me unexpectedly. The thought of it had long been torturing me. But I will arrange the funeral for this body; do you assist. Remain and chant the paean to the implacable lord of Hell. All Thessalians over whom I hold sway: I bid you participate in the mourning for this woman with shorn hair and black attire. You who harness teams or single horses: cut the manes of their necks with steel. Let there be no sound of flutes or of the lyre throughout the city for twelve full months. Never shall I bury a body dearer or more generous to me than this. Worthy is she of my honor, for she alone has died in my stead.

*[Exeunt into house Admetus with children, and servants bearing the body of Alcestis.]*

CHORUS. *Daughter of Pelias, fare you well in the home of Hades, when you dwell in the sunless house. Let Hades the dark-haired god know, and the old man who sits at oar and rudder, the ferryman of the dead, that he has carried in his two-oared boat across the gulf of Acheron the noblest of women by far, by far.*

*Often will the servants of the Muses sing of you, celebrating your fame upon the seven-toned shell of the mountain tortoise and in chants unaccompanied by the lyre; in Sparta when the cycle of the seasons returns to the Carneian month, when the moon rides high throughout the night, and in Athens the brilliant and blessed. Such a theme for song have you left by your death for the singers of songs.*

*Would it were in my power, would I could row you back across the infernal river and return you to the light from the mansion of Hades, from the streams of Cocytus! For you alone, dear among women, had the hardihood to save your husband from Hades by giving your life in exchange. May the earth rest light upon you, dear lady. If ever your husband were to take to himself a new mate, surely then will he be hateful to me and to your children.*

*His mother would not hide her body in the ground for her son's sake, his aged father would not. Basely they lacked the courage to deliver him they had borne, though their hair was hoary. But you have died in the flower of your youth and have left the light. Had I but the luck to find a wife who would cleave to me like that—the type is rare—then without pain, certainly, would we abide together throughout life.*

*[The body is borne into the house, followed by Admetus and the children. Enter Heracles with lion skin and club.]*

HERACLES. Friends, countrymen of this land of Pherae, do I find Admetus at home?

LEADER. The son of Pheres is within the house, Heracles. But say, what need sends you to the land of the Thessalians, to come to this city of Pherae?

HERACLES. I am performing a certain task for Eurystheus of Tiryns.

LEADER. Where are you going? On what errand are you bound?

HERACLES. To fetch the four-horse team of Diomede of Thrace.

LEADER. However will you be able? You are not ignorant of his kind of hospitality?

HERACLES. I am. I have never gone to the land of the Bistones.

LEADER. It is not possible to become master of those horses unless you fight for them.

HERACLES. Neither is it possible for me to renounce my tasks.

LEADER. You will slay and return, or die and there remain.

HERACLES. This will not be the first such race that I have run.

LEADER. What will be your profit if you overcome their master?

HERACLES. I shall drive the horses off to the Tirynthian land.

LEADER. It is no easy matter to put the bit into their jaws.

HERACLES. Why not? Unless they breathe fire from their nostrils.

LEADER. It's not that. They tear men with their swift jaws.

HERACLES. Flesh is the food of mountain beasts, not of horses.

LEADER. You may see their cribs spattered with blood.

HERACLES. Whose son does their keeper boast that he is?

LEADER. Son of Ares, and lord of the all-golden Thracian shield.

HERACLES. This you describe is just another labor, part of my fate. Always is it hard and always uphill, if I must do battle with all the sons whom Ares begot. First, it was Lycaon, then Cycnus, and now I come to this third contest, to engage with those horses and their master. But there is none who will ever see Alcmena's offspring flinch at an enemy's hand.

LEADER. But look, the master of this land himself, Admetus, comes forth from the house.

[Enter Admetus, in mourning and with head shorn; servants follow.]

ADMETUS. Hail, child of Zeus, of the blood of Perseus.

HERACLES. Rejoice, Admetus, lord of the Thessalians.

ADMETUS. I wish I could. But I know you mean kindly.

HERACLES. Why do you appear with the shorn head of mourning?

ADMETUS. I am about to bury a dead body this day.

HERACLES. God avert evil from your children!

ADMETUS. The children I begot are alive in the house.

HERACLES. Your father is of a ripe old age, if it is he that is departed.

ADMETUS. He too is alive, and so is my mother, Heracles.

HERACLES. Your wife Alcestis isn't dead?

ADMETUS. I could tell a two-fold story about her.

HERACLES. What do you mean? Is she dead or alive?

ADMETUS. She is alive and she is not, and that is what grieves me.

HERACLES. I know as much as I did. Your words are obscure.

ADMETUS. Do you not know the fate which she is doomed to meet?

HERACLES. I know; she has agreed to die for you.

ADMETUS. How then is she still alive if she has acquiesced in this?

HERACLES. Oh that's it! Don't weep for her too early. Put it off till the time comes.

ADMETUS. He that is doomed is dead, and he that is dead no longer lives.

HERACLES. But to be and not to be are considered separate things.

ADMETUS. That is your judgment, Heracles; I think otherwise.

HERACLES. But why *are* you weeping? Who of your friends is dead?

ADMETUS. A woman, a woman we were lately speaking of.

HERACLES. A stranger, or some blood relation?

ADMETUS. A stranger, but a connection of my household.

HERACLES. How did she come to die in your house?

ADMETUS. Her father was dead, and she lived here as an orphan.

HERACLES. Ah, would I had found you, Admetus, free from sorrow.

ADMETUS. Why do you speak like that? What do you mean to do?

HERACLES. I shall move on to the hearth of another host.

ADMETUS. It cannot be, my lord; may so great a wrong not come to pass!

HERACLES. A guest that comes into a house of mourning is troublesome.

ADMETUS. The dead have died. Do go into the house.

HERACLES. It is shameful for guests to feast while the host weeps.

ADMETUS. The guest chambers to which we shall take you are in a separate wing.

HERACLES. Let me go, and I shall be infinitely grateful.

ADMETUS. It cannot be. You shall not go to another man's hearth. [To servant.] Take this gentleman to the guest rooms apart from the house and open them, and tell those in charge to provide plenty of food. [To other servants as Heracles moves off with his guide.] Shut the doors of the central court well. It is not seemly for guests that are feasting to hear groans or to be disturbed.

LEADER. What are you about? With such a calamity before you, Admetus, have you the heart to entertain guests? Why are you so foolish?

ADMETUS. But if I had driven from my house and from the city the guest that came to me, would you have praised me more? No; my misfortune would grow no smaller and I should only be the more inhospitable. Then would this new evil be added to the others, that my house should be called guest-hating. I myself find this man an excellent host whenever I go to the thirsty land of Argos.

LEADER. How could you hide the fate that is upon you when a man comes who was, as you called him yourself, a friend?

ADMETUS. He would never have been willing to enter my house if he had discovered a hint of my grief. To some, I suppose, I should appear foolish in doing such a thing, and they would not praise me. But my halls have not learnt how to repulse or dishonor guests.

[Exit into palace.]

CHORUS. *House of many guests, house of a hero, ever free: in you even Pythian Apollo of the goodly lyre deigned to dwell; in your pastures he condescended to become a herdsman, piping to your flocks shepherds' wedding songs upon the sloping hills.*

*For the joy of this minstrelsy the spotted lynxes fed with them; there came too the tawny troop of lions, forsaking the glen of Othrys. About thy cither, Phoebus, there danced the dappled fawn tripping with a dainty ankle out from amongst the pines of lofty foliage ravished by your gladdening melody.*

*That is how he owns a seat rich in flocks by the fair-flowing Boebian lake and sets as a boundary for the fields of his tilth and the spread of his plains the dusky depot of the horses of the sun, the clime of the Molossians; and unto the Aegean Sea, to the havenless shore of Pelion, does he hold sway.*

*And now again he has opened his house wide and received a guest, though with eyelids moist, bewailing within his palace the body of his dear wife, but lately dead. But such is the gentleman; even his errors are honorable. In nobility is all wisdom. I wonder, but in my soul abides the trust that the god-fearing man shall do well.*

[Enter Admetus followed by servants bearing the body of Alcestis upon a bier, and by others with various offerings. They set the bier down at the approach of Pheres.]

ADMETUS. Men of Pherae, it is kind of you to come. My attendants are now bearing aloft the corpse and all its appurtenances to the funeral pyre. Salute the departed as she goes forth upon her last journey, as custom requires.

LEADER. I see your father approaching with an old man's gait, and his henchmen bearing in their hands adornments for your wife, due offerings for the dead.

[Enter from the right Pheres, an old man, followed by attendants bearing offerings.]

PHERES. I come, my child, grieving with you in your afflictions. A noble and chaste wife have you lost—none will gainsay it. But such things must be borne, unfortunate though they be. Accept these ornaments, and let them go into the grave. It is right that we should honor her body, for she died to save your life, my son, and did not make me childless or suffer me to pine away in a sorrowful old age bereft of you. To the lives of all womankind has she brought great glory in daring this noble deed. [Extends hand toward body in formal salutation.] You who have preserved this man, who have raised us up when we were fallen, fare you well, and may it be well with you in the house of Hades. Such marriages are profitable to mankind, I declare, or to marry is not worth while.

ADMETUS. Not at my bidding do you come to this funeral, and I do not count your presence here as friendly. Those ornaments of yours she will never wear. Nothing of yours will she want for her burial. Then was the time for you to sympathize with me, when I was at the point of death. But you stood aloof and let another die, though she was young and you were old. And will you now weep over the corpse? Were you really the father of this body of mine? Did she really bear me who declares she did and is called my mother? Or was I fathered by a slave and put at your wife's breast secretly? You showed your character when it came to the test. I do not count myself your son. Truly, you surpass all men in cowardice; for at your age, when you had reached the end of life, you had not the will or the courage to die for your own child. You suffered this woman to do so, a stranger in blood. Her alone might I rightly regard as both mother and father.

And yet you might so honorably have striven in this trial by dying for your own son, for brief in any case was the span of life remaining to you, and you had had all the happiness a man may expect. You had spent your prime in kingship, and you had me for a son and heir of your house, so that you were not going to die childless and leave an orphaned house for strangers to plunder.

You cannot say that you left me to die because I had dishonored your old age, for I was most respectful toward you. And this is the thanks you give me, you and she that bore me! You had better lose no time in begetting children to care for your old age and to deck you out in death and to order the burial of your dead body. Never shall hands of mine bury you. I am dead as far as you are concerned. If I look upon the light because I have found another deliverer, I declare that I am that person's child and the loving guardian of that person's old age.

Falsely, it seems, do old men pray for death, complaining of age and tiresome length of life. When death comes near none wishes to die, and old age ceases to be a burden.

LEADER. Admetus, the trouble we have is enough. Stop; do not enrage your father.

PHERES. Boy, on whom do you suppose you are heaping your abuse? Some Lydian or Phrygian bought with your money? Don't you know that I am a Thessalian, the true born son of a Thessalian father, and a free man? You are too insolent; you have injured me by flinging boys' talk at me, and you will not get off with it.

I brought you into the world to be master of this house, and I raised you up; I am not obliged to die for you. I have received no such tradition from my ancestors that fathers should die for their children; it's not a Greek custom. For yourself were you born, for better or for worse. You got from me all you were entitled to. You rule many people, and I shall leave you broad acres of land; these same things I got from my father. How am I wronging you? Of what am I depriving you? Don't you die for my sake, and I shan't die for yours. You are glad to see the light: do you suppose your father isn't? Yes, I reckon the time to be spent below is long, and life is short, yet it is sweet. You fought shamelessly to save your life and you are alive because you eluded the lot that was fated for you and killed this woman. Then do you speak of my cowardice, you vilest of cowards, who are worsted by a woman, who died for the sake of a fine young felow like you?

You have discovered a clever method of living for ever if you will always persuade your current wife to die for you. Then will you insult your friends who will not do the same? You yourself are the coward. Hold your tongue. Remember, if you love your life, so does everyone else. If you speak evil of us you will hear much evil of yourself and that true.

LEADER. Too much evil has been spoken, now and before. Stop reviling your son, old man.

ADMETUS. Talk on, I have had my say. If it pains you to hear the truth you ought not to have done me wrong.

PHERES. If I had died for you it would have been a greater wrong.

ADMETUS. Is it the same thing for a man in his prime to die as for an old man?

PHERES. We have one life to live, not two.

ADMETUS. Live longer than Zeus, then!

PHERES. And aren't you burying this corpse instead of yourself?

ADMETUS. Proof of *your* cowardice, vile creature.

PHERES. But she didn't die at my hands: that you cannot say.

ADMETUS. Ah, may you sometime come to need my help!

PHERES. Do you curse your parents when you have suffered no wrong?

ADMETUS. I noticed you were in love with long life.

PHERES. Court many women so that more may die for you.

ADMETUS. *Yours* is this reproach, *you* were not willing to die.

PHERES. Precious is this god-given light, precious.

ADMETUS. Base is your spirit, and most unmanly.

PHERES. But you are not gloating over carrying an old man to his grave.

ADMETUS. Yet you will die, and ingloriously, when you die.

PHERES. Ill fame does not concern me when I am dead.

ADMETUS. Ah, how full of shamelessness is old age!

PHERES. *She* was not shameless; her you found foolish.

ADMETUS. Go away and let me bury my dead!

PHERES. I go. You murdered her, and you will bury her. But you will yet answer for it to her relatives. Surely Acastus is no longer a man if he does not avenge his sister's blood.

[*Exit with attendants, deliberately.*]

ADMETUS [*shouting after him*]. Begone, you and she that houses with you. Grow old childless, as you deserve, though your child is alive. Never will you come under the same roof with me. If it were necessary to renounce your paternal hearth through heralds I would do so.

But now let us move on—the evil which is before us must be borne—so that we may set this body upon its pyre.

CHORUS. *Woe, woe, unhappy for your hardihood, noble and best of women by far, farewell. Kindly may Hermes of the Dead and Hades receive you. If in that place too there is any advantage for the good may you partake of it, and take your seat beside the bride of Hades.*

[*Exeunt Admetus and cortege in procession. Enter Butler.*]

BUTLER. Many strangers who came to Admetus' house from all sorts of places have I known and waited on at table, but never have I received at this hearth a worse rascal than today's guest. In the first place, though he saw Master in mourning he came in and crossed the threshold without a scruple. Secondly, he had not the decency to accept whatever fare we happened to have, realizing our trouble, but if there was something we did not serve he hurried us on to serve it. He took in his hands the ivy cup and swilled the

neat juice of the dark grape until the wine's fire wrapped him
about and heated him. He crowned his head with branches
of myrtle and howled discordant tunes. Two strains could be
heard: he kept singing, caring nothing for Admetus' troubles,
and we servants bewailed our mistress. But we did not let the
guest see that our eyes were wet, for so had Admetus bidden
us. Now here I am at home, feasting this stranger, some
rascally thief or highwayman, but she is gone forth from
the house, and I did not follow the funeral or stretch my
hand out to lament my mistress, who was a mother to me and
to all the servants. She saved us from a thousand difficulties
by mollifying her husband's anger. Am I not right in loathing this stranger who has intruded on our troubles?

[*Enter Heracles, garlanded, goblet in hand, drunk.*]

HERACLES. You there, why that sober and anxious look?
A servant ought not to glower at a guest, but receive him
affably. You see a man here who is your master's comrade,
and you receive him with a morose and frowning look, making much of a trouble not your own. Come here and learn a
thing or two. Do you understand the nature of mortality? I
suppose you don't; how should you? But listen to me. All
men have to pay the debt of death, and there is not a mortal
who knows whether he is going to be alive on the morrow.
The outcome of things that depend on fortune cannot be
foreseen; they can neither be learnt nor discovered by any
art. Hearken to this and learn of me, cheer up, drink, reckon
the days yours as you live them; the rest belong to fortune.
Pay honor too to Cypris, most sweetest of goddesses to men;
she is a gracious deity. Let these other things go, and heed
my words—if I seem to you to be talking sense; I think I am.
Won't you then get rid of this inordinate grief? Come away
from the door there, bind your head with garlands, and drink
with me. I know well enough that the splash of the wine in
the cup will shift you from this dour, tight, moodiness. We
are only human, and our thoughts ought to be human. Life
for all you sober and frowning folk, if you take my opinion,
is not really life but a calamity.

BUTLER. I know all this. But our situation doesn't call for
revelry and mirth.

HERACLES. The woman who died was a stranger. Don't
grieve over-much. The masters of the house are alive.

BUTLER. What, alive? Don't you know the trouble of this house?

HERACLES. If your master didn't lie to me.

BUTLER. He is much too hospitable, much.

HERACLES. Ought I to suffer just because some stranger woman is dead?

BUTLER. A stranger she was, yes indeed, too much so!

HERACLES. There wasn't some trouble of which he didn't tell me?

BUTLER. Go in peace. *We* are involved in our masters' misfortune.

HERACLES. This talk does not sound like a stranger's woes!

BUTLER. Otherwise I should not have been annoyed when I saw you hilarious.

HERACLES. Have I been tricked by my host?

BUTLER. You did not come at a suitable time to be received in this house. We have been bereaved. You see that our clothing is deep mourning and that our hair is shorn.

HERACLES. Who has died? Is it one of the children—his old father?

BUTLER. The wife of Admetus has died, stranger.

HERACLES. What is it you say? And did he then entertain me?

BUTLER. He was ashamed to turn you away from his house.

HERACLES. Poor man, what a wife you have lost!

BUTLER. We are all ruined, not she alone.

HERACLES. I did notice something. I saw that his tears were flowing and his hair shorn and the look of his face; but he persuaded me, saying he was taking a stranger's corpse to its burial. Against my better feeling I entered these gates, and I was drinking in the house of a hospitable man while he was in such a state! And am I yet revelling with garlands on my head? [*Tears off garland, throws goblet down.*] And you— a calamity like this in the house, and you didn't tell me! Where is he burying her? Where shall I go to find him?

BUTLER. Straight along the road that leads to Larissa. Outside the city you will see a hewn tomb.

HERACLES. Heart much-enduring and hand of mine, show now the sort of son that Tirynthian Alcmena, Electryon's daughter, bore to Zeus. I must save the woman that is newly dead. I must establish Alcestis in this house again. I must render this gratitude to Admetus. I shall go and watch for Death, the gloomy-garbed lord of the dead; methinks I shall find him drinking the libations of the dead hard by the tomb.

If I rush upon him from ambush and seize him and pin him with the hoops of my arms, however much his sides heave, none can deliver him from my bone-crushing hold until he surrenders this woman to me. But if I miss this quarry and he come not to the bloody offering, I will betake me to the sunless mansions of Cora and her lord below, and I will make my request. I am certain I shall bring Alcestis up and place her in the hands of my host, who received me into his house and thrust me not away though he was smitten with a grievous calamity; noble as he is, he concealed it, and showed regard for me. Who of the Thessalians is more hospitable than this man? Who that dwells in Hellas? He shall not say it was a base man he showed kindness to, himself so noble.

[*Exit: the funeral procession with Admetus returns.*]

ADMETUS. *Ah, hateful is this homecoming, hateful the sight of these widowed halls. Alas for me, alas! Woe! Woe! Whither shall I go? Where stand? What shall I say? What not? Would I might perish! To a heavy doom did my mother bring me forth. I envy the dead, I yearn for them, in their houses I crave to dwell. I take no joy in looking upon the sunlight, or in treading the ground underfoot. Such a hostage has Death robbed me of and delivered to Hades!*

SOME OF CHORUS. *Go forward! Go forward! Step into the house!*

ADMETUS. *Alas! Alas!*

OTHERS. *Worthy of groans are your sufferings.*

ADMETUS. *Ah! Ah!*

OTHERS. *Through tortures have you passed, I know it well.*

ADMETUS. *Alack! Alack!*

OTHERS. *You are in no way helping her below.*

ADMETUS. *Woe is me! Woe is me!*

OTHERS. *Bitter it is never again to behold the face of your beloved wife.*

ADMETUS. *You have mentioned that which has bruised my soul. What greater evil can befall a man than to lose his faithful wife? Would I had never married, never lived with her in this house! I envy those mortals who do not marry, who have no children; their life is single, and its grief a burden within measure. But to have to look upon the sicknesses of children, or bridal beds devastated by death, is unendurable when it is possible to go through life childless and unwed.*

SOME OF CHORUS. *Fate, fate hard to wrestle against, has come upon you.*

ADMETUS. *Alas! Alas!*

OTHERS. *No bound have you set to your griefs.*

ADMETUS. *Ah! Ah!*

OTHERS. *Heavy are they to bear, and yet—*

ADMETUS. *Alack! Alack!*

OTHERS. *Bear up! You are not the first to lose—*

ADMETUS. *Woe is me. Woe is me!*

OTHERS. *A wife. Calamity has various faces and smites various mortals.*

ADMETUS. *Ah, the long sorrow and the grief for friends that are under the earth! Why did you prevent me from flinging myself into her hollowed grave, from lying dead with her who was so far the best? Then would Hades have had instead of one soul two, the most faithful that ever crossed the infernal lake together.*

CHORUS. *I have a certain kinsman whose only son, a young man worthy of lamentation, was taken from his house. Nevertheless he endured his misfortune with moderation, childless though he was, though his hair was turning hoary and he was far advanced in life.*

ADMETUS [*pauses at the doors of the palace*]. *Ah, my fine house! How can I enter you? How live in you, with my changed fortune? Ah me! Great is the change. Then with Pelian torches and with bridal songs did I enter in, holding the hand of my beloved wife. There followed a merry, shouting crowd, congratulating her that is dead and me, and acclaiming the union of gentle folk, both of noble descent. But now with wailing instead of hymeneals and with deep mourning instead of bright garments I am ushered into my deserted couch.*

CHORUS. *Your life was happy, you did not know what sorrow was, and then came this blow. But you have saved your life. Your wife has died, has left her love behind. Is this so strange? Many men has death separated from their wives.*

ADMETUS. Friends, I regard my wife's fate as happier than my own, though it might not seem to be so. Her no pain will ever touch again; she has surcease of many toils, and with glory. I, on the other hand, who ought not to have lived, have escaped destiny, but shall drag out a bitter life. Too late I realize it.

How can I bear to enter this house? Whom should I speak to, by whom should I be addressed, that I may find joy in going out? Whither shall I turn? The loneliness within will drive me out when I see my wife's bed empty, and the seats upon which she used to sit, and the floor all through the house unswept. The children will fall about my knees and weep for their mother, and the servants lament the gentle mistress they have lost.

Such are the things that will happen in the house. Abroad, marriages of Thessalians will drive me away, and their gatherings crowded with women. I shall not bear to look at the young women who were my wife's companions. Any man that happens to be unfriendly to me will say: "Look at the fellow who keeps alive so shamefully; he had not the courage to die, but gave in exchange the woman he married, in his cowardice, and escaped Hades. Do you call that a man? He hates his parents, though he himself was not willing to die." Such is the reputation I shall have, beside my other troubles. What have I to gain by living, friends, with a wretched reputation *and* a wretched life?

CHORUS. *I have surveyed the Muses and the heavens on high; of many doctrines have I laid hold, but I have found nothing mightier than Necessity. For it there is no remedy in the Thracian tablets which the word of Orpheus prescribed, nor among the drugs which Phoebus gave to the Asclepiads, dispensing medicines to suffering mortals.*

*This goddess alone has no altars or image to approach; she heeds no sacrifices. Reverend goddess, come not upon me more mightily than in time past. Your aid even Zeus must have to work his will. The iron of the Chalybes is less strong than you; in your rugged spirit is no respect of persons.*

*You, Admetus, this goddess has gripped in the inescapable bond of her arms. But be brave; never can you bring the dead up from below by weeping. Even the gods' offspring go down to the darkness of death. Dear was she when she was among us, dear will she be though dead. The noblest wife of them all did you join to your bed.*

*Not as a mound over the dead that have perished shall the tomb of your wife be accounted, but it shall be honored like the shrines of the divinities, an object of reverence for passers by. The traveller shall go up the winding path and say, "This woman once died for her husband; now she is a blessed divinity. Hail, lady revered, and grant us blessing!" Such are the salutations that shall greet her.*

LEADER. But here as it seems, Admetus, is Alcmena's son; he is coming toward your hearth.

*[Enter Heracles leading a veiled woman.]*

HERACLES. To a friend a man should speak freely,
Admetus, and not keep reproaches in his bosom in silence.
I thought that when I arrived in your hour of sorrow I
should be accounted a friend. But you did not tell me that
the body which you had to bury was your wife's. You entertained me in your house as if your mourning were for
some stranger's grief. And I crowned my head and poured
libations to the gods in this house of yours while it was in
sorrow. I blame you, yes, I blame you for this treatment. But
I do not wish to trouble you in your misfortune.

I shall tell you why I turned and came here again. Take
this woman and keep her for me until I kill the king of the
Bistones and come back with the Thracian horses. If I fare as
I hope I shan't—I pray I do come home again—I give this
woman to serve in your house. She came into my hands as
the result of hard work. I found certain men had arranged a
public contest, a proper toil for athletes. From there I bring
this woman, whom I received as a prize of victory. Those
who won the lighter contests had horses to lead off; those
who won the heavy events, boxing and wrestling, had cattle,
and with them went a woman. It was shameful for me to
neglect this honorable prize when I had happened on it. But
now, as I said, you must take care of this woman. She is not
stolen, but won by labor. Perhaps in time you too will
thank me.

ADMETUS. Not because I misjudged you, not because I was
ashamed, did I keep my poor wife's fate hidden. But it would
have been sorrow added to sorrow if you had gone on to the
house of some other host: I had enough trouble to weep for,
as it was.

I beg of you, my lord, if it is at all possible, bid this woman
stay with some other Thessalian who has not suffered as I
have; you have many friends among the Pheraeans. Do not
remind me of my sorrow. I should not be able to see her in
my house without weeping. Do not add a disease to my sickness—I am weighed down enough with my calamity.

Where could a young woman be cared for in my house? She
is young, as her dress and ornaments indicate. Shall she
live under the same roof with men? How can she remain pure
if she will be in the company of young men? It is not
easy, Heracles, to restrain a young man in his prime. I am

thinking of your interests. Shall I bring her into the chamber of her that is dead and keep her there? How can I bring this woman into *her* bed? I fear a two-fold reproach: some citizen may charge me with betraying my benefactress and falling upon the bed of another young woman; and she that is dead would not like it. She has deserved my respect, and I must be very prudent.

Know you, lady, whoever you are, that you have the same stature as Alcestis, and you resemble her in figure. Ah me! 'Fore the gods, take this woman out of my sight; do not press on my weakness! When I look at her I seem to be looking at my own wife. It confuses my heart; springs of tears gush forth from my eyes. Ah, wretch that I am, at last I have begun to taste the bitterness of my loss.

LEADER. I cannot call your lot happy, but the dispensation of heaven, however it strikes us, we must accept with fortitude.

HERACLES. Would I had the power to bring your wife from the abodes of the dead into the light, and bestow this kindness upon you!

ADMETUS. Well I know you have the will. But how can this be? It is not possible that the dead should come into the light.

HERACLES. Don't overdo it; bear your trouble decently.

ADMETUS. It is easier to advise someone else than to be firm when you are suffering.

HERACLES. What would be your advantage if you determine to keep groaning forever?

ADMETUS. I know that myself, but a sort of passion drives me frantic.

HERACLES. Loving a person that is dead makes for tears.

ADMETUS. She has ruined me, more than I can say.

HERACLES. You have lost a splendid wife; who will deny it?

ADMETUS. So splendid that I can no longer enjoy life.

HERACLES. Time will soften your trouble; now it is still fresh.

ADMETUS. Time will, if by time you mean death.

HERACLES. A woman, the desire for a new union, will put an end to your sorrow.

ADMETUS. Hush! What a thing to say! I did not expect that of you!

HERACLES. Why? Won't you marry? Will you keep a widowed bed?

ADMETUS. The woman who will lie with me does not exist.

HERACLES. You don't expect you are helping her that is dead in any way?

ADMETUS. Her I must honor wherever she is.

HERACLES. Splendid! Splendid! But you are liable to be called foolish.

ADMETUS. But know you will never call me bridegroom.

HERACLES. I admire your faithful love to your wife.

ADMETUS. May I die if I betray her, even if she is dead.

HERACLES. Receive this woman now into your noble house.

ADMETUS. Nay, I beseech you, by Zeus who begot you!

HERACLES. You will be making a mistake if you don't do this thing.

ADMETUS. And if I do my heart will be gnawed with sorrow.

HERACLES. Trust me; this favor may turn out to your advantage.

ADMETUS. Ah, would you had never won her in that contest!

HERACLES. But I did win, and now you share in my winning.

ADMETUS. I appreciate it; but let the woman leave this place!

HERACLES. She will go away if she must, but first consider whether she must.

ADMETUS. She must, unless it will make you angry with me.

HERACLES. I know what I am about; that is why I insist.

ADMETUS. Have it your way, then, but I am not pleased with what you are doing.

HERACLES. The time will come when you will thank me; only trust me.

ADMETUS [to attendants]. Bring this woman in, if she must be received in my house.

HERACLES. I would not hand this woman over to servants.

ADMETUS. Then do you yourself lead her into the house if you will.

HERACLES. I shall put her into *your* hands.

ADMETUS. I won't touch her. There's the house; she may enter.

HERACLES. To your right hand alone will I entrust her.

ADMETUS. My lord, you are forcing me to do this against my will.

HERACLES. Venture to put out your hand and touch the stranger.

ADMETUS [*stretching his hand, with head averted*]. I am putting it out—as if I were beheading the Gorgon.

HERACLES. Have you got her?

ADMETUS. I have, yes.

HERACLES. Keep her, then, and one day you will say that Zeus' son is a noble guest. [*Approaches Woman and raises her veil.*] Look at her and see whether she has any resemblance to your wife. Be happy and leave off your grief.

ADMETUS. Gods! What shall I say? A marvel beyond hope! Is this my wife I see? Really mine? Or is some mockery of delight from a god distracting me?

HERACLES. No; this is your own wife that you see.

ADMETUS. See that this isn't some phantom from the shades!

HERACLES. Don't make your guest out a necromancer.

ADMETUS. But am I looking at my own wife that I buried?

HERACLES. You are indeed. I don't wonder you distrust your luck.

ADMETUS. May I touch her, may I speak to her as my living wife?

HERACLES. Speak to her. You have all that you desired.

ADMETUS. Dearly beloved wife! Dear face and form! Beyond all hope I possess you. I thought I should never see you again.

HERACLES. You do possess her. May none of the gods be jealous.

ADMETUS. Noble son of greatest Zeus, be ever blessed! May the Father that begot you preserve you. You alone have raised my state. How did you restore her to the light from the shades?

HERACLES. I joined battle with the power that has charge of such matters.

ADMETUS. You say you fought this fight with death? Where?

HERACLES. At the tomb. I seized him from ambush with my hands.

ADMETUS. But why does she stand here speechless?

HERACLES. It is not permitted for you to hear her voice until her consecration to the powers below be removed and the third day come. But take her into the house. And in future, Admetus, show respect for guests, as is right. Farewell; I go to perform the labor that is before me for the king, the son of Sthenelus.

ADMETUS. Stay with us, and share our hearth.

HERACLES. I will, another time; now I must be getting on.

ADMETUS. Good luck go with you then, and a happy return.

*[Exit Heracles.]*

To all the citizens of my realm I ordain that dances be instituted for these happy events and that the altars be made to steam with atoning sacrifices of cattle. We have changed our state of life from its former condition for the better. I shall not deny that I am fortunate.

*[Exit to palace, holding Alcestis.]*

CHORUS. *Many are the forms of divine intervention; many things beyond expectation do the gods fulfil. That which was expected has not been accomplished; for that which was unexpected has god found the way. Such was the end of this story.*

*[Exeunt.]*

# Medea

◆

MEDEA is a masterly study of an intense woman's passion. Immoderate love has given way to immoderate hate, and lust for vengeance now overcomes love of children. The struggle in the heart of Medea and its refractions upon the other dramatis personae are in themselves convincing and illuminating enough to make great drama; but the role of Jason adds another dimension. Moderns can understand that a young noble abroad on a dangerous mission might have become involved with a passionate barbarian who saves his life and honor, and in later years, returned to conventional society, have grown weary of her erotic intensity. But for Euripides' audience Jason had a better case: the children of such a union possessed no civic rights, and Jason was in fact securing their future by marrying a Greek princess. But when he puts the unquestioned assumptions which justify his treatment of Medea into words—women in love must subordinate themselves, and residence in Greece outweighs the advantages of royalty elsewhere—then even a stupid audience might begin to question assumptions. That Euripides intended a social lesson is clear from Medea's first speech, which is a fine feminist harangue but not appropriate to her own situation.

Medea's conduct is by no means justified. Having done what she did she must be punished, but she need not have done it if convention had not justified brutality like Jason's.

And she will be punished; her escape from the mob bent on lynching her is made intentionally incredible. Surely a woman who has to beg the King of Athens for protection will not have a dragon-chariot at her disposal.

Among the subtler effects lost to the English reader is the sibilant quality of Medea's angry speeches. When she reproaches Jason, for example, she says *esosa se esosa hos isasi hosoi*—one long hiss.

# MEDEA

## CHARACTERS

| | |
|---|---|
| NURSE | JASON |
| CREON, *King of Corinth* | CHORUS, *Corinthian Women* |
| CHILDREN OF MEDEA | AEGEUS, *King of Athens* |
| MEDEA | MESSENGER |
| TUTOR | |

The scene represents the home of Medea at Corinth.

Medea was acted 431 B.C.

———◆———

*[Enter Nurse.]*

NURSE. How I wish that the ship Argo had never winged its way through the grey Clashing Rocks to the land of the Colchians! How I wish the pines had never been hewn down in the glens of Pelion, to put oars into the hands of the Heroes who went to fetch for Pelias the Golden Fleece! Then Medea my mistress would not have sailed to the towers of Iolcus, her heart pierced through and through with love for Jason, would not have prevailed on the daughters of Pelias to murder their father, would not now be dwelling here in Corinth with her husband and children. When she fled here she found favor with the citizens to whose land she had come and was herself a perfect partner in all things for Jason. (And therein lies a woman's best security, to avoid conflict with her husband.) But now there is nothing but enmity, a blight has come over their great love.

Jason has betrayed his own children and my mistress to sleep beside a royal bride, the daughter of Creon who rules this land, while Medea, luckless Medea, in her desolation invokes the promises he made, appeals to the pledges in which she put her deepest trust, and calls Heaven to witness the sorry recompense she has from Jason. Ever since she realized her husband's perfidy, she has been lying there prostrated, eating no food, her whole frame subdued to sorrow, wasting away

with incessant weeping. She has not lifted an eye nor ever
turned her face from the floor. The admonitions of her friends
she receives with unhearing ears, like a rock or a wave of the
sea. Only now and then she turns her white neck and talks to
herself, in sorrow, of her dear father and her country and the
home which she betrayed to come here with a husband who
now holds her in contempt. Now she knows, from bitter experience, how sad a thing it is to lose one's fatherland. She hates
her own children and has no pleasure at the sight of them. I
fear she may form some new and horrible resolve. For hers is
a dangerous mind, and she will not lie down to injury. I know
her and she frightens me [lest she make her way stealthily
into the palace where his couch is spread and drive a sharp
sword into his vitals or even kill both the King and the bridegroom and then incur some greater misfortune]. She is cunning. Whoever crosses swords with her will not find victory
easy, I tell you.

But here come the children, their playtime over. Little
thought have they of their mother's troubles. Children do not
like sad thoughts.

*[Enter Tutor, with boys.]*

TUTOR. Ancient household chattel of my mistress, why are
you standing here all alone at the gates, muttering darkly to
yourself? What makes Medea want you to leave her alone?

NURSE. Aged escort of Jason's children, when their master's
affairs go ill, good slaves find not only their misfortune but
also their heart's grief. My sorrow has now become so great
that a longing came over me to come out here and tell to earth
and sky the story of my mistress's woes.

TUTOR. What? Is the poor lady not yet through with weeping?

NURSE. I wish I had your optimism. Why, her sorrow is only
beginning, it's not yet at the turning point.

TUTOR. Poor foolish woman!—if one may speak thus of
one's masters. Little she knows of the latest ills!

NURSE. What's that, old man? Don't grudge me your news.

TUTOR. It's nothing at all. I'm sorry I even said what I said.

NURSE. Please, I beg of you, don't keep it from a fellow
slave. I'll keep it dark, if need be.

TUTOR. I had drawn near the checkerboards where the old
men sit, beside the sacred water of Pirene, and there, when
nobody thought I was listening, I heard somebody say that
Creon the ruler of this land was planning to expel these chil-

dren *and* their mother from Corinth. Whether the tale is true or not I do not know. I would wish it were not so.

NURSE. But will Jason ever allow his children to be so treated, even if he *is* at variance with their mother?

TUTOR. Old loves are weaker than new loves, and that man is no friend to this household.

NURSE. That's the end of us then, if we are to ship a second wave of trouble before we are rid of the first.

TUTOR. Meanwhile you keep quiet and don't say a word. This is no time for the mistress to be told.

NURSE. O children, do you hear what love your father bears you? Since he is my master, I do not wish him dead, but he is certainly proving the enemy of those he should love.

TUTOR. Like the rest of the world. Are you only now learning that every man loves himself more than his neighbor? [Some justly, others for profit, as] now for a new bride their father hates these children.

NURSE. Inside, children, inside. It will be all right. [*To the Tutor.*] And you keep them alone as much as you can, and don't let them near their mother when she's melancholy. I have already noticed her casting a baleful eye at them as if she would gladly do them mischief. She'll not recover from her rage, I know well, till the lightning of her fury has struck somebody to the ground. May it be enemies, not loved ones, that suffer!

MEDEA [*within.*] *Oh! my grief! the misery of it all! Why can I not die?*

NURSE. *What did I tell you, dear children? Your mother's heart is troubled, her anger is roused. Hurry indoors, quick. Keep out of her sight, don't go near her. Beware of her fierce manner, her implacable temper. Hers is a selfwilled nature. Go now, get you inside, be quick. Soon, it is clear, her sorrow like a gathering cloud will burst in a tempest of fury. What deed will she do then, that impetuous, indomitable heart, poisoned by injustice?*

[*Exeunt children with Tutor.*]

MEDEA [*within*]. *O misery! the things I have suffered, cause enough for deep lamentations! O you cursed sons of a hateful mother, a plague on you! And on your father! Ruin seize the whole household!*

NURSE. *Ah me, unhappy me! Why will you have your sons partake of their father's guilt? Why hate them? Ah children, your danger overwhelms me with anxiety. The souls of royalty are vindictive; they do not easily forget their resentment, possibly because being used to command they are seldom checked. It is better to be used to living among equals. For myself, at any rate, I ask not greatness but a safe old age. Moderation! Firstly, the very name of it is excellent; to practise it is easily the best thing for mortals. Excess avails to no good purpose for men, and if the gods are provoked, brings greater ruin on a house.*

[*Enter Chorus.*]

CHORUS. *I heard a voice, I heard a cry. It was the unhappy Colchian woman's. She is not yet calm. Pray tell us, old woman. From the court outside I heard her cries within. I do not rejoice, woman, in the griefs of this house. Dear, dear it is to me.*

NURSE. *It is a home no more; the life has gone out of it. Its master a princess' bed enthralls, while the mistress in her chamber is pining to death, and her friends have no words to comfort her heart.*

MEDEA [*within*]. *Oh! Would that a flaming bolt from Heaven might pierce my brain! What is the good of living any longer? O Misery! Let me give up this life I find so hateful. Let me seek lodging in the house of death.*

CHORUS. *O Zeus, O Earth, O Light, hear what a sad lament the hapless wife intones. What is this yearning, rash woman, after that fearful bed? Will you hasten to the end that is Death? Pray not for that. If your husband worships a new bride, it is a common event; be not exasperated. Zeus will support your cause. Do not let grief for a lost husband waste away your life.*

MEDEA [*within*]. *Great Zeus and Lady Themis, see you how I am treated, for all the strong oaths with which I bound my cursed husband? May I live to see him and his bride, palace and all, in one common destruction, for the wrongs that they inflict, unprovoked, on me! O father, O country, that I forsook so shamefully, killing my brother, my own!*

NURSE. *Hear what she says, how she cries out to Themis of Prayers and to Zeus whom mortals regard as the steward of oaths. With no small revenge will my mistress bate her rage.*

CHORUS. *I wish she would come into our presence and hear the sound of the words we would speak. Then she might forget the resentment in her heart and change her purpose. May my zeal be ever at the service of my friends. But bring her here, make her come forth from the palace. Tell her that here too are friends. Make haste before she does any harm to those within. Furious is the surge of such a sorrow.*

NURSE. *I shall do so, though I am not hopeful of persuading the mistress. But I freely present you with the gift of my labor. Yet she throws a baleful glare, like a lioness with cubs, at any servant who approaches her as if to speak. Blunderers and fools! that is the only proper name for the men of old who invented songs to bring the joy of life to feasts and banquets and festive boards, but never discovered a music of song or sounding lyre to dispel the weary sorrows of humanity, that bring death and fell havoc and destruction of homes. Yet what a boon to man, could these ills be cured by some! At sumptuous banquets why raise a useless strain? The food that is served and the satisfaction that comes to full men, that in itself is pleasure enough.*

[*Exit Nurse.*]

CHORUS. *I hear a cry of grief and deep sorrow. In piercing accents of misery she proclaims her woes, her ill-starred marriage and her love betrayed. The victim of grievous wrongs, she calls on the daughter of Zeus, even Themis, Lady of Vows, who led her through the night by difficult straits across the briny sea to Hellas.*

[*Enter Medea.*]

MEDEA. Women of Corinth, do not criticize me, I come forth from the palace. Well I know that snobbery is a common charge, that may be levelled against recluse and busy man alike. And the former, by their choice of a quiet life, acquire an extra stigma: they are deficient in energy and spirit. There is no justice in the eyes of men; a man who has never harmed them they may hate at sight, without ever knowing anything about his essential nature. An alien, to be sure, should adapt himself to the citizens with whom he lives. Even the citizen is to be condemned if he is too selfwilled or too uncouth to avoid offending his fellows. So I . . . but this unexpected blow which has befallen me has broken my heart.

It's all over, my friends; I would gladly die. Life has lost its savor. The man who was everything to me, well he knows it, has turned out to be the basest of men. Of all creatures that feel and think, we women are the unhappiest species. In the first place, we must pay a great dowry to a husband who will be the tyrant of our bodies (that's a further aggravation of the evil); and there is another fearful hazard: whether we shall get a good man or a bad. For separations bring disgrace on the woman and it is not possible to renounce one's husband. Then, landed among strange habits and regulations unheard of in her own home, a woman needs second sight to know how best to handle her bedmate. And if we manage this well and have a husband who does not find the yoke of intercourse too galling, ours is a life to be envied. Otherwise, one is better dead. When the man wearies of the company of his wife, he goes outdoors and relieves the disgust of his heart [having recourse to some friend or the companions of his own age], but we women have only one person to turn to.

They say that we have a safe life at home, whereas men must go to war. Nonsense! I had rather fight three battles than bear one child. But be that as it may, you and I are not in the same case. You have your city here, your paternal homes; you know the delights of life and association with your loved ones. But I, homeless and forsaken, carried off from a foreign land, am being wronged by a husband, with neither mother nor brother nor kinsman with whom I might find refuge from the storms of misfortune. One little boon I crave of you, if I discover any ways and means of punishing my husband for these wrongs: your silence. Woman in most respects is a timid creature, with no heart for strife and aghast at the sight of steel; but wronged in love, there is no heart more murderous than hers.

LEADER. Do as you say, Medea, for just will be your vengeance. I do not wonder that you bemoan your fate. But I see Creon coming, the ruler of this land, bringing tidings of new plans.

*[Enter Creon.]*

CREON. You there, Medea, looking black with rage against your husband; I have proclaimed that you are to be driven forth in exile from this land, you and your two sons. Immediately. I am the absolute judge of the case, and I shall not go back to my palace till I have cast you over the frontier of the land.

MEDEA. Ah! Destruction, double destruction is my unhappy lot. My enemies are letting out every sail and there is no harbor into which I may flee from the menace of their attack. But ill-treated and all, Creon, still I shall put the question to you: Why are you sending me out of the country?

CREON. I am afraid of you—there's no need to hide behind a cloak of words—afraid you will do my child some irreparable injury. There's plenty logic in that fear. You are a wizard possessed of evil knowledge. You are stung by the loss of your husband's love. And I have heard of your threats—they told me of them—to injure bridegroom and bride and father of the bride. Therefore before anything happens to me, I shall take precautions. Better for me now to be hateful in your eyes than to relent and rue it greatly later.

MEDEA. Alas! Alas! Often ere now—this is not the first time—my reputation has hurt me and done me grievous wrong. If a man's really shrewd, he ought never to have his children taught too much. For over and above a name for uselessness that it will earn them, they incur the hostility and envy of their fellow men. Offer clever reforms to dullards, and you will be thought a useless fool yourself. And the reputed wiseacres, feeling your superiority, will dislike you intensely. I myself have met this fate. Because I have skill, some are jealous of me, others think me unsociable. But my wisdom does not go very far. However, you are afraid you may suffer something unpleasant at my hands, aren't you? Fear not, Creon; it is not my way to commit my crimes against kings. What wrong have you done me? You have only bestowed your daughter on the suitor of your choice. No, it is my husband I hate. You, I dare say, knew what you were doing in the matter. And now I don't grudge success to your scheme. Make your match, and good luck to you. But allow me to stay in this country. Though foully used, I shall keep my peace, submitting to my masters.

CREON. Your words are comforting to hear, but inside my heart there is a horrible fear that you are plotting some mischief, which makes me trust you even less than before. The hot-tempered woman, like the hot-tempered man, is easier to guard against than the cunning and silent. But off with you at once, make no speeches. My resolve is fixed; for all your skill you will not stay amongst us to hate me.

MEDEA. Please no, I beseech you, by your knees, by the young bride . . .

CREON. You are wasting your words; you will never convince me.

MEDEA. Will you drive me out and have no respect for my prayers?

CREON. Yes, for I love you less than I love my own family.

MEDEA. O fatherland, how strongly do I now remember you!

CREON. Yes, apart from my children, that is *my* dearest love.

MEDEA. Alas! the loves of men are a mighty evil.

CREON. In my opinion, that depends on the circumstances.

MEDEA. O Zeus, do not forget the author of this wickedness.

CREON. On your way, vain woman, and end my troubles.

MEDEA. The troubles are mine, I have no lack of troubles.

CREON. In a moment you will be thrust out by the hands of servants.

MEDEA. No, no, not that. But Creon I entreat you. . . .

CREON. You seem to be bent on causing trouble, woman.

MEDEA. I shall go into exile. It is not *that* I beg you to grant me.

CREON. Why then are you clinging so violently to my hand?

MEDEA. Allow me to stay for this one day to complete my plans for departure and get together provision for my children, since their father prefers not to bother about his own sons. Have pity on them. You too are the father of children. It is natural that you should feel kindly. Stay or go, I care nothing for myself. It's them I weep for in their misfortune.

CREON. My mind is not tyrannical enough; mercy has often been my undoing. So now, though I know that it is a mistake, woman, you will have your request. But I give you warning: if to-morrow's divine sun sees you and your children inside the borders of this country, you die. True is the word I have spoken. [Stay, if you must, this one day. You'll not have time to do what I dread.]

[*Exit Creon.*]

CHORUS. *Hapless woman! overwhelmed by sorrow! Where will you turn? What stranger will afford you hospitality? God has steered you, Medea, into an unmanageable surge of troubles.*

MEDEA. Ill fortune's everywhere, who can gainsay it? But it is not yet as bad as that, never think so. There is still heavy weather ahead for the new bride and groom, and no little trouble for the maker of the match. Do you think I would ever have wheedled the king just now except to further my own plans? I would not even have spoken to him, nor touched him either. But he is such a fool that though he might have thwarted my plans by expelling me from the country he has allowed me to stay over for this one day, in which I shall make corpses of three of my enemies, father and daughter and my own husband.

My friends, I know several ways of causing their death, and I cannot decide which I should turn my hand to first. Shall I set fire to the bridal chamber or make my way in stealthily to where their bed is laid and drive a sword through their vitals? But there is one little difficulty. If I am caught entering the palace or devising my bonfire I shall be slain and my enemies shall laugh. Better take the direct way and the one for which I have the natural gift. Poison. Destroy them with poison. So be it.

But suppose them slain. What city will receive me? Whose hospitality will rescue me and afford me a land where I shall be safe from punishment, a home where I can live in security? It cannot be. I shall wait, therefore, a little longer and if any tower of safety shows up I shall carry out the murders in stealth and secrecy. However, if circumstances drive me to my wits' end, I shall take a sword in my own hands and face certain death to slay them. I shall not shirk the difficult adventure. No! by Queen Hecate who has her abode in the recesses of my hearth—her I revere above all gods and have chosen to assist me—never shall any one of them torture my heart with impunity. I shall make their marriage a torment and grief to them. Bitterly shall they rue the match they have made and the exile they inflict on me.

But enough! Medea, use all your wiles; plot and devise. Onward to the dreadful moment. Now is the test of courage. Do you see how you are being treated? It is not right that the seed of Sisyphus and Aeson should gloat over you, the daughter of a noble sire and descendant of the Sun. But you realize that. Moreover by our mere nature we women are helpless for good, but adept at contriving all manner of wickedness.

CHORUS. *Back to their sources flow the sacred rivers. The world and morality are turned upside-down. The hearts of men are treacherous; the sanctions of Heaven are undermined. The voice of time will change, and our glory will ring down the ages. Womankind will be honored. No longer will ill-sounding report attach to our sex.*

*The strains of ancient minstrelsy will cease, that hymned our faithlessness. Would that Phoebus, Lord of Song, had put into woman's heart the inspired song of the lyre. Then I would have sung a song in answer to the tribe of males.*

*History has much to tell of the relations of men with women.*

*You, Medea, in the mad passion of your heart sailed away from your father's home, threading your way through the twin rocks of the Euxine, to settle in a foreign land. Now, your bed empty, your lover lost, unhappy woman, you are being driven forth in dishonor into exile.*

*Gone is respect for oaths. Nowhere in all the breadth of Hellas is honor any more to be found; it has vanished into the clouds. Hapless one, you have no father's house to which you might fly for shelter from the gales of misfortune; and another woman, a princess, has charmed your husband away and stepped into your place.*

*[Enter Jason.]*

JASON. Often and often ere now I have observed that an intractable nature is a curse almost impossible to deal with. So with you. When you might have stayed on in this land and in this house by submitting quietly to the wishes of your superiors, your forward tongue has got you expelled from the country. Not that your abuse troubles *me* at all. Keep on saying that Jason is a villain of the deepest dye. But for your insolence to royalty consider yourself more than fortunate that you are only being punished by exile. I was constantly mollifying the angry monarch and expressing the wish that you be allowed to stay. But in unabated folly you keep on reviling the king. That is why you are to be expelled.

But still, despite everything, I come here now with unwearied goodwill, to contrive on your behalf, Madam, that you and the children will not leave this country lacking money or anything else. Exile brings many hardships in its wake. And even if you do hate me, I could never think cruelly of you.

MEDEA. Rotten, heart-rotten, that is the word for you. Words, words, magnificent words. In reality a craven. You come to me, you come, my worst enemy! This isn't bravery, you know, this isn't valor, to come and face your victims. No! it's the ugliest sore on the face of humanity, Shamelessness. But I thank you for coming. It will lighten the weight on my heart to tell your wickedness, and it will hurt you to hear it. I shall begin my tale at the very beginning.

I saved your life, as all know who embarked with you on the Argo, when you were sent to master with the yoke the fire-breathing bulls and to sow with dragon's teeth that acre of death. The dragon, too, with wreathed coils, that kept safe watch over the Golden Fleece and never slept—I slew it and raised for you the light of life again. Then, forsaking my father and my own dear ones, I came to Iolcus where Pelias reigned, came with you, more than fond and less than wise. On Pelias too I brought death, the most painful death there is, at the hands of his own children. Thus I have removed every danger from your path.

And after all those benefits at my hands, you basest of men, you have betrayed me and made a new marriage, though I have borne you children. If you were still childless, I could have understood this love of yours for a new wife. Gone now is all reliance on pledges. You puzzle me. Do you believe that the gods of the old days are no longer in office? Do you think that men are now living under a new dispensation? For surely you know that you have broken all your oaths to me. Ah my hand, which you so often grasped, and oh my knees, how all for nothing have we been defiled by this false man, who has disappointed all our hopes.

But come, I shall confide in you as though you were my friend, not that I expect to receive any benefit from you. But let that go. My questions will serve to underline your infamy. As things are now, where am I to turn? Home to my father? But when I came here with you, I betrayed my home and my country. To the wretched daughters of Pelias? They would surely give me a royal welcome to their home; I only murdered their father. For it is how it is. My loved ones at home have learned to hate me; the others, whom I need not have harmed, I have made my enemies to oblige you. And so in return for these services you have made me envied among the women of Hellas! A wonderful, faithful husband I have in you, if I must be expelled from the country into exile, deserted by my friends, alone with my friendless children! A fine story to tell of the new bridegroom, that his children and the woman who saved his life are wandering about in aimless beggary! O Zeus, why O why have you given to mortals sure means of knowing gold from tinsel, yet men's exteriors show no mark by which to descry the rotten heart?

LEADER. Horrible and hard to heal is the anger of friend at strife with friend.

JASON. It looks as if I need no small skill in speech if, like a skilful steersman riding the storm with close-reefed sheets, I am to escape the howling gale of your verbosity, woman. Well, since you are making a mountain out of the favors you

have done me. I'll tell *you* what *I* think. It was the goddess of
Love and none other, mortal or immortal, who delivered me
from the dangers of my quest. You have indeed much sub-
tlety of wit, but it would be an invidious story to go into,
how the inescapable shafts of Love compelled you to save my
life. Still, I shall not put too fine a point on it. If you helped
me in some way or other, good and well. But as I shall
demonstrate, in the matter of my rescue you got more than
you gave.

In the first place, you have your home in Greece, instead of
in a barbarian land. You have learned the blessings of Law
and Justice, instead of the Caprice of the Strong. And all the
Greeks have realized your wisdom, and you have won great
fame. If you had been living on the edges of the earth, nobody would ever have heard of you. May I have neither gold
in my house nor skill to sing a sweeter song than Orpheus if
my fortune is to be hid from the eyes of men. That, then, is
my position in the matter of the fetching of the Fleece. (It
was you who proposed the debate.)

There remains my wedding with the Princess, which you
have cast in my teeth. In this connection I shall demonstrate,
one, my wisdom; two, my rightness; three, my great service
of love to you and my children. (Be quiet, please.) When I
emigrated here from the land of Iolcus, dragging behind me
an unmanageable chain of troubles, what greater windfall
could I have hit upon, I an exile, than a marriage with the
king's daughter? Not that I was weary of your charms
(that's the thought that galls you) or that I was smitten with
longing for a fresh bride; still less that I wanted to outdo my
neighbors in begetting numerous children. Those I have are
enough, there I have no criticism to make. No! what I
wanted, first and foremost, was a good home where we
would lack for nothing (well I knew that the poor man is
shunned and avoided by all his friends); and secondly, I
wanted to bring up the children in a style worthy of my
house, and, begetting other children to be brothers to the
children born of you, to bring them all together and unite
the families. Then my happiness would be complete. What do
*you* want with more children? As for me, it will pay me to
advance the children I have by means of those I intend to
beget. Surely that is no bad plan? You yourself would admit it, if jealousy were not pricking you.

You women have actually come to believe that, lucky in
love, you are lucky in all things, but let some mischance be-

fall that love, and you will think the best of all possible worlds a most loathsome place. There ought to have been some other way for men to beget their children, dispensing with the assistance of women. Then there would be no trouble in the world.

LEADER. Jason, you arrange your arguments very skilfully. And yet in my opinion, like it or not, you have acted unjustly in betraying your wife.

MEDEA. Yes! I do hold many opinions that are not shared by the majority of people. In my opinion, for example, the plausible scoundrel is the worst type of scoundrel. Confident in his ability to trick out his wickedness with fair phrases he shrinks from no depth of villainy. But there is a limit to his cleverness. As there is also to yours. You may as well drop that fine front with me, and all that rhetoric. One word will floor you. If you had been an honorable man, you would have sought my consent to the new match and not kept your plans secret from your own family.

JASON. And if I had announced to you my intention to marry, I am sure I would have found you a most enthusiastic accomplice. Why! even now you cannot bring yourself to master your heart's deep resentment.

MEDEA. That's not what griped you. No! your foreign wife was passing into an old age that did you little credit.

JASON. Accept my assurance, it was not for the sake of a woman that I made the match I have made. As I told you once already, I wanted to save you and to beget princes to be brothers to my own sons, thereby establishing our family.

MEDEA. May it never be mine . . . a happiness that hurts, a blessedness that frets my soul.

JASON. Do you know how to change your prayer to show better sense? "May I regard nothing useful as grievous, no good fortune as ill."

MEDEA. Insult me. *You* have a refuge, but I am helpless, faced with exile.

JASON. It was your own choice. Don't blame anyone else.

MEDEA. What did I do? Did I betray you and marry somebody else?

JASON. You heaped foul curses on the king.

MEDEA. And to your house also I shall prove a curse.

JASON. Look here, I do not intend to continue this discussion any further. If you want anything of mine to assist you or the children in your exile, just tell me. I am ready to give it with an ungrudging hand and to send letters of introduction to my foreign friends who will treat you well. If you reject this offer, woman, you will be a great fool. Forget your anger, and you will find it greatly to your advantage.

MEDEA. I would not use your friends on any terms or accept anything of yours. Do not offer it. The gifts of the wicked bring no profit.

JASON. At any rate, heaven be my witness that I am willing to render every assistance to you and the children. But you do not like what is good for you. Your obstinacy repulses your friends; it will only aggravate your suffering.

MEDEA. Be off with you. As you loiter outside here, you are burning with longing for the girl who has just been made your wife. Make the most of the union. Perhaps, god willing, you are making the kind of marriage you will some day wish unmade.

[Exit Jason.]

CHORUS. *Love may go too far and involve men in dishonor and disgrace. But if the goddess comes in just measure, there is none so rich in blessing. May you never launch at me, O Lady of Cyprus, your golden bow's passion-poisoned arrows, which no man can avoid.*

*May Moderation content me, the fairest gift of Heaven. Never may the Cyprian pierce my heart with longing for another's love and bring on me angry quarrelings and never-ending recriminations. May she have respect for harmonious unions and with discernment assort the matings of women.*

*O Home and Fatherland, never, never, I pray, may I be cityless. It is an intolerable existence, hopeless, piteous, grievous. Let me die first, die and bring this life to a close. There is no sorrow that surpasses the loss of country.*

*My eyes have seen it; not from hearsay do I speak. You have neither city nor friend to pity you in your most terrible trials. Perish, abhorred, the man who never brings himself to unbolt his heart in frankness to some honored friends! Never shall such a man be a friend of mine.*

[Enter Aegeus, in traveler's dress.]

AEGEUS. Medea, good health to you. A better prelude than that in addressing one's friends, no man knows.

MEDEA. Good health be yours also, wise Pandion's son, Aegeus. Where do you come from to visit this land?

AEGEUS. I have just left the ancient oracle of Phoebus.

MEDEA. What sent you to the earth's oracular hub?

AEGEUS. I was enquiring how I might get children.

MEDEA. In the name of Heaven, have you come thus far in life still childless?

AEGEUS. By some supernatural influence I am still without children.

MEDEA. Have you a wife or are you still unmarried?

AEGEUS. I have a wedded wife to share my bed.

MEDEA. Tell me, what did Phoebus tell you about off-spring?

AEGEUS. His words were too cunning for a mere man to interpret.

MEDEA. Is it lawful to tell me the answer of the god?

AEGEUS. Surely. For, believe me, it requires a cunning mind to understand.

MEDEA. What then was the oracle? Tell me, if I may hear it.

AEGEUS. I am not to open the cock that projects from the skin. . . .

MEDEA. Till you do what? Till you reach what land?

AEGEUS. Till I return to my ancestral hearth.

MEDEA. Then what errand brings your ship to this land?

AEGEUS. There is one Pittheus, king of Troezen. . . .

MEDEA. The child of Pelops, as they say, and a most pious man.

AEGEUS. To him I will communicate the oracle of the god.

MEDEA. Yes, he is a cunning man and well-versed in such matters.

AEGEUS. Yes, and of all my comrades in arms the one I love most.

MEDEA. Well, good luck to you, and may you win your heart's desire.

AEGEUS. Why, what's the reason for those sad eyes, that wasted complexion?

MEDEA. Aegeus, I've got the basest husband in all the world.

AEGEUS. What do you mean? Tell me the reason of your despondency, tell me plainly.

MEDEA. Jason is wronging me; I never did him wrong.

AEGEUS. What has he done? Speak more bluntly.

MEDEA. He has another wife, to lord it over me in our home.

AEGEUS. You don't mean that he has done so callous, so shameful a deed!

MEDEA. Indeed he did. Me that used to be his darling he now despises.

AEGEUS. Has he fallen in love? Does he hate your embraces?

MEDEA. Yes, it's a grand passion! He was born to betray his loved ones.

AEGEUS. Let him go, then, since he is so base, as you say.

MEDEA. He became enamored of getting a king for a father-in-law.

AEGEUS. Who gave him the bride? Please finish your story.

MEDEA. Creon, the ruler of this Corinth.

AEGEUS. In that case, Madam, I can sympathize with your resentment.

MEDEA. My life is ruined. What is more, I am being expelled from the land.

AEGEUS. By whom? This new trouble is hard.

MEDEA. Creon is driving me out of Corinth into exile.

AEGEUS. And does Jason allow this? I don't like that either.

MEDEA. He says he does not, but he'll stand it. Oh! I beseech you by this beard, by these knees, a suppliant I entreat you, show pity, show pity for my misery. Do not stand by and see me driven forth to a lonely exile. Receive me into your land, into your home and the shelter of your hearth. So may the gods grant you the children you desire, to throw joy round your deathbed. You do not know what a lucky path you have taken to me. I shall put an end to your childlessness. I shall make you beget heirs of your blood. I know the magic potions that will do it.

AEGEUS. Many things make me eager to do this favor for you, Madam. Firstly, the gods, and secondly, the children that you promise will be born to me. In that matter I am quite at my wits' end. But here is how I stand. If you yourself come to Athens, I shall try to be your champion, as in duty bound. This warning, however, I must give you! I shall not consent to take you with me out of Corinth. If you yourself come to my palace, you will find a home and a sanctuary. Never will I surrender you to anybody. But your own efforts must get you away from this place. I wish to be free from blame in the eyes of my hosts also.

MEDEA. And so you shall. But just let me have a pledge for these services, and I shall have all I could desire of you.

AEGEUS. Do you not trust me? What is your difficulty?

MEDEA. I do trust you. But both the house of Pelias and Creon are my enemies. Bound by oaths, you would never hand me over to them if they tried to extradite me. But with an agreement of mere words, unfettered by any sacred pledge, you might be won over by their diplomatic advances to become *their* friend. For I have no influence or power, whereas they have the wealth of a royal palace.

AEGEUS. You take great precautions, Madam. Still, if you wish, I will not refuse to do your bidding. For me too it will be safer that way, if I have some excuse to offer to your enemies, and *you* will have more security. Dictate the oath.

MEDEA. Swear by the Floor of Earth, by the Sun my father's father, by the whole family of the gods, one and all——

AEGEUS. To do or not do what? Say on.

MEDEA. Never yourself to cast me out of your country and never, willingly, during your lifetime, to surrender me to any of my foes that desire to seize me.

AEGEUS. I swear by the Earth, by the holy majesty of the Sun, and by all the gods, to abide by the terms you propose.

MEDEA. Enough! And if you abide not by your oath, what punishment do you pray to receive?

AEGEUS. The doom of sacrilegious mortals.

MEDEA. Go and fare well. All is well. I shall arrive at your city as soon as possible, when I have done what I intend to do, and obtained my desire.

LEADER [*as Aegeus departs*]. May Maia's son, the Lord of Journeys, bring you safe to Athens, and may you achieve the desire that hurries you homeward; for you are a generous man in my esteem.

MEDEA. O Zeus and his Justice, O Light of the Sun! The time has come, my friends, when I shall sing songs of triumph over my enemies. I am on my way. Now I can hope that my foes will pay the penalty. Just as my plans were most storm-tossed at sea, this man has appeared, a veritable harbor, where I shall fix my moorings, when I get to the town and citadel of Pallas.

Now I shall tell you all my plans; what you hear will not be said in fun. I shall send one of my servants to ask Jason to come and see me. When he comes, I shall make my language submissive, tell him I approve of everything else and am quite contented [with his royal marriage and his betrayal of me, that I agree it is all for the best]; I shall only ask him to allow my children to remain. Not that I wish to leave them in a hostile land [for my enemies to insult]. No! I have a cunning plan to kill the princess. I shall send

them with gifts to offer to the bride, to allow them to stay in
the land—a dainty robe and a headdress of beaten gold.
If she takes the finery and puts it on her, she will die in
agony. She and anyone who touches her. So deadly are the
poisons in which I shall steep my gifts.

But now I change my tone. It grieves me sorely, the horrible deed I must do next. I shall murder my children, these
children of mine. No man shall take them away from me.
Then when I have accomplished the utter overthrow of the
house of Jason, I shall flee from the land, to escape the consequences of my own dear children's murder and my other
accursed crimes. My friends, I cannot bear being laughed at
by my enemies.

So be it. Tell me, what has life to offer them. They have
no father, no home, no refuge from danger.

My mistake was in leaving my father's house, won over
by the words of a Greek. But, as god is my ally, he shall pay
for his crime. Never, if I can help it, shall he behold his
sons again in this life. Never shall he beget children by his
new bride. She must die by my poisons, die the death she deserves. Nobody shall despise *me* or think me weak or passive.
Quite the contrary. I am a good friend, but a dangerous
enemy. For that is the type the world delights to honor.

LEADER. You have confided your plan in me, and I should
like to help you, but since I also would support the laws of
mankind, I entreat you not to do this deed.

MEDEA. It is the only way. But I can sympathize with your
sentiments. You have not been wronged like me.

LEADER. Surely you will not have the heart to destroy your
own flesh and blood?

MEDEA. I shall. It will hurt my husband most that way.

LEADER. But it will make you the unhappiest woman in
the world.

MEDEA. Let it. From now on all words are superfluous.
[*To the nurse.*] Go now, please, and fetch Jason. Whenever loyalty is wanted, I turn to you. Tell him nothing of my
intentions, as you are a woman and a loyal servant of your
mistress.

[*Exit Nurse.*]

CHORUS. *The people of Erechtheus have been favored of
Heaven from the beginning. Children of the blessed gods are
they, sprung from a hallowed land that no foeman's foot has
trodden. Their food is glorious Wisdom. There the skies are
always clear, and lightly do they walk in that land where once*

*on a time blonde Harmony bore nine chaste daughters, the Muses of Pieria.*

*Such is the tale, which tells also how Aphrodite sprinkled the land with water from the fair streams of Cephissus and breathed over it breezes soft and fragrant. Ever on her hair she wears a garland of sweet-smelling roses, and ever she sends the Loves to assist in the court of Wisdom. No good thing is wrought without their help.*

*How then shall that land of sacred rivers, that hospitable land receive you the slayer of your children? It would be sacrilege for you to live with them. Think. You are stabbing your children. Think. You are earning the name of murderess. By your knees we entreat you, by all the world holds sacred, do not murder your children.*

*Whence got you the hardihood to conceive such a plan? And in the horrible act, as you bring death on your own children, how will you steel your heart and hand? When you cast your eyes on them, your own children, will you not weep that you should be their murderess? When your own children fall at your feet and beg for mercy, you will never be able to dye your hands with their blood. Your heart will not stand it.*

[*Enter Jason, followed by the Nurse.*]

JASON. I come at your bidding. Though you hate me, I shall not refuse you an audience. What new favor have you to ask of me, woman?

MEDEA. Jason, please forgive me for all I said. After all the services of love you have rendered me before, I can count on you to put up with my fits of temper. I have been arguing the matter out with myself. Wretched woman (thus I scolded myself), why am I so mad as to hate those that mean me well, to treat as enemies the rulers of this land and my husband who, in marrying a princess and getting brothers for my children, is only doing what is best for us all? What is the matter with me? Why am I still furious, when the gods are showering their blessings on me? Have I not children of my own? Am I forgetting that I am an exile from my native land, in sore need of friends? These reflections let me see how very foolish I have been and how groundless is my resentment. Now, I want to thank you. I think you are only doing the right thing in making this new match. I have been the fool. I ought to have entered into your designs, helped you to accomplish them, even stood by your nuptial couch and been glad to be

of service to the new bride. But I am what I am . . . to say no
worse, a woman. You ought not therefore to imitate me in
my error or to compete with me in childishness. I beg your
pardon, and confess that I was wrong then. But now I have
taken better counsel, as you see.

Children, children, come here, leave the house, come out
and greet your father as I do. Speak to him. Join your mother
in making friends with him, forgetting our former hate. It's
a truce; the quarrel is over. Take his right hand. Alas! my
imagination sickens strangely. My children, will you stretch
out loving arms like that in the long hereafter? My grief!
How quick my tears are! My fears brim over. It is that long
quarrel with your father, now done with, that fills my tender
eyes with tears.

LEADER. From my eyes, too, the burning tears gush forth.
May Sorrow's advance proceed no further.

JASON. That is the talk I like to hear, woman. The past I can
forgive. It is only natural for your sex to show resentment
when their husbands contract another marriage. But your
heart has now changed for the better. It took time, to be sure,
but you have now seen the light of reason. That's the action
of a wise woman. As for you, my children, your father has
not forgotten you. God willing, he has secured your perfect
safety. I feel sure that you will yet occupy the first place here
in Corinth, with your brothers. Merely grow up. Your father,
and any friends he has in heaven, will see to the rest. May I
see you, sturdy and strong, in the flower of your youth, triumphant over my enemies.

You there, why wet your eyes with hot tears, and avert
your pale cheek? Why are you not happy to hear me speak
thus?

MEDEA. It's nothing. Just a thought about the children
here.

JASON. Why all this weeping over the children? It's too
much.

MEDEA. I am their mother. Just now when you were wish-
ing them long life, a pang of sorrow came over me, in case
things would not work out that way.

JASON. Cheer up, then. I shall see that they are all right.

MEDEA. Very well, I shall not doubt your word. Women are
frail things and naturally apt to cry.

But to return to the object of this conference, something
has been said, something remains to be mentioned. Since it
is their royal pleasure to expel me from the country—oh yes!

it's the best thing for me too, I know well, not to stay on here in the way of you and the king; I am supposed to be their bitter enemy—*I* then shall go off into exile. But see that the children are reared by your own hand, ask Creon to let *them* stay.

JASON. I don't know if he will listen to me, but I shall try, as I ought.

MEDEA. At least you can get your wife to intercede with her father on their behalf.

JASON. Certainly, and I imagine I shall persuade her.

MEDEA. If she is a woman like the rest of us. In this task, I too shall play my part. I shall send the children with gifts for her, gifts far surpassing the things men make to-day [a fine robe, and a head-dress of beaten gold]. Be quick there. Let one of my maids bring the finery here. What joy will be hers, joys rather, joys innumerable, getting not only a hero like you for a husband, but also raiment which the Sun, my father's father, gave to his children. [*Medea takes the casket from a maid who has brought it, and hands it to the children.*] Here, my children, take these wedding gifts in your hands. Carry them to the princess, the happy bride, and give them to her. They are not the kind of gifts she will despise.

JASON. Impetuous woman! Why leave yourself thus empty-handed? Do you think a royal palace lacks for raiment and gold? Keep these things for yourself, don't give them away. If my wife has any regard for me at all, she will prefer me to wealth, I'm sure.

MEDEA. Please let me. They say that gifts persuade even the gods, and gold is stronger than ten thousand words. Hers is the fortune of the hour; her now is god exalting. She has youth, and a king for a father. And to save my children from exile, I would give my very life, let alone gold.

Away, my children, enter the rich palace and entreat your father's young wife, my mistress, to let you stay in Corinth. Give her the finery. That is most important. She must take these gifts in her hands. Go as fast as you can. Success attend your mission, and may you bring back to your mother the tidings she longs to hear.

[*Exeunt Children with Tutor, and Jason.*]

CHORUS. *Now are my hopes dead. The children are doomed. Already they are on the road to death. She will take*

*it, the bride will take the golden diadem, and with it will
take her ruin, luckless girl. With her own hands she will put
the precious circlet of death on her blonde hair.*

*The beauty of it, the heavenly sheen, will persuade her to
put on the robe and the golden crown. It is in the halls of
death that she will put on her bridal dress forthwith. Into
that fearful trap she will fall. Death will be her portion,
hapless girl. She cannot overleap her doom.*

*And you, poor man. Little luck your royal father-in-law is
bringing you. Unwittingly, you are bringing death on your
children, and on your wife an awful end. Ill-starred man,
what a way you are from happiness.*

*And now I weep for your sorrow, hapless mother of these
children. You will slaughter them to avenge the dishonor of
your bed betrayed, criminally betrayed by your husband
who now sleeps beside another bride.*

[Enter Children with their Tutor.]

TUTOR. Mistress, here are your children, reprieved
from exile. Your gifts the royal bride took gladly in her
hands. The children have made their peace with *her*. What's
the matter? Why stand in such confusion, when fortune is
smiling? [Why do you turn away your cheek? Why are you
not glad to hear my message?]

MEDEA. Misery!

TUTOR. That note does not harmonize with the news I have
brought.

MEDEA. Misery, and again Misery!

TUTOR. Have I unwittingly brought you bad news? I thought
it was good. Was I mistaken?

MEDEA. Your message was . . . your message. It is not you
I blame.

TUTOR. Why then are your eyes downcast and your tears
flowing?

MEDEA. Of necessity, old man, of strong necessity. This is
the gods' doing, and mine, in my folly.

TUTOR. Have courage. Some day your children will bring
you too back home.

MEDEA. Ah me! Before that day I shall bring others to another home.

TUTOR. You are not the first woman to be separated from
her children. We are mortals and must endure calamity with
patience.

MEDEA. That I shall do. Now go inside and prepare their usual food for the children.

[*Exit Tutor.*]

O my children, my children. For you indeed a city is assured, and a home in which, leaving me to my misery, you will dwell for ever, motherless. But I must go forth to exile in a strange land, before I have ever tasted the joy of seeing *your* happiness, before I have got you brides and bedecked your marriage beds and held aloft the bridal torches. Alas! my own self-will has brought me to misery. Was it all for nothing, my children, the rearing of you, and all the agonizing labor, all the fierce pangs I endured at your birth? Ah me, there was a time when I had strong hopes, fool as I was, that you would tend my old age and with your own hands dress my body for the grave, a fate that the world might envy. Now the sweet dream is gone. Deprived of you, I shall live a life of pain and sorrow. And you, in another world altogether will never again see your mother with your dear, dear eyes.

O the pain of it! Why do your eyes look at me, my children? Why smile at me that last smile? Ah! What can I do? My heart is water, women, at the sight of my children's bright faces. I could never do it. Goodbye to my former plans. I shall take my children away with me. Why should I hurt their father by *their* misfortunes, only to reap a double harvest of sorrow myself? No! I cannot do it. Goodbye to my plans.

And yet . . . what is the matter with me? Do I want to make myself a laughing-stock by letting my enemies off scot-free? I must go through with it. What a coward heart is mine, to admit those soft pleas. Come, my children, into the palace. Those that may not attend my sacrifices can see to it that they are absent. I shall not let my hand be unnerved.

Ah! Ah! Stop, my heart. Do not you commit this crime. Leave them alone, unhappy one, spare the children. Even if they live far from us, they will bring you joy. No! by the unforgetting dead in hell, it cannot be! I shall not leave my children for my enemies to insult. [In any case they must die. And if die they must, *I* shall slay them, who gave them birth.] My schemes are crowned with success. She shall not escape. Already the diadem is on her head; wrapped in the robe the royal bride is dying, I know it well. And now I am setting out on a most sorrowful road [and shall send these on one still more sorrowful]. I wish to speak to my children.

Give your mother your hands, my children, give her your hands to kiss.

O dear, dear hand. O dear, dear mouth, dear shapes, dear noble faces, happiness be yours, but not here. Your father has stolen this world from you. How sweet to touch! The softness of their skin, the sweetness of their breath, my babies! Away, away, I cannot bear to see you any longer. [*Children retire within.*] My misery overwhelms me. O I *do* realize how terrible is the crime I am about, but passion overrules my resolutions, passion that causes most of the misery in the world.

CHORUS. *Often ere now I have grappled with subtle subjects and sounded depths of argument deeper than woman may plumb. But, you see, we also have a Muse who teaches us philosophy. It is a small class—perhaps you might find one in a thousand—the women that love the Muse.*

*And I declare that in this world those who have had no experience of paternity are happier than the fathers of children. Without children a man does not know whether they are a blessing or a curse, and so he does not miss a joy he has never had and he escapes a multitude of sorrows. But them that have in their home young, growing children that they love, I see them consumed with anxiety, day in day out, how they are to rear them properly, how they are to get a livelihood to leave to them. And, after all that, whether the children for whom they toil are worth it or not, who can tell?*

*And now I shall tell you the last and crowning sorrow for all mortals. Suppose they have found livelihood enough, their children have grown up, and turned out honest. Then, if it is fated that way, death carries their bodies away beneath the earth. What then is the use, when the love of children brings from the gods this crowning sorrow to top the rest?*

MEDEA. My friends, all this time I have been waiting for something to happen, watching to see what they will do in the royal palace. Now I see one of Jason's attendants coming this way. His excited breathing shows that he has a tale of strange evils to tell.

[*Enter Messenger.*]

MESSENGER. What a horrible deed of crime you have done, Medea. Flee, flee. Take anything you can find, sea vessel or land carriage.

MEDEA. Tell me, what has happened that I should flee.

MESSENGER. The princess has just died. Her father Creon, too, killed by your poisons.

MEDEA. Best of news! From this moment and for ever you are one of my friends and benefactors.

MESSENGER. What's that? Are you sane and of sound mind, woman? You have inflicted a foul outrage on a king's home, yet you rejoice at the word of it and are not afraid.

MEDEA. I too have a reply that I might make to you. But take your time, my friend. Speak on. How did they die? You would double my delight, if they died in agony.

MESSENGER. When your children, both your offspring, arrived with their father and entered the bride's house, we rejoiced, we servants who had been grieved by your troubles. Immediately a whisper ran from ear to ear that you and your husband had patched up your earlier quarrel. And one kisses your children's hands, another their yellow hair. I myself, in my delight, accompanied the children to the women's rooms. The mistress, whom we now respect in your place, did not see the two boys at first, but cast a longing look at Jason. Then, however, resenting the entrance of the children, she covered her eyes with a veil and averted her white cheek.

Your husband tried to allay the maiden's angry resentment, saying, "You must not hate your friends. Won't you calm your temper, and turn your head this way? You must consider your husband's friends your own. Won't you accept the gifts and ask your father to recall their sentence of exile, for my sake?" Well, when she saw the finery, she could not refrain, but promised her husband everything, and before Jason and your children were far away from the house she took the elaborate robes and put them on her. She placed the golden diadem on her clustering locks and began to arrange her coiffure before a shining mirror, smiling at her body's lifeless reflection. Then she arose from her seat and walked through the rooms, stepping delicately with her fair white feet, overjoyed with the gifts. Time and time again, standing erect, she gazes with all her eyes at her ankles.

But then ensued a fearful sight to see. Her color changed, she staggered, and ran back, her limbs all atremble, and only escaped falling by sinking upon her chair. An old attendant, thinking, I suppose, it was a panic fit, or something else of divine sending, raised a cry of prayer, until she sees a white froth drooling from her mouth, sees her rolling up the pupils of her eyes, and all the blood leaving her skin. Then, instead of a cry of prayer, she let out a scream of lamenta-

tion. Immediately one maid rushed to Creon's palace, another to the new bridegroom, to tell of the bride's misfortune.
From end to end, the house echoed to hurrying steps. A
quick walker, stepping out well, would have reached the end
of the two hundred yard track, when the poor girl, lying there
quiet, with closed eyes, gave a fearful groan and began to
come to. A double plague assailed her. The golden diadem on
her head emitted a strange flow of devouring fire, while the
fine robes, the gifts of your children, were eating up the poor
girl's white flesh. All aflame, she jumps from her seat and
flees, shaking her head and hair this way and that, trying to
throw off the crown. But the golden band held firmly, and
after she had shaken her hair more violently, the fire began
to blaze twice as fiercely. Overcome by the agony she falls on
the ground, and none but her father could have recognized
her. The position of her eyes could not be distinguished,
nor the beauty of her face. The blood, clotted with fire,
dripped from the crown of her head, and the flesh melted
from her bones, like resin from a pine tree, as the poisons ate
their unseen way. It was a fearful sight. All were afraid
to touch the corpse, taught by what had happened to her.

But her father, unlucky man, rushed suddenly into the
room, not knowing what had happened, and threw himself
on the body. At once he groaned, and embracing his daughter's form he kissed it and cried, "My poor, poor child, what
god has destroyed you so shamefully? Who is it deprives this
aged tomb of his only child? Ah! let me join you in death, my
child." Then, when he ceased his weeping and lamentation
and sought to lift his aged frame upright, he stuck to the fine
robes, like ivy to a laurel bush. His struggles were horrible.
He would try to free a leg, but the girl's body stuck to his.
And if he pulled violently, he tore his shrunken flesh off his
bones. At last his life went out; doomed, he gave up the
ghost. Side by side lie the two bodies, daughter and old
father. Who would not weep at such a calamity?

It seems to me . . . I need not speak of what's in store for
you; you yourself will see how well the punishment fits the
crime . . . it's not the first time the thought has come, that the
life of man is a shadow. [I might assert with confidence that
the mortals who pass for philosophers and subtle reasoners are
most to be condemned.] No mortal man has lasting happiness. When the tide of fortune flows his way, one man may
have more prosperity than another, but happiness never.

[*Exit Messenger.*]

LEADER. It seems that this day Fate is visiting his sins on
Jason. Unfortunate daughter of Creon, we pity your calamity.
The love of Jason has carried you through the gates of death.

MEDEA. My friends, I am resolved to act, and act quickly
[to slay the children and depart from the land]. I can delay
no longer, or my children will fall into the murderous hands
of those that love them less than I do. In any case they must
die. And if they must, I shall slay them, who gave them birth.
Now, my heart, steel yourself. Why do we still hold back?
The deed is terrible, but necessary. Come, my unhappy hand,
seize the sword, seize it. Before you is a course of misery, life-
long misery; on now to the starting post. No flinching now,
no thinking of the children, the darling children, that call
you mother. This day, this one short day, forget your children.
You have all the future to mourn for them. Aye, to mourn.
Though you mean to kill them, at least you loved them. Oh!
I am a most unhappy woman.

[*Exit Medea.*]

CHORUS. *O Earth, O glorious radiance of the Sun, look and
behold the accursed woman. Stop her before she lays her
bloody, murderous hands on her children. Sprung are they
from your golden race, O Sun, and it is a fearful thing that
the blood of a god should be spilt by mortals. Nay, stop her,
skyborn light, prevent her. Deliver the house from the misery
of slaughter, and the curse of the unforgetting dead.*

*Gone, gone for nothing, are your maternal pangs. For noth-
ing did you bear these lovely boys, O woman, who made the
inhospitable passage through the grey Clashing Rocks! Why
let your spleen poison your heart? Why this murderlust, where
love was? On the man that spills the blood of kinsmen the
curse of heaven descends. Go where he may, it rings ever in
his ears, bringing sorrows and tribulations on his house.*

[*The Children are heard within.*]

*Listen, listen. It is the cry of the children. O cruel, ill-starred
woman.*

ONE OF THE CHILDREN [*within*]. Ah me! What am I to do?
Where can I escape my mother's murderous hands?

THE OTHER [*within*]. I know not, my dear, dear brother. She is killing us.

CHORUS. *Should we break in? Yes! I will save them from death.*

ONE OF THE CHILDREN [*within*]. Do, for god's sake. Save us. We need your help.

THE OTHER [*within*]. Yes, we are already in the toils of the sword.

CHORUS. *Heartless woman! Are you made of stone or steel? Will you slaughter the children, your own seed, slaughter them with your own hands?*

*Only one woman, only one in the history of the world, laid murderous hands on her children, Ino whom the gods made mad, driven from home to a life of wandering by the wife of Zeus. Hapless girl, bent on that foul slaughter, she stepped over a precipice by the shore and fell headlong into the sea, killing herself and her two children together. What crime, more horrible still, may yet come to pass? O the loves of women, fraught with sorrow, how many ills ere now have you brought on mortals!*

[*Enter Jason, attended.*]

JASON. You women there, standing in front of this house, is Medea still within, who wrought these dreadful deeds? Or has she made her escape? I tell you, she had better hide under the earth or take herself off on wings to the recesses of the sky, unless she wishes to give satisfaction to the family of the king. Does she think she can slay the rulers of the land and get safely away from this house? But I am not so anxious about her as I am about the children. The victims of her crimes will attend to her. It's my own children I am here to save, in case the relatives of the king do them some injury, in revenge for the foul murders their mother has committed.

LEADER. Jason, poor Jason, you do not know the sum of your sorrows, or you would not have said these words.

JASON. What is it? She does not want to kill me too, does she?

LEADER. Your children are dead, slain by their mother's hand.

JASON. For pity's sake, what do you mean? You have slain me, woman.

LEADER. Your children are dead, make no mistake.

JASON. Why, where did she slay them? Indoors or out here?

LEADER. Open the doors and you will see their bodies.

JASON. Quick, servants, loosen the bolts, undo the fastenings. Let me see the double horror, the dead bodies of my children, and the woman who . . . oh! let me punish her.

[*Medea appears aloft in a chariot drawn by winged dragons. She has the bodies of the children.*]

MEDEA. What's all this talk of battering and unbarring? Are you searching for the bodies and me who did the deed? Spare yourself the trouble. If you have anything to ask of me, speak if you will, but never shall you lay a hand on me. I have a magic chariot, given me by the Sun, my father's father, to protect me against my enemies.

JASON. You abominable thing! You most loathsomest woman, to the gods and me and all mankind. You had the heart to take the sword to your children, you their mother, leaving me childless. And you still behold the earth and the sun, you who have done this deed, you who have perpetrated this abominable outrage. My curses on you! At last I have come to my senses, the senses I lost when I brought you from your barbarian home and country to a home in Greece, an evil plague, treacherous alike to your father and the land that reared you. There is a fiend in you, whom the gods have launched against me. In your own home you had already slain your brother when you came aboard the Argo, that lovely ship. Such was your beginning. Then you married me and bore me children, whom you have now destroyed because I left your bed. No Greek woman would ever have done such a deed. Yet I saw fit to marry you, rather than any woman of Greece, a wife to hate me and destroy me, not a woman at all, but a tigress, with a disposition more savage than Tuscan Scylla. But why all this? Ten thousand reproaches could not sting you; your impudence is too engrained. The devil take you, shameless, abominable murderess of your children. I must bemoan my fate; no joy shall I have of my new marriage, and I shall never see alive the children I begot and reared and lost.

MEDEA. I might have made an elaborate rebuttal of the speech you have made, but Zeus the Father knows what you received at my hands and what you have done. You could not hope, nor your princess either, to scorn my love, make a fool of me, and live happily ever after. Nor was Creon, the matchmaker, to drive me out of the country with impunity. Go ahead, then. Call me tigress if you like, or Scylla that haunts the Tuscan coast. I don't mind, now I have got properly under your skin.

JASON. You too are suffering. You have your share of the sorrow.

MEDEA. True, but it's worth the grief, since you cannot scoff.

JASON. O children, what a wicked mother you got!

MEDEA. O children, your father's sins have caused your death.

JASON. Yet it was not *my* hand that slew them.

MEDEA. No, it was your lust, and your new marriage.

JASON. Because your love was scorned you actually thought it right to murder.

MEDEA. Do you think a woman considers that a small injury?

JASON. Good women do. But you are wholly vicious.

MEDEA. The children here are dead. That will sting you.

JASON. No! they live to bring fierce curses on your head.

MEDEA. The gods know who began it all.

JASON. They know, indeed, they know the abominable wickedness of your heart.

MEDEA. Hate me then. I despise your bitter words.

JASON. And I yours. But it is easy for us to be quit of each other.

MEDEA. How, pray? Certainly I am willing.

JASON. Allow me to bury these bodies and lament them.

MEDEA. Certainly not. I shall bury them with my own hands, taking them to the sanctuary of Hera of the Cape, where no enemy may violate their tombs and do them insult. Here in the land of Sisyphus we shall establish a solemn festival, and appoint rites for the future to expiate their impious murder. I myself shall go to the land of Erechtheus, to live with Aegeus, the son of Pandion. You, as is proper, will die the death you deserve, [struck on the head by a fragment of the Argo,] now you have seen the bitter fruits of your new marriage.

JASON. May you be slain by the Curse of your children, and Justice that avenges murder!

MEDEA. What god or power above will listen to you, the breaker of oaths, the treacherous guest?

JASON. Oh! abominable slayer of children.

MEDEA. Get along to the palace and bury your wife.

JASON. I go, bereft of my two sons.

MEDEA. You have nothing yet to bemoan. Wait till you are old.

JASON. My dear, dear children!

MEDEA. Yes, dear to their mother, not to you.

JASON. And yet you slew them.

MEDEA. I did, to hurt you.

JASON. Alas! my grief! I long to kiss their dear mouths.

MEDEA. Now you speak to them, now you greet them, but in the past you spurned them.

JASON. For god's sake, let me touch my children's soft skin.

MEDEA. No! You have gambled and lost.

JASON. O Zeus, do you hear how I am repelled, how I am wronged by this foul tigress, that slew her own children? But such lament as I may and can make, I hereby make. I call upon the gods. I invoke the powers above to bear me witness that you slew my children and now prevent me from embracing their bodies and giving them burial. Would that I had never begotten them, to live to see them slain at your hands.

CHORUS. *Zeus on Olympus hath a wide stewardship. Many things beyond expectation do the gods fulfil. That which was expected has not been accomplished; for that which was unexpected has god found the way. Such was the end of this story.*

[*Exeunt.*]

# Hippolytus

———

SEVERAL earlier tragedies involved the passion of love: *Hippolytus* is the first in which it is central. The hero is himself the battleground between love and anti-love, and his fate underscores the folly of attempting withdrawal from any essential aspect of life. It is easy but wrong to see Hippolytus as a saint who dies for his purity and Phaedra as a lascivious woman whose death is deserved. Poor Phaedra yields her secret only in delirium induced by long fasting. And Hippolytus is as objectionable in his priggishness as he is appealing in his naive devotion to Artemis. But only when he speaks of Aphrodite or to women are his speeches so outrageous; with others he is a wholly charming young man. Hippolytus becomes a tragic figure because his personality is warped, and his personality is warped because of the stain of his illegitimacy—he regularly speaks of himself as *nothos,* bastard. That is why he hates Aphrodite. But Aphrodite cannot be ignored. Even Artemis, as she explains at the end of the play, cannot protect her devotee from her colleague. The only comfort she can give is that she will one day avenge herself on a devotee of Aphrodite. Hippolytus is a beautiful play and a sad one; the reader appreciates the chorus' vain wish for wings wherewith to fly away to some flowery and still untainted region of the world.

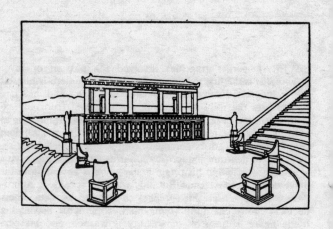

# HIPPOLYTUS

## CHARACTERS

APHRODITE

HIPPOLYTUS

CHORUS *of Huntsmen*

ATTENDANT *of Hippolytus*

CHORUS *of Troezenian Women*

NURSE

PHAEDRA

THESEUS

MESSENGER

ARTEMIS

The scene represents the palace of Theseus at Troezen. At either side are the statues of Aphrodite and Artemis.

Hippolytus was acted in 428 B.C., and obtained first prize.

———◆———

[*Enter Aphrodite upon the speaking platform reserved for Gods.*]

APHRODITE. Great is my power and wide my fame among mortals and also in heaven; I am the Goddess Cypris. All men that look upon the light of the sun, all that dwell between the Euxine Sea and the boundaries of Atlas are under my sway: I bless those that respect my power, and disappoint those who are not humble toward me. Yes, even the family of gods have this trait: they are pleased when people respect them. I shall demonstrate the truth of this forthwith. Theseus' son Hippolytus, born of the Amazon and brought up by temperate Pittheus, is the only inhabitant of this land of Troezen who declares that I am the very vilest of divinities. He spurns love and will have nothing to do with sex. *He* honors Phoebus' sister Artemis, Zeus' maiden, and thinks her the greatest of goddesses. He consorts with her continually in the green forests, clearing away the beasts of the earth with his swift dogs, pursuing a more than mortal companionship. Of course I don't grudge them that: why should I? It is his sinful neglect of *me* for which I shall punish Hippolytus this very day. The ground was prepared long ago: there is not much left for me to do. Once when he was going from Pittheus' house to the land of Pandion to see the Mysteries and be initiated, his father's noble wife

Phaedra saw him, and her heart was smitten with a fearful
love—all by my scheming. [Even before she came to this
land of Troezen she built a shrine of Cypris there on the
rock of Pallas, commanding a view of this land, because she
loved an absent love; and the place she established she
called Hippolytus' Belvedere in his honor for ever more.]
Then Theseus left the land of Cecrops and sailed to this
land with his wife. To expiate his guilt in the murder of
Pallas' sons, he has consented to a year's banishment from
home. And here the wretched woman, moaning and distraught with the pricks of love, love undeclared, is dying.
None of her maids understands her trouble. But this passion
must not end so simply. I will reveal the thing to Theseus,
to everybody. The young man who is hostile to me will be
killed by his father's curses. Poseidon, the master of the
sea, has granted a boon to Theseus: thrice shall he have
fulfilment for his prayers to him. Phaedra dies though she
saves her good name. Yes, she must die; I shall not let the
thought of her suffering stop me from punishing my enemies
to my heart's content.

But I see Hippolytus striding on after his work at the
chase, so I will leave this place. Behind him there comes a
great crowd of henchmen, doing honor to Goddess Artemis
with ringing hymns. Little he knows that the gates of Hades
are wide open, and that he is looking at this light for the
last time.

> [*Aphrodite disappears. From the left there enters Hip-
> polytus with javelin and garland, attended by a
> crowd of Huntsmen; they pay no notice to the
> statue of Aphrodite.*]

HIPPOLYTUS. *Follow, follow, sing heavenly Artemis, Zeus'
child, whose charge we are.*
HUNTSMEN. *Revered, revered, hallowed daughter of
Zeus, hail Artemis, hail maiden of Leto and Zeus, most
beautiful of maidens by far. You dwell in heaven in your
noble sire's hall, in the house of Zeus bedecked with gold.
Hail most beautiful, most beautiful of maidens in Olympus,
hail Artemis!*

> [*Hippolytus advances, bows to the statue of Artemis,
> and places his garland upon her altar.*]

HIPPOLYTUS. For you, dear Lady, I bring this garland, this lovely chain of flowers, from a virgin meadow, where no shepherd presumes to pasture his flock, nor has iron ever come there. Virgin it is, and in summer the bees frequent it, while Purity waters it like a garden. He whose fortune it is to be in all things wholly virtuous, not by teaching of men but by nature, may cull flowers in that meadow; for others it is not lawful. From a reverent hand, then, dear Lady, accept this diadem for your golden tresses. To me alone of mortals does this grace belong—to live with you and converse in words; I hear your voice though I do not see your face. May I round the goal of life even as I have begun.

[*An Attendant who has come out of the house and watched Hippolytus steps forward.*]

ATTENDANT. Prince—for only gods may be addressed as Lords—would you accept a word of sound advice from me?

HIPPOLYTUS. To be sure: it would seem foolish not to.

ATTENDANT. You know, of course, the general tendency of men——

HIPPOLYTUS. I do not. What are you getting at?

ATTENDANT. To hate haughtiness and reserve.

HIPPOLYTUS. And rightly; are not all haughty people hateful?

ATTENDANT. Affable people have a certain charm?

HIPPOLYTUS. A great deal; and what's more, they get on in the world with little effort.

ATTENDANT. Don't you expect the same thing is true with the gods?

HIPPOLYTUS. Yes; for men act on the same principles as gods.

ATTENDANT. Why then are you so haughty, in not worshipping a deity that——

HIPPOLYTUS. What deity? Mind your mouth doesn't stumble.

ATTENDANT. This goddess here, this Cypris that stands at your gates.

HIPPOLYTUS. I keep at a respectful distance; *I* am chaste.

ATTENDANT [*soothingly*]. Yes, yes; and reverend, and famous among men.

HIPPOLYTUS. With gods and men tastes vary.

ATTENDANT. Good luck to you; you have your share of wisdom.

HIPPOLYTUS. I don't like deities who are marvellous after dark.

ATTENDANT [*half aside*]. You should have respect for religion, my boy.

HIPPOLYTUS. Forward, comrades, enter the house and see about some food. A full table is a delight after hunting. And the horses must be groomed, so that I may harness them to my car and give them a proper work-out when I have had my fill. As for this Cypris of yours—I bid her a long farewell.

[*Exit; enter Chorus of Troezenian Women, right and left.*]

CHORUS. *There is a certain rock (from Ocean, they say, its waters distill), which sends forth from its crannies a flowing stream in which pitchers can be dipped. There a friend of mine was washing her bright colored clothes in the running water, and putting them to dry in the sun on the face of a warm rock. From her I heard the first rumor that my mistress was keeping to her house, wasting away on a bed of sickness, her blonde head veiled in dainty fabrics. I hear that for three days now her lovely lips have not been profaned by Demeter's grain. Some secret trouble makes her yearn to put into the sad haven of death.*

SOME WOMEN. *You must be possessed, young woman, whether it is Pan or Hecate, or the dread Corybants, or the mountain Mother, that haunts you.*

OTHERS. *Or perhaps you are pining away for sins against the huntress Dictynna, who afflicts you for offerings withheld. For she can go in pursuit over the land and also across the sea, through the eddies of the briny surge.*

OTHERS. *Or has some one in the house beguiled your husband, the first chief of the Erechtheids, the nobly born, to steal away to another woman's love?*

OTHERS. *Or has some sailor man outward bound from Crete voyaged to this harbor so friendly to sailors, and brought a rumor to the queen prostrating her on a bed of grief, Sorrow's prisoner?*

OTHERS. *This agony of grief, this feeling of desperation, is a common symptom of the delirium which attends travail, in women whose constitution is highstrung. I experienced this thrill, this chill, in my own womb, but I cried to the*

*heavenly archer, Goddess Artemis, who presides over child-*
*birth. And always, much wanted, by god's grace, she comes.*

THE LEADER. *But here she is, being carried outside the*
*doors by her old nurse. The cloud on her brow lowers dark.*
*My spirit is most eager to know what it is that has thus*
*ravaged my queen's face and driven away her color.*

[*Enter, from the house, Nurse, followed by Phaedra,*
*supported by female attendants.*]

NURSE. *Oh, the troubles and hateful sicknesses of mortals!*
*What shall I do with you, what not do? Here you have the*
*clear light, here is the fresh air. The bedding of your sick*
*couch is now outdoors. You could speak of nothing but*
*coming out here; soon enough you will be eager to go to*
*your room again. You are easily put out, nothing pleases*
*you. You are not satisfied with what you have; it takes ab-*
*sence to make your heart grow fonder.*

*Rather be sick than be nurse. The one is simple, but the*
*other combines mental worry with manual labor. But all*
*man's life is grievous; there is no rest for the weary. If*
*there is anything dearer than life, darkness swathes it and*
*clouds it over. So we find ourselves hopelessly in love with*
*the thing we see, this world of brightness, because we have*
*no experience of any other mode of living, and no proof of*
*the other world; myths merely lead us astray.*

PHAEDRA [*to attendants*]. *Raise my body, hold my head*
*up. The joints of my limbs are paralyzed. Take hold of my*
*pretty arms and hands. My tiara is too heavy on my head.*
*Take it off and spread my curls out on my shoulders.*

NURSE. *Cheer up, child. Don't toss about; it hurts. You will*
*bear your troubles more easily if you are quiet and brave.*
*Man is made to mourn.*

PHAEDRA. *Ah, ah! Oh to drink a cup of pure water from a*
*dewy spring! Oh to lie down and rest under the poplars in a*
*leafy meadow!*

NURSE. *Child, what are you shrieking? Don't talk that*
*way before people, blurting out mad, nightmarish words.*

PHAEDRA. *Take me to the mountain! I go to the forest, to*
*the pines, where the hounds chase their prey to the death,*
*and leap upon the dappled hinds. Gods, I yearn to urge on*
*the dogs, to poise the Thessalian dart beside my yellow*
*hair and fling it, to hold a barbed lance in my hand!*

NURSE. *What in the world are you raving about now,*

*child? What concern have* you *with hunting? What is this hankering for mountain streams? Right here next door to the castle is a well of water from which you could get a drink.*

PHAEDRA [*paying no attention to Nurse*]. *Artemis, Queen of Limna by the sea, queen of the tracks that echo with the hooves of horses, would I were there now, breaking colts of Enetia.*

NURSE. *What new raving is this you are uttering? A moment ago you were heading for the mountain and yearning for wild animals. Now you hanker for colts on the level sands. It would take a deal of prophesy to discover which of the gods is wrenching your reins and upsetting your mind, girl.*

PHAEDRA [*falls back and clasps her head*]. *Wretched me! What in the world have I done? How far have I wandered from good sense? I was mad, I have been overthrown by some god's spite. Dear, dear, what misery! Nanna, hide my head again. I'm ashamed of what I've said. Hide it. From my eyes tears are trickling. My eyes are fascinated by my shame. To come to one's senses brings pain. To be mad is an evil, but it is better to remain mad and perish.*

NURSE. *I am covering you. But when will death cover my body? Long life teaches me many things. Friendship between mortals should be taken in moderation. Don't let it get down into the marrow of the soul. Bonds of affection ought to be elastic, for letting apart or drawing together. It's a heavy load for one soul to be in pain for two, as I am now in anguish for her. Too strict regimentation brings more breakdowns than triumphs, I am told, and is bad for the health. So I have less praise for extremes than for "nothing in excess"; and you will find that the sages agree with me.*

LEADER. *Old woman, loyal nurse to the queen, we perceive the sad misfortune of Phaedra, but the nature of her disease is not clear. We should like to inquire and learn from you.*

NURSE. *I do not know, though I keep questioning her. She does not choose to tell.*

LEADER. *Not even what the beginning of her pains was?*

NURSE. *It amounts to the same thing. She keeps quiet about it all.*

LEADER. *How feeble she is, how wasted her figure!*

NURSE. *How could it be otherwise when she hasn't eaten for three days?*

LEADER. *Is it madness, or is she trying to die?*

NURSE. She is; she is starving herself to death.

LEADER. It's a wonder that her husband is content with such behavior.

NURSE. She hides her troubles and doesn't say she is ill.

LEADER. Does he not surmise it from the look of her face?

NURSE. He happens to be out of the country.

LEADER. But you—haven't you tried to *force* her to tell you what this illness, this madness, is?

NURSE. I have tried everything, but have had no success. But I'll not abate my zeal even now, so that you can appear and testify to my loyalty toward my mistress in her affliction. [*She turns back to Phaedra.*] Come now, precious child, let us both forget our earlier talk. You be more amiable. Smooth out your gloomy brow; change the direction of your thoughts. I too took the wrong road with you, but I'll leave it and turn to a better course. If your trouble is one of the unmentionable passions, here are women to help you out. If your affliction can be communicated to men, speak and your case can be referred to physicians.

Ah, why are you silent? You ought not to stay silent, child. Disprove me if I am saying anything out of place, or give in to my reasonable pleas.

Say something! Look at me!—Women, we are giving ourselves all this trouble for nothing. We are as far off as ever. She was not touched by our words before, and she pays no attention now.

But mark this. You may be stubborner than the sea, if you like, but if you die you will betray your children and deprive them of their father's house, as sure as the horse-loving Amazon queen bore a master for your own children, a bastard, but with no bastard heart—you know well whom I mean, Hippolytus—

PHAEDRA. Ah me!

NURSE. It touches you, does it?

PHAEDRA. You have undone me, Nanna. I beseech you, 'fore the gods, do not mention that man again.

NURSE. You see. You are sane enough; but for all your sanity, you are unwilling to benefit your children and save your own life.

PHAEDRA. I do love my children. I am storm-tossed by another misfortune.

NURSE. Surely your hands are pure of blood?

PHAEDRA. My hands are pure, but my heart is defiled.

NURSE. Is it a spell brought on by some enemy?

PHAEDRA. It is a friend that destroys me; but it is not his choice any more than mine.

NURSE. Has Theseus wronged you in any way?

PHAEDRA. May it turn out that I do not wrong him!

NURSE. What then is this terrible thing which compels you to die?

PHAEDRA. O let me sin! It's not against you I sin!

NURSE. I will not, but it is your fault if I fail.

PHAEDRA. What are you doing? Will you force me, clinging to my hand?

NURSE. Yes, and to your knees, and shall never let go!

PHAEDRA. These woes will be yours too when you learn them, poor woman.

NURSE. What can be a greater woe than to be rebuffed by you?

PHAEDRA. You will be my death. But the thing does me credit.

NURSE. Then will you hide your good deeds when I implore you to tell me?

PHAEDRA. Yes, for it is out of evil that I am contriving good.

NURSE. Speak then, and make your goodness known.

PHAEDRA. Go away, 'fore the gods, and let go my hand.

NURSE. I will not, for you do not give me the gift you should.

PHAEDRA. I will; I must respect the sanctity of your suppliant hand.

NURSE. I am silent at once. From now on *you* speak.

PHAEDRA. My poor mother, how strange was your love—

NURSE. For the bull, you mean? Or what?

PHAEDRA. And you, poor sister, bride of Dionysus—

NURSE. What ails you, child? You are maligning your relatives!

PHAEDRA. And I am the third—how sadly I perish!

NURSE. I am dumbfounded. What is coming next?

PHAEDRA. There, not here, my misery began.

NURSE. I am no nearer knowing the things I want to hear.

PHAEDRA. Ah, would you could say for me what I must say!

NURSE. I am not a prophet, to have sure knowledge of the unseen.

PHAEDRA. What sort of a thing do they mean when they say that people . . . love?

NURSE. A sweet thing, girl; yes, and painful too.

PHAEDRA. I have known only the pain.

NURSE. What are you saying? You are in love, child? With a *man?*

PHAEDRA. If he is a man, that Amazon's—

NURSE. Hippolytus are you saying?

PHAEDRA. From your lips it came, not mine.

NURSE. Oh, what *will* you say, child? Ah, but you have ruined me. It is intolerable, women. I will not endure it and live. Hateful is the day, hateful is the light I see. I shall fling, I shall hurl this body, I shall quit this life and die. Farewell, I no longer live. Good people fall in love with evil —despite all their good intentions. It's not a goddess that Cypris is, it seems, but whatever there is more powerful than a goddess; she has ruined this woman, and me, and the house.

SOME WOMEN OF THE CHORUS. *You have heard, O you have heard the queen confessing her unspeakable, miserable woe.*

OTHERS. *May I perish before I reach your state of mind, dear to me as you are. Woe is me! Alas! Alack!*

OTHERS. *Poor woman! Such agony!*

OTHERS. *O Misery, man's daily bread!*

OTHERS. *You are ruined. You have shown your evils forth to the light.*

OTHERS. *How will this long day end for you?*

OTHERS. *Some strange evil is coming to a head in this household.*

OTHERS. *It is no longer doubtful how far the luck of love has waned, poor child of Crete.*

PHAEDRA. Women of Troezen, who live in this outpost of the land of Pelops, I have often meditated in the long hours of the night how the life of man is wrecked. It seems to me that it is not by any natural defect in judgment that men fare ill; for many have good sense. But this is how we must look at it. We understand and know what is right, but we do not carry it out in practice, some of us through indolence, others from preferring some other kind of pleasure to duty. And there are many pleasures of life, [, long talks, and leisure, that delightful evil. And there is shame. This is of two sorts, one not bad, the other the bane of houses. But if the distinction were clear, there would not have been the same word for both meanings].

So in this case. Once I saw how my trouble was developing, I knew there was no medicine with which I could combat it; there was no changing my mind. Now I will tell you the way I reasoned it out. When love had wounded me I looked about how I might best put up with it. I began with the resolve to keep quiet and hide my disease. You cannot trust the tongue, which knows well enough how to rebuke the wilfulness of other people but is its own worst enemy. Next, I intended to overcome my folly by my self-control, and so endure it.

And thirdly, when I could not master Cypris by these means I thought it the best plan—none will gainsay me—to die. As I would not wish my good deeds to pass unnoticed, so I did not want a crowd of witnesses to my sin. To own the passion, I knew, would be no less disgraceful than if I gratified it. Besides, I realized full well that I was that object of universal detestation, a Woman. A foul curse on the woman who first committed adultery with strange men! It was from noble families that this evil first started, and when shameful things seem to be approved by the fáshionable, then the common people will surely think them correct. Those women who talk chastity, but secretly have their disreputable affairs, I hate. Sea-Goddess Cypris! How in the world can they look their husbands in the face, without quaking for fear lest the darkness, the partner in their crimes, some day take voice; or the walls of their chamber?

There you have my reason for killing myself: the desire to spare my husband and children that shame. Free in fact and free in speech may they live and flourish in illustrious Athens, glorious in their mother! It makes a man cringe, however stout-hearted he may be, when he knows his mother's or his father's baseness. This only, they say, stands the stress of life: a good and just spirit in a man. Time, like a young girl, has a mirror, wherein, in his own good time, he shows the base their baseness. Among such may *I* never be seen!

LEADER. Ah, how fair is chastity everywhere, what fruit of noble reputation does it produce!

NURSE. Mistress, that trouble of yours just now gave me a terrible fright at the moment. Now on reflection, I see I was stupid. People's second thoughts are somehow saner. It's nothing odd or inexplicable that has happened to you. Love's passions have swooped down over you. You are in love. What is remarkable in that? Many people are in the same state. Will you throw your life away because of love? Little will it profit those who are or ever will be in love with others if they have to die for it. You cannot withstand Cypris if she rushes upon you full tilt. When she finds a person yielding she comes on gently, but when she finds a person too high and mighty she takes him and—what do you think? —knocks the pride out of him. She roves through the air. She is in the waves of the sea; from her do all things spring. It is she that sows love and bestows it, and all we who are upon earth are born of love.

Those who possess the writings of the ancients and spend all their time with the Muses know that Zeus was once madly in love with Semele, they know that Dawn of the lovely light carried Cephalus off to the gods for the sake of love. Still they live in Heaven and do not shun the presence of the gods. They acquiesce, I imagine, in the fate that has mastered them.

Will *you* not yield? Your father ought to have begotten you by special arrangement, or with different gods for masters, if you will not acquiesce in the present dispensation. How many men, and very sensible men too, do you think, look the other way when their wives are unfaithful? How many fathers, do you think, play pander to their own amorous sons? The wise men of this world hold this principle: Don't notice what you don't like. People ought not to work out their lives too precisely. Why, they cannot even make a roof with rafters that would stand precise measuring! When you have got in as deep as you have, how can you expect to swim out unscathed? No! If you have more good than evil in your character, being only human, you will be doing well enough.

Now, dear girl, don't be wrongheaded, don't be presumptuous. Yes, that is just what it is, pure presumption, wanting to be better than the gods. Have the courage to love: a god has willed it. You are sick; find some way to cure your sickness. There are charms and soothing spells. Some remedy for this affliction will turn up. Believe me, men would be slow in making discoveries if we women did not contrive devices.

LEADER. Phaedra, this woman is the more practical, things being as they are; but it's you I approve. But this approval may be less welcome to you than her talk, and more painful to hear.

PHAEDRA. This it is which ruins well ordered cities and houses of men: words too plausible. One ought not to speak to tickle the ear; eloquence should promote virtue.

NURSE. Why this unctuous talk? This is no time to mince words. It's time to use plain talk about you. With all speed we must determine the *man's* feelings. He must be told the blunt truth about you. If you had not got your affairs into this tangle, if you had been a really good woman, I should never have urged you to this course, merely to gratify your lust. But now the struggle is to save your life, and there's no disgrace in that.

PHAEDRA. Horrible things you say!—Will you not shut your mouth? Don't start that wicked, wicked talk again.

NURSE. Wicked, perhaps, but better for you than your fine principles. Better the deed if it can save you than an empty name in the pride of which you perish.

PHAEDRA. Please don't, by the gods—you speak so well, your words are so shameful—do not go further. Already my heart is prepared to receive love, and if you put so fair a face on what is shameful, my reserves of resistance will be exhausted.

NURSE. If that is your mind you ought not to have sinned. But things being as they are, hear me. This is the next best thing I can do for you. I have at home a philtre, a soothing charm for love—I just now thought of it—which will put an end to this malady neither on disgraceful terms nor to the injury of your mind, if only you do not turn coward. [We must get hold of some token from the man you crave, some of his hair or some scrap from his clothing, to conjoin one willing love out of two.]

PHAEDRA. Is this medicine a salve, or is it to be swallowed?

NURSE. I do not know; try to be helped, not educated, child.

PHAEDRA. I am afraid you may turn out too much a sophist for me.

NURSE. You would be afraid of anything, you know. What is your worry?

PHAEDRA. That you may hint something of my state to Theseus' son.

NURSE. Let be, girl. I shall fix that up. [*Turns to statue of Aphrodite*] Be my fellow-worker, Lady Cypris, Sea-Goddess! The other things I am minded to do it will be enough to tell our friends within.

[*Exit Nurse.*]

CHORUS. *Eros, Eros, you make the eye misty with longing; you import a sweet delight into the hearts of those against whom you march: may you never show yourself to me to my hurt, may you never come inordinately. Neither the*

flash of fire nor the bolt of the stars is more deadly than
the shafts of Aphrodite which Eros, Zeus' boy, hurls from
his hands.

In vain, in vain, has Hellas multiplied the slaughter of
cattle on the banks of the Alpheus and at the Pythian shrine
of Phoebus; all in vain if we revere not Eros, tyrant over
men, chamberlain of the dearest bowers of Aphrodite, the
destroyer that brings all manner of calamities on mortals
when he attacks.

There was a maiden in Oechalia, a filly unbroken,
loverless. But Cypris drove her far from the house of
Eurytus, like a flying Naiad or a Bacchant, and bestowed
her on Alcmena's son, with blood and flame and gory bridals: O woeful wedlock!

O sacred wall of Thebes, O mouth of Dirce,-you might
well tell how Cypris creeps on. The mother of divine Bacchus she gave as a bride to the forked thunderbolt and
brought her to bed with murderous Death. Fearfully does
Cypris breathe upon all the world, like some bee ever hovering.

PHAEDRA [who has approached the door and there lis-
tened during the last lines of the Chorus]. Be still, women.
I am ruined.

LEADER. What is it, Phaedra? What is so fearful in the
house?

PHAEDRA. Silence! Let me hear what they are saying inside.

LEADER. I am silent. But I do not like this prelude.

PHAEDRA. Alas! Alas! Oh! Oh! O wretched me! What sufferings are mine!

LEADER. What means this cry? What are you shrieking?
Tell us what you've heard that frightens you, that startles
your senses?

PHAEDRA. I am ruined. Stand at the door here and listen
to the brawl going on indoors.

LEADER. You are nearest the door: attend to the sound
coming from within. Tell me, O tell me, what evil has come
to pass?

PHAEDRA. The horse-loving Amazon's son, Hippolytus, is
shouting. He is saying dreadful things to my maid.

LEADER. The sound I hear, but I do not catch the words
distinctly. You must have heard what came through the door.

PHAEDRA. Only too well. He is calling her a pander of sin,
a betrayer of her master's bed.

LEADER. *O Misery! You are betrayed, my dear. How can I counsel you? Your secret is out; you are utterly ruined.*

PHAEDRA. Oh! Oh! Ah! Ah!

LEADER. *Betrayed by your friends.*

PHAEDRA. She has ruined me; she has divulged my trouble. She meant well but she has made a sorry cure of my disease.

LEADER. What now? What will you do? Your case is desperate.

PHAEDRA. One thing I know: to die as soon as possible is the only cure for my present troubles.

[*Enter from the house Hippolytus followed by the Nurse.*]

HIPPOLYTUS. O mother earth! O eye of the sun! What unspeakable words I have heard!

NURSE. Quiet, boy, before anyone hears your noise!

HIPPOLYTUS. I cannot be silent when I have heard such horror.

NURSE. Do, by your lovely right hand!

HIPPOLYTUS. Don't lay your hand on me! Don't touch my clothes!

NURSE. Oh, by your knees, do not ruin me!

HIPPOLYTUS. How ruin, if, as you say, you have spoken no wrong?

NURSE. This story, boy, is not for every ear.

HIPPOLYTUS. Fair deeds become fairer when spoken in public.

NURSE. Child, do not disregard your oath.

HIPPOLYTUS. My tongue swore, my mind is unsworn.

NURSE. Boy, what are you about? Will you kill your own?

HIPPOLYTUS. I spit the word out! No unjust person can be "my own".

NURSE. Be charitable. To err is human, child.

HIPPOLYTUS. Zeus! Why did you let women settle in this world of light, a curse and a snare to men? If you wished to propagate the human race you should have arranged it without women. Men might have deposited in your temples gold or iron or a weight of copper to purchase offspring, each to the value of the price he paid, and so lived in free houses, relieved of womankind. Here is a proof that woman is a great nuisance. The father who begot her and brought her up pays a great dowry to get her out of his house and be rid

of the plague. The man who receives the poisonous weed
into his home rejoices and adds beautiful decorations to the
useless ornament and tricks her out in gowns—poor fool,
frittering away the family property. [He is under constraint:
if his in-laws are good people he must keep his cheerless
bed; if his spouse is agreeable but her relatives useless, the
evil he must accept oppresses the good.] Happiest is he who
has a cipher for a wife, a useless simpleton to sit at home.
A clever woman I hate; may there never be in my house a
woman more intellectual than a woman ought to be. Mischief
is hatched by Cypris in clever women; the helpless kind is
kept from misconduct by the shortness of her wit. No maids
should be allowed near a wife; beasts that can bite but cannot talk should be their only company in the house, so that
they could neither address anyone or receive speech in return. As it is, the vile women weave their vile schemes within, and the maids carry word outdoors.

So you, sorry wretch, come to me to procure incest in my
father's bed. But I will scour it away, sluicing fresh running
water into my ears. How could I be base, who feel polluted
by the mere hearing? Know well, woman, it's only my piety
that saves you. If I had not been taken unaware by sacred
oaths I should never have kept from telling my father this.
Now I will stay away from the house as long as Theseus is
out of the country, and I shall keep my mouth shut. But I
shall watch, when I come back with my father, how you
will look at him, you and that mistress of yours. Then I shall
know fully the brazenness of which I have had the taste.

Curse you! *Let* people say I am always harping on the
same theme. Still I shall never tire of hating women. For
that matter, *they* never tire of wickedness. Either teach
them to be chaste or leave me to assail them always.

[*Exit.*]

PHAEDRA. *Miserable, unhappy doom of women! What skill
have we, what words, when we have fallen, to break the hold
of scandal? I have got my deserts. O earth! O light! How can
I avoid my doom? How shall I hide my calamity, friends?
What god will be my helper, what mortal will appear as my
advocate and ally in this unfair procedure? This suffering
that comes upon my life is inescapable. Most unhappy of
women am I.*

LEADER: Alas, alas, it is over and done. Your maid's devices have not succeeded, lady; things have gone awry.

PHAEDRA. Vilest of vile women, ruin of your friends, what have you done to me! May father Zeus uproot and blast and shatter you with fire! Did I not bid you—did I not foresee your purpose?—to keep silent about the thing which is now my dishonor? But you could not refrain, and now I can no longer die with honor.

But I need some new scheme. That man's heart is whetted with rage: he will blame *me* to Theseus for *your* mistakes. [He will relate these happenings to the old man Pittheus.] He will fill the whole land with the worst sort of scandal. Curse you and whoever else is over-zealous to render dishonorable service to friends who don't wish it!

NURSE. Mistress, of course you can blame me and miscall me—the sting of grief warps your judgment—but I too have an answer to make, if you will listen. I raised you and am devoted to you. I sought a drug for your malady, and I lost. If it had worked, I would now be among the wise ones, no doubt. According to success do we gain a reputation for judgment.

PHAEDRA. Is this fair, will this suffice me, to wound me first and then calmly admit it?

NURSE. We talk too long. I was not wise. But there is an escape even from this, child.

PHAEDRA. Stop your talk. Your first advice was not good; your first attempt was fatal. Get out of my way and look out for yourself. I will set my own affairs to rights.

[*Exit Nurse.*]

And do you, noble daughters of Troezen, grant me this petition: enfold in silence what you have here heard.

LEADER. I swear by revered Artemis, Zeus' maiden, never to reveal your sins to the light.

PHAEDRA. Thank you. I have thought it over; there is only one solution to my problem, if I am to bequeath an honorable life to my children and turn this disaster to my own credit. Never will I disgrace my Cretan home, nor will I face Theseus on so vile a charge,—not for the sake of one little life.

LEADER. Are you about to do some irretrievable evil?

PHAEDRA. Die. But I must plan how.

LEADER. Don't say such a thing!

PHAEDRA. You too lecture me! I shall pleasure Aphrodite (it is she who has destroyed me) by departing from life this

day. I am worsted by bitter love. But I shall become a bane to
another when I am dead. He may learn not to be superior
about my troubles; when he has shared this trouble with
me he shall learn to be reasonable.

[*Exit.*]

CHORUS. *Sink me beneath earth's deepest abysses! Or make
me a winged bird, O god, among the feathered flocks! Let
me fly over the waves to the Adriatic shore, to the waters of
Eridanus, where the sad daughters of the Sun, mourning for
Phaethon, distil amber splendors of tears into the dark
flood.*

*To that orchard on the shore, where the Hesperides sing,
would I take me; where the Sea Lord of the darkling deep
no longer vouchsafes a path for mariners, fixing there the holy
boundary of heaven which Atlas holds; where ambrosial fountains gush by the couches of the halls of Zeus; where divine
earth, the good giver, multiplies blessings for the gods.*

*Cretan barque white-winged, through the resounding wave
of the briny surge you carried my lady from her happy home
to the joy of a joyless marriage. Verily, ill luck attended the
departure, as the barque flew from the Cretan land to glorious Athens; and ill luck was there, on the shores of
Munychus, as they knotted the ends of their cables, and set
foot on the mainland.*

*True were the omens; she has been smitten to the heart
by Aphrodite's dread plague, the plague of incestuous love.
And now, overwhelmed in the surge of calamity, to the
beams of her bridal chamber she will fix a hanging noose and
fit it to her white neck, from shame and loathing of life,
choosing rather the glory of a fair name and seeking to rid
her heart of the pains of love.*

NURSE [*within*]. Help! To the rescue, all that are near
the house! In the noose is our mistress, Theseus' wife.

SOME WOMEN OF THE CHORUS. Alas, alas, it is done. The
royal lady no longer lives. She is caught in the swinging
noose.

NURSE [*within*]. Will you not hurry? Will nobody bring
a sharp knife to loosen the knot from her neck?

OTHERS OF THE CHORUS. Friends, what shall we do? Do
you think we should enter the house and loosen the queen
from the suicide's noose?

OTHERS. Why? Aren't there young serving women? Meddling is not a safe way of life.

NURSE [*within*]. Straighten her limbs, arrange the poor body. A bitter housewifery is this for my masters.

CHORUS. She is dead, poor woman, if I hear right. They are already arranging her corpse.

[*Enter Theseus, garlanded as one returning from an oracle.*]

THESEUS. Women, do you know the meaning of the commotion in the house? A grievous sound from the maidservants reached me. Nor does the house deign to open its doors and welcome me with joy, as coming from the oracle. Has any ill befallen old Pittheus? He is well on in life, yet I should be sorry if he left us.

LEADER. This misfortune, I tell you, pertains not to the old, Theseus; the death of the young will grieve you.

THESEUS. Ah me! The life of my children is not taken from me?

LEADER. They are alive, but their mother is dead: how sad for you!

THESEUS. What are you saying? My wife dead? How?

LEADER. She fastened a suicide's noose about her neck.

THESEUS. Was she chilled with grief? Or what was the trouble?

LEADER. That is all we know. I have but just come to your house, Theseus, to mourn for your sorrow.

THESEUS [*flinging away his garland*]. Ah! why is my head crowned with these twisted leaves, sorry pilgrim that I am! Loosen, servants, the bars of the gates, undo the bolts, that I may see the bitter spectacle of my wife, who by her death has ruined me.

[*The palace doors are thrown open, and the body of Phaedra, surrounded by wailing domestics, is revealed.*]

SOME WOMEN OF THE CHORUS. *Alas, poor woman, for your bitter woes! Victim of your own deed, a deed to confound this house!*

OTHERS. *Woe, woe, for your boldness! Ruthlessly slain by an unholy chance, a sorry triumph over your own self!*

OTHERS. *What is it, poor woman, that darkened your life?*

THESEUS. *Alas for my woes! I have suffered, O my city, the greatest sorrow I ever suffered. How heavily have you tram-*

*pled upon me and my house, O fortune, mysterious blight of
some avenging fiend, nay, very annihilation of life! A sea of
evils do I behold, unhappy, so wide that I shall never see the
shore again, never rise above the flood of this calamity. Unhappy me! What words can rightly describe your heavy fortune, my wife? Like some bird have you vanished out of my
hands, launching yourself with a sheer leap to Hades, woe is
me! Oh, Oh! Oh, Oh! Pitiable, pitiable, is my affliction.
From some far off time, from the sins of someone long ago,
the gods bring disaster home to me.*

LEADER. Not upon you alone has this disaster fallen, O
King; many beside you have lost excellent wives.

THESEUS. *Below earth, in the shades below earth, I would
abide in darkness, wretchedly dying; for I am bereft of your
dearest companionship. Your death has destroyed much more
than yourself.*

*Who will tell me? Whence came this deadly doom to your
heart, poor wife? Will someone tell me what has happened?
Is it to no purpose that my lordly house shelters a crowd of
domestics? Alas for you, woe is me! Such a grief have I seen
for my house, unendurable, unspeakable! I am ruined. Desolate is my house and my children are orphaned. You have
forsaken me, forsaken me, O dearest and best of women
whom the light of the sun and the starry radiance of night
behold!*

CHORUS. *Alas! Unhappy, unhappy, man! What sorrow
reigns in your house! My eyes are wet with blinding tears for
your loss. But for the woe to follow I have been trembling
long.*

THESEUS. Ah! Ah! What is this tablet clutched in that dear
hand? Will it tell some new sorrow? Has the poor woman
written her desires, her requests, about remarriage, about the
children? Reassure yourself, hapless one, the woman does not
live who will enter the bed of Theseus or his home. Look!
the imprint of the golden seal of her who is no more smiles
up at me. Come, let me unroll the string of the seal and see
what this tablet would say to me.

SOME WOMEN OF THE CHORUS. [*Woe, woe, here is another, a new evil sent by a god to succeed the former. For me
life has become unlivable in the face of what has happened.*

OTHERS. *Ruined, utterly overthrown, alas, alas, do I call the
house of my lords.*

OTHERS.] *O god, if it is in any wise possible, do not con-*

*found this house; hear my petition. I see, like a prophet, an omen of further evil.*

THESEUS. Ah, a new evil is this added to the old—unendurable, intolerable! Ah, poor devil that I am!

LEADER. What is it? Tell me if I may hear.

THESEUS. *The tablet cries aloud, it cries aloud of horrors. Whither can I flee this weight of woe? I am undone, utterly ruined. Such an elegy I have read, ah me! It has a tongue, this writing.*

LEADER. Alas, your words are harbingers of evil.

THESEUS. No longer will I keep it back behind the gates of my reluctant lips. This abominable, abominable crime! O my city, my city, Hippolytus has laid violent hands on my wife, brazenly despising the awful eye of Zeus! Father Poseidon, with one of those three curses which once you promised me destroy my son; let him not escape this day, if the curses you granted me are genuine.

LEADER. For the gods' sake, king, recall that prayer! You will come to realize the mistake you have made; believe me!

THESEUS. It cannot be. Further, I drive him forth from this land. By one of two fates will he be smitten. Either Poseidon will honor my curses and send him dead to the house of Hades, or exiled from here, wandering from land to land, a homeless stranger, he will drain the cup of life's bitterness to the dregs.

LEADER. Here he comes himself, most opportunely—your son, Hippolytus. Bate your fierce rage, Lord Theseus. Consider what is best for your house.

*[Enter Hippolytus from the right.]*

HIPPOLYTUS. I heard your cries, father, and have come in haste. What thing is making you groan I do not know, but I should like to hear it from you. Ha! What's this? Your wife, father. Dead. This is a terrible shock. Just a little while ago I left her; no long time ago she was looking on the light.

What happened to her? How did she die? Father, I want to learn about it from you. You keep silent. But there's no use of silence in trouble. The heart which yearns to be told all inquires as eagerly in time of trouble too. It is not right to hide your grief from friends, indeed more than friends.

THESEUS. Mankind, vain and misguided, why do you teach ten thousand arts and contrive and invent all manner of devices, yet do not understand and have not investigated the one thing—how to teach sense to people who have no mind?

HIPPOLYTUS. You posit a wise sage indeed, to be able to compel those who have no sense to have good sense. But you are spinning fancies, father, at an unfitting time; I fear your tongue is running wild from grief.

THESEUS. Ah, men ought to have a true yardstick of friendship, deposited somewhere, some means of discerning the heart, to know who is the true friend and who is not. And all men should have two separate voices, one a just voice and the other so-so. Then the one which was dishonest would be convicted by the just one, and we should not be liable to error, as we are.

HIPPOLYTUS. Has some friend got your ear for slander against me? Am I infected though altogether innocent? I am astonished. Yes, your words astound me: they wander far from the seat of reason.

THESEUS. Ah, the heart of man—how far can it go? What limit is there to brazenness and effrontery? If it is to expand generation by generation, and the new transcend the old in rascality, the gods will have to add some new land to the earth to make room for the rogues that are born.

Look at this man. My own son, yet he tried to seduce my wife. He is manifestly proven most base by the hand of her who is dead. [*Hippolytus covers his face in horror.*] Show your face here to your father: your company has already polluted me. *You* are that superior creature that associates with gods? *You* are temperate and uncontaminated by evil? Your high claims will never convince me; I won't be such a fool as to attribute to the gods such a lack of discernment. Go then and brag, cry up your vegetarian diet like a quack. Hold Orpheus your master, rant away, revere the vaporings of your many screeds. But you are caught. I charge you all, shun such men as this. They ensnare with pious words, but their aims are evil. She is dead: do you think that will save you? You are only the more caught, you utter villain. What oaths, what arguments could outweigh this tablet to deliver you from the charge?

You will say that she hated you: you will plead the natural antipathy of bastard and true born. You are making her a bad bargainer in the business of lives, if for hatred of you she sacrificed the dearest thing she had. Well, will you say that folly resides not in men but is innate in women? I have known young men no more proof against temptation than women when Cypris troubled their adolescent spirits. [But the epithet "masculine" is their excuse.]

But why do I stand here arguing with you when this corpse lies here, a most irrefragable witness? Go to your ruin, an exile from this land, and go at once. Go not to divinely built Athens nor to the bounds of any land where my spear holds sway. If I lie down to the wrongs you have done me, Sinis of the Isthmus will swear that I never slew him, that I have been making an empty boast; and the rocks of Sciron, beside the sea, will deny that I am dangerous to evildoers.

LEADER. I know not how I can call any mortal happy. They that were exalted are debased.

HIPPOLYTUS. Father, this passion, this emotional intensity, is dreadful. That sort of thing makes for a plausible harangue, but when you get to the bottom of it, it is not a good thing. I have no skill in speaking before the crowd; I am cleverer, on the other hand, with my friends, and those few. That too is quite natural; those who are accounted of no consequence among the wise are eloquent before the mob. But the predicament which has come upon me forces me to loosen my tongue. I shall begin my speech at the point where you first assailed me, thinking to crush me beyond reply.

You see this light, this earth: within their range there lives not a man of chaster heart than mine, deny it as you will. I have learnt, first, to reverence the gods, and next, to have as friends not those who would attempt iniquity but those who would blush to suggest evil to their friends, or to act on a base suggestion. I am not a mocker of my companions, father; I am always the same to my friends, whether present or absent. And if there is one thing of which I am without spot it is the thing in which you think you have caught me. Of sexual intercourse I am to this day pure. I know nothing of the deed except what I have heard people say or seen in pictures. And I am not keen to look at such things, for I have a virgin soul.

Suppose my chastity fails to convince you. Then it is for you to demonstrate how I was corrupted. Was it because this woman excelled all other women in beauty of person? Or did I expect to rule your house, attaching myself to a woman that was an heiress? I must then have been a fool, quite out of my wits. But "it is delightful to be king"? Not at all, at least not for the temperate man, unless dominion has corrupted the minds of mortals that take pleasure in it. While I might like to be first in the Games, in the city I should prefer to take a back seat, living a contented life with the help of my friends among the best people. In that way there is freedom of conduct, and the absence of danger provides a greater joy than kingship.

Of my arguments one is yet unspoken; you have the rest. If I had a witness to my innocence, if this woman were alive to be present at my trial, then an examination of the facts would reveal the guilty. As things are, I can but swear by Zeus, guardian of oaths, by this land's level plain, that I have never touched the wife of your bed, never would have desired it, never even have thought of it. Yea, may I perish unhonored, unknown, without a city, without a house, an exile wandering over the earth; may neither sea nor land receive the flesh of me when I am dead, if I am a guilty man.

Whether it was through fear that she destroyed her life, I know not; for me it is not lawful to say more. Right has she done when she could not do right; right I had, and it has done me wrong.

LEADER. The oaths you have offered by the gods, no mean pledge, are a sufficient rebuttal of the charge against you.

THESEUS. Is not this fellow a wizard and a mountebank to believe that nonchalance will help him to prevail over me, after making a cuckold of his father?

HIPPOLYTUS. And I am equally surprised at you, father. If you were my son and I your father I should have killed you on the spot, and would not now be punishing you with exile if you had presumed to touch my wife.

THESEUS. A characteristic suggestion! But not so shall you die. A quick death is easiest for a poor wretch. But an exile wandering far from your native soil, as you pronounced the terms for yourself—

HIPPOLYTUS. Ah me! What will you do? Will you not await time's testimony about me? Will you drive me out of the land?

THESEUS. Ay, beyond the sea and the Atlantic limits, if I could: so utterly do I hate you.

HIPPOLYTUS. Will you cast me out of the land untried, without examination of oath or pledge or prophet's oracle?

THESEUS. This tablet here, though it has no oracular cachet, authenticates the charge against you. For the birds of omen which fly overhead—I bid them a long farewell.

HIPPOLYTUS. Ye gods! Why do I not open my mouth, when I am being destroyed by you whom I worship? But I cannot. In any case, I should not persuade the one I must, and I should be violating to no purpose the oaths that I swore.

THESEUS. Your cant is killing me. Out from your country's soil, and at once!

HIPPOLYTUS. Whither shall I turn my unhappy steps? What host will receive me in his house, exiled on such a charge?

THESEUS. One who is pleased to entertain ravishers of wives and partners of evil.

HIPPOLYTUS. Ah, me! This strikes me to the heart and brings me nigh to tears, that I should appear unrighteous and that *you* should believe me so.

THESEUS. Then was the time to groan and to realize what you were about, when you shamelessly and brutally defiled your father's wife.

HIPPOLYTUS. O halls, would that you could utter forth a clear voice, and bear witness whether I am a base man!

THESEUS. You take refuge in speechless witnesses—quite clever. This deed, though it speak not, testifies to your villainy.

HIPPOLYTUS. Alas! If only I could stand apart and look myself in the face, that I might weep at the evils I have suffered!

THESEUS. You've had much more practice at regarding yourself than doing your duty by your parents as you ought.

HIPPOLYTUS. Unhappy mother! Bitter hour of birth! May none of my friends ever be a bastard!

THESEUS. Drag him away, slaves, won't you? Did you not hear me long since decreeing banishment for this man?

HIPPOLYTUS. At his peril shall any of them touch me. Do you yourself thrust me out of the land, if you have the moral courage.

THESEUS. I will so, if you do not heed my words. No pity at all for your exile moves me.

[*Hippolytus moves off; exit Theseus. Hippolytus pauses at the statue of Artemis.*]

HIPPOLYTUS. It is settled, it seems, and I am ruined. I know these things, but I know not how to say them. O dearest of deities, maiden daughter of Leto, companion at home, companion in the woods, I am banished from glorious Athens. Farewell, city and land of Erechtheus. O plain of Troezen, what a delightful land for lads to grow up in! Farewell. For the last time I see you, address you.

Come, lads, my age-fellows in this land, bid me good

speed, escort me forth from the land. Never will you see a man more chaste, even if my father thinks otherwise.

[*Exit Hippolytus with his following.*]

CHORUS OF HUNTSMEN. *Verily, it is a great thing, to believe in gods that care; it soothes the griefs of the believer. Though my secret heart hopes in an intelligent Providence, yet when I look at the fortunes of men and their actions, the hope fails me. One thing comes, another goes, and life for man is ever shifting, ever wandering.*

CHORUS OF WOMEN. *Heaven hear my prayer and Fate grant me this boon: good fortune and wealth, and a mind ungrieved, unanxious! May my opinions be neither uncompromising nor (on the other hand) mere glosses. May my disposition be easy, adjusting itself to every new morrow, in life-long happiness.*

CHORUS OF HUNTSMEN. *My temper is no longer orthodox, when I behold the frustration of my hopes. We have seen the star of Athens, the most brilliant of Hellas, we have seen him sent forth to a strange land by his father's fury.*

*O sands of my country's shore, O mountain thickets, where with swift hounds he used to slay the wild beasts, in the company of revered Dictynna!*

CHORUS OF WOMEN. *No more shall you mount the car of Enetian coursers, holding the hooves of your trained steed to the chariot course at Limna! The Muse that was ever wakeful within the frame of the lyre will be heard no more in your father's house. The retreats of Leto's maiden in the green forest depths will stand ungarlanded. Your exile has killed the competition of the maidens for the prize of your love.*

A MATRON OF THE CHORUS. *But I—with tears for your calamity I shall endure a life that is no life. You had no joy of your son, poor mother. Alas! I am angry with the gods. Woe! Triad of Graces, why do you let him go forth from his fatherland, from these halls, the poor sufferer? He was not the cause of the calamity.*

LEADER. Look! I see a henchman of Hippolytus, gloomy-visaged, striding toward the house in haste.

[*Enter Messenger.*]

MESSENGER. Where might I go to find Theseus, ruler of this land, women? Tell me, if you know. Is he within the house?

LEADER. Here is himself, coming out of it.

[*Enter Theseus.*]

MESSENGER. Theseus, I bring a story which should cause concern to you and to the citizens that live in the city of Athens or at the ends of the land of Troezen.

THESEUS. What is it? No sudden calamity has befallen the two neighboring cities?

MESSENGER. Hippolytus is dead, or practically so. He yet looks upon the light, but it is touch and go.

THESEUS. By whose hand? In a feud with someone whose wife he had defiled, like his father's?

MESSENGER. His own chariot team destroyed him, and the curses of your mouth, with which you cursed your son to your father who is lord of the sea.

THESEUS. Ye gods! Poseidon! So you *are* my father right enough. For you have heeded my prayers.

How did he die? Tell me. How did Justice bring her cudgel down upon him that wronged me?

MESSENGER. Hard by the wave-beaten shore we were combing the horses' manes with currycombs, all in tears; for a messenger had come saying that Hippolytus might no longer set foot in this land because you had doomed him to miserable exile. Then he came, bringing the same sad song to us on the shore. A countless following of his friends, a throng of his age-fellows, came with him. After a time, when he had ceased from his groans he spoke: "Why am I so distracted? My father's behests must be obeyed. Harness the yoke-bearing steeds to my car. This city is no longer mine".

Then did every man bestir himself, and quicker than you could say the word we set the mares all harnessed before their master. He grasped the reins in his hand from the rim of the car and fitted his feet neatly into the sockets, but first he spread out his hands in prayer to the gods: "Zeus, may I live no longer if I am a man that is base. Let my father realize how he has abused me, either after I am dead or while I still see the light". With that he took the goad in his hand and whipped up the horses. We servants followed our master close to the car, near the horses' heads, out the road which leads directly to Argos and Epidauria. When we had come to a deserted stretch, there is a beach beyond this land,

sloping toward the Saronic Sea. From there came a noise,
like an earthquake, a deep roar, horrible to hear. The horses
held their heads erect and pointed their ears toward heaven.
Upon us broke a mighty dread, whence that sound could be.
When we looked toward the sea-beaten shores we saw an un-
earthly wave reaching to the sky in a pillar, preventing me
from seeing the headland of Sciron beyond; it hid all the
Isthmus and the Rock of Asclepius. And then swelling up and
splashing quantities of foam with a snorting of the sea it
proceeds toward the shore, where the four-horse chariot was.
Together with the breaker and its triple surge the wave set
forth a bull, a prodigious monster. With its bellowing the
whole land was filled, and it re-echoed horribly; to the on-
lookers it was a sight more than eyes could bear.

Straightway a dreadful fright falls upon the mares. Their
master, who was quite at home with the ways of horses,
seized the reins in his hands and strained at them as a sea-
faring man pulls at his oar, and he planted his body to lean
backward with the reins. But the mares bit down on the fire-
begotten bits in their jaws and bore on violently, paying no
heed either to the steersman's hand nor to the traces nor to
the jointed chariot. When he steered the course with his
reins to the soft ground the bull appeared in front to head him
off, throwing a frenzy into the four-horse team. And when
they careered madly toward the rocks it kept close to the
rail in silence, and kept up until it fouled the chariot and
overturned it, striking its wheel-rim against a rock. Then
everything was in confusion. The hubs of the wheels flew up,
and the linch-pins of the axles. Himself, poor man, tangled in
the traces, is caught in an inextricable bond and dragged
along, dashing his dear head against the rocks, lacerating his
flesh; and he cried out in a voice dreadful to hear: "Stand,
you that were fattened at my stalls; do not crush me out! O
my father's unhappy curses! Who here wills to save a good
man?"

Many of us willed to, but we were left far behind. Meanwhile he is freed from his bonds, the traces neatly cut, I
know not how, and he falls, breathing yet some little life. The
horses vanished, and that ill-starred monster of a bull, I
know not where in the rocky ground.

I am a slave of your house, Sire, but so much I can never
do—be persuaded that your son is base; nay, not even if the
whole race of womankind hang themselves or if someone fill

all the pines of Ida with accusations; for I know that he is a good man.

LEADER. Alas, the disaster of new evils is consummated. There is no refuge from destiny and the inevitable.

THESEUS. Hatred of the man who suffered these things gave me pleasure in the account. But now I respect the gods and him too, because he is of my body, and so I am neither rejoiced nor grieved by these evils.

MESSENGER. Well then? Shall we bring the sufferer here, or what shall we do with him to please you? Think it over. If you take my advice, you will not be cruel to your boy in his misfortune.

THESEUS. Bring him to me, so that I may look with my own eyes upon him who denies he defiled my bed, and may confute him with words and with the dispensations of the gods.

[Exit Messenger.]

CHORUS. *Thou, Cypris, dost ply the stubborn hearts of gods and mortals, and with thee is he of varied plume that circles round on swiftest wing. He darts over the earth and the tuneful briny deep, Eros the winged, gleaming with gold. He enchants with a heart-frenzy all whom he assails; he charms the natures of the young beasts on the mountains, and those of the sea, as many as earth sustains and the gleaming sun beholds, and men also. Over these all, Cypris, dost thou alone hold queenly sway.*

[Artemis appears aloft.]

ARTEMIS. *You, the nobly born child of Aegeus, do I bid hearken: Leto's maiden Artemis addresses you.*

*Theseus, why, miserable man, do you take pleasure in these circumstances, when you have slain your son unrighteously, crediting for things secret the lying tales of your wife? But not secret is the retribution that has over-taken you. Why do you not hide your body in shame in Tartarus beneath the earth, or change your being to a bird of the sky, to fly far from this woe? You can have no por-tion in the life of good men.*

Hear, Theseus, the state of your sorrows; I shall not make it easy for you, but cause you pain. For this purpose have I come, to reveal to you the righteous heart of your son that he may die with honor, and also the frenzy of your wife and, in a sense, her nobleness.

Stung by the pricks of that goddess most hateful to us who delight in virginity, your wife became enamored of your son. With her will she tried to overcome Cypris, but was ruined, unwittingly, by the devices of her nurse, who revealed her passion to your son, under pledge of secrecy. As became à righteous man, he yielded not to her proposals. But neither did he repudiate the oath he had sworn, though vilely treated by you; for a pious man he was. But she feared an investigation, and wrote lying writings, and destroyed your son by guile. Yet you believed her.

THESEUS. Woe is me!

ARTEMIS. Does the tale sting you, Theseus? But stay quiet and hear what happened thereafter, that you may groan the more. You know that you had three true curses from your father? Of these you have misused one, against your own son, base villain, when you could have used it against some enemy. Your father of the sea, though kindly disposed, granted as much as he was bound to; for he had promised. But to him and to me alike do you appear base; for you awaited neither pledge nor sign of oracles, you neither made examination nor left proof to length of time; but quicker than became you, you hurled curses upon your son and slew him.

THESEUS. Lady, let me perish!

ARTEMIS. Dreadful was your act. Nevertheless, even for you it is possible to attain forgiveness. It was Aphrodite, sating her wrath, who willed these things to happen. The gods have this rule: none will cross the course of another's humor; we stand aside always. Yet, if I did not fear Zeus, I would never have stooped to this dishonor—to let die the man I loved most of all mortals. As for your sin, in the first place your ignorance acquits you of malice; secondly, your wife's death beggared argument and forced your judgment.

Upon you in chief have these woes burst forth, but the sorrow is mine too. The gods have little joy in the death of the pious; but the wicked we destroy with their children and their houses.

[*Enter Hippolytus supported by attendants.*]

CHORUS. *Lo! Hither comes the pitiable man: mangled are his youthful flesh and his fair head. O the misery of this house! What a double grief, launched from Heaven, has been fulfilled for these halls!*

HIPPOLYTUS. *Ah! Ah! Oh! Oh! An unfortunate am I. By the*

*unjust imprecations of an unjust father am I mangled, ah, miserably. Woe is me, woe! Pains shoot through my head, a spasm darts through my brain. Hold, I will rest my failing body.*

*O hateful chariot team, fed by my own hand, you have utterly destroyed me, you have utterly slain me. Alas, alas! 'Fore the gods, gently, slaves, take hold of my wounded body with your hands. Who stands at my side to the right? Carefully raise me, carry me evenly, the ill-starred, accursed by my father's errors. Zeus, Zeus, do you see this? Here am I, the pious, the reverent, here am I, who excelled all in temperance—to Hades manifest I go; I have lost my life utterly. In vain have I toiled at the labors of piety toward men.*

*Ah, ah! Ah, ah! The pain, now the pain is come: let me go, ah me! Let Death the Healer come upon me. Come, come and destroy the unhappy wretch. For a two-edged sword I yearn, to cut myself in pieces and lay my life to rest. O ill-starred curse of my father! The evil of bloodguilty kinsmen, ancestors of old, finds its issue in me and tarries not; it comes upon me—why, when I am in no way guilty of evil? Woe is me, woe! How can I free my life from these unfeeling sufferings? Masterful Death, lay my miseries to rest in the blackness of thy night!*

ARTEMIS [*who has remained upon her platform unobserved*]. Ah, unhappy man! To what a calamity are you yoked! Your own nobility of heart has destroyed you.

HIPPOLYTUS. Ah, breath of divine fragrance! Even in the midst of evils I perceive thee, and my body is alleviated. Artemis the goddess is in this place.

ARTEMIS. She is, hapless man; and of the gods most friendly to you.

HIPPOLYTUS. You see how it is with me, Lady,—how pitiful—

ARTEMIS. I see. But gods may not weep.

HIPPOLYTUS. Your huntsman, your henchman, is no more—

ARTEMIS. Ah, no. Very dear to me you are, even in your death.

HIPPOLYTUS. The keeper of your horses, the guardian of your images.

ARTEMIS. Pernicious Cypris has devised it so.

HIPPOLYTUS. Ah me! I recognize the deity that ruined me.

ARTEMIS. She was aggrieved for the worship she missed; she hated you for your chastity.

HIPPOLYTUS. The three of us has Cypris destroyed; I perceive it.

ARTEMIS. Your father and you and the third, his wife.

HIPPOLYTUS. I mourn too for my father's catastrophe.

ARTEMIS. He was deceived by a deity's scheming.

HIPPOLYTUS. Ah, unhappy father! What a calamity is yours!

THESEUS. I am ruined, child; life has no pleasure for me.

HIPPOLYTUS. For your sake rather than for mine do I groan for this mistake.

THESEUS. Would that *I* were a corpse, child, instead of you.

HIPPOLYTUS. Ah, bitter gifts of your father Poseidon!

THESEUS. O that the prayer had never come to my mouth!

HIPPOLYTUS. Why? You would have killed me in any case; you were so infuriated.

THESEUS. Yes; my wits were confused by the gods.

HIPPOLYTUS. Ah! Would that the human race might bring a curse on the gods!

ARTEMIS. Let be. Though you are buried in the darkness of earth, I shall not forget Goddess Cypris. It was she who willed the wrath that has fallen on you, because you were pious and pure of heart. With these arrows of mine from which there is no escape I will wreak vengeance with my own hand upon another mortal—whoever is most dear to her. To you, sore sufferer, I shall vouchsafe in return for these evils the highest of honors in the city of Troezen. Maidens unwed shall shear their tresses for you before their bridal night, and you shall reap as your reward through the long ages to come the bountiful sorrow of tears. Ever shall virgins cherish you, singing songs in your honor, and Phaedra's love for you shall not fall into silent oblivion.

And you, son of ancient Aegeus, take your child into your arms and clasp him close. Unwittingly did you destroy him. It is but natural for humans to err when gods put it in their way. And you I bid, Hippolytus, not to hate your father. You understand the doom by which you were ruined.

Farewell! For me it is not lawful to look on death or to pollute my eyes with the gasps of the dying. I see that you are now near that sad case.

[*Artemis vanishes.*]

HIPPOLYTUS. Farewell, blessed maiden, in thy going! Right easily do you forsake our long companionship. My father I absolve from all blame, as you request; for in the past also I obeyed your counsels.

Ah! Ah! Already the darkness is shrouding my eyes. Take me, father, raise me up.

THESEUS. Ah me, child, what are you doing to wretched me?

HIPPOLYTUS. I am gone. Already I see the gates of the dead.

THESEUS. Will you leave me with my hands defiled?

HIPPOLYTUS. Nay, I free you from guilt for this death.

THESEUS. What do you say? Do you set me free of this bloodshed?

HIPPOLYTUS. I call to witness Artemis, mistress of the bow.

THESEUS. Best beloved, how noble do you show yourself to your father!

HIPPOLYTUS. Pray to obtain such sons—true-born.

THESEUS. Woe for your good and pious heart!

HIPPOLYTUS. Farewell, a long farewell, to you, my father.

THESEUS. Forsake me not, child; bear up!

HIPPOLYTUS. My bearing up is done. Father, I have died. Quickly hide my face with garments.

THESEUS. O glorious Athens, realm of Pallas, what a man you are losing! My grief! Long will I remember the evil you have done, O Cypris!

CHORUS. *Upon all the citizens has this common grief come unexpected: there shall be a downpouring of many a tear. The fame of the great endures, commanding sorrow.*

[*Exeunt.*]

# Andromache

THE plot of *Andromache* appears to be disjointed, with little obvious connection between its episodes. But the essential theme of the play, which is the inhumanity of Spartan *Kultur*, runs through all its parts. *Andromache* is indeed primarily a piece of anti-Spartan propaganda, written near the beginning of the Peloponnesian War, but it is a real tragedy, not merely a political squib, thanks to Euripides' unfailing sympathy for the oppressed and his passionate conviction that the war was not merely a quarrel between two cities but a clash between two ways of life. Menelaus is an unprincipled brute and a coward, Hermione luxurious and lecherous, Orestes a sneaking cad. All are unconscionably arrogant and unconscionably cruel to people less happily situated than themselves; and all are ready to cringe before firm opposition. Athens is not directly praised, but we assume that it maintains the more civilized ideals represented by Andromache and Peleus and Neoptolemus. It is in his sympathetic understanding of these victims of heartlessness that the Euripides we know appears. Apollo, who at the beginning of the war had given public notice that "invoked or not he would side with Sparta," proves to be a proper god for these unprincipled Spartan twisters.

# ANDROMACHE

## CHARACTERS

ANDROMACHE, *widow of Hector, slave of Neoptolemus*
ATTENDANT
HERMIONE, *wife of Neoptolemus, daughter of Helen and Menelaus*
MENELAUS, *father of Hermione*

MOLOSSUS, *son of Andromache*
PELEUS, *grandfather of Neoptolemus*
NURSE, *of Hermione*
ORESTES, *nephew of Menelaus*
MESSENGER
THETIS, *goddess, once wife of Peleus*

The scene represents the front of Thetis' Temple between Phthia and Pharsalia in Thessaly.

Andromache was acted sometime between 430 and 424 B.C.

———◆———

*[Andromache is seated at the altar of Thetis.]*

ANDROMACHE. O lovely Asia, O city of Thebes! Long ago I left you, a proud young bride with a dowry of much gold, and went to Priam's royal hearth, to be the wife of Hector and the mother of his children. Yes, in those olden days Andromache was a name to envy, but now—in all the world can any woman match her misery? My husband Hector I saw slain by Achilles, and Astyanax, his son and mine, hurled from the soaring battlements when the Greeks had taken Troyland. And I myself, daughter of a house that never knew constraint, was brought to Greece a slave, the pick of the plunder of Troy, given to the islander Neoptolemus in reward for his prowess. Here I live in Phthia and the neighboring fields of Pharsalia, where the sea-nymph Thetis shared house with Peleus, shunning the world and its bustle. (The people of Thessaly call the place Thetideum to commemorate the bridals of the goddess.) This house the son of Achilles occupied, leaving Peleus to rule over Pharsalia. He refuses to assume the throne till the old man

101

dies. Here in this house I have lain with the son of Achilles,
my lord and master, and borne him a son.

In those days, though my lot was hard, I was always sustained by the hope that while the boy was spared, I might have some bulwark and defense against trouble. But ever since my master spurned my slave's bed to marry Hermione of Sparta, she has been persecuting me with wicked slanders. She says that I have used secret spells to make her barren and hated by her husband, that I want to step into her place in the house myself, and drive her by force from her husband's bed. Yet, great Zeus be my witness, only under bitter constraint did I occupy that bed in the beginning, and now I have quite left it. But she refuses to believe me. Indeed she seeks my life; and in this her father Menelaus is acting in concert with his daughter. At this very moment he is in the palace, having come from Sparta for this and nothing else. In my terror, I came and took my seat here in the shrine of Thetis, in the hope that she may save me from death. For Peleus and the descendants of Peleus revere this memorial of the Nereid's marriage. My only son I have sent away secretly to another house, because I fear for his life. His father is not at hand either to help me, or to do anything for the boy. Far away in the land of Delphi, he is offering satisfaction to Loxias for that mad act of his when he went to Pytho and demanded from Phoebus an explanation of his father's murder. He hopes that if he asks pardon for his earlier trespass he may secure the god's goodwill for the future.

[Enter Handmaid.]

HANDMAID. Mistress—you see, I will not deny you the title with which I showed my respect for you in your own home, when we lived in Troy, myself a loyal servant both to you and, in his lifetime, to your husband. Now I come with more news for you—pity overcomes my fear of detection. Menelaus and his daughter are hatching a fearful plot against you. You must watch out.

ANDROMACHE. My dearest fellow slave (for fellow slave you are with her who was once your queen, but is now in distress), what are they doing? What new webs of trickery are they weaving? Do they mean murder? I have suffered everything else.

HANDMAID. It's your boy, whom you spirited away from the palace, that they mean to kill, unhappy woman.

ANDROMACHE. My grief! Has she learned of his escape? But how, how? My misery! I am lost.

HANDMAID. I do not know. That is all I heard, and Menelaus has left the house to get him.

ANDROMACHE. Then I *am* lost. O my child, these two vultures will catch you and kill you. And he that is called your father is still waiting at Delphi.

HANDMAID. If only *he* were here, I'm sure you would not be treated like this. As it is, you have no friends.

ANDROMACHE. Is there no word of Peleus coming either?

HANDMAID. He is too old to help even if he came.

ANDROMACHE. And yet I have sent for him more than once.

HANDMAID. You don't think that any of your messengers was concerned about *you*, do you?

ANDROMACHE. Why should they be? Will *you* take my message?

HANDMAID. But what excuse shall I give for so long an absence from the house?

ANDROMACHE. You will hit upon any number of expedients, being a woman.

HANDMAID. It's a risk, with Hermione so much on the lookout.

ANDROMACHE. You see? You desert your friends in their hour of need.

HANDMAID. Not I. Don't cast that reproach at me. I'll go. Nobody takes much notice of what happens to a slave woman, supposing I do get into trouble.

ANDROMACHE. Go, then. And I shall fill the wide sky with the lamentations and wailings and weepings that are now my constant companions.

[*Exit Handmaid.*]

It is in the nature of woman, when sorrows surround her, to find a joy in giving voice and tongue continually to her griefs. And I do not lack for topics of lament: the city of my fathers in ruins, my Hector dead, myself saddled with a cruel destiny, and slavery, foul slavery my portion. Call no man happy till he is dead, till you have seen how he has passed the last hour of his life on earth.

*It was no bride but rather a destroying fiend that Paris brought home to lofty Ilium, when he led Helen to the bridal chamber. On her account, O Troy, the warriors of Greece came in a thousand swift ships and ravaged you*

*with fire and sword, and slew Hector, my Hector, alas;*
*whom the son of the sea-nymph Thetis dragged round the*
*walls behind his chariot. I myself was taken from my cham-*
*ber down to the seashore, the hateful yoke of slavery on my*
*neck. Many were the tears that coursed down my cheeks,*
*as I left my city and my home and my husband in the dust.*
*O my grief, my grievous grief, why must I still look upon the*
*light, Hermione's slave? My torments have driven me forth*
*to this statue of the goddess which I embrace with suppliant*
*arms, while my tears gush forth like a fountain welling*
*from a rock.*

[Enter Chorus.]

CHORUS. *O woman, you who have been seated all this*
*time on the holy floor of Thetis, never leaving your post,*
*Phthian though I am, I have come to you, a daughter of*
*Asia, to see if I might compound an antidote for your hard*
*trials, that have engaged you and Hermione in a poisonous*
*feud, a sorry competition of two loves for the son of*
*Achilles, possessed by both.*

*Realize your position, think how hopeless is the hard lot*
*to which you are come: a slave against her masters, a*
*daughter of Ilium against the inhabitants of Lacedaemon.*
*Leave the altar and shrine of the sea-goddess. Why this*
*frenzy, what is the use of weeping your beauty away, just*
*because masters are masterful? Might will overtake you.*
*Why all this striving? You are nothing.*

*Come now, leave the splendid seat of the Lady of the Sea.*
*Realize that you are a slave in a foreign land, in a city*
*which is not your city, where you see none of your friends,*
*hapless girl, most wretched of all women.*

*O woman of Ilium, my heart grieved greatly for you when*
*you came to my master's house. It is fear that keeps me*
*silent—though I feel real pity for you—fear that the child*
*of Zeus' daughter learn of the goodwill I bear you.*

[SOME LINES HAVE FALLEN OUT HERE.]
[Enter Hermione.]

HERMIONE [to the Chorus]. These gorgeous golden ornaments on my head, these elaborate robes that clothe my
body, these are no gifts from the stores of Achilles or Peleus.
No, I brought them here with me from Laconia, the land of
the Spartans, them and all the rest of my dowry, given me

by my father Menelaus. So I have the right to speak freely. That is my answer to you.

[*To Andromache.*] As for you, you slave, won in war, you want to drive me out of this house and take possession yourself. Thanks to your spells, my husband hates me. Thanks to you, my womb is barren and dead. You are all very clever at that sort of thing, you continental women. But I'll put a stop to your tricks. The house of the Nereid here will do you no good, nor the altar nor the temple. You will die. But if it be that some god or mortal consents to rescue you, you must give up the high notions of the dignity you once enjoyed. You will have to crouch low and fall at my feet; you will have to sweep my floors and with your own hands sprinkle the house with river water from vessels of beaten gold; in short, you will have to learn just where in the world you are. This is not Hector, you know, or Priam and his gold. This is a Greek city. But you, poor wretch, have so little sensibility that you can stoop to sleep with the son of the man who slew your husband, and have children by his murderer. The whole tribe of barbarians is like that. Fathers have intercourse with daughters, sons with mothers, brothers with sisters. Kinsman slaughters closest kinsman, no law preventing. Don't introduce these practices here. It's a bad thing for one man to hold the reins over two women. The man who wants a happy home is content to confine his attention to one woman's bed.

LEADER. Woman is naturally a jealous creature; her intensest hatred is always kept for her husband's mistresses.

ANDROMACHE. Alas! youth is the world's plague, youth and its injustice. For my part, I am afraid that my being a slave may deny me the right to reply to you, though I have many truths to utter; or that if I speak and win, my victory may be to my cost. The great ones of the world resent being beaten in argument by their inferiors. Still, nobody will accuse me of scamping my own case.

Tell me, young woman, what considerations could have made me so confident of expelling you from your legitimate marriage? Is the city of Sparta less important than Phrygia? Does my fortune exceed yours? Are you looking at a free woman? Or is it youthfulness, or a fresh, young body, or great wealth, or a multitude of friends, that encourage me to seek to supplant you in this house? And why? In order that I, in your place, may give birth to slaves who will hang to my skirts in wretchedness? Will any man tolerate my

children as kings of Phthia, if you have no children? I suppose the Greeks love me and Hector's line. Perhaps they have
never heard of the queen of Phrygia.

It is not because of any spells of mine that your husband
hates you. No! it's your incompatibility. There is your philtre;
it is not our beauty, woman, but our virtues that delight
our husbands. If anything ever annoys you, then the city of
Laconia is extolled, and Scyrus is nowhere with you. You
are rich in a poor country. In your eyes Menelaus is greater
than Achilles. This is what your husband hates in you. Even
if she gets a humble husband, a woman ought to be content
and not start a competition of pretensions. If you had married a prince somewhere in Thrace, land of blizzards, where
one husband shares his bed with many wives in turn, would
you have slain these others? Then the sexual incontinence,
manifest in you, would have been extended to all womankind. A shameful imputation, and yet we do suffer worse
than men from that disease; though we hide it beautifully.

O dear, dear Hector, I at least for your sake actually
joined you in loving the occasional objects of your roaming
fancy. Many a time in the past did I offer my breasts to your
bastards, to avoid causing you any offence. And so doing
I attached myself to my husband and was a good wife to
him. But you are so full of fears, you would not suffer even a
drop of heaven's rain to visit your husband's face. Woman,
do not seek to outdo your mother's amorousness. When
mothers are wicked, sensible children should avoid taking
after them.

LEADER [to Hermione]. Mistress, take my advice, carry
your dispute with her no further than you feel you must.

HERMIONE [to Andromache]. Stop moralizing. And don't
bandy words with me as if you, forsooth, are the good woman and my conduct the opposite.

ANDROMACHE. As it is, in the light of your present attitude.

HERMIONE. May I never be cursed with a mind like yours,
woman!

ANDROMACHE. You are young to be talking about such
shameful things!

HERMIONE. You don't merely talk, you do them, as much
as you can.

ANDROMACHE. At it again? Must you keep harping on this
thwarted passion of yours?

HERMIONE. Why not? Doesn't love come first with all women?

ANDROMACHE. Yes, the right kind of love. Otherwise, it is not a good thing.

HERMIONE. Our city is not run on barbarian lines.

ANDROMACHE. Shameful is shameful, both in Greece and abroad.

HERMIONE. You are glib, glib; but you must die, none-the-less!

ANDROMACHE. Do you see the statue of Thetis looking at you?

HERMIONE. Yes, and hating your country where Achilles was slain.

ANDROMACHE. It was Helen caused his death. *Your* mother, not I.

HERMIONE. No further, please. Will you probe my wounds further?

ANDROMACHE. See, I am silent, I shut my mouth.

HERMIONE. Tell me what I came out here to learn.

ANDROMACHE. I tell you that you are not as wise as you ought to be!

HERMIONE. Will you leave this holy precinct of the sea goddess?

ANDROMACHE. Yes, if my life is to be spared. Otherwise, I shall never leave it.

HERMIONE. Then my resolve is fixed. I shall not wait for my husband to come home.

ANDROMACHE. But neither shall I surrender to you before then.

HERMIONE. I shall bring fire to play on you. I care nothing for your agony.

ANDROMACHE. Start your fire. The gods will know your crime.

HERMIONE. Your flesh, too, will suffer the tortures of cruel wounds.

ANDROMACHE. Slaughter me, defile the altar of the goddess with blood. She will punish you.

HERMIONE. You barbarous creature, hardened in impudence, does death not appall you? Very well. I shall soon get you to shift from your seat here, and of your own accord. I have the kind of bait that will fetch you. But enough. Enough of words. The deed will speak for itself, and soon. Sit on in your seat. Though molten lead soldered you all around, I shall shift you, before the son of Achilles, in whom you trust, comes home.

[*Exit Hermione.*]

ANDROMACHE. I do trust in him. It's a strange thing that whereas there are antidotes, revealed to men by some god, against the venom of fierce serpents, nobody has yet discovered a remedy for a plague worse than fire or any viper —the plague of Women. Such a curse our sex is to mankind.

CHORUS. *Yes, that was the beginning of great tribulation, when the son of Maia and Zeus came to that glen on Ida with a team of three beautiful goddesses, arrayed for a fatal contest of beauty; came to the cowherd's steading, to the young man plying his lonely shepherding, to the farm which was his home in the wilderness.*

*When they had come to that leafy glen, they washed their shining bodies in the waters of the mountain springs, and thus came to the son of Priam, each one seeking to outbid the others in the bitterness of their rivalry. The Cyprian was victorious with her deceitful words, words sweet to hear but bringing the bitterness of overthrow on the hapless city of the Phrygians and the citadel of Troy.*

*Would that his mother had hurled him far from her, like a thing of ill omen, before ever he made his home on the crags of Ida, that day when Cassandra beside the divine laurel cried out, "Kill him, kill this terrible bane of Priam's city." Did she not approach all the elders of the people? Did she not beseech them all to slay the babe?*

*Then the yoke of slavery would not have come upon the daughters of Troy, and you, woman, would have gotten a throne in the palace of kings. Greece would have been spared the grievous tribulations of those ten years when her young men fought a restless war round the walls of Troy. Wives would not have been left desolate, nor old fathers childless.*

[*Enter Menelaus.*]

MENELAUS. Here I come with that son of yours whom you spirited away to another house, without my daughter's knowledge. Yes, you flattered yourself that the statue of the goddess here would guarantee your own safety, and the people that hid him, the boy's. But we have discovered that you are not so wise as Menelaus, woman. And if you refuse to rid this spot of your presence, this boy here will be slaughtered instead of you. Reflect, then, whether you will die yourself or have *him* die for your crimes against me and my daughter.

ANDROMACHE. O Reputation, Reputation, to multitudes of worthless mortals you lend the illusion of greatness. Honorable fame, truly won, I admire; but there's a spurious glory which I will not deign to call glory; it is merely a chance reputation for discretion.

Was it really you that led the flower of Greece to war and wrested Troy from Priam, was it really this poor specimen that is now cajoled by his childish daughter and, snorting with fury, enters into the lists with a helpless woman, a slave? You were not worthy of Troy, I tell you. Troy did not deserve to be taken by you. [On the surface they are brilliant, those who are reputed to be wise; but inside they are no better than anybody else, unless, perhaps, in wealth. There's where their great strength lies.] Come, Menelaus, let us talk this matter out. Suppose your daughter has had my life, suppose I am dead. She will not escape any longer the pollution of blood-guilt. And in the opinion of most men you too will be chargeable with my murder; it must be so, for you are an accomplice. But suppose I escape death, will you slay my child? Then, tell me, how will the father not resent his son's murder? His reputation in Troy is not so unmanly. No! he will go to the proper quarter for satisfaction—you will see, he will not disgrace Peleus and Achilles his own father—and he will thrust your daughter out of his house. And what will *you* say when you offer her to somebody else? Will you say that it was her chastity led her to escape from a wicked husband? The truth will be known. Then, who will wed her? Or will you keep her in your house, to grow grey in her widowhood?

O poor man, don't you see the multitudinous sea of troubles that is surging towards you? How many betrayals of your daughter's bed would you rather discover than suffer the fate I describe? It is not right to commit great crimes for trifles. We women may be a bane and a plague, but men ought not to imitate us. For my part, if I am putting spells on your child and making her womb abortive, as she herself says, then freely and with a will, not throwing myself on any altars, I shall stand my own trial according to the verdict of your son-in-law, to whom I equally owe damages if I am making him childless. Such is *my* attitude. But there is *one* thing in your character that frightens me: it was in a woman's quarrel also that you sacked the hapless city of the Phrygians.

LEADER. For a woman speaking to a man you have said more than enough. You are right; but you have shot beyond the mark of discretion.

MENELAUS. Woman, this quarrel, as you say, is a small thing, not worthy of a king like me, or of Greece. But you must learn that it is a greater thing for a man to attain the object of the moment than to capture Troy. So I am my daughter's ally, for I consider the loss of one's husband a very serious matter. Anything else that happens to a woman is secondary; when she loses her man she loses her life. Neoptolemus is entitled to command my slaves; and my child and I too are entitled to command his. Friends, who are really and truly friends, have nothing private; their possessions are held in common. If I wait for the absent master and refuse to help myself, I am a worthless, foolish creature. Come now, get up from the shrine of the goddess here. If you die, the boy here escapes death; but if you refuse to die, I shall kill *him*. One or the other of you must forfeit life.

ANDROMACHE. Alas! you offer me a hard choice, his life or mine, a bitter lottery, in which, win or lose, I get misery and sorrow. O listen to me. You are committing a great crime for a trivial cause. Why slay me? What have I done? What city have I betrayed? What child of yours did I kill? What palace did I set afire? I *did* sleep, on compulsion, with my master. And yet you will kill me, not him, the responsible party. Ignoring the cause, you attack the subsequent effect. What a sorry situation! O my hapless country, how I am being wronged! Why did I have to have a child, to add to the burden of slavery a second burden? [But why weep thus? Why shed tears over the present? Why count death an evil?] I saw Hector dragged in death behind the wheels, I saw Ilium (the pity of it!) in flames. Myself enslaved, aboard the ships of the Argives I went, dragged off by the hair. Then brought to Phthia, I become the bride of Hector's murderers. What pleasure, then, has life for me? Where should I look? The present or the past? This boy alone was left me, the light of my life. Him they are about to slay; such is their pleasure. No! he shall not die, not if *my* life can save him. For him, if he escape, there is hope; for me, not to die for my child would be a disgrace.

There! I quit the altar. Here I am, at your mercy, to kill, to slay, to imprison, to hang. O my child, I your mother am

going to the house of Death, that you may not die. If you
get off with your life, remember your mother, what she endured and how she died. Tell your father how I fared and,
as you tell him, kiss him and hold his hands and weep. With
all mankind their children are their very life. I see that now.
The man who criticizes the family, having none himself,
may feel less pain, but his very happiness is a misfortune.

LEADER. Your words touch my heart. Men must pity misfortune, even in a stranger. Menelaus, you should try to rec-
oncile your daughter and this woman and deliver her from
sorrow.

MENELAUS. Seize her, slaves, throw your arms around her.
She will hear something she won't like. It was to make you
leave the altar of the goddess that I used your son's life as a
bait. Thereby I induced you to hand yourself over to me, for
slaughter. And that is what is in store for you; make no mistake. The fate of the child here my daughter will decide,
whether to kill him or not. Off with you into the house. A
slave like you must learn never to insult free folks.

ANDROMACHE. Woe is me! It was a trick, an underhand
trick. I have been deceived.

MENELAUS. Broadcast it to the world. I don't deny it.

ANDROMACHE. Is this what you on the Eurotas call clever?

MENELAUS. Yes, and you in Troy also: to return evil for
evil!

ANDROMACHE. Don't you believe in the gods and a day of
retribution?

MENELAUS. When that day comes, I'll stand it. But you I
shall kill.

ANDROMACHE. And this little chick also, snatched from
under my wing?

MENELAUS. Oh no! I'll give him to my daughter to slay, if
she wishes.

ANDROMACHE. Alas! Why do I not now mourn over you
as dead, my child?

MENELAUS. And why not? I cannot encourage you to be
optimistic about *his* future.

ANDROMACHE. O ye inhabitants of Sparta, the whole
human race loathes you. Your counsels are full of treachery.
Masters of the lie you are, ever planning wickedness. Your
minds are crooked, hypocritical, always devious. Justice is
thwarted by your successes in Greece. What crimes are not
found among you? Where does murder thrive more? Or sor-
did greed? Are you not always found saying one thing and

thinking another? My curse on you! For me this death sentence is not so hard as you expect. I died long ago, on that day when the hapless city of the Phrygians was destroyed and my noble husband, whose spear often drove you to your ship, making a craven sailor out of a craven soldier. Now it is to a woman that the warrior shows his grim face. You will slay me. Then slay. With no flatteries on my tongue I will take leave of you and your daughter. You are great in Sparta. Well, I was great in Troy. If I am now in misery, don't you gloat; you too may some day fare likewise.

[*Menelaus and his attendants leading Andromache depart.*]

CHORUS. *Never shall I approve of two loves for one man, or two women in a house where one son is. It means strife in the home, and enmity and pain. I would have the husband content himself with one wife, sharing his bed with none other.*

*So also in cities two rulers are worse to bear than one. It means civil strife, and burden on burden for the people. So between two craftsmen, creators of song, the Muses love to cause strife.*

*When the swift winds sweep the sailors along, two minds in control are inimical to good steering. A whole crowd of the most skilled helmsmen is less useful than a single mind in supreme command, though its skill be less. Therein lies efficiency, in houses and cities alike, whenever decisions are to be made.*

*Witness the Laconian, the daughter of prince Menelaus. In a blaze of fury against her rival, she means to kill the unlucky daughter of Ilium and her child for spiteful jealousy. Such murder is hideous, against the laws of god and man. Some day, lady, you will be overtaken by sorrow for these deeds.*

*But look what I see. Here in front of the palace comes the pair, tied close together, condemned to die. O unhappy woman, and you too, poor child, who will be slain on account of your mother's love, though you have no part in this affair and are guilty of no crime against the rulers.*

[*Enter Menelaus, and Andromache and Molossus in bonds.*]

ANDROMACHE. *Here I go, my bleeding hands bound fast with knotted ropes, on my way beneath the earth.*

MOLOSSUS. *Mother, mother, I too go with you, under your wing.*

ANDROMACHE. *A murderous sacrifice, ye lords of Phthia.*

MOLOSSUS. *O father, come and help your dear ones!*

ANDROMACHE. *There you will lie, my child, my dear one, close to your mother's breast, your body with hers, beneath the earth.*

MOLOSSUS. *Ah me! What will they do? Poor me, and you too, mother.*

MENELAUS. *Off with you to the dead. You come from a city I hate. A double compulsion demands your two deaths. My vote destroys you, and my daughter Hermione your son here. It is the height of nonsense to leave your enemies' children to carry on the enmity, when you have the power to kill them and free your house from fear.*

ANDROMACHE. *My husband, my husband, if only I had the help of your hand and spear, son of Priam!*

MOLOSSUS. *O misery! What spell can I invent to turn death aside?*

ANDROMACHE. *Pray to him, my child. Clasp your master's knees.*

MOLOSSUS. *Dear, dear man, let me go! Don't kill me!*

ANDROMACHE. *My eyes are wet with tears. They flow down like a sunless spring from a slippery rock. My misery!*

MOLOSSUS. *Ah me! Is there no remedy for my woes?*

MENELAUS. *Why entreat me? I am like a sea-swept rock or a relentless wave to all your prayers. To my own folk I give assistance, but you I have no cause to love. I tell you, I wasted no small part of my life to win Troy and your mother. She is the one to thank for your descent to infernal Hades.*

LEADER. Look, I see Peleus approaching, hurrying his old legs hither.

[*Enter Peleus with escort.*]

PELEUS [*to Menelaus*]. It's you I am asking—you who are supervising this slaughter—what are you up to? What is the meaning of it? Whose word started this rebellion? What do you mean by taking the law into your own hands? Menelaus, stop. Don't let haste outrun justice.

[*To his escort.*] And you lead me more quickly. This

is no time for loitering, I see. I would be thankful if I could recapture the strength of youth, now or never.

Firstly then, like a following wind that fills a ship's sails, I'll breathe courage upon her. Tell me, what right had they to bind your arms with ropes and hale you off, you and your child? You are going to your death, like a ewe with its lamb, while I and your owner are away.

ANDROMACHE. Old man, these men are leading me and my child to our death, just as you see. Why need I tell you? Not once only, but by message after message, I appealed to you, earnestly, to come. You have been told, I suppose, of the quarrel in the palace, started by this man's daughter; you know why I am being killed. And now they have torn me away from the altar of Thetis, the mother of your noble son, the goddess whom you worship and revere. They hale me off, denying me a regular trial, not waiting for the return of the absent owner. They know we are helpless, I and the child here, the innocent child whom they intend to slay with his unhappy mother. Ah, old man, I beseech you, falling before your feet (my hand is not free to touch your dear dear beard), save me, for heaven's sake. Otherwise, we die, which will be ill-luck for me, but disgrace for you and yours.

PELEUS. Loose her, I command you, before somebody is sorry. Untie the ropes that bind her hands together.

MENELAUS. But I forbid it. I am stronger than you and have far better right to dispose of her.

PELEUS. How? Will you come here and meddle in my affairs? Isn't it enough for you to lord it over the Spartans?

MENELAUS. It was I who took her prisoner in Troy.

PELEUS. Yes, but it was *my* son's son who got her as his prize.

MENELAUS. Well, is not mine his, and his mine?

PELEUS. Of course, but only to treat well, not to injure, and not to insult and kill.

MENELAUS. Take my word for it, you will never wrest her from my hands.

PELEUS. See this staff? I'll bloody your head for you.

MENELAUS. Touch me then, and see what happens. Just take a step towards me.

PELEUS. What! Do you count as a man, a coward like your fathers before you? Where is your place in the catalogue of men? Weren't you robbed of your wife by a mere Phrygian? You left the rooms of your house without bolts or duennas, as if that wife you had, the wickedest of her sex, were a chaste woman!

Spartan girls could not be chaste even if they wanted to. They leave home, and with naked thighs and their dresses loosened, they share the running tracks and gymnasiums with the young men. I call it intolerable. And then are we to be surprised that the women you bring up are not chaste? Helen might well have asked that question when she left your palace and your sanctified love and went gallivanting off to another country with her young man. And what followed? For her sake you assembled all that throng of Greeks and led them to Ilium. When you discovered her wickedness, you ought to have rejected her with loathing, instead of starting a war for her. Yes, you should have let her stay where she was and even paid money *not* to take her back home. But your mind took a different tack; you sacrificed many good lives, you made old women look in vain for their children's return, you robbed old grey fathers of their noble sons. I myself, alas! am one of these. In my eyes you are the devil who murdered Achilles. You alone came back from Troy without even a sword-scratch. Your untarnished armor in its fair coverings returned with you as good as it went.

I warned Neoptolemus, before the marriage, not to form any connection with you or take into his home the foal of an unchaste woman. The maternal disease tends to come out in them. (There's something I advise you to consider, suitors: pick the daughter of a good mother.) But there's more. Think of the hideous wrong you did your brother, when you stupidly demanded the sacrifice of his daughter. You were so afraid you would lose your worthless wife. And when you had taken Troy, (yes, I'll go as far as that with you,) you did not slay the woman when you had her at your mercy. No! as soon as you saw her breasts, you threw away your sword and took a kiss, fawning on the treacherous bitch, quite unable to resist her charms, you spineless creature! And after all that, you come to my grandson's house, in his absence, and pillage it. An unfortunate woman you put to a shameful death, and her son too. He will make you and your daughter that is in the house sorry for this, even if he is a bastard three times over. Many a time, mark you, poor soil yields a better harvest than rich, and bastards are often better men than legitimate sons. Take your daughter back home with you. Men had better choose their friends and relations from the humble and honest than from the wealthy and wicked. But you are nothing at all.

LEADER. From small beginnings the tongue produces mighty feuds, and wise men take good care not to start quarrels with friends.

MENELAUS. How can one say the old are wise, or those who in the old days passed for men of sense among the Greeks, seeing that you, who are Peleus and the son of a noble father, after allying yourself to our family thus insult us and shame yourself because of a foreign woman? This woman here you should have chased further than Nile's water, further than the Phasis. You should have spurred me on to do the same. She is from the continent, where so many corpses of Greeks were strewn on the ground before the spear. She had her share in the blood of your own son; for Paris, who slew your son Achilles, was the brother of Hector, and she is Hector's wife. Yet you go into the same house with her, and stoop to eat at the same table. You let her bear children, our enemies, in your house. And when I, looking out for your interests as well as my own, wish to put a stop to this, I find the woman snatched from my grasp.

Yet think—I may touch on the subject without immodesty. If my daughter has no children and this woman has, will you make them kings here in Phthia? Will a foreign family rule over Greeks? Is it not I who show good sense, in hating injustice, and you who are witless? [And now consider another thing. If you had given *your* daughter to some countryman. of yours and she had then been treated like this, would you have sat idly by and said nothing? I think not. Yet in defense of a foreigner you talk like this to friends and relatives. Moreover, man and woman are equally susceptible to grief, the woman when she is wronged by the man, and similarly the man when he has an unchaste woman in his home. Yet the man's own hands are his great strength, but the woman's resources are in her parents and her family. Am I not then entitled to give assistance to my own people?] You're an old man, just an old man. You spoke of my war service; that helps my case more than if you had kept quiet about it. Helen got into trouble involuntarily; it was heaven's doing. And yet it was the best thing that could have happened to Greece. They knew nothing of arms and war; they were taught valor. Experience teaches men everything. If at the sight of my wife I restrained myself from killing her, that was moral strength. Indeed, I could wish that you had had the same when you slew (your brother) Phocus.

I make this criticism not out of spleen, but out of kindness. If you lose that quick temper of yours your wagging tongue will only hurt you more. My motto is "Profit by Precaution."

LEADER. Now, stop this wild talk, both of you; that will be much better. You may both hurt yourselves.

PELEUS. Ah me! How stupid is our Greek custom! When armies raise trophies over an enemy, we do not regard the victory as the work of the toiling privates; it is the general who carries off the laurels. Yet he is only one man, wielding his lance with ten thousand others, doing no more than any one, but getting more credit than all. Seated solemnly in office, wherever they go, they think they are better than the common people; but they are themselves nobodies. The ordinary man is a thousand times cleverer than they; he only lacks their effrontery and ambition. So you and your brother sit back swollen with pride because of Troy and the service you saw there, but your glory rests on the labors and sacrifices of others. I shall teach you never to think Trojan Paris a more dangerous enemy than Peleus, if you don't get to the devil out of this house as fast as you can, and your barren daughter with you. My grandson will drag her by the hair from room to room. A barren cow herself, with no children of her own, she cannot stand others having any. If she has the bad luck to be barren, is that a reason why we should be deprived of descendants? Take your cursed hands off her, you slaves. Let me see if anybody will stop me from untying this woman's hands.

[*To Andromache.*] Lift yourself up. Trembling though I am, I shall loosen the twisted, knotted thongs. Oh look! you scoundrel, how you have disfigured her hands! Did you think you were roping a steer or a lion? Or were you afraid that she might seize a sword and drive you off? Come here, my child, come under my arms. Help me to untie your mother's bonds. I shall yet raise you up in Phthia to be an enemy to these Spartans. Take away their martial glory, their prowess in war, and in all other respects [*turning to Menelaus*], believe me, you are no better than anybody else.

CHORUS. Old age is an unbridled sort of thing, quick to anger and hard to handle.

MENELAUS. You are too prone to abuse. You let yourself be carried away. I am an unwilling visitor to Phthia. Consequently, I shall not do anything unpleasant, nor shall let anybody act unpleasantly to me. So now, since my time is not unlimited, I'll be off home. Not far from Sparta there's a . . . a city which has been friendly in the past, but is now showing hostility. I will lead an army into the field against it and reduce it to subjection. When I have things there settled to my liking, I shall return. Then I shall confront my son-in-law face to face; I shall inform him of my attitude and learn his. If he punishes this woman and behaves with moderation towards me in future, he will find me moderate too. But anger will provoke anger; I shall take my cue from him. These empty words of yours do not weigh on me. You are no man, but only a talking shadow, unable to do anything but talk.

[*Exit Menelaus.*]

PELEUS. Lead on, my child. Stand here under my arms, and you too, poor woman. You ran into a fierce storm, but you have reached a sheltered anchorage.

ANDROMACHE. Ah, old man, may the gods bless you and yours for saving my child and my ill-starred self. But look out lest these men lurk in ambush in a lonely part of the road and carry me off by force. They see that you are old, and I am weak, and the boy here is only an infant. For the moment we have escaped; take care we are not taken prisoner later.

PELEUS. Don't mention such womanish fears. Go. Who will touch you? Whoever does will be sorry for himself. By the favor of heaven I have hosts of horsemen and many foot-soldiers at my command in Phthia. I am not yet bowed down by age, as you imagine. A man like *that* I shall face alone and triumph over him, elderly though I be. Even an old man, if his heart is in the right place, is a better man than many a youngster. What's the use of physique to a craven?

[*Exeunt Peleus, Andromache, Molossus, and Attendants.*]

CHORUS. *Better never to be born, unless of ancestors that are noble, and to a house that is rich in possessions! For if hard times come along, the well-born have no lack of resources. Honor and glory are for the scions of noble families; their name is published abroad. Time does not obliterate the traces of the gentleman. Even in death his greatness is undimmed.*

*It is better not to win a victory of dishonor than to overthrow justice by violence and be hated for it. Such a triumph is dear to men's hearts at first, but time withers it away. It be-*

comes a burden on a man and a reproach to his house. Here is
the life I praise, the life I hope to win: to wield no power that
is unjust either at home or in the city.

O aged son of Aeacus, now I do believe that you, in company with the Lapithae, did glorious battle with the Centaurs;
that on the deck of the Argo you crossed the Inhospitable Sea,
out through the Clashing Rocks, on that famous voyage; that
in the earlier days, when the renowned son of Zeus threw a
net of slaughter over the city of Ilium, you shared in the
glory of the deed, on your return to Europe.

[Enter Nurse.]

NURSE. [to Chorus]. My dear friends, how this day does
produce evil on the heels of evil! The mistress of the house
(Hermione I mean), now that her father has left her alone and
she has time to think of the dreadful thing she has done,
plotting the death of Andromache and her child, wishes to
kill herself for fear of her husband. She is afraid he may drive
her ignominiously from his home to punish her for her misconduct, or even put her to death for seeking to kill those she
had no right to. The servants who are watching her can hardly
keep her from hanging herself or snatch the sword out of the
grip of her hand. Such is her remorse; she realizes that what
she did was not right. Indeed, I am worn out keeping her
from the halter, my friends. You must go into the palace
here and save her from death. She may be more ready to
listen to new friends than old.

LEADER. Listen! We can hear the cries of the servants you
came to report. I think the poor girl is going to show us how
sorry she is for her dreadful deeds. Here she comes out. She
has escaped the hands of the servants in her longing for death.

[Hermione rushes in.]

HERMIONE. O my misery! I will tear my hair. My nails
will rend and lacerate my cheeks.

NURSE. My child, what are you about? Will you disfigure
your person?

HERMIONE. Ah! Ah! This delicate veil, off with it from my
hair, into the air with it.

NURSE. My child, cover your bosom, fasten your dress!

HERMIONE. But why should I cover my bosom with robes?
The thing I have done is not covered, not concealed, not hidden from my husband.

NURSE. Are you grieving for the murderous plot against your rival?

HERMIONE. *Grieving! I am overwhelmed with sorrow at my murderous attempt. I am accursed, accursed in men's eyes.*

NURSE. Your husband will forgive you this mistake.

HERMIONE. *Why did you snatch the sword from my hand? Give it back to me, dear woman, give it back to me. Let me thrust the sword home into my breast. Why do you keep me from hanging myself?*

NURSE. What! let you go when you are out of your senses and might kill yourself?

HERMIONE. *My dreary fate! Where is consuming fire? I yearn for it! Oh! let me go to some soaring crag, beside the sea or on the wooded mountains, where I may die and find comfort in the grave!*

NURSE. Why trouble yourself like this? Divine visitations come on all mortals, at one time or another.

HERMIONE. *O my father, you have left me, you have left me desolate on the shore like a boat left without oars. He will kill me, kill me. No longer shall I live in this house, my husband's house. Shall I rush for protection to some god's statue? Shall I throw myself, like a slave, at the feet of a slave? I wish I were a dark-winged bird, to fly far from Phthia, or that pine-built hull that passed through the Dark Beaches, first of ships to sail the sea.*

NURSE. My child, you are far too impetuous for my liking, both in your crime against the Trojan woman and now again in this excessive panic which now possesses you. Your husband will never put your love aside like that. The worthless pleas of a barbarian woman will not win him over. You are no prisoner of war got in Troy. In you he got a noble man's daughter, and a rich dowry beside, from a city that enjoys no small prosperity. My child, your father will not abandon you, as you fear; he will not allow you to be thrown out of this house. Come now, get indoors. Don't make a spectacle of yourself in front of the palace here. You may cause a scandal if you are seen out here.

LEADER. Here comes a stranger, a foreign-looking man, making for us with hurried steps.

[*Enter Orestes.*]

ORESTES. Alien women, are these the halls of Achilles' son? Is this the royal palace?

LEADER. That's right. But tell me, who are you that ask this question?

ORESTES. The son of Agamemnon and Clytemnestra, my name Orestes. I am on my way to the oracle of Zeus at Dodona. When I got to Phthia, I thought I would inquire after my kinswoman, Hermione of Sparta. Is she alive and happy? Though she lives in a land far from mine, she is still dear to me.

HERMIONE. O Agamemnon's son, your appearance means a haven for the sailor storm-tossed. I beseech you by these knees, have pity on my misfortune. You see my plight. I throw my arms about your knees; let them do for suppliant branches.

ORESTES. Hullo! what's this? Am I mistaken or do I really see the queen of the palace here, the daughter of Menelaus?

HERMIONE. You do, unless Tyndarid Helen had other daughters in my father's house. You *must* know me.

ORESTES. O Healer Phoebus, grant release from sorrows! What is the matter? Is it gods or men that afflict you?

HERMIONE. Partly myself, partly the man whose wife I am, partly some god. I am utterly ruined.

ORESTES. What misfortune, except trouble with her husband, could befall a woman who has no children?

HERMIONE. That is just my difficulty. You prompt me well.

ORESTES. Is your husband in love with some other woman instead of you?

HERMIONE. His slave woman, Hector's wife.

ORESTES. That's bad. One man and two women.

HERMIONE. That is how things are. And then I counterattacked.

ORESTES. You didn't plot against the woman, did you, as a woman would?

HERMIONE. I did. I plotted death against her and her bastard son.

ORESTES. And did you kill them, or did some mischance rob you of your victims?

HERMIONE. Yes, old Peleus. He defended the worthless pair.

ORESTES. Had you any accomplice in your attempt at murder?

HERMIONE. My father. He came from Sparta for that very purpose.

ORESTES. And was he then worsted at the hands of the old man?

HERMIONE. Yes, in reverence for his age. And he has gone away and left me desolate.

ORESTES. I see. You are afraid of your husband because of what you have done.

HERMIONE. That's it. He will kill me, as I deserve. That's obvious. But I beseech you, by the God of Kindred, get me out of this country, to the ends of the earth. Or take me to my father's halls. This house seems to cry aloud "Drive her out". The land of Phthia hates me. If my husband finds me here on his return from the oracle of Phoebus, he will make me die a criminal's death. Or else I shall become the slave of this bastard wife of his, whose mistress I used to be. Perhaps you may ask how I came to make this mistake. Listening to bad women was my ruin. They flattered my vanity with words like these. "Will you allow the most unworthy slave in the whole house, a captive in war, to share your husband's bed? By the Queen of Heaven, if it were in my house, if it were my husband she had been enjoying, she would be dead now."

And I, listening to their siren words [their glib, unprincipled, cunning chatter] became swollen with folly. Why should I be keeping jealous watch over a husband? I had everything I needed, ample wealth and complete authority in the palace. Any children I had would be legitimate, whereas hers would be bastards and, through their mother, slaves to mine. But never, let me say it again, never should men of sense who have a wife at home, allow other wives to visit her frequently. They teach mischief. One woman seeks to undermine her love for some private profit of her own. Another, faithless herself, wants a companion in wickedness. In many cases it may be merely pruriency. There is the source of all the infidelity in men's homes. Therefore, guard your housedoors well, with bolts and bars. When other women get in, they do no good, and much mischief.

LEADER. You let your tongue run on too freely against our sex and its ways. In the circumstances I can sympathize with you, but still, women should gloss over women's failings.

ORESTES. He had a good idea, whoever taught mortals to listen to what the other side has to say. That was why, knowing the trouble that was upsetting this house and the feud between you and Hector's wife, I kept waiting and watching, to see if you would stay on the spot or take fright at what you had done to the captive woman and decide to get out of the house. So, ignoring your express commands, I came here, meaning to take you away with me if you gave me any pretext. And you do. You who were once *my* wife are now living with this fellow, thanks to your father's dishonesty. Before ever he set foot on Trojan territory, he gave you to me for my wife. Later, he promised you to your present lord, if ever he took the city of Troy.

Then when Achilles' son returned home here, I forgave your father and begged Neoptolemus to release him from the promise he made about you. I mentioned the misfortunes of my family, and the cruel fate that still haunted me. I pointed out that I might be able to marry into a family related to my own, but hardly into a strange family, being the sort of exile that I was. But he became insulting and taunted me with my mother's murder and the gory-visaged goddesses. I, humiliated by the fate of my family, was hurt, deeply hurt; but on account of my misfortunes I put up with it, and reluctantly went away, robbed of you, my wife. Now therefore, since your luck has veered round and you find yourself in a hopeless predicament, I shall take you away from your home and give you into your father's keeping. Kinship is a strange thing. In trouble there's nothing better than one of your own family.

HERMIONE. Of my betrothals my father will take care; it's no business of mine to decide. But quick, get me out of this house, lest my husband gets back home before I am away or Peleus hears that I am deserting his son's house and comes in pursuit on horses.

ORESTES. Don't be afraid of what an old man can do. As for Achilles' son you have nothing to fear from him, after the outrageous wrongs he has done me. A pretty trap has been set for him and stands right in his path, a murderous, inescapable web, devised by my hand. Until then, I'll say nothing. When the deed is doing, the rock of Delphi will witness it. A matricide am I? If my bravoes keep their word in the Pythian land, the matricide will teach him to marry no women meant for me. He will rue the day he asked Lord Phoebus to give him satisfaction for his father's death. No change of mind will help him; to-day the god gives him his deserts. Thanks to Phoebus and my accusations he will die a horrible death. He will learn how I can hate. God brings reversal of fortune on his enemies and stops their presumption.

[*Exeunt Orestes and Hermione.*]

CHORUS. *O Phoebus that built the well-walled towers on the hill of Ilium, and sea-god Poseidon that drives a car of grey horses over the waves, why did you deliver to war-loving Enyalius the work which your hands had built, abandoning hapless, hapless Troy and honoring it no more?*

*On the banks of Simois many were the chariots of noble horses you yoked. Many were the contests of men you established, contests of death, not for garlands. The princes of Ilium are dead and gone. Nowhere now in Troy does fire burn bright on the altars of the gods with smoke of incense.*

*Gone is the son of Atreus, by the hand of his wife. She herself, at the hands of her own children, has got her reward, paying for the murder with her own life. Out of heaven, out of heaven came the oracular command against her, when Agamemnon's son, after visiting the sanctuary, journeyed to Argos and slew her, murdered his own mother. O god, O Phoebus, how am I to believe?*

*In the market-places of all Hellas countless widows have sung dirges for their husbands, as they left their homes for a stranger's bed. Not on you alone, not on your family alone, has cruel agony come. A plague smote Greece, a plague. And across to the fruitful fields of Phrygia the thunderstorm passed, raining bloodshed and death.*

[*Enter Peleus, with attendants.*]

PELEUS. Women of Phthia, tell me what I ask. I heard a vague report that the daughter of Menelaus had quit this house and departed, and I hurried over here eager to find out if it were true. The folks at home must look out for the affairs of their friends that are abroad.

LEADER. Peleus, what you heard is true. I cannot, in honor, conceal the mischief that is going on around me. The queen has fled, she has left the house.

PELEUS. What was the fear that possessed her? Please, tell me all.

LEADER. She was afraid of her husband, afraid he would cast her out.

PELEUS. For her plots against the life of his son?

LEADER. Yes, and she was afraid of the captive woman.

PELEUS. Did she leave home with her father? Or with whom?

LEADER. Agamemnon's son escorted her out of the country.

PELEUS. What does he hope to accomplish by that? Does he want to marry her?

LEADER. He does, and also to cause the death of your grandson.

PELEUS. By lurking in ambush or meeting him face to face in battle?

LEADER. In the holy temple of Loxias, assisted by the Delphians.

PELEUS. Ah me! This is terrible news. Quick, quick, go to Pytho's altar, somebody, and tell your friends there what has happened here. Hurry, before the son of Achilles is slain by his enemies.

[Enter Messenger.]

MESSENGER. Alas, alack! Alas that I come to tell a story so painful to you, old man, and to my master's friends.

PELEUS. Ah! ah! my prophetic soul bodes ill.

MESSENGER. Your son's son is dead, old Peleus. Now you know. So deadly were the wounds he received from the swords of the Delphians and their friend from Mycenae.

[Peleus half faints.]

LEADER. Aged sir, what are you about? Don't collapse. Rouse yourself.

PELEUS. It's all over with me. My life is ended. My voice is gone, my legs are gone under me.

MESSENGER. If you really wish to help your friends, rise up and listen to the story of the deed.

PELEUS. O Fate, how cruelly you have gripped my suffering heart in the last years of extreme old age. How has my only son's only son been taken from me? Tell me. The tale is intolerable, but I will hear it.

MESSENGER. When we had arrived in the famous land of Phoebus, we devoted three radiant circuits of the sun to sightseeing, feasting our eyes on everything. And, as it proved, this incurred suspicion. The god's tenants began to gather together; little circles kept forming, while the son of Agamemnon went round the town filing each man's ears with words of hate. "Do you see this fellow stalking about the god's treasuries where all the gold and costly offerings are? He's back here again with the same intentions as before, when he came here to sack the temple of Phoebus."

This started a dangerous uproar in the city. The magis-

trates came flocking into the council chambers and, of their
own accord, those who were in charge of the god's treas-
ures posted sentries in the colonnaded halls. Meanwhile,
knowing nothing of all this, we had taken sheep, raised on
the grass of Parnassus, and we went and stood before the
altar fire, along with our Delphian agents and the priests of
Pytho. Then somebody said: "Young man, what prayer are
we to make to the god for you? What have you come here
for?" And Neoptolemus said: "I wish to make amends to
Phoebus for my past error, when I demanded of him satisfaction for my father's blood". There and then it was seen how
effective was Orestes' tale that my master was lying and
really meant mischief. The latter crosses the threshold of the
temple, to make his prayer to Phoebus before the prophetic
seat, and begins to busy himself with the burnt offering.
There, hidden in the shadow of the laurels, was a band
of men with swords, of whom Clytemnestra's child was one.
It was he planned the whole murder. While Achilles' son
stood facing the shrine and made his prayer, the armed men
drew their sharp whetted swords and, without warning,
stabbed the defenceless son of Achilles. He recoils—his
wounds were not deep, nothing fatal—and snatching some
weapons that hung on pegs on the temple-front he takes
his stand on the altar, showing fight, menacing. In a loud
voice he asks the sons of Delphi: "Why do you kill me when
my mission here is pious? What am I supposed to have done
to deserve death?"

There were thousands of them at hand, but no man spoke
a word. Instead, they began to pelt him with stones from
their hands, raining them on him like hailstones from all
sides. With his weapons held in front of him he tried to keep
off the showering missiles, reaching his shield this way and
that. It was of no avail. A whole storm of missiles at once,
arrows, javelins, light altar forks, and sacrificial knives, came
flying about him. *There* was a war dance you would have
shuddered to see, as your grandson kept dodging their aim.
But they surrounded him and hemmed him in and gave him
no breathing space, till at last he quitted the altar top with
that leap that Troy knew so well and rushed at his assailants,
who turned tail and fled, like pigeons at the sight of a hawk.
In the confusion many were killed, either by the sword of
Neoptolemus or crushed to death by one another in the
narrow exit. The temple's hush was desecrated by the babel,
echoed to the rocks. Then there was a moment of peace, my

master standing there, his armor glittering in the sunlight, till a mysterious voice came, blood-curdling, awful, from the heart of the shrine, which roused the armed crew and brought them back to the fight. The son of Achilles fell, stabbed in the side by a sharp sword, slain by a man of Delphi, like his father before him and countless others. As he lay on the ground, there was none who did not stab him or stone him, striking and mutilating his corpse. His body, his beautiful body, was quite disfigured by savage wounds. The corpse (I suppose it was too near their altar) they threw out of the shrine to which men do sacrifice. We picked it up with all speed and have brought him back to you, to lament over him with groans and tears and do him the honor of interment.

That is what Phoebus who issues oracles to others, the lord to whom the whole world looks for justice, did to Achilles' son when he offered to make amends. Like any base mortal, he remembered an ancient quarrel. How can he be wise?

[*The body of Neoptolemus is brought in.*]

CHORUS. *And now the prince approaches, borne shoulder-high from Delphi to his home. Unhappy is the victim, unhappy are you too, old man. This is not the welcome home you hoped to give to the son of Achilles. This evil blow hits you too and makes his calamity yours.*

PELEUS. *Ah woe is me! What a sorrow I see before me and take into my hands and my house! Woe is me! Alas and alas! O city of Thessaly, we are ruined, we are lost. My race is extinct, no children are left in my halls. O the wretchedness of my sorrow! What friend have I left to look upon and be happy? Dear mouth, dear cheek, dear hands, would that fate had slain you under the walls of Ilium, by the banks of Simois!*

LEADER. In that case, old man, he would have been honored more in death, and your life would be happier.

PELEUS. *O marriage, marriage, that has destroyed my home, destroyed my city. Alas, alàs! O that my family had never for the sake of children and heirs, involved itself with your wife Hermione (name of evil), thus bringing death on you, my child! Would that a thunderbolt had struck her first. And oh that you, a mere mortal, had never laid on Phoebus, a god, the guilt of spilling your father's heroic blood by (Paris') deadly archery.*

CHORUS. *Wail and wail again. I shall lead off the keening over my dead master with the Song of the Dead.*

PELEUS. *Wail and wail again. I take up the strain of sorrow. A sad old man, I weep.*

CHORUS. *Nay, it was a god's dispensation. A god brought this mishap to pass.*

PELEUS. *Dear boy, you have left my house desolate, you have abandoned me to childlessness in my wretched old age.*

CHORUS. *Old man, you should have died before your children, you should have died.*

PELEUS. *Shall I not rend my hair? Shall my hands not beat my head? A sorry sound! Ah my city, Phoebus has robbed me of my two children.*

CHORUS. *Old man, you have suffered grief, you have looked upon misery. What sort of life will you have hereafter?*

PELEUS. *Childless and helpless, in sorrow unending, I shall know no respite from misery till the day I die.*

CHORUS. *Vain then were the good wishes of the gods at your marriage.*

PELEUS. *My fortunes took a lofty flight, but now they lie in the dust, far from their former boasts.*

CHORUS. *Lonely you live in a lonely house.*

PELEUS. *I have lost my city, I have lost it. Let me throw this scepter to the ground. And you, daughter of Nereus in the caves of night, you will see me prostrate, my destruction complete.*

CHORUS. *Oh! Oh! What is that moving? What miracle do I see? Girls, look, see. This is some spirit, ferrying across the bright air, to settle on the pasture lands of Phthia.*

[Thetis appears.]

THETIS. Peleus, I am Thetis: for the sake of our sometime marriage I come to you from the house of Nereus. First I admonish you, do not take too hard the sorrows that lie before you. I too, who should surely never have known grief for children perished, lost the son I bore you, swift-footed Achilles, who was foremost among Hellenes.

I shall explain my errand here; do you but hearken. Him that is dead, this child of Achilles, take to the Pythian hearth and there bury him. It shall be a blot on Delphi; his tomb shall proclaim the crime of Orestes' bloody hand. As for the captive woman, Andromache I mean, she must settle in the

Molossian country, old man, united to Helenus, (Hector's brother,) in proper wedlock. And with her must go this boy, the last of the house of Aeacus. From him shall spring the kings of Molossia, one succeeding another in unbroken prosperity. It is not destined that your stock and mine should perish like this from the earth, old man, no, nor Troy's. For her line too heaven provides, although she has been overthrown by the will of Pallas.

That you may have reason to be grateful for your marriage with me [—I am a goddess born and my father before me—] I will deliver you from all mortal ills and make you a god, free from death and decay. And then in the house of Nereus you shall dwell with me for all time, god and goddess together. Then with feet unwetted you shall rise from the sea to look upon our son Achilles, your darling and mine, where he dwells in his island home on the White Strand within the Euxine Sea.

Now take this body and make your way to the Delphians' god-built city. When you have committed it to the earth, go to the hollow cave of the ancient rock of Sepias and there take your seat. Wait till I come from the brine with my choir of fifty Nereids to fetch you. That which is fated you must needs bring to pass; this is Zeus' pleasure.

Cease from your sorrow for the dead. For all mankind this decree is ordained by the gods: death is a debt that all must pay.

PELEUS. Lady, noble sharer of my bed, offspring of Nereus, hail! These things you do are worthy of yourself, and of your children. I do stop my grief at your bidding, goddess. When I have buried Neoptolemus I shall go to the glens of Pelion, where once my arms clasped your form so fair.

*[Thetis disappears.]*

Now does it not behoove a prudent man to marry into a noble house and to give in marriage to men that are well-born? A vulgar match is not to be desired, not even if it brings a man an enormous dowry. Then the gods would never bring men bad luck.

CHORUS. *Many are the forms of divine intervention; many things beyond expectation do the gods fulfil. That which was expected has not been accomplished; for that which was unexpected has god found the way. Such was the end of this story.*

*[Exeunt.]*

# Ion

———◆———

ION is a highly dramatic piece, full of arresting incident and emotional crisis. The picture of Ion's disillusionment as he suddenly matures and finds he must leave the shelter of the temple for the bad world outside is masterful and unique of its kind in Euripides. If Apollo is exhibited as a knave more plainly than elsewhere, yet the morning splendor of his shrine and the devotion of the Greek Samuel who serves it communicates a real sense of the beauty of holiness. The rather complicated plot runs as follows:

Creusa, the sole survivor of the line of Erechtheus, the founder of Athens, had been ravished by Apollo and had given birth to a son whom she abandoned in the cave where she had been ravished. Subsequently she married Xuthus, a soldier of fortune who had rendered the Athenians great service in war. Years pass but the couple remain childless. When the play opens Creusa and Xuthus have brought their trouble to Delphi, where the temple servant was a young man of unknown parentage who had been brought up from infancy in the temple's service. Xuthus is informed that this young man, Ion, is his own son, begotten before his marriage to Creusa. When Creusa learns of this response of the oracle she naturally imagines that Apollo has allowed her son and his to perish while he has preserved in his own temple a son of Xuthus and some Delphian woman. She makes an attempt on Ion's life but her agent is discovered. She herself, condemned to death by the Delphians, barely escapes Ion's vengeance by taking refuge at the god's altar. Now the priestess gives Ion the ark by which he may discover his mother. The tokens are identified by Creusa, and the two are reconciled as mother and son. Ion is determined to enter the temple to demand of the god whether Xuthus (as the oracle first proclaimed) or Apollo (as appears from the tokens) is his real father. He is prevented from doing so by the appearance of Athena, who assures him that Apollo is indeed his father, that Apollo had changed his plans, that he had done all things well.

If we like, we can think that Creusa's lover was human and that her child perished; that Ion was the son of the priestess, who is now eager to settle him well in life; and that the tokens were fabricated by the priestess to prevent Ion from killing Creusa and to make sure that he would indeed become prince of Athens. But whether or not *Ion* was intended as an expression of scepticism, it justifies itself completely as drama.

# ION

## CHARACTERS

HERMES

ION, *son of Creusa and Apollo, sacristan at Apollo's temple at Delphi*

CHORUS, *women attendants of Creusa*

CREUSA, *wife of Xuthus, queen of Athens*

XUTHUS, *king of Athens*

OLD RETAINER, *of Creusa*

SERVANT, *of Creusa*

THE PYTHIAN PRIESTESS

ATHENA

The scene represents the front of the temple of Apollo at Delphi.

The date of the Ion is uncertain; 418 B.C. is not unlikely.

———◆———

[*Hermes appears on the platform reserved for gods.*]

HERMES. Atlas that wears heaven, the old homestead of the gods, on his brazen back, begot Maia out of one of the goddesses, and she bore me, Hermes, to Zeus the greatest: I am the runner of the deities. I have come to this land of Delphi where Phoebus sits at the Earth's navel and gives oracles to mortals; he is always prophesying the things that are and the things that are to be.

Now there is a city of the Hellenes, not an obscure one, called after Pallas of the gold-tipped spear. There Phoebus mated with Creusa, Erechtheus' child, by force, under the hill of Pallas in the land of the Athenians, by the northerly rocks which the rulers of Attica call the Tall Cliffs. Unknown to her father—so the god preferred it—she bore her belly's burden to the end. When her time came she gave birth to a boy at home and carried the infant to the very same cave where she had lain with the god, and exposed him to die, as she thought, in the lightly rocking embrace of a sheltering ark. But she did not forget a tradition of her ancestors, back to earth-born Erichthonius. To him Zeus' Maid assigned a brace of serpents as a body-guard when she gave him to

Aglaurus' daughters to keep. Hence derives that Erechthid use of gold snakes in the children's nurseries. Well, Creusa attached to her child such finery as a young girl possesses, and left it to die.

Phoebus, who is my brother, makes this request of me: "Brother, go to the autochthonous people of glorious Athens —you know Athena's city—get a new born infant out of the hollow rock, together with his cradle and swaddling clothes, bring him to my oracle at Delphi, and put him right at the doorstep of my house. For the rest—the boy, if you wish to know, is mine—I shall take care."

To oblige my brother Loxias I took the wicker casket and brought it, and I put the child on the steps of this very temple; I turned open the lid of the cradle so the child could be seen. Now it is the regular practice of the priestess to enter the shrine of the god at the hour when the disk of the sun begins its course. When she cast her eye on the new-born babe she wondered whether any Delphian girl had dared fling her clandestine offspring into the temple of the god, and she was ready to thrust it out of the sacred place. But pity cast out cruelty—the god too was with him and did not allow his child to be thrown out of his house—and she took the child up and cared for it. She did not know it was Phoebus that begot him, nor who was the mother. Nor does the boy know anything of his parents.

When he was young he used to wander about the altars of his boyhood home in childish play. When he grew a man the Delphians made him treasurer of the god and the trusted custodian over all; and so he continues to lead a holy life in the temple of the god until this day.

Creusa, the mother of this young man, is married to Xuthus. It happened this way. The storm of war burst upon the Athenians and the folk of Chalcedon who hold Euboea. Because he lent them aid and assisted them to victory, he received the honor of Creusa's hand, though he was not of the same race, but an Achaean born, son of Aeolus the son of Zeus. Though striving long for offspring he is childless, as is Creusa; and for this reason they have come to this oracle of Apollo, because they yearn for children. Loxias is guiding their destiny in this; his plan is not so secret as he thinks. When Xuthus enters this shrine he will give him his own child and declare that Xuthus is the father, so that the boy will come to his mother's house and be acknowledged by Creusa. Thus Loxias' amours remain secret, and at the same

time the boy attains his rights. He will cause him to be called
Ion throughout Hellas, Ion that is to colonize the Asian
land. But I shall betake me to yonder laurel planted close, to
learn what will be done about the child. I see the son of
Loxias coming to brighten the portals of the Temple with
laurel branches. First of the gods do I call his name *Ion*, the
name which shall be his.

[*Exit; enter from Temple, Ion, followed by servants.*]

ION. *See the gleaming car of the sun! His brilliance
streams over the earth; before his fire the stars flee from
the sky into mysterious night. Parnassus' untrodden peaks,
kindling into flame, receive for mortals the wheels of light.*

*The fumes of the myrrh of the desert are wafted upward
to Phoebus' roof. Upon the sacred tripod the Delphian
priestess sits, and chants to the Hellenes the oracles which
Apollo murmurs in her ears.*

*But come, O Delphians, servants of Phoebus, go to the
silvery eddies of Castalia, and when you have bathed in
its pure dew enter the temple. Keep your lips clean from ill
omened speech. Let your own tongues set an example of
propriety to those who would consult the god.*

*As for me, I shall perform the tasks at which I have
labored from childhood. With laurel sprays and sacred
wreaths, I shall make pure the entry-way of Phoebus; with
drops of moisture I shall sprinkle his floor. The flocks of
birds that befoul the sacred offerings I shall make flee with
my arrows. No mother, no father have I; I serve the temple
of Phoebus that has nurtured me.*

*Come, fresh branch of lovely bay. You too are his serv-
ant. Here, before the temple, you sweep the altar of Phoebus.
You were grown in deathless gardens where the sacred waters,
sending forth their gushing, ever-flowing stream, bedew the
holy myrtle-shrubs. With you I sweep the god's pavement
the livelong day. As soon as the sun's swift wing appears, I
begin my daily task.*

*O Healer! Healer! Blessed, blessed be thou, O son of Leto!*

*Fair is the task wherewith I minister before your house, O
Phoebus, and honor your oracular habitation. Glorious is my
task; I tender the hand of service to gods, not to mortals
but to immortals. To toil at labors so blessed I weary not.
Phoebus is as the father that begot me; as such I praise him*

*that sustains me. I call my benefactor by title of father, even
Phoebus, the temple's lord.*

*O Healer! Healer! Blessed, blessed be thou, O son of Leto!
I end my task with the broom of bay. From a golden
ewer I shall pour out the spring water which Castalia
eddies gush forth. The dewy moisture I may sprinkle, for
I am pure and chaste. May this my service to Phoebus never
cease; or if it cease, may it be with a happy lot!*

*Ha! Here they come already, the feathered tribe leaving
behind their nests on Parnassus. Don't there, I tell you.
Get away from the cornices. Don't make these golden halls
your. . . . And you're back again: just let my arrows get
at you, you herald of Zeus, that vanquish with your talons
the strongest birds. Here's another one, a swan, flapping
down to the altar. Take your bright purple feet away from
here! Your tunefulness, vying with Phoebus' own, will not
save you from my arrows. Be off, fly away; settle upon the
Delian lake. If you don't do as I say, your blood will drown
that pretty song of yours.*

*Ha! What new bird is this that has come? What! Would
you build for your younglings a nest of sticks and straw
under the eaves? The twang of my bow shall keep you at
your distance. Will you not heed me? Go and breed your
young by the eddyings of Alpheus or in the Isthmian grove.
Don't spoil the offerings and the temple of Phoebus. I
scruple to slay you; for you birds announce to mortals the
will of the gods. But I will be Phoebus' servant and labor at
my appointed tasks, and I shall not cease ministering to
them that sustain me.*

> [*Enter Chorus, composed of Creusa's maids; they ad-
> mire the sculptures along the temple walls, until
> they arrive at the center door where they accost
> Ion.*]

CHORUS [*the mark at the beginning of each paragraph
indicates a change of speaker*]. *Not in holy Athens alone
then are there fair-columned courts of the gods and homage
done to the God of Good Roads. With Loxias, too, Leto's
son, there is the fair-faced brightness of twin facades.*
—*Look here, see! Here is Zeus' son slaying the Lernaean
Hydra with his golden scimitar. Friend, just look into this.*
—*I see, and near him someone else is raising a blazing torch.
Can it be he whose story is told in my embroidery, Iolaus, the*

*shield bearer, who undertook to share in Zeus' son's labors
and endured them with him?*

*—O but do look at this man mounted on a winged horse! He
is slaying a fire-breathing three-bodied monster.*

*—I am darting my eyes in every direction. Look at the
furious battle of the giants upon the marble wall!*

*—Friends, let us look at it like this.*

*—Do you see her that is standing over Enceladus and
brandishing the gorgon-faced shield? . . .*

*—I see Pallas, my Goddess.*

*—So it is! And the mighty thunderbolt flaming at each end,
in the far-darting hands of Zeus?*

*—I see it. That horrible man, that's Mimas. The flame is
burning him to ashes.*

*—And Bromius, the reveller Bacchus, is slaying another of
the children of the Earth with his ivy-decked thyrsus, never
meant for war.*

[To Ion.]

*—Sir, to you that stand by the temple I speak: is it lawful
to pass into this sanctuary with bare feet?*

Ion. *It is not lawful, strangers.*

Chorus. *I don't suppose you could tell me if——*

Ion. *Speak,* what do you wish?

Chorus. *Is it true that this shrine of Phoebus holds
within it the center navel of the earth?*

Ion. *Yes, it is decked with garlands, and there are gorgons
around it.*

Chorus. *That's what we have been told.*

Ion. *If you have offered a sacred cake in front of the
temple and you wish to make some inquiry of Phoebus,
you may approach the altar. You may not enter within the
temple without the sacrifice of a sheep.*

Chorus. *I understand. We shall not transgress against the
god's law. What is on the outside will feast our eyes.*

Ion. *You may look at everything, everything that is lawful.*

Chorus. *My mistress let me off to come and see the sights
of this sanctuary of the god.*

Ion. *What house do you say you are the servants of?*

Chorus. *My queen was born and reared in a palace at
Athens. But the lady of whom you ask is here.*

[Enter Creusa.]

Ion. You have nobility, lady, whoever you are; and your bearing indicates your character. Usually one may recognize whether a person is well born by noticing his bearing. Ah, but you amaze me. Your eyes are shut, and you moisten your noble cheek with tears at the sight of Loxias' holy oracle. Why are you so worried, lady? Why, when all others take pleasure at the sight of the god's sanctuary, are your eyes wet with tears?

Creusa. Stranger, it cannot be rudeness in one like you to express wonder at my tears. When I looked upon this house of Apollo, I retraced the path of an old, old memory. I was standing here, but my thoughts were of something at home. Ah, that women must suffer for the sins of gods! But enough. To whom shall we carry our case, when it is our masters' crimes that are our undoing?

Ion. Why this mysterious sadness, lady?

Creusa. It is nothing. I have shot my shaft. For the rest, I shall be silent, and you think no more of it.

Ion. Who are you? Where is your home? Of what father were you born? What name must we call you?

Creusa. Creusa is my name. My father was Erechtheus, my country is the city of Athens.

Ion. You live in a glorious city, your upbringing is of noble parents. Accept my compliments, lady.

Creusa. Only so far am I blessed, stranger; no further.

Ion. Please, now! Is it true then, the story men tell that——

Creusa. What are you asking, stranger? What do you want to know?

Ion. Was your father's father sprung of the Earth?

Creusa. Yes, Erichthonius was. But my ancestry helps me little.

Ion. And did Athena really raise him up from the ground?

Creusa. Yes, into her maiden arms: she did not bear him.

Ion. Is it the way the pictures usually show it? Did she give him——

Creusa. To the children of Cecrops to preserve; but they were not to look at him.

Ion. I have heard that the maidens opened Athena's casket.

Creusa. And so they died and the rocky cliff ran red with their blood.

Ion. Ah, yes. But is *this* story true or false?

Creusa. What is your question? I have plenty of leisure.

Ion. Did your father Erechtheus sacrifice your sisters?

CREUSA. He did not hesitate to kill those girls. It was a sacrifice for his country.

ION. And how were you the only sister saved?

CREUSA. I was a new-born babe in my mother's arms.

ION. Did a chasm of the earth really engulf your father?

CREUSA. The strokes of the Sea's trident destroyed him.

ION. Is there a place there called the Tall Cliffs?

CREUSA. Why ask that? What memories you recall!

ION. That place the Pythian god and the Pythian wild fire honor.

CREUSA. Honor indeed! Would I had never seen that place.

ION. Why do you hate what the god holds most dear?

CREUSA. It is nothing. That cave and I know a shameful story.

ION. What Athenian married you, lady?

CREUSA. My husband is not a citizen, but an alien, from abroad.

ION. Who is he? He must be somebody of good birth.

CREUSA. Xuthus, son of Aeolus, descended from Zeus.

ION. How could a foreigner marry a native?

CREUSA. There is a city next door to Athens, Euboea—

ION. Separated, they say, by a boundary of waters.

CREUSA. That city Xuthus sacked, making common cause with Cecrops' sons.

ION. He came as an ally, and then took you in marriage?

CREUSA. My dowry was the prize of his prowess.

ION. Have you come to this oracle with your husband or alone?

CREUSA. With my husband. He is visiting the caverns of Trophonius.

ION. As a sightseer or to consult the god?

CREUSA. He wishes to learn one thing from Trophonius and from Phoebus.

ION. Is it for crops you have come? Is it about children?

CREUSA. We are childless though we have been married long enough.

ION. Have you never borne a child at all? Are you barren?

CREUSA. Phoebus knows how barren I am.

ION. Unhappy woman, all the rest does not make up for that.

CREUSA. But who are you? Your mother must be proud of you.

ION. I am called the god's slave, and so I am, lady.

CREUSA. The offering of some city? Sold by some one?

ION. I know only one thing. I am called Loxias'.

CREUSA. Then I in my turn, stranger, pity you.

ION. Yes, for I know neither mother nor father.

CREUSA. Do you live in the temple here or under your own roof?

ION. All god's house is mine; I sleep where sleep overtakes me.

CREUSA. Was it as a child you came to the temple or as a youth?

ION. An infant, say those who seem to know.

CREUSA. What Delphian woman gave you suck?

ION. I have never known the breast. She who cared for me . . .

CREUSA. Who was she, poor lad? Misery has found her fellow.

ION. Phoebus' prophetess. I count her as my mother.

CREUSA. How did you support yourself till you reached manhood?

ION. The altars fed me; and the constant stream of visitors.

CREUSA. Unhappy is your mother! Whoever was she?

ION. Perhaps my mother is some wronged woman.

CREUSA. You do make a living, don't you? At least, you are well-dressed.

ION. My clothes are from the store of the god whom I serve.

CREUSA. Have you never pressed a search to discover your parents?

ION. I have no clue, lady.

CREUSA. Ah! I know another woman who was wronged as your mother was.

ION. Who was she? I should be pleased if she would join in the task with me.

CREUSA. It is for her sake I come here ahead of my husband.

ION. What request have you? I am at your service, lady.

CREUSA. I wish to obtain an oracle from Phoebus in secret.

ION. Speak, then. I shall manage the rest for you.

CREUSA. Then hear my story. No! I am ashamed.

ION. Then you will accomplish nothing. Shame is a futile goddess.

CREUSA. Phoebus lay with her—so says this friend of mine.

ION. A woman? With Phoebus? Stranger, do not say such a thing.

CREUSA. Yes, and she bore a son to the god unknown to her father.

Ion. It cannot be. Some man seduced her. She is ashamed.

Creusa. She denies it herself. Her sufferings were pitiable.

Ion. How so, if her lover was a god?

Creusa. The child she bore she cast forth from her home.

Ion. The child that was cast out—where is he? Does he look upon the light of day?

Creusa. Nobody knows. It is this, in fact, that I am asking the god.

Ion. If the child is no more, how did he perish?

Creusa. She expects wild beasts killed the poor thing.

Ion. What evidence led her to suppose this?

Creusa. She came where she had put him, and did not find him there any more.

Ion. Were there any drops of blood along the path?

Creusa. She says there were not. And certainly she searched the ground carefully.

Ion. How long is it since the child was made away with?

Creusa. If he were alive, he would be the same age as you.

Ion. The god deals unfairly with him. I am sorry for the mother.

Creusa. Yes, for never thereafter did she bear another child.

Ion. What if Phoebus has taken him and is bringing him up secretly?

Creusa. It is not fair of him to keep to himself a joy he should share.

Ion. Ah me! This case sounds so like my own.

Creusa. For you too, stranger, I think your poor mother is yearning.

Ion. Do not bring back to me a forgotten sorrow.

Creusa. I shall be silent. Proceed with what I ask you.

Ion. Don't you see the weakness of your position?

Creusa. Was she not all too weak, that wretched woman?

Ion. Will the god's oracle give away the god's secret?

Creusa. Why not? His tripod is for *all* Greeks, without favor.

Ion. He is ashamed of the business. Do not embarrass him.

Creusa. But the woman he wronged is more than *ashamed*.

Ion. Nobody will ever give you an answer in this matter. If he were proven a villain in his own temple, Phoebus would justly inflict some calamity on him who passed the judgment. Desist then, lady. The oracle must not antagonize the god. That would be the height of absurdity, to expect to wring their secrets from reluctant gods, either by the slaughter of sheep at their altars or by the flight of birds. When the gods are niggards, the blessings we wrest from them by force are niggardly. Only in that which they give willingly do we find profit.

LEADER. Many are the calamities that befall mortals; their forms vary. In all the world it would be hard to find a single case of happiness.

CREUSA. Ah Phoebus! Then and now have you been unfair to her that pleads with you here, though absent. You did not save your own child, as you should have done. And though you are a prophet you will make no answer to his mother that inquires for him, so that if he is dead he may be honored with a tomb, and if he is alive. . . . But I must let this be, if the god himself prevents me from learning what I would know.

But I see my noble husband, Xuthus, approaching, stranger; he has come from Trophonius' cavern. Say nothing to him of the words we have spoken lest I be put to shame for meddling with secret matters. Then our plot would have a different meaning. It's difficult for women to get on with men. The good are lumped together with the bad and we are all detested. That's what makes life hard.

[*Enter Xuthus.*]

XUTHUS. First to the god who must receive the first fruits of my bidding, I bid hail. Next, hail to you, my wife. Has my delay alarmed you?

CREUSA. No, but I was thinking of you. Tell me, what oracle do you bring from Trophonius? How may our seed be joined to produce children?

XUTHUS. He did not think fit to anticipate the response of the god. One thing he said: neither I nor you shall go home from the oracle childless.

CREUSA. Revered mother of Phoebus, grant that our coming be auspicious; may our previous dealings with your son fall to a happier issue.

XUTHUS. So be it. Who speaks for the god here?

ION. I do, outside the temple: within the charge belongs to others, who sit near the tripod, stranger. They are the noblest of the Delphians, chosen by lot.

XUTHUS. Good! I understand all that I require.

I shall go within. I hear that a general sacrifice has been offered before the temple for all the visitors. I wish to receive the god's oracles this very day, for it is an auspicious one. Do you, my wife, make a round of the altars with laurel branches in hand and pray the gods that I may bring home from Apollo's temple the happy promise of children.

CREUSA. These things shall be, so they shall.

*[Exit Xuthus into temple.]*

If Loxias will now at least be willing to retrieve his former sins, though I shall never be able to forgive him wholly, yet will I bow to his will, whatever he grants—for he *is* a god.

*[Exit Creusa.]*

ION. Why does this woman rail against the god in dark and riddling speech? Is it out of affection for the woman on whose behalf she is consulting the oracle? Or has she some guilty secret?

But what have I to do with Erechtheus' daughter? She is nothing to me. No, I will take these golden ewers and go and fill the lavers with water. But I must admonish Phoebus. What ails him? He ravishes girls and betrays them! Begets children by stealth and callously leaves them to die! Not you, Phoebus, surely! You are mighty; pursue virtue! When men are wicked, the gods punish them. How then can it be just for you yourselves to flout the laws you have laid down for men? If the day ever comes—of course the supposition is absurd—when you have to make amends to men for your rapings and whorings, you and Poseidon, and Zeus the King of Heaven, you will bankrupt your temples to pay for your sins. You follow your whims without a second thought; that is wicked. One can no longer blame men for imitating the splendid conduct of the gods; blame those who set us the example.

*[Exit Ion.]*

CHORUS. *You, Athena, my Athena, you who were born without help of our Lady of Travail, without pangs of childbirth, you I implore, Blessed Lady of Victory, brought to birth by Titan Prometheus from the lofty forehead of Zeus, come to the Pythian dwelling from the golden chambers of Olympus. Come winging down to the town where Phoebus' hearth at earth's navel vouchsafes unerring oracles, where the choirs dance round the tripod: come you and Leto's child, goddesses both, both virgins, holy sisters of Phoebus. Make it your prayer, maidens, that the ancient race of Erechtheus may at last obtain fair posterity by a clear oracle.*

*It is a constant source of rare felicity for mortals, when ancestral halls are radiant with children of good promise, with lives young and vigorous, to inherit their fathers' wealth and keep it for the children of the next generation. They are our strength in time of trouble, and in happiness our delight; in war they are a tower of strength to preserve their native land. Far dearer than wealth, far dearer than princely halls to me are children to care for, children to rear in virtue. The life that is childless I abhor; the man who chooses such a life I condemn. May my wealth be but moderate, and my life happy with children.*

*O haunt of Pan! O secret cave out there beside the Tall Cliffs! There the three daughters of Aglaurus still tread the measures of their dance, on the green lawns before the shrine of Pallas to the lively sound of the music of the pipes, which you, Pan, play in your sunless caves. There it was that a maiden became a mother—ah, unhappy girl—and bore to Phoebus a babe; and there she exposed it to be a feast for the fowls and bloody banquet for beasts. O the bitterness of that forced union! Never have I heard it told in loom or legend that children born of gods to mortals had any share in happiness.*

[*Enter Ion.*]

ION. Serving women who keep watch to await your mistress about the steps of this fragrant temple, has Xuthus already left the sacred tripod and oracle or is he still waiting within to consult about his childlessness?

LEADER. He is still within, stranger; he has not yet passed this threshold. But I hear the sound of the gates as if someone were coming out; yes, our master can now be seen coming out.

[*Enter Xuthus, greeting Ion effusively.*]

XUTHUS. My child! Happiness to you! It is proper that this should be my first word to you.

ION. I am quite happy. *You* be sensible, and then it will be well with both of us.

XUTHUS. Give me your hand's dear greeting, let me embrace you.

ION. Are you in your right mind? Has some god-sent stroke demented you?

XUTHUS. I am in my senses. I have found my nearest and dearest and I do not want you to get away.

ION. Stop! Do not touch, do not crush the god's chaplets.

XUTHUS. I *will* touch you. I am no robber; I have found my own, my precious own.

ION. Won't you keep away, before you get an arrow in your ribs?

XUTHUS. Why do you avoid me? Just when you have discovered your own dearest. . . .

ION. I am not fond of teaching reason to boorish and lunatic aliens.

XUTHUS. Kill me, burn my body. If you kill me you will be your father's murderer.

ION. How can you be my father? Is this some joke for my benefit?

XUTHUS. No. The words come rushing forth that will make my meaning clear to you.

ION. And what have you to say?

XUTHUS. I am your father and you are my child.

ION. Who says so?

XUTHUS. He who reared you, Loxias, reared you for me.

ION. We have just your word for that.

XUTHUS. I have heard the god's oracle.

ION. It was a riddle and you misunderstood it.

XUTHUS. Not if I hear correctly.

ION. What did Phoebus say?

XUTHUS. That the man who would meet me . . .

ION. How, meet you?

XUTHUS. As I came out of the god's temple . . .

ION. What about him?

XUTHUS. Is my own son.

ION. Really your own, or only a gift?

XUTHUS. A gift, yes; but my own son.

ION. And your first step brought you to me?

XUTHUS. None other, my child.

ION. How on earth could this thing happen?

XUTHUS. We both marvel at the same thing.

ION. If you are my father, who is my mother?

XUTHUS. I cannot say.

ION. Didn't Phoebus tell you?

XUTHUS. I was so delighted I did not go on to ask.

ION. Then I must have been born of mother Earth.

XUTHUS. The ground doesn't bear children.

ION. How then could I be yours?

XUTHUS. I don't know. I leave that to the god.

ION. Come, let us discuss it another way.

XUTHUS. That will be better, my child.

ION. Have you ever had any irregular relations?

XUTHUS. When I was young and foolish.

ION. Before you married Erechtheus' daughter?

XUTHUS. Certainly never since.

ION. So it was then you begot me?

XUTHUS. The time fits in.

ION. Then how did I come here . . .

XUTHUS. I am at a loss.

ION. I must have made a long journey.

XUTHUS. It puzzles me.

ION. Did you ever come to the Pythian rock before?

XUTHUS. Yes, to the torch-light procession of Bacchus.

ION. Did you lodge with some public host?

XUTHUS. Yes, and there were some Delphian girls that he . . .

ION. He introduced you to their company? Was that what you were about to say?

XUTHUS. Yes, some of Bacchus' Maenads.

ION. Were you sober, or drunk?

XUTHUS. There was wine and merriment. . . .

ION. That's it; that was my begetting.

XUTHUS. But fate has discovered you, my child.

ION. How did I get to the temple?

XUTHUS. Perhaps the girl cast you out.

ION. I have at least escaped the servile taint.

XUTHUS. Receive your father, child.

ION. However it is, it is not right for me to distrust the god.

XUTHUS. Now you are being reasonable.

ION. What more can I desire . . .

XUTHUS. At last you are seeing it in the right light.

ION. Than to be born the son of a son of Zeus.

XUTHUS. That distinction is yours.

ION. Shall I touch him that begot me?

XUTHUS. If you trust the god.

ION. Hail, father . . .

XUTHUS. Dear is the greeting; I accept it.

ION. And hail this day.

XUTHUS. It has made me happy.

ION. Ah, dear mother, when will I see *your* face? I yearn to see you more than ever, whoever you are. Perhaps you are dead, and I shall never be able to.

LEADER. We too share in the happiness of the royal house.

Nevertheless I wish that my mistress could have been blessed with children too, and the house of Erechtheus.

XUTHUS. O my child, I have found you; the god has kept his word. He has brought us together. And you have found what is nearest and dearest to you, though you did not know it before. But your eagerness just now was right; I too am filled with that longing. How are you, my boy, to discover your mother? How am I to find what sort of woman bore you to me? Perhaps we may leave it for time to reveal. But leave the god's ground; give up this homeless life. Suit your mind to your father's and come to Athens where your father's illustrious scepter awaits you, and great wealth. There you shall not be handicapped by either of the twin blots, humble birth and straitened circumstances. On the contrary, you shall be both noble in birth and rich in substance.

Have you nothing to say? Why do you keep your eyes downcast to the ground, and retire into thought? Your change from cheerfulness casts dread into your father.

ION. Things do not have the same look when they are far away as when they are seen near at hand. I do not despise the fortune that has found me a father in you. But hear, my father, what is in my mind. Famous Athens, they say, is sprung from the soil; it is no immigrant race. I shall intrude under a double handicap: my father is an immigrant and I myself a bastard. If I am under this reproach and am moreover without position. . . . But if I push myself forward to the front rank of the state and try to be somebody I shall be hated by the incompetent crowd, for superiority is always odious. Then there are those honest and able men who in their wisdom keep quiet and do not rush into the limelight —with them I should get the reputation of being a silly fool, because I would not hold my peace in a city full of disquiet. If I seek my rightful place I shall be hemmed in by the voting power of the demagogues who make free with the city. It always happens so, father: those who hold in their hands the cities and their offices are most hostile to all rivals.

I shall come to a strange house, an intruder, and to a woman that is childless. In the past she shared her sorrow with you; now that she is left quite alone with all her hopes frustrated she will feel all the bitterness of her lot. How can I avoid being hated by her, and rightly, when I stand close to your side and she, still childless, looks bitterly on your happiness? Then you will either have to cast me off and regard only your wife, or respect my claims and have your home broken up.

How many murders, how many deaths by deadly drugs have women contrived for their husbands? Besides, I pity your wife, father; she is getting older and has no child. It isn't right that the descendant of such a noble line should be cursed with barrenness.

Men's eulogies of monarchy are undeserved; it has a fair face, but it is bitter within. Who can be happy, who can be fortunate, if he must drag out the years of his life in an eternity of dread and sidelong glances? I had rather live happy as a common citizen than be a ruler, who must seek bad men for friends and hate good men for fear of being assassinated. Perhaps you will say that gold overweighs these inconveniences, that it is pleasant to be rich. But I have no desire to hold tight to wealth, agonized by every noise I hear. May mine be a moderate station, free from worry.

Hear now, father, the blessings I have enjoyed here. First of all I had leisure, a precious gift to man. Here there was no great tumult. No scurvy fellow ever jostled me from the road. It is an intolerable thing to yield the road in deference to inferiors. My energies were expended in prayer to the gods and conversation with my fellow men. I ministered to people that were cheerful, not complaining. While I was speeding some on their way other visitors would come, so that there was always the charm of a fresh face meeting fresh faces. Justice is good for mortals whether they like it or not, and both nature and custom conspired to make me a just servant of the god.

When I think these things over, father, I reckon I am better off here than there; let me live here. The pleasure is the same whether one exults in greatness or is content with little.

LEADER. I approve your speech if those I love shall find happiness as a result of your preference.

XUTHUS. Stop this sort of talk. Learn to carry your good luck. Here where I found you, my son, let us share a feast, the first of many that we shall partake of together. I will offer the birth sacrifices which I have not yet offered for you. I shall feast you as if you were some friend I was bringing home, and I shall take you with me to Athens pretending you are a mere sightseer and not my own true son. I do not wish to annoy my wife who is childless with my own happiness. In time I will find an opportunity to prevail over my wife to allow you to hold my scepter over the land.

I name you *Ion*, a name suitable to the event, for it was when I came out of the god's shrine that your track crossed mine. Now gather a crowd of your friends for this happy sacrifice, and bid them farewell on the eve of your departure from the city of Delphi.

You women I bid keep silent in this matter; it is death if you speak of it to my wife.

ION. Well, I shall go. One thing is wanting in my fortune: unless I find the mother who bore me, father, life will be unlivable. If I may make the prayer, I wish my mother would be a woman of Athens, so that I may have the right of free speech on my mother's side. If a foreigner comes to a city of pure blood, even though he is a citizen in theory, his lips are enslaved; he does not have free speech.

[*Exeunt Xuthus and Ion.*]

CHORUS [*The mark at the beginning of a paragraph indicates a change of speaker*]. *I foresee tears and sharp cries of sorrow and many an access of grief when my lady learns her husband is blessed with a child, while she herself is barren and without offspring. Prophet, child of Leto, what oracle is this you have chanted? Whence comes this child who was reared about your temple? Of what woman was he born? The oracle mislikes me and I fear it conceals some treachery. I dread the issue. How will it end? Strange is the god's word, and strange this tale he tells. There is something underhand, something fortuitous about this child of an unknown woman. Who will not agree in this?*
—*Friends, shall we mention these things plainly in our mistress' ear? Shall we tell her that the husband who was her all in all, with whom she shared her hopes, poor woman——*
—*Now her life is ruined while he has happiness.*
—*She has fallen on a grey old age, while her husband——*
—*Dishonors his own wife.*
—*The wretch! An outsider he came into the house, into great wealth; but he has disgraced his fortune.*
—*May he perish! May he perish!*
—*He deceived my lady.*
—*May the gods frustrate his prayers when he burns on the fire the wafer of purification. She shall know my attitude, she shall know how devoted I am to my queen.*

—*Already they will be at the feast, this new son and his new father.*
—*O ridges of Mount Parnassus with your cliffs and lofty uplands, where in the night Bacchus leaps nimbly along with his train of Bacchants and raises his pine torches with both ends flaming! May that boy never arrive at my city, but die on the first day of his new life! If the city were in straits, it would have grounds for admitting aliens, as did King Erechtheus, our leader of old.*

[*Enter Creusa and Old Retainer, laboriously ascending.*]

CREUSA. Old man, guardian of my dear father Erechtheus while he was yet alive, heave yourself up to the shrine of the god, and share my joy if Lord Loxias prophesies the birth of children. Pleasant it is to share in the happiness of friends; and if—god forbid—any evil befall, it is sweet to look into the eyes of a loyal comrade. Though I am your mistress, I cherish you like a father, as you once cherished my father.

OLD RETAINER. Daughter, you hold fast to ways that are worthy of your worthy forebears. You do not disgrace your ancient ancestry, sprung of Earth itself. Help me up, help me up to the halls, lead me on. It's a stiff climb, this oracle is, as you see. Be physician to my old age, assist my toiling limbs.

CREUSA. Follow then. Mind where you put your step.

OLD RETAINER. See, my foot is slow, but my spirit swift.

CREUSA. Lean on your staff and watch the turns of the road.

OLD RETAINER [*stumbling*]. This too is blind work when my sight is so short.

CREUSA. You are right, but do not yield to weariness.

OLD RETAINER. Not willingly. I cannot control what I haven't got.

[*Creusa and Old Retainer arrive near the Chorus.*]

CREUSA. Women, faithful servants of my web and spindle, what fortune did my husband carry away? What about children, our reason for coming here? Tell me. If you give me good news you will be giving joy to a mistress who will not forget it.

LEADER. Oh, fate!

OLD RETAINER. This introduction is not a happy one.

LEADER. Ah, unhappy!

OLD RETAINER. Is there something distressing in the oracle?

LEADER [to Chorus]. Well, what are we to do? We are under threat of death if . . .

CREUSA. What tune is this? This fear—what is it about?

LEADER. Shall we speak or be silent? What shall we do?

CREUSA. Speak. You have some bad news for me, I see.

LEADER. You shall be told, even if I must die twice over. Mistress, you shall never hold children in your arms or strain them to your breast.

CREUSA. *Woe is me, let me die!*

OLD RETAINER. Daughter!

CREUSA. *Ah me for my trouble. I have received, I have suffered, dear friends, a sorrow I cannot live through. I am ruined.*

OLD RETAINER. My child!

CREUSA. *Ah, me! Ah, me! This agony has stabbed me to the heart.*

OLD RETAINER. Do not moan . . .

CREUSA. *But there is reason for lamentation.*

OLD RETAINER. Before we learn . . .

CREUSA. *What is there still for me to learn?*

OLD RETAINER. Whether the master shares the same doom as you, or whether you alone are unfortunate.

LEADER. To him, old man, Loxias has given a son. He is holding a private celebration from which *she* is excluded.

CREUSA. *What have you said? What have you said? This surpasses all, a crowning sorrow for me to groan over.*

OLD RETAINER. Is he to be born of some woman, this child of whom you speak, or did the oracle declare he was already born?

LEADER. Indeed he is born: a young man full grown has Loxias given him. I was there myself.

CREUSA. *What do you say? Unspeakable, unspeakable, unutterable is the thing you keep dinning in my ears.*

OLD RETAINER. And in mine too. But how does the oracle work out? Tell me more plainly. And who is the child?

LEADER. The first person your husband should meet on leaving the temple the god gave him as a son.

CREUSA. *Alas, alas, alas! And what becomes of me? A childless life he promises me, a childless life, in a house forsaken and solitary.*

OLD RETAINER. Of whom then did the oracle speak? Whom

did my poor lady's husband meet? How, where did he see
him?

LEADER. You remember, dear lady, the young man who
was sweeping this temple? He is the child.

CREUSA. *Would I might fly through the liquid air, far
from the land of Hellas, to the stars of the west! What
anguish, what anguish I suffer!*

OLD RETAINER. What name did his father call him? Do
you know, or are they not saying till it is settled?

LEADER. He called him *Ion*, because he was the first to
meet his father.

OLD RETAINER. What sort of-woman is his mother?

LEADER. I cannot say. But to tell you all I know, the husband of our lady has stolen off to the sacred tabernacles to
make sacrifices of friendship and birthday offerings on the
boy's behalf. He is sitting down at table beside his new son.

OLD RETAINER. Mistress, we have been betrayed—I suffer
with you in this—betrayed by your husband. This is outrageous; it is a deliberate plot to thrust us out of the halls of
Erechtheus. It is not because I hate your husband that I say
this, but because I love *you* more than him. He came to the
city an alien. He married you and took possession of your
house and all your heritage. Now he is shown up: getting
children by another woman and deceiving you. I shall tell
you how the deception was worked. When he perceived you
were barren he was not content to bear the burden of your
fate equally with you; but he took some slave girl to his bed,
and by this clandestine union begot that child whom he gave
to one of his friends at Delphi to bring up. Here, to maintain the deception, he is reared in the god's temple, roaming at will. When Xuthus learned that his son was grown to
young manhood, he persuaded you to come here to consult
about your childlessness. The god didn't lie, it was *he* that
lied. He has been bringing up the child all these years. This
was the plan he had concocted. If discovered, he intended
to lay the responsibility on the god; but if the deception succeeded he meant to invest the child with royal power, to
disarm criticism. [And this new-fangled name Ion was
coined on the spot, to suit the pretence that he met him as
he went.]

LEADER. Ah, I always hate scoundrels who do wrong and
then trick it out with lies. In a friend I should prefer honest
dullness to clever knavery.

OLD RETAINER. A worse evil than all this must you suffer.

You must take into your house as master a motherless nobody, some slave woman's brat. It would have been bad
enough if he had brought into the house the son of a well-
born mother, and had first prevailed on you by pleading your
barrenness. If this was not agreeable to you he ought to have
sought a union with the house of Aeolus.

Consequently, you must do a deed worthy of your sex.
Grasp a sword or use some trick or poison and kill your
husband and the child before death comes to you from
them. [If you fail in this you will lose your life. When two
enemies are beneath the same roof the one or the other
must succumb.] For my part I am ready to share this labor
with you and to murder the boy: I shall go to the house where
he is banqueting, and whether I die or live to enjoy the light,
I shall repay you, mistress, for all you have given me. One
thing only brings shame to slaves—the name. In all else the
slave that's honest is as good as the free man.

LEADER. I, too, dear mistress, am willing to share this lot,
either to die or to live honorably.

CREUSA. *O my soul, how can I keep silence? Yet how un-
veil that dark amour and lose the name of honor? But what
is left to stop me? Why strive any longer for virtue? Has not
my husband proved false? And I am robbed of home, robbed
of children: gone are the fair hopes which I tried to realize
by keeping my union secret, keeping secret that lamentable
birth, but I could not. No! By the starry throne of Zeus, by
the goddess that haunts our mountains, by the holy shore
of the waters of Triton's lake, no longer will I hide my lover.
When the load is lifted from my breast I shall be easier. My
eyes drop tears, my soul is in anguish; gods and men have
conspired against me. But I shall expose them, ingrates and
seducers of women.*

*You that make music from the seven voices of the lyre,
drawing from the lifeless horns of oxen strains of lovely
music—yours is the reproach, son of Leto, that I will publish
to the bright light of day. You came to me with the sunlight
in your golden hair when I was gathering the yellow flowers
in the folds of my robe, the flowers that shone like golden
suns. You caught the white wrists of my hands and drew me
screaming "Mother, Mother" to the bed in that cave. Divine
seducer, you drew me there and shamelessly you worked the
pleasure of Cypris. And I bore you a son—O Misery!—and in
fear of my mother I cast him upon your bed, upon the cruel
couch where cruelly you ravished me, the hapless girl. Woe*

*is me, woe! And now my boy is gone, fowls of the air have
torn and devoured him, my boy—and yours, cruel god. But
you only play your lyre and sing songs of triumph!*

*Ho, son of Leto, you I call, you who sit on your throne
of gold and give holy answers from earth's center: I will
shout a word into your ear. Vile seducer! To my husband,
who has done you no kindness, you have given a son and
heir; but my child, yes and yours (where is your heart?) is
gone, the prey of the birds, reft from his mother's swaddling
clothes. Delos hates you, the young laurels hate you, beside
the soft-leaved palm, where Leto bore you in a holy birth by
the seed of Zeus.*

[*Creusa collapses.*]

LEADER. Ah me! What a treasure of tribulation is here laid
open! Who would not shed a tear?

OLD RETAINER. Daughter, I gaze at your face and find no
satisfaction. I am beyond thought. When I had just now
bailed a sea of troubles from my soul, another wave swamped
me astern as I heard your story. You had emerged from the
troubles that were at hand, only to pursue further the hard
road of trouble. What is this you say? What charge is this
you make against Apollo? What sort of child do you say
you bore? Where in the city did you say you put him, a
welcome thing for beast to devour? Go over it again.

CREUSA. You make me feel ashamed, old man, but I shall
speak nevertheless.

OLD RETAINER. Do; I can feel generous sympathy for
friends in sorrow.

CREUSA. Hear then. You know the cave to the north of
Cecrops' rocks which we call the Tall Cliffs?

OLD RETAINER. I know it. There is a shrine of Pan and
his altar hard by.

CREUSA. It was there I underwent that fearful trial.

OLD RETAINER. What trial? How my tears start to meet
your words!

CREUSA. Against my will, ah me, I lay with Phoebus.

OLD RETAINER. Daughter, can this have been what I myself noticed?

CREUSA. I do not know. If you speak frankly, so will I.

OLD RETAINER. Was it when you were stifling your sighs
for some mysterious complaint?

CREUSA. That was when the trouble happened which I am
now revealing to you.

OLD RETAINER. How then did you keep your affair with Apollo hidden?

CREUSA. I gave birth . . . contain yourself and hear me out, old man.

OLD RETAINER. Where was it? Who brought the baby forth? Did you go through that agony alone?

CREUSA. Alone, in the cave where I had been ravished.

OLD RETAINER. The child, where is he? Then you will no longer be barren!

CREUSA. He is dead, old friend; he was exposed to the beasts.

OLD RETAINER. Dead? And Apollo—did the poltroon not help you?

CREUSA. He did not. The boy's days are spent in the house of Hades.

OLD RETAINER. Who exposed him? Surely it was not you!

CREUSA. It was I. In the dark I swathed him in my garments.

OLD RETAINER. Did no one share your secret of his exposure?

CREUSA. Only Misery and Stealth.

OLD RETAINER. How could you bring yourself to leave your child in the cave?

CREUSA. Ah, how indeed! Many pitiful words I flung from my lips.

OLD RETAINER. Ah, hard, hard! But the god's heart was harder still.

CREUSA. If you had seen the babe stretch his hands out to me!

OLD RETAINER. Looking for your breast? To nestle in your arms?

CREUSA. That was his place, and I was wrong to keep him from it.

OLD RETAINER. What did you think to gain by casting your own child out?

CREUSA. I thought the god would save his own son.

OLD RETAINER. Ah me, what a storm has overtaken your once prosperous house!

CREUSA. Why do you hide your head, old man? Why do your tears gush forth?

OLD RETAINER. Because I see you and your father both unblessed.

CREUSA. Such is mortality. Nothing remains the same.

OLD RETAINER. Let us hug our griefs no longer, my daughter.

CREUSA. Why, what is to be done? Misery is helpless.

OLD RETAINER. Avenge yourself on him who first injured you—on the god.

CREUSA. How can a mortal such as I prevail against the stronger powers?

OLD RETAINER. Burn Loxias' sacred oracle!

CREUSA. I am afraid. I have enough trouble already.

OLD RETAINER. Then dare the thing you *can* do: kill your husband.

CREUSA. I respect the love that once was ours, when he was true.

OLD RETAINER. At any rate kill the boy who has risen against you.

CREUSA. How? If it were only possible! How I would like to!

OLD RETAINER. Arm your attendants with daggers.

CREUSA. I shall set about it. But where is this thing to be?

OLD RETAINER. In the sacred tabernacles where he is entertaining his friends.

CREUSA. The murder would be public; and slaves are irresolute.

OLD RETAINER. Ah, me, your courage fails. But come, you devise some scheme.

CREUSA. Ah, I *have* it. It is cunning and it will work.

OLD RETAINER. With head and hand I am at your service.

CREUSA. Hear then. Do you know the Battle of the Giants?

OLD RETAINER. Yes, the battle in which they opposed the gods at Phlegra.

CREUSA. There Earth gave birth to Gorgon, a fearful monster.

OLD RETAINER. To be ally to her own sons and to the gods a stumbling block.

CREUSA. Yes, and Goddess Pallas, Zeus' daughter, killed her.

[OLD RETAINER. What shape of creature was she, that fierce Gorgon?

CREUSA. Her breast was armed with circling snakes.]

OLD RETAINER. Is this the tale which I heard long ago?

CREUSA. Yes, it is this monster's skin that Athena wears upon her breast.

OLD RETAINER. Is it what they call the Aegis, Pallas' armor?

CREUSA. Yes, it got its name when she rushed with the gods to battle.

OLD RETAINER. But where is the harm in this for your enemies, daughter?

CREUSA. Do you know Erichthonius or—but of course you must, old man.

OLD RETAINER. Your first progenitor, whom the Earth brought forth.

CREUSA. When he was a new born babe Pallas gave him . . .

OLD RETAINER. What? You hesitate to say.

CREUSA. Two drops of the blood of the Gorgon.

OLD RETAINER. What power have they over human beings?

CREUSA. The one has a deadly power, the other is a remedy for disease.

OLD RETAINER. How did she attach them to the child's person?

CREUSA. With a golden chain. He gave it to my father.

OLD RETAINER. And when your father died it came to you?

CREUSA. Yes, I wear it here on my wrist.

OLD RETAINER. How does this divine gift work its double effect?

CREUSA. The drop that flowed from the hollow vein at the slaying . . .

OLD RETAINER. How is it used? What is its efficacy?

CREUSA. It wards off disease and sustains life.

OLD RETAINER. The second one you mentioned—what does it do?

CREUSA. It kills; it is venom from the Gorgon's snakes.

OLD RETAINER. Do you carry it mingled with the first, or separate?

CREUSA. Separate. Good does not mingle with evil.

OLD RETAINER. Dearest girl, you have all that you need.

CREUSA. By this shall the boy die, and you will be the slayer.

OLD RETAINER. Where? How is it to be done? It is yours to say, mine to dare.

CREUSA. In Athens, when he comes to my house.

OLD RETAINER. That's not so good—you criticized *my* plan you know.

CREUSA. Why? Do you suspect what occurs to me too?

OLD RETAINER. You will be thought to have destroyed the boy even if you do not kill him.

CREUSA. Right. They say the step-mother hates the children.

OLD RETAINER. Kill him here, so you may deny the murder.

CREUSA. At least I taste the pleasure all the sooner.

OLD RETAINER. Yes, you will trick the husband that is trying to trick you.

CREUSA. Do you know then what you must do? Take from my hand this gold trinket of Athena's, this ancient vessel; go where my husband is offering his stealthy sacrifice, and when they have finished the feast and are about to pour libations, take this from your robe and drop it hastily into the young man's cup—only his, not everyone's; keep his drink separate —this young man who would be lord over my house. If it passes his throat he shall never come to glorious Athens, but die and remain here.

OLD RETAINER. You step into the house of the public hosts; I shall carry out the task assigned me.

[*Exit Creusa.*]

Come, old foot, become young in deeds in spite of the years. March against the enemy. Assist your mistress to slay her enemy, and rid her home of him.

To honor piety is a good thing for the successful; but when a man wants to injure enemies no law stands in the way.

[*Exit.*]

CHORUS. *Enodia, daughter of Demeter, queen of apparitions of night and of day, guide to its goal the cup which my lady, my own dear lady has filled with deadly poison, distilled from the earth-born Gorgon's severed throat; guide it against him that grasps at the house of Erechtheus. Never may a stranger from a strange house reign over my city; may none but noble Erechthids rule it.*

*If this murder fails and my mistress' purpose is unfulfilled, if no opportunity is found for this enterprise which now seems hopeful, then will the spirit move her to pierce her throat with a whetted sword or suspend it in a noose; ending her sorrows with new sorrows she will pass over into another world. Never while she lives in the world of light will she suffer strangers and aliens to rule over her house; she is an aristocrat born.*

*I blush for the god of our many hymns, if this boy shall be among the pilgrims by the springs of Callichorus, keeping vigil through the night to see the torches blaze forth on the Twentieth, when the stars in the divine ether start the dance, and the moon joins in, and the fifty daughters of Nereus,*

*that whirl in the depths of the sea and in the eddies of the*
*everlasting rivers, dance in honor of the Maid with the*
*golden diadem and her holy mother. Yet it is there that he*
*hopes to be king, to enter upon the labor of others—Phoebus'*
*begging missionary!*

*All you followers of the Muse, whose slanderous songs cele-*
*brate the criminal loves and sinful passions of woman, see*
*how much more virtuous we are than brutal, lecherous man.*
*Sing your palinode, let your Muse assail men, let her pro-*
*claim the evil they inflict on women. Witness this son of*
*a son of Zeus: what ingratitude he shows. Not in the bed*
*my mistress shared did he beget his son and heir; to another*
*woman he made himself pleasant and got himself a bastard.*

[*Enter servant of Creusa hurriedly.*]

SERVANT. Good women, where can I find our mistress,
Erechtheus' daughter? I have gone over the whole city looking for her but I cannot find her.

LEADER. What is the matter, fellow slave? What eagerness
possesses your feet? What tidings do you bring?

SERVANT. The hunt is on. The rulers of the land are searching for her to stone her to death.

LEADER. Woe is me! What do you say? Has somebody discovered our secret plot to kill the lad?

SERVANT. That is it. And you are in it; you will be among
the first to suffer for it.

LEADER. How was the dark scheme detected?

SERVANT. The god exposed it; [he would not let right defeat wrong] because he did not want his temple defiled.

LEADER. How? I beseech you on my knees, tell me the tale.
Let me hear it and I shall die more happily if die I must—or
perhaps we may be spared.

SERVANT. When Creusa's husband left the god's shrine and
took his new son with him to the feast and the sacrifices
which he was preparing for the gods, he went to the twin
rocks of Dionysus where the god's Bacchic fire flickers, to
sprinkle the blood of a victim in acknowledgment of his new-
found son. To his son he said: "My child, remain here and set
laborers to work on building a commodious tent. If I tarry
long over my sacrifices to the gods of Birth, let the feast go on
for the friends that are there." He took his heifers and went
his way. The young man religiously fixed on the poles the
canvas that served the tent for walls; he took careful pre-

cautions against the sunlight so that the tent should not face
the shafts of light from noon till dying day. He measured the
length of one hundred feet for each side of his rectangle;
[this made the area within ten thousand square feet, according to the experts] for he wanted to invite all the folk of
Delphi to the feast. Then he took sacred tapestries from the
treasury and hung them as a screen, a marvel for men to see.
First he threw a fold of drapery over the roof-tree; this had
been dedicated to the god by Zeus' son, Heracles, part of the
spoils of the Amazons. There were among them webs woven
with figures like these: Heaven mustering his stars in ether's
vault; Helios driving his horses toward the dying day, bringing in his train the brilliant light of Hesperus; Night the dark-
robed goddess swinging her chariot onward, drawn by two
horses unassisted, while the stars kept her company; the
Pleiad moving along her path in mid-sky with Orion and
his sword; and above all the Bear wheeling round in heav-
en with his golden tail; the disk of the full Moon, that divides
the month, shooting her arrows upward; the Hyades, the
mariner's surest sign; and Dawn, the harbinger of day, chasing the stars. Upon the walls he hung other tapestries of
foreign workmanship: well-oared ships bearing down on a
Greek fleet; creatures half man half beast; horsemen hunting
stags or stalking fierce lions. At the entry way he hung the offering of some Athenian, Cecrops coiling his spiral folds near
his daughters. In the midst of the feasting place he set golden
mixing bowls.

Then a herald strutted forth and announced that any native
Delphian that desired might come to the banquet. When the
pavilion was filled they decked themselves with garlands and
partook of abundant viands to their heart's content. When
they had put from them the pleasure of food, an old man
stepped forward and took his stand in the middle of the floor;
he moved the banqueters to much laughter by his officious
zeal. From the pitchers he ceremoniously poured water for
washing the hands; he swung the censers of myrrh resin; he
took charge of the golden goblets: a self-appointed
factotum. When they came to the part of the feast where the
flutes are played and a common bowl is set out, the old man
said: "We ought to do away with these small wine cups and
bring in large ones, so that these gentlemen might grow jovial
sooner." Then there was work to do, carrying round the silver
and gold goblets.

The old man took a special cup, as if to do pleasure to his
new master and handed it to him full. But first he put into the
wine the potent drug which, they say, our mistress gave him,
so that her husband's new son might perish. Now nobody
knew this, but when the newly revealed son and the rest of the
company were holding up the cups for libations, one of the
domestics uttered an unlucky word. As the young man had
been brought up in the temple with expert diviners, he con-
strued it as an omen and bade a fresh bowl be filled. The
first libation he poured on the ground and he told all the
others to spill theirs. Then, in solemn silence, we filled the
sacred bowls with water and wine of Byblus. While we were
thus engaged, new guests arrived—a flight of doves; they live
in Loxias' temple unafraid. When the guests had poured their
cups out the birds greedily dipped their beaks into the drink
and drew it down their feathered throats. The other birds suffered no harm from the god's libation; but the dove that settled on the spot where the new master's glass had been
emptied, no sooner tasted the wine than she quivered all
through her feathered frame and staggered and screamed
an unintelligible note, a cry of anguish. The entire throng of
feasters marvelled at the bird's agony. At last she died in convulsions, her pink claws and legs relaxed.

Then the child of the oracle threw his cloak back from
his limbs and leaped over the table, crying: "What man was
going to kill me? Tell me, old man. You were the one who
was so eager; from your hand I received the cup." Straightway he seized the wrinkled arm and searched the old man,
to catch him in the act, with the poison on him. So he was detected, and in spite of himself was forced to reveal Creusa's
crime and the trick of the cup. Immediately the young man
whose birth Loxias' oracle had revealed ran forth and with
him the feasters, and he stood among the Pythian lords and
said: "Sacred Earth, the daughter of Erechtheus, an alien
woman, would destroy me with poisons." The rulers of the
Delphians determined, by the majority of votes, that my mistress should be flung from the rock and die for trying to
slay the temple child and attempting murder in the sanctuary.
The whole city is seeking her whom sorrow brought to this
sorry pass. For desire of children she came to Phoebus' temple; now she has lost all hope of children and her own life.

[Exit]

CHORUS. *Unhappy me! There is no escape from death. The truth is out; the murderous potion has revealed it, the juice of the Bacchic grape mixed with the viper's deadly venom. Revealed is our offering to the gods of the grave. A calamity for me, but death on the rock for my mistress. Give me wings to carry me away, or let me take hiding in the bowels of the earth to escape the horror of the rocks. Put me on a car drawn by the swiftest of trampling horses. Put me on a ship that sails.*

*But how can we hide, unless god in his goodness helps to conceal us? What suffering, poor mistress, still awaits your soul? Is it because we wished to harm our neighbor that we ourselves suffer, as justice demands?*

[*Creusa comes dashing in, veiled.*]

CREUSA. They are after me, women, they will kill me, slaughter me. I am doomed by the Pythian vote. I am given over to execution.

LEADER. We know your troubles, poor woman, we know your plight.

CREUSA. Where shall I take refuge? I scarcely got myself out of the house before my executioners arrived. But I eluded them and here I am.

LEADER. Where else than at the altar?

CREUSA. What good will that do me?

LEADER. Heaven does not allow suppliants to be killed.

CREUSA. True; but I have been legally condemned to die.

LEADER. Yes, if they catch you.

CREUSA. Ah, here they come rushing up with drawn swords; what a bitter race we are running.

LEADER. Take your seat on the altar; if they kill you there, your blood will haunt your murderers. But fortune must be endured.

[*Creusa sits on the altar, clutching the statue; enter Ion with armed followers. He does not see Creusa.*]

ION. Ah father Cephisus, in shape of bull, what viper is this you have begotten? What serpent whose eyes blaze forth murder? In her is every crime; she is as poisonous as those drops of Gorgon's blood with which she was going to kill me. Seize her, and Parnassus' rocks will card the locks of her pretty hair, when we hurl her like a discus down the cliff.

[*Sees Creusa.*] It was a piece of good luck that this happened before I arrived at Athens and fell under a stepmother's power. I was still among friends when I got your measure and realized how dangerous an enemy you could be. If you had ensnared me within your own house you would have sent me to the house of Hades without more ado.

But neither Apollo's altar nor his temple will save you. I pity you; but I pity myself more, and my mother; her body may be far away from me, but her name never.

Look at her. What will she not stoop to? Ruse after ruse! Now she cowers at god's altar, hoping to escape the penalty for her crimes.

[*Ion motions guards to advance.*]

CREUSA. I warn you not to kill me, in my own name and in the name of the god at whose altar I stand.

ION. What is there in common between you and Phoebus?

CREUSA. I consecrate my body; I surrender it to the god.

ION. And yet you tried to kill the god's servant with poison?

CREUSA. You were no longer Loxias' but your father's.

ION. My father begot me, but it was Loxias who *owned* me.

CREUSA. He *did* own you. But now I, not you, am his.

ION. But without the piety that was mine.

CREUSA. You were an enemy of my house; I had to kill you.

ION. I did not come against your country in arms.

CREUSA. Indeed you did; and you would have set fire to the house of Erichthonius.

ION. With what torches, with what firebrands?

CREUSA. You meant to take forcible possession of my house.

ION. The land belonged to my father; it was his to give.

CREUSA. What portion have the sons of Aeolus in the land of Pallas?

ION. With his arms he delivered it, not with his tongue.

CREUSA. A country's hired soldier cannot be its possessor.

ION. So you would have killed me for fear of what was waiting for you?

CREUSA. Yes, I feared for my own life, in case *you* should not wait.

ION. Because *you* have no child, you hate to see *me* finding a father.

CREUSA. Because I have no child, must my house be pillaged by you?

ION. At least you will concede me my patrimony.

CREUSA. Yes, a shield and a spear—there is your whole heritage!

ION. Leave the altar and the hallowed seats!

CREUSA. Admonish your own mother, wherever she is.

ION. Are *you* not to be punished for your murderous attempt?

CREUSA. Not unless you want to slaughter me here in this holy place.

ION. Why do you seek to die with the holy chaplets on you?

CREUSA. I shall wound One that wounded me.

ION. Alas! It's a crazy world where the laws of god are neither good nor wise. It ought not to be right for the wicked to find refuge at altars; they ought to be driven away. It is not seemly that the god should be defiled by the hand of crime. Only the blameless victims of oppression should get sanctuary at the altar. As things are, the good and the bad are not distinguished; they both get equal treatment from the gods.

[*Enter the Pythian prophetess, carrying a basket wrapped in woollen bands.*]

PROPHETESS. Forbear, my son. I leave the tripod of prophecy and step over this threshold—I, the prophetess of Phoebus, chosen from among all the women of Delphi to preserve the ancient usage of the tripod.

ION. Hail, dear mother to me, though you did not bear me.

PROPHETESS. Indeed, you may call me that; I do not dislike the name.

ION. Have you heard that this woman laid a treacherous plot to kill me?

PROPHETESS. I have. And you too sin, by cruelty.

ION. Should I not meet murder with murder?

PROPHETESS. Wives are ever hostile to stepchildren.

ION. And so are we to stepmothers when we suffer at their hands.

PROPHETESS. No more of this. Leave the sanctuary and return to your country.

ION. What should I do? Advise me.

PROPHETESS. Go to Athens with pure hands and good omens.

ION. Pure are his hands who kills his enemies.

PROPHETESS. You must not. Listen to me; I have something to tell you.

ION. Speak on. Whatever you say will be said in kindness.

PROPHETESS. Do you see this basket in my folded arms?

ION. I see an ancient ark with woollen bands.

PROPHETESS. This is the ark in which I found you long ago, a new-born babe.

ION. What do you say? This is a new story you are telling now.

PROPHETESS. I kept it in silence, now I reveal it.

ION. How could you keep it hidden all these years?

PROPHETESS. The god wanted you to minister in his house.

ION. And now he no longer wants me? How shall I be sure of this?

PROPHETESS. He has revealed your father, and is sending you away.

ION. Did you keep these things by command, or why?

PROPHETESS. Loxias caused me to have scruples at that time.

ION. To do what? Tell me, go on with your story.

PROPHETESS. To keep this find until this present time.

ION. Does it hold some advantage for me . . . some harm?

PROPHETESS. In it are hidden the swaddling clothes in which you were wrapped.

ION. Are you bringing me clues for seeking my mother?

PROPHETESS. Yes, since the deity so wishes. He forbade it before.

ION. O day of blessed sights!

PROPHETESS. Take it now and strive to find her that bore you.

ION. I will, if I have to traverse all Asia, and the limits of Europe.

PROPHETESS. That is for you to decide. For the god's sake I reared you, child, and now I give these things back to you which he wished me, unbidden, to take and keep. Why he so wished it I cannot say. No mortal man knew that I had these things, or where they were hidden. Farewell. Fondly I salute you, like a mother losing her son.

Begin now the search for your mother. Begin it right. First ask if it was any Delphian girl that bore you and left you in this temple. If not, was it a Greek. You have heard all you

will hear from me, or from Phoebus, who has interested himself in your fate.

*[Exit.]*

ION. Ah, me! The tears stream from my eyes as I think of
my mother on that day, trying to keep the secret of her
shame, casting out her own unsuckled son. In the god's house
I got my living, a nameless servant. Though the god was kind,
my lot was hard. During all those years when I might have
known the luxury of a mother's arms and got some delight in
life, I was deprived of a mother's love and care. Hapless
too is she that bore me. She has suffered no less than I; for
she lost the joy of a son.

*[Turns to go into temple but pauses.]*

Now I shall take this ark and dedicate it to the god. I don't
wish to discover something I might not like. Suppose my
mother is really some slave woman. It is better to leave the
matter unexplored than discover such a mother. Phoebus,
to your shrine I devote this. . . . What ails me? I am thwart-
ing the god's purpose; it was he who preserved for me these
tokens of my mother. I must open this, I must take the
risk. I cannot escape my destiny. O sacred bands, O wrappings
that have kept my mother's secret, what are you hiding?

*[Removes the woollen bands.]*

Look, a round wicker ark! By some miracle it has not
grown old, there is no mould on the plaitings. Yet a long
time has passed since these things were stored away.

CREUSA. Ah! What vision, what unexpected sight do I see?

*[Creusa shows speechless joy.]*

ION. Be quiet. You have already shown me clearly that
you know how.

. CREUSA. There is no need for silence in my case; do not
chide me. I see the chest where I once exposed *you*, my
child, when you were yet a silly babe, in Cecrops' cave, at the
Tall Cliffs with their rocky roofs. I shall leave this altar, yes,
even if I must die.

*[She leaps from the altar and embraces Ion.]*

ION. Seize her! The god has driven her mad; she has left the altar and the images. Tie her arms!

CREUSA. Slay me, slay me. But I will cling to this ark and to you and to those things that are hidden in it.

ION. Isn't this monstrous? I am being talked out of my claims.

CREUSA. No, you are being discovered by those that love you.

ION. You love me? And yet you tried to kill me by treachery.

CREUSA. You are my son. Whom could a mother love more?

ION. Stop those lies. In a moment I shall have you.

CREUSA. I hope you will. That is my goal.

ION. Is the chest empty or does it contain something?

CREUSA. Your wrappings, in which I exposed you.

ION. Will you name them before you see them?

CREUSA. If not, I agree to die.

ION. Speak. There is something uncanny in your assurance.

CREUSA. Look, then. There is a web I once wove when I was a girl.

ION. What kind? There are plenty of girls' webs.

CREUSA. An unfinished thing; the sort of thing we are taught to weave at first.

ION. What is the design on it? This way you will not take me in.

CREUSA. There was a Gorgon in the middle threads of the cloth.

ION. Zeus, the hounds of fate are catching up with me!

CREUSA. The Gorgon is fringed with serpents, as in the aegis.

ION. Look, there is the web. It's come true . . . like an oracle.

CREUSA. How well it has lasted, the loom work of my girlhood!

ION. Is there anything else? Was this just one lucky hit?

CREUSA. Serpents, an antique sort of thing, all of gold, the gift of Athena, who likes all children to have them. It is in imitation of ancient Erichthonius.

ION. What is the purpose, tell me, what is the use of this golden trinket?

CREUSA. It is for the new born child to wear as a necklace, son.

ION. Here it is! But I am eager to learn about the third thing here.

CRESUA. A crown of olive which I then put about your head, the olive which Athena first brought to our Rock. If that crown is there it has not lost its greenness, but is yet vigorous, for the olive of which it is made is sacred.

ION. My own dear mother! O the joy of seeing you, the joy of kissing your joyous face!

CREUSA. O my child, O light brighter than the sun to your mother (the god will understand), I hold you in my arms. *My treasure, I never hoped for this. I thought you had gone to your long home with Persephone and the shades below.*

ION. Ah, dearest mother, your arms are around me! You see me alive that was dead.

CREUSA. *Ah, ye expanses of brilliant ether! What words, what cry shall I utter? Whence came this joy, this unexpected joy? How did I attain this rapture?*

ION. This was the last thing I dared hope for . . . to find myself yours.

CREUSA. *I still tremble with fear.*

ION. That you do not have me? But you do.

CREUSA. *I had cast all hope away, far away. Lady, how, how did my babe come into your arms? What hands brought him to the house of Loxias?*

ION. It was an act of god. But for the future may our fortune be as happy as it was unhappy in the past.

CREUSA. *My child, not without tears was your birth; with lamentations were you separated from your mother's arms. Now, cheek to cheek, I breathe again; happiness, blissful happiness has come to me.*

ION. You speak for me too.

CREUSA. *No longer am I childless, no longer barren. In my house the flame of hope is kindled; my land has got a ruler, Erechtheus is young again; the house of the Earth-born no longer looks on darkness, but lifts up its eyes to the shining of the sun.*

ION. Mother, my father is here also; let him share this pleasure which I give you.

CREUSA. *Hush, my child! The truth, the horrible truth comes out.*

ION. What are you saying?

CREUSA. *Other is your origin, far other.*

ION. Ah me! Am I a bastard? Did you get me out of wedlock?

CREUSA. *No torches, no dances, my child, graced the union that gave birth to your dear self.*

ION. Alas! I am of base birth. But mother, of whom?

CREUSA. *Be witness the Gorgon-slayer . . .*

ION. What does this mean?

CREUSA. *Whose seat is on the hill of olives, on the cliffs of home . . .*

ION. Your words are dark. I cannot make them out.

CREUSA. *By the Rock of the Nightingales, with Phoebus . . .*

ION. Why do you mention Phoebus?

CREUSA. *I lay upon a secret couch.*

ION. Tell on. It is good news, happy news you bring me.

CREUSA. *In the tenth month I bore you to Apollo. Nobody knew.*

ION. O words of joy, if what you say is true!

CREUSA. *In fear of my mother I wrapped you in these swaddling clothes which covered you, the unsteady work of a young girl's shuttle. No mother's breast had you to give you milk, no mother's hands to wash you. You were left to die; in a cave in the wilderness you were cast away, a thing for birds with their talons to slay and devour.*

ION. What horrible courage, mother!

CREUSA. *It was terror, my child, that constrained me to fling your life away. In spite of myself, I became your murderer.*

ION. And I yours, O horror!

CREUSA. *Ah, dreadful was our lot then, dreadful too the present lot. We are tossed this way and that, the playthings of fortune now fair, now foul. The winds change; may good winds abide. O for calm after storm, my child! The evils we have had are enough.*

LEADER. Let no one ever think anything impossible, in view of the present happenings.

ION. O Fortune that rings the changes of mortal success and failure, how close I came to slaying my mother, O awful doom! Ah, is it possible in the space of one day to read all this in the sun's golden scroll? At any rate, a treasure of love have I found in you, my mother. Certainly I have no fault to find with my birth. But there is something else, which I wish to say to you in private. Come here. I will whisper in your ear what I have to say, and wrap the matter in darkness. Are you sure, mother, that you did not yield like any frail girl to a secret lover and then put the blame on the god? Are you not perhaps trying to escape the shame of my birth by claiming that Phoebus, and not some mortal, is my father?

CREUSA. No! By Athena of Victory who of old in her chariot fought side by side with Zeus against the Earth-born, no mortal alive is your father, my child, but he that reared you, lord Loxias.

ION. How was it then that he gave his own son to another father and declared that I was born the son of Xuthus?

CREUSA. Not born his son, but *given* to Xuthus, *born* of Apollo. A friend may give another friend his own son to be his heir in his house.

ION. Is the god true or are his oracles lies? My heart is troubled, mother, and with reason.

CREUSA. Hear what has occurred to me, child. It was to benefit you that Loxias established you in a noble house. If you had been called the god's, you would never have possessed the heritage of a home or a father's name. How could you when I, myself, kept the union secret and tried secretly to kill you? For your own happiness he is assigning you to another father.

ION. That is not good enough: I am going after the truth. I shall go into the Temple and inquire of Phoebus whether I am born of a mortal father or of Loxias.

[*Athena appears above the Temple.*]

Ha! Who is hovering over the halls of incense, outfacing the sun in brilliance?—What god? Let us flee, mother, and not look upon sights divine— [*Athena makes a sign to detain them*] unless it be opportune for us to look on.

ATHENA. Do not flee. I am no enemy that you should flee from me, but gracious toward you, both in Athens, and here. I am Pallas that come to you, the namesake of your land. I hurry here to represent Apollo; he did not see fit to face you two, lest upbraidings about bygones be bandied about. So he sent me to you to recite his message: that this woman is your mother and Apollo your father; that he bestowed you as he did, not because that man was your father, but so that you might be brought into a noble house. But when the truth came out and Creusa was informed, he was afraid you would die by your mother's devices, or she be murdered by you, and so he schemed to save you. King Apollo meant to hush the matter up till you were in Athens, and then inform you that this woman is your mother and that you are her son, and Apollo's.

Now let me finish my task. Hear, both of you, the god's oracles which I harnessed my chariot to bring you.

Take this boy and go to the land of Cecrops, Creusa, and set him on the royal throne He is sprung from the sons of Erechtheus and is worthy to rule over my land; he shall be famous throughout Hellas The sons born to him, four out of a single stock, will give their names to the tribal peoples of the land, who dwell upon my cliff. Geleon will be the first, then will come the Hopletes. then the Argades, and the Aegicores, the tribe named from my aegis The children born of these shall at the time appointed settle the island towns of the Cyclades and the shores of the mainland. and this will give strength to my land Facing across the straits they will inhabit the plains of two continents the lands of Asia and of Europe. They shall be named Ionians because of the name of this lad and they shall achieve renown.

To Xuthus and you shall be born sons: Dorus, from whom shall spring the fame and glory of the Dorian state in the land of Pelops, the second, Achaeus who will be ruler of the seacoast by Rhion and the people thereof shall be his namesakes, and be distinguished thereby.

Apollo has managed all things well. First he gave you an easy birth, so that your friends knew nothing. And when you had given birth to this boy and had wrapped him in his swaddling clothes, he bade Hermes snatch the infant in his arms and transport him here; and he fed him. and did not allow his life to expire Now be quiet about his child being your own; let Xuthus cherish his pleasant fancy, and you your blessings. Farewell After this respite from troubles I proclaim a happy lot for you.

ION. O Pallas. daughter of Zeus the greatest, with no want of faith do we receive your words. I do believe that my father is Loxias and this woman my mother. Nay, even before this I could have believed it.

CREUSA. Now hear my words. I praise Phoebus whom I did not praise before because he is restoring to me the child he once neglected. Fair to me now is the face of these gates and the shrine of the god, though they were hateful before. Now I am glad to cling to the door knocker and to salute his gates.

ATHENA. I commend that change of tone; now you praise the god. Ay, the gods act late perhaps, but always at the end with power.

CREUSA. My child, let us go home.
ATHENA. Go, and I will attend you.
CREUSA. Worthy is the guardian of our path.
ATHENA. And friendly to your city.
CREUSA. Sit you upon the ancient throne.
ION. It is a possession to be prized.

[*Athena disappears; exeunt Creusa and Ion.*]

CHORUS. *Hail Apollo, child of Zeus and Leto! He whose house is vexed by misfortunes ought to revere the deities and be of good courage! For at the last the good shall attain their deserts, but the evil, as their nature is, will never fare well.*

[*Exeunt.*]

# The Trojan Women

————◆————

AT the end of his fifth book Thucydides tells how the Athenians destroyed the ancient Greek city of Melos, which had wished to remain neutral in the Peloponnesian War, slaughtering its men and enslaving its women and children. Then his sixth book describes the feverish enthusiasm with which the Athenians were embarking on their ruinous Sicilian expedition. It was at the height of this enthusiasm that Euripides presented *Trojan Women*—a passionate and poetic expression of the horror and futility and degradation of war at any time, but desperately urgent in its particular setting. The culminating horror of Melos had shattered the patriotic idealism of the poet of *Andromache*. The Athenian audience must surely have been startled and sobered when, in the prologue, their own patron deity Athena asks Poseidon, who was Troy's champion, to bring disaster upon the Greeks on their long voyage. Perhaps the best evidence of the soundness of the Athenian democracy is that it could give such a play official sponsorship at such a time.

In the background a great and rich city with ancient traditions is burning, and in the cold dawn a broken old woman, once queen of this city, is lying on the ground. Over her there sweeps one piece of gruesome heartlessness after another, each more wanton than the last, each politically expedient in the conviction of the conquerors. Yet this crushing of humanity does not lend the conquerors the glory they expected; they are plainly uneasy and frightened—to the point of sacrificing Polyxena to a ghost and dashing Astyanax to his death. Even so there is a touch of desperate humanity in the pity of Talthybius and in the gift of Hector's shield, the Greeks' most valuable prize, to be Astyanax' coffin. The final stroke is the appearance of self-assured and bedizened Helen among the havoc she had caused. It was for this paltry toy that vanquished and victors alike had suffered degradation.

# THE TROJAN WOMEN

## CHARACTERS

POSEIDON
ATHENA
HECUBA
CHORUS of Trojan Women
TALTHYBIUS, Herald of the
    Greeks

CASSANDRA, daughter of
    Hecuba, and Priestess
    of Apollo
ANDROMACHE, widow of
    Hector
MENELAUS, husband of
    Helen
HELEN

The scene is the camp of the Greeks before Troy, in the background the smoking ruins of the city. At the entrance of one of the tents Hecuba is stretched on the ground.

The play was produced in 415 B.C.

———◆———

*[Poseidon enters, unseen by Hecuba.]*

POSEIDON. I am Poseidon, come from the salt depths of the Aegean sea, where the bands of Nereids ply their lovely feet in the intricacies of the dance. Ever since Phoebus and I threw the stone circle of towers, true and plumb, round this Troy, my goodwill toward the city of my Phrygians has not failed. Now the city is a smoking ruin, sacked by the Argive spear. That man of Parnassus, Epeius the Phocian, aided by the devices of Pallas, constructed a horse teeming with armed men, and sent the fatal monster inside the towers. Therefore men of after time will call it the Horse of Spears.

The sacred groves are abandoned. The shrines of the gods run with human blood. On the steps of the altar of Zeus the Protector, Priam lies dead. All the gold, all the spoils of Phrygia are being transported to the Achaean ships. They are now waiting for a following wind: after ten winters and summers they yearn to see their wives and children, those Greeks that came in war against this city. I too, vanquished by Hera the Argive goddess and Athena, who united to destroy the Phrygians, now leave famous Ilium and my altars.

When the evil of desolation overtakes a city, a blight falls on the cult of the gods; they delight no more in their worship. Scamander echoes to the loud wailings of multitudes of captured women being allotted their masters. Some have fallen to the Arcadians, others to the Thessalians, others to the two sons of Theseus, princes of Athens. All the Trojan women that are not to be assigned by lot are within these tents, specially picked for the first men of the army. With them is the daughter of Tyndareus, Helen the Laconian, rightly regarded as a captive woman.

If any one wants to see an unhappy woman, here is Hecuba prostrate before the entrance, weeping many tears for many miseries. Her daughter Polyxena has been slain at the tomb of Achilles, bravely dying, hapless girl. Priam is gone and the children, all but the virgin Cassandra, whom Lord Apollo has given over to prophetic frenzy. And now Agamemnon, religion and reverence forgot, forces her to be his concubine.

O city that once was fortunate, O shining battlements, farewell! If Pallas, daughter of Zeus had not willed your ruin, you would still be standing on firm foundations.

[*Enter Athena.*]

ATHENA. You who are nearest in lineage to my father, god powerful and respected in heaven, may I end our ancient feud and address you?

POSEIDON. You may, queen Athena. The company of kinsfolk is a great charm to the heart.

ATHENA. I thank you for your courtesy. My lord, I have a plan for you and me to discuss.

POSEIDON. Do you bring some news from heaven? Is it from Zeus or some other god?

ATHENA. No, it is for Troy's sake, whose soil we tread. I have come to enlist your might in a common cause.

POSEIDON. Have you renounced your former hatred and taken compassion on the city, now it is in flames and ashes?

ATHENA. First get back to where we were. Will you share my plan and help me to work out my will?

POSEIDON. I will. But I wish to learn your purpose in coming here. Does it concern the Achaeans, or the Phrygians?

ATHENA. I wish to bring gladness to my former enemies, the Trojans, and to inflict on the host of the Achaeans a sorrowful homecoming.

POSEIDON. Why do you jump like this from mood to mood and rush to excesses of hate and love?

ATHENA. Have you not heard of the insult to me and my temples?

POSEIDON. I have: Ajax dragged Cassandra off with violence.

ATHENA. Yes, and nothing was done to him by the Achaeans, nothing even said to him.

POSEIDON. And yet it was thanks to your might that they captured Ilium.

ATHENA. That is why, with your help, I will do them an injury.

POSEIDON. Anything you want from me is at your disposal. But what do you mean to do?

ATHENA. I mean to give them a homecoming they will not recognize.

POSEIDON. While they are still on land, or when they are on the salt sea?

ATHENA. Whenever they sail off home from Ilium. Zeus will send torrents of rain and hail and hurricanes that will black out the sky. He says he will lend me the fire of his thunderbolts to smite the Achaeans and set their ships ablaze. You, on the other hand, must do your part. Make the crossing of the Aegean a din of monstrous waves, a maelstrom of waters. Fill the sheltered straits of Euboea with drowned bodies. The Achaeans must learn in future to stand in proper awe of my shrines and to respect the other gods.

POSEIDON. So shall it be. You need make no long speech to get this favor. I shall stir up the waters of the Aegean sea. The shores of Myconus, the reefs of Delos, Scyros, Lemnos, and the promontories of Caphareium will receive innumerable bodies of drowned men. But go to Olympus, get the Father's thunderbolts in your hands and be on watch when the Argive fleet loosens its cables.

                                          [*Exit Athena.*]

The mortal is mad who sacks cities and desolates temples and tombs, the holy places of the dead; his own doom is only delayed.

            [*Exit Poseidon. Hecuba begins to rise, slowly.*]

HECUBA. *Up, poor soul, lift your head, your neck, from the ground. This is no longer Troy nor we Troy's royal fam-*

*ily. Fortune veers; be brave. Sail with the stream, sail with
the wind of fate. Do not run your ship of life head-on into
the billows of disaster. Alas! I weep. And why may I not
weep in my misery? My country is lost, my children, my husband. O ancestry, with your spread of pride lowered, you
come to nothing after all.*

*What should I tell of, what leave untold? What a sorry
bed on which I lay my heavy, weary limbs, lying stretched
on my back, in a hard, hard couch! Oh my head, my temples, my sides! Oh how lovely, to shift my bony back, to let
my body keel over to this side and that, to the rhythm of my
complaints, my unceasing tears. This is the music of the sorrowful—to chant the jarring dirges of their doom.*

*O prows of ships, to the horrid call of the trumpet and the
loud scream of fifes you came on swift oars over the purple
brine, across the safe seas of Hellas to sacred Ilium, and in
the bay of Troy (alas!) you dropped your cable ropes, produce of Egypt. You came to fetch Menelaus' loathsome wife,
that affront to Castor, that scandal of the Eurotas. It is she
who has murdered the father of fifty sons and grounded me
on these sorry shoals of disaster.*

*Ah me! Here I sit, a sorry seat, beside the tents of Aga-
memnon. They carry me off to slavery, an old woman like
me, my poor head laid bare by sorrow's cutting edge.
Enough! Woeful widows of Troy's warriors, and you virgin
brides of violence, Troy is in smoke, let us weep for Troy.
Like a mother hen clucking over her fluttering chicks, I shall
lead your song, ah how unlike those songs I used to lead in
honor of the gods, leaning on Priam's sceptre as my foot
gave the loud stamp, and the dance started to the Phrygian
strains.*

[*Enter Chorus in two halves, one consisting of the
older women, the other of the younger.*]

LEADER. *Hecuba, why those shouts, why those cries? Has
word come for one of us? I heard your piteous lamentations
ringing through the tents. And shuddering fear grips the
hearts of the Trojan women within, who are bemoaning their
slavery.*

HECUBA. *My child, the crews of rowers are stirring down
by the Argive ships.*

LEADER. *Ah me! What does that mean? The time has come,*

*I suppose, when the ships will carry me away from my native land.*

HECUBA. *I do not know, but I suspect the worst.*

LEADER. *Ho! woeful women of Troy, come and hear your doom, out of the tents with you, the Argives are setting sail for home.*

HECUBA. *Ah! do not bring frenzied, fey Cassandra out here, for the Argives to insult. Spare me grief on grief. O Troy, hapless Troy, this is your end. Hapless are they that have lost you, the living and the dead.*

CHORUS. *Ah me! In fear and trembling I quit these tents of Agamemnon to hear your words. O queen. Have the Argives made their decision? Is it death for hapless me? Or are the sailors already preparing to push off and ply their oars?*

HECUBA. *My child, I have been here since daybreak, my heart in a swoon of dread.*

CHORUS. *Has some herald of the Greeks been here already?*

HECUBA. *The hour of allotment must be near.*

CHORUS. *Oh! Oh! Will it be to Argos or Phthia or one of the islands that they will take me, unhappy me, far from Troy?*

HECUBA. *Alas! Alas! Whose wretched slave shall I be? Where, where on earth shall this old woman toil, useless as a drone, poor counterpart of a corpse, a feeble, ghastly ornament? To be posted to watch at the door, to become a children's nurse—I who in Troy was paid the honors of a queen?*

CHORUS [*the mark at the beginning of a line indicates a change of speaker*]. *Alas! Alas! How piteous are the lamentations with which you bemoan your indignities!*

—*No more shall I ply my flying shuttle in Trojan looms.*

—*For the last time I see the graves of my parents, for the very last time.*

—*I shall have worse sorrows, forced to lie in the bed of Greeks—*

—*my curse on the night when that is my fate.*

—*or kept as a slave woman to draw water from holy Pirene.*

—*May I come to Theseus' land, the glorious, the blessed.*

—*Never, never, I pray, to the swirling Eurotas, the cursed abode of Helen, there to look upon Menelaus as my master, the sacker of Troy.*

—*I have heard tales of the loads of wealth, the profusion of fine fruitfulness, in the grand land of Peneus, the beautiful pedestal of Olympus. There let me come; that is my second choice, after Theseus' land, holy, august.*

—*Then there is the land of Etna and Hephaestus, Sicily, mother of mountains, looking across to Phoenicia; I have heard of its fame, of its crowns of valor. Likewise its neighbor, as you sail over the Ionian sea, the land watered by the loveliest of rivers, Crathis, whose mysterious waters (waters that put yellow fire in your hair) bring prosperity to the land and a breed of valiant men.*

—*And now here comes a herald from the army of the Danaans; he comes, quickening his steps at his journey's end, to dispense his budget of news. What does he bring? What has he to tell? What matter? We are already slaves of the Dorian land.*

*[Enter Talthybius.]*

TALTHYBIUS. Hecuba, you know I made many trips to Troy as messenger from the Greek army. That makes me an acquaintance of yours, of long standing. I am Talthybius, here to announce the latest news.

HECUBA. *Here it comes, my Trojan friends. This is what I have long been dreading.*

TALTHYBIUS. The assignments have already been made, if that was your dread.

HECUBA. *Ah! Where do we go? Some city in Thessaly or in Phthia or in the land of Cadmus?*

TALTHYBIUS. You were each assigned individually to separate masters.

HECUBA. *Then who got whom? Is there good luck ahead for any of Troy's daughters?*

TALTHYBIUS. I can tell you, but you must particularize your questions, one at a time.

HECUBA. *Then tell me, who got my daughter, poor Cassandra?*

TALTHYBIUS. King Agamemnon took her, as a special prize.

HECUBA. *What? To be the slave of his Lacedaemonian wife? Ah me!*

TALTHYBIUS. No, she is to be his concubine.

HECUBA. *His concubine? The virgin of Phoebus, the girl on whom the golden-haired god bestowed virginity, as a peculiar favor?*

TALTHYBIUS. Love's shafts pierced him for the prophetic maiden.

HECUBA. *O my daughter, throw away the holy branches, throw off the sacred livery of chaplets that deck your person.*

TALTHYBIUS. Why? Isn't it a great thing to get a king for a lover?

HECUBA. *And what of the daughter you lately took away from me? Where is she?*

TALTHYBIUS. You mean Polyxena? Or whom do you speak of?

HECUBA. *Just her. To whom did the lot yoke her?*

TALTHYBIUS. She has been appointed to serve at the tomb of Achilles.

HECUBA. *Ah me! My daughter? To serve at a tomb? But what new usage or ordinance is this that the Greeks have?*

TALTHYBIUS. God bless your child. She rests well.

HECUBA. *What words are these? Tell me, does she see the sun?*

TALTHYBIUS. She is in the hands of fate; her troubles are over.

HECUBA. *And what of fire-eating Hector's wife, unhappy Andromache? What luck had she?*

TALTHYBIUS. Achilles' son took her also, as a special gift.

HECUBA. *And whose servant am I, this ancient body who needs a staff in her hand to help her two legs to walk?*

TALTHYBIUS. The king of Ithaca, Odysseus, got you for his slave.

HECUBA. *Ah! Hecuba, smash your shaven head, tear your two cheeks with your nails. Ah me! An abominable, treacherous scoundrel I have got for master, an enemy of justice, a lawless beast, whose double tongue twists all things up and down and down and up, who turns every friendship to hate, who—O women of Troy, wail for me. I go to my doom, ruin and misery are mine. The unluckiest lot has fallen to me.*

LEADER. Mistress, you know *your* fate, but which of the Peloponnesians, which of the Thessalians, is the master of my life?

TALTHYBIUS. On, servants, you must fetch Cassandra out here at once. I will put her into my general's hands and then come for the others.

Ha! What is that torch flame blazing inside? What are these Trojan women up to? Now that they are about to be carried abroad to Argos, are they starting a fire in the heart of the tents? Are they deliberately burning themselves to death? Truly, in people like these the love of freedom does not offer an easy neck to misery. Open up! Open up! Their death may be all very fine for them, but the Achaeans won't like it, and I don't want it to get me into any trouble.

HECUBA. It is not that. It is no fire. It is my child, frantic Cassandra; here she comes hurrying out.

[*Enter Cassandra, dressed as Apollo's priestess, and waving a nuptial torch. She fancies she is about to be married in Apollo's temple, while the god himself leads the choir.*]

CASSANDRA. *Lift up the torch, bring it to me. I bear the flame, I do reverence, and look! look! I light up this temple with the blaze. O King hymeneal, blessed is the bridegroom, blessed too am I; in Argos I am to marry a royal lover. Hymen, O King hymeneal! Poor mother, your time is all taken with mourning for my dead father and our dear country, with tears and lamentations. Therefore I now must hold aloft the blazing torch myself, for my own wedding. See its radiance, see its brilliance, giving light to thee, Hymenaeus, and thee, Hecate, as custom prescribes for the weddings of maidens.*

*Lift high the light foot. On, on with the dance. Evan! Evoe! Let it be as in the proudest days of my father's prosperity. The choir is sacred; lead it, Phoebus, in honor of thy priestess, in thy temple among the laurels. Hymen, O Hymen hymeneal! Sing, mother, sing and dance, whirling mazily in and out, trip it with me, as you love me. Shout the marriage greeting to the bride, wish her joy with songs and shouts. Come, daughters of Phrygia, in your loveliest robes, sing my wedding, sing the husband that Fate brings to my bed.*

LEADER. Queen, will you not seize your frantic daughter before she trips lightly off to the Argive host?

HECUBA. Hephaestus, you carry the torches at the weddings of mortals, but this was cruel of you to fan this flame. How unlike the high hopes I had!

Ah me! my child, never, never did I think your nuptials would be held amidst the spears and lances of Argives. Give me that light. In your frantic haste you do not hold the torch straight. Our disasters have not made you sober; you are still the same.

Women of Troy, take the torches; let your tears answer her wedding songs.

CASSANDRA. Mother, crown my conquering head; rejoice in the royal match I make. Escort me; if you do not find me

eager, push me by force. As Loxias exists, Agamemnon, the
Achaeans' noble king, will find me a more fatal bride than
Helen ever was. For I shall kill him; *I* shall ruin *his* house.
I shall take vengeance for my brothers and my father—

But these things can wait: I shall not sing of the axe which
will fall on my neck and another's, or of the matricidal
tournament which my wedding will start, or of the utter overthrow of Atreus' house.

But I will show that our city is more fortunate than the
Achaeans. Possessed though I am, I shall for once emerge
from my frenzy. For the sake of one woman and one woman's passion, the Greeks went chasing after Helen and perished in their thousands. Their general, their clever general,
to help those he should hate most, sacrificed the dearest thing
he owned; his own child, the joy of his house, he gave up for
his brother; and that for a woman, who had not been carried off by force, but had left home willingly. Then after
they had come to the banks of Scamander, they met their
deaths, not resisting any encroachments on their border lands
nor in defence of their towering cities. Those that Ares
took never saw their children; no wives' hands wrapped them
in their cerements; they lie in a foreign land. And back home
the misery was no less: widows dying lonely, old men left
childless in their halls, the sons they reared serving others,
none to visit their graves and make them blood offerings. This
is the praise the expedition has earned. . . . Of their crimes
it is better to say nothing; may my muse never lend her voice
to sing of evil things.

As for the Trojans, in the first place, what fame could be
more glorious than theirs? They died for their country. When
any fell in battle, their bodies were brought home by their
comrades; they were dressed for the grave by the proper
hands, and the soil of their native land wrapped them about.
All that did not fall in battle spent their every day with
their wives and children in their own homes. The Achaeans
were denied those pleasures. Hector's fate brought you grief,
but hear the truth of it; he is gone, but he lived long enough
to win a hero's fame. And it was the coming of the Achaeans
that brought this to pass. If they had stayed at home, his
virtues would have remained unknown. Paris, too, married
the daughter of Zeus. If he had not done so, nobody would
have heard of him or the bride in his house.

It comes to this: if a man is wise he will shun war. But if
war must come, it is a crown of honor for a city to perish in

a good cause; in an evil cause there is infamy. Therefore, mother, you must not feel sorry for our country or my concubinage. This wedlock of mine is the means by which I shall destroy our worst enemies, mine and yours.

LEADER. It is fine to be able to laugh at your own miseries and sing riddling songs. Perhaps some day you will show your meaning.

TALTHYBIUS [who has been listening, at first in amazement, then with impatience]. It's as well Apollo gave you crazy wits. Otherwise it would have cost you dear to be speeding my commanders from the land with such maledictions.

Right enough, the grand folks in the world, the folks everybody thinks so clever, are no better than the nobodies. Witness Atreus' precious son, the all powerful king of united Greece, saddled with a peculiar passion for this daft creature. I'm a poor man, to be sure, but I would never have taken a woman like this to *my* bed.

[To Cassandra.] Here you, since you are not quite right in the head, I'll let your words go down the wind, this reviling of the Argives and praising of the Phrygians. Come with me to the ships, a fine bride for the general.

[To Hecuba.] And you, be ready to come when Laertes' son wants you brought. It's a virtuous woman whose servant you will be, judging by the reports that have come to Ilium.

CASSANDRA. What a rogue of a servant. Why do heralds have such an honorable name, that profession which the whole world unites in detesting, these go-betweens of kings and states?

So you say my mother will go to the halls of Odysseus? Where then are the declarations of Apollo, made plain to me, which say she will die here?—The insulting details I omit. Hapless Odysseus, he does not know the dreadful trials in store for him. The day will come when my woes and my city's will seem to him like golden joys. Ten weary years must roll by, in addition to the years spent here, before he gets back to his native land, companionless. He must see dread Charybdis, whose dwelling is in the ebb and flow of that rockbound strait, and that cannibal of the mountains the Cyclops, and Ligurian Circe who changes fine men into swine; he must endure shipwreck on the salt sea, and the temptations of the lotus, and the holy cows of the Sun, whose flesh will take voice and utter a tale of agony for Odysseus. To cut a long story short, he will descend alive to Hades, and when he finally escapes from the clutches of the sea he will come home to a multitude of sorrows in his house.

But why launch forth all the sorrows of Odysseus? [*To Talthybius.*] March; let me lose no time, let me fly to my bridegroom's bed—of death. Great general of the Greeks, miserable will be your interment, in the night, not by day. O you whose fortune seems so grand! I too, of course, must die; my body will be thrown naked down a ravine, into a torrent of winter floods, near the grave of my bridegroom; I shall be given to the wild beasts to devour, I Apollo's servant. O chaplets of the god whom I love most of any, O raiment of exaltation, farewell; I leave the feasts in which once I gloried. Go, I wrench you from my skin. While my body is still undefiled I give them to the rushing winds, to carry them to you, O Lord of Prophecy.

Where is the general's ship? Where must I embark? There is no time to lose, be on the look-out for a breeze to fill your sails, to carry me off, one of three Furies. Farewell, mother, do not weep. O dear country, O my brothers under the earth and my father that begot me, you will not have long to wait for me. But I shall descend to the dead a conquering hero, having destroyed the house of Atreus, by whom our house was destroyed.

[*Exeunt Cassandra and Talthybius. Hecuba collapses.*]

LEADER. Nurses of old Hecuba, don't you see that your mistress has fallen, prostrate and speechless? Take hold of her. Will you leave the old woman lying? O cruel! Lift her upright.

HECUBA. Leave me, my daughters; an unwanted service is no service. Let me lie where I have fallen. I have full cause for falling, the things I have to endure and have endured and shall endure. O ye gods! It's poor helpers indeed I am now invoking; but still it's the fashion to call upon the gods when trouble overtakes us. This is my swan-song; first I will sing of my blessings and thus accentuate the pity of my woes.

I was a queen, I married into a king's house, and there I bore my excellent children, no mere figures but the best of the Phrygians [, of whose like no mother can boast, Trojan or Greek or barbarian]. These children I saw fall in battle with the Greeks, and I cut my hair over their tombs. And Priam their father—his loss was not reported to me by others; with

my very own eyes I saw him slaughtered at his own hearth,
the hearth of Zeus Protector. I saw my city taken. The virgin
daughters whom I reared to bestow on bridegrooms of the
highest rank, have been snatched out of my hands; another
type of bridegroom had the fruits of my care. No hope have
I that they will ever see me again or I them. And finally, the
crown of wretched misery, I go to Greece to an old age of
slavery. They will put me to all the tasks that are most intolerable to the aged. I shall be a door servant, looking after
the keys, I the mother of Hector! Or I shall have to bake
bread, and lay to rest on the hard ground the wrinkled back
that slept in palace beds. This poor battered body of mine
will be dressed in rags and tatters, an insult to my former
prosperity. Unhappy woman that I am, what a present, what a
future, and all because of one woman's marriage.

O my child, O Cassandra and your divine ecstasies, how
horrible the circumstances that have destroyed your sacred
purity! And O Polyxena, poor girl, where, where are you?
Of all my many children neither son nor daughter is here to
help their poor mother. Why then do you lift me up? What is
there to hope for? Lead me, me that once walked delicately
in Troy and am now a slave, lead me to some grovelling lair,
where the stones will be my pillow. Let me fling myself on
the ground there and waste out my cursed life in weeping.
Never hold any man happy, even the favorites of fortune,
this side of death.

CHORUS. *Sing me, O Muse, of Ilium. Sing a new strain, a
strain of weeping, a funeral dirge. The song I shall now
utter I dedicate to Troy. It was that four-footed wagon of the
Greeks that was our sad undoing, that made us prisoners
of war, from that moment when the Achaeans left at our
gates that horse, accoutered in gold and rattling to heaven
with the armor within. The population of Troy, standing on
rocks around, cried out, "Come, men, your troubles are
over, lead in this idol, consecrate it to the Maiden of Ilium,
daughter of Zeus." All the young women left their homes,
and all the old men. With singing and rejoicing they took
possession of the deadly trap.*

*Every son and daughter of Phrygia rushed to the gates to
do honor to the Immortal Virgin, to give to the goddess the
cunning fabrication of mountain pine, wherein lurked the
Argive ambush and Troy's destruction. They threw hempen
ropes around it, as if it were some black ship they were
launching, and brought it to the stone abode of Goddess*

Pallas and set it on the floor, the floor that was to cost our
land its lifeblood. On this labor of joy the darkness of night
descended. Then the Libyan flute shrilled forth and the
ringing songs of Phrygia. The air was filled with the patter
of dancing feet, with the gladsome choruses of maidens.
Everywhere was the glare of torch fire; even within the
houses the rooms of the sleepers glowed darkly.

I myself that night was singing in the choirs before the
temple of the Virgin of the Mountains, the daughter of
Zeus, when suddenly the castle and all the city rang with
cries of havoc. Darling infants clung in terror to their
mothers' skirts. Ares issued from his ambush; the will of
Pallas was accomplished. Phrygian blood ran on every altar.
In their lonely beds the young women shore off their
tresses, crowns of triumph for the Grecian breed, offerings of
sorrow for the land of the Phrygians.

[A wagon enters. In it are Andromache and her young
        son Astyanax, also Trojan spoils, among them Hec-
        tor's armor.]

Hecuba, look. Here comes Andromache in an enemy wagon, bound for a foreign land. Clutched to her heaving breast
is her darling Astyanax, Hector's son. Hapless woman, where
are they taking you on this wagon's top, seated amid Hector's
bronze armor and the spoils of sacked Ilium, with which
Achilles' son will adorn the temples of Phthia, far, far from
Troy.

ANDROMACHE. Our masters, the Greeks, are haling me off.
HECUBA. Ah me!
ANDROMACHE. Why do you lament? Lamentation is mine—
HECUBA. Ah! Ah!
ANDROMACHE. —for grief is mine—
HECUBA. O Zeus!
ANDROMACHE —and misery is mine.
HECUBA. My children—
ANDROMACHE. —now no longer.
HECUBA. Gone is the glory, gone is Troy——
ANDROMACHE. O grief!
HECUBA. —and gone my children, my noble children.
ANDROMACHE. Alas! Alas!
HECUBA. Alas indeed, and again alas for what was
mine——
ANDROMACHE. Ah me!

HECUBA. *The splendor, the fortune——*

ANDROMACHE. *—of the city——*

HECUBA. *—in smoke.*

ANDROMACHE. *O come, my husband, I beseech you——*

HECUBA. *You cry on one that lies with Hades, a son of mine, unhappy me!*

ANDROMACHE. *—come and save your wife.*

HECUBA. *And you, O you, whose foul murder dishonored Greece——*

ANDROMACHE. *—father of my Hector, Priam old and venerable——*

HECUBA. *—lull me asleep, the sleep of death.*

ANDROMACHE. *Deep are our yearnings——*

HECUBA. *Deep also (O cruel!) are the griefs we bear——*

ANDROMACHE. *—for the city that is gone——*

HECUBA. *Grief on grief accumulates.*

ANDROMACHE. *—destroyed by the illwill of the gods, from that hour when your infant son escaped death, the son who for a wicked woman destroyed the towers of Troy. Before the temple of Pallas the bloody bodies of our dead are exposed, for the vultures to harry. The end has come and the yoke of slavery for Troy.*

HECUBA. *O my country, my poor country——*

ANDROMACHE. *I weep at leaving you——*

HECUBA. *—now you see the bitter end.*

ANDROMACHE. *—and my own home, where my baby was born.*

HECUBA. *O my children, you have gone and left your mother in a deserted city—to the bitterness of dirges and lamentations and tears, fountains of tears, in our home. The dead shed no tears; they have forgotten their griefs.*

LEADER. What a sweet thing tears are to the miserable, dirges and lamentations and songs burdened with pain.

ANDROMACHE. O mother of Hector, of the hero whose spear destroyed so many Argives, do you see this sight?

HECUBA. I see the hand of the gods; some men they raise from nothingness to towering heights, others they humiliate and destroy.

ANDROMACHE. Away we are led like stolen cattle, I and my son. Nobility enslaved! O the heavy change!

HECUBA. Strange are the ways of Necessity. They have just now torn Cassandra away from me with violence.

ANDROMACHE. Alas! A second Ajax, I suppose, another ravisher, awaits your daughter. And you have other sorrows.

HECUBA. Ay, I have, beyond measure, beyond my counting. Sorrow outsorrows sorrow.

ANDROMACHE. Your child Polyxena is dead, slain at the tomb of Achilles, an offering to the lifeless dead.

HECUBA. Unhappy me! It becomes clear; this is what Talthybius meant just now with his dark riddle.

ANDROMACHE. I saw her myself. I got off this carriage and covered her with her robes and beat my breast for the dead.

HECUBA. Ah, my child! Brutally butchered! Ah and again ah! How shameful a death!

ANDROMACHE. She died as she died.—And yet in death she was luckier than I who live.

HECUBA. Death and life are not the same, my child. Death is nothingness; in life there is hope.

ANDROMACHE. [Lady, mother of Polyxena, listen to my words of comfort; let me breathe gladness into your heart.] The dead, I say, are as if they had not been born. It is better to die than to live in pain; the dead have no sorrows to hurt them, but when a man passes from happiness to misery his heart hankers restlessly after the joys he once knew. Polyxena is as dead as if she had never seen this life; she knows nothing of her sorrows. I aimed at fame, and the more I won the more I had to lose. In Hector's house I toiled to master all the accomplishments of a virtuous wife. In the first place I kept to the house and had no longing for those places where her mere presence is enough to earn a woman who does not stay at home an evil name, whether she is that sort of woman or not. I did not admit inside my doors the smart talk of women. I had my native wit to teach me virtue; I needed no more. My tongue was still and my countenance serene in my husband's presence. I knew when to insist with my husband and when to allow him to overrule me.

This was the reputation that reached the Achaean host and ruined me. For when I was captured, the son of Achilles wanted to make me his wife. I shall slave in the house of my husband's murderers. And if I forget dear Hector and open my heart to my present lord, I shall seem a traitor to the dead. On the other hand if I cherish Hector's love, I shall get myself hated by my lord and master. However, they say that a single night abates a woman's aversion for a man's bed. But I abominate the woman who marries again and forgets her first husband in the arms of the second. Why, even the draught-horse, separated from his old partner in the yoke, will pull reluctantly. And yet brutes have neither speech nor use of reason and are lower than man.

In you, dear Hector, I had all the husband I wanted: wise, noble, wealthy, brave, a great man. You got me virgin from my father's house; you were the first to enter my innocent bed. And now you are dead, and I am being shipped captive to the yoke of slavery in Greece. [*To Hecuba.*] Do you not think that the death of Polyxena, whom you weep for, is a lesser evil for her than my evils? Even hope, that remains to all the living, stays not with me; I nurse no delusion that things will ever be all right for me—it would be pleasant if I could even think so.

LEADER. Your misery is mine. As you bewail *your* lot, you teach me the depth of my own sorrows.

HECUBA. Never in my life have I set foot on a ship myself, but the pictures I have seen and the stories I have heard have taught me. If sailors have to face a storm that is not too great, they rally eagerly to the task of saving themselves from peril; one man takes the helm, another looks to the sails, another keeps out the sea water. But if the waves are too high, the storm too fierce, they give in to fate and submit to the mercy of the running seas. So I who have sorrows aplenty am dumb; I submit, I have no use for words. The waves of misery, heaven-sent, overpower me.

My dear child, think no more of Hector's fate. Your tears will not save him. Respect your present master; ply your husband with the allurements of your ways. If you do that, you will have a happiness in which all your friends will share, and you will bring up this grandson of mine to be a mighty aid to Troy; some day descendants of his may return and settle here, and Troy be again a city.

But what is this? One thing after another. Here I see the servant of the Achaeans, with word of new decisions. What brings him back?

[*Enter Talthybius and armed escort.*]

TALTHYBIUS. Wife of Hector who was the bravest of the Phrygians in days gone by, do not hate me. It is not of my choice that I bring you word of the common purpose of the Danaans and the sons of Pelops——

ANDROMACHE. What is it? I feel you are beginning a song of sorrows.

TALTHYBIUS. They have decided that the boy here. . . . How can I speak the word?

ANDROMACHE. What? Is he not to have the same master as I?

TALTHYBIUS. None of the Achaeans will ever be this boy's master.

ANDROMACHE. Are they leaving him here, sole survivor of the Phrygians?

TALTHYBIUS. I don't know how to break the sorrowful news gently.

ANDROMACHE. I thank you for your consideration. But I will not thank you for a tale of sorrows.

TALTHYBIUS. They are going to kill your child. Now you know the extent of your sorrow.

ANDROMACHE. Ah me! This word you bring me is a greater sorrow than my new marriage.

TALTHYBIUS. Odysseus prevailed in the general council with his advice——

ANDROMACHE. Alas and alas! My sorrows are too much.

TALTHYBIUS. He advised them not to allow the son of a heroic father to grow up——

ANDROMACHE. May his advice be applied to his own children.

TALTHYBIUS. But to hurl him from the battlements of Troy. Come now, let things take their course, and you will show wisdom. Don't hold on to the boy. Bear the agony of sorrow gallantly. You are powerless; don't think you are strong. There is no help for you anywhere. Just look around. Your city is destroyed, your husband dead, yourself overpowered. We are quite able to contend with a solitary woman. Therefore, do not invite a struggle; don't do anything that will humiliate you and just make things more objectionable. And another thing: I don't want you to utter imprecations against the Achaeans. If you say anything to provoke the army, this boy may get no burial, no service of tears. Say nothing; make the best of the situation, and you will not leave this boy's body unburied, and you yourself may find the Achaeans kindlier to you.

ANDROMACHE. My dearest child, my special care, you will leave your hapless mother, you will be slain by our enemies. Your father's gallantry, that brought salvation to others, has brought death to you. Your father's virtues flowered unseasonably for you.

Ah my luckless bridals, the luckless wedding that brought me long ago to Hector's hall [, not to bear a son to be slaughtered by Greeks, but one to rule over the broad acres

of Asia]. My child, are you crying? Do you realize your
evil fate? Why do your hands clutch me, why do you hang
on to my skirts, like a little bird cowering under my wings?
Hector cannot come to you, snatching up his famous spear;
he cannot leave his grave to succor you. Your father's kinsmen cannot help you, nor the strength of Phrygia. A dolorous
leap you must make; mercilessly hurled head first from the
heights, your broken body will give up the ghost. O young
thing, your mother's lovely armful! How sweet the fragrance
of your body! So it was in vain that this breast suckled you,
as you lay in your baby clothes. In vain I labored, in vain I
wore myself out with toil. Greet your mother, now, it is your
last chance. Embrace her that gave you birth. Wrap your
arms around me, right around me. Press your lips to mine.

O you Greeks, un-Greek are the tortures you devise. Why
are you killing this innocent child? O scion of Tyndareus,
Zeus was never your father. I declare you are the daughter
of many fathers, first the Spirit of Evil, then Hate, and Murder, and Death, and every monster that earth rears. Never
shall I affirm that Zeus begot you, to be the death of Greeks
and barbarians innumerable. Be damned! The loveliness of
your eyes has brought hideous ruin on the famous fields of
Phrygia.

[*She hands Astyanax to Talthybius.*]

There! take him, take him away, hurl him to his death, if
that is your will. Feast on his flesh. It is the gods who are
destroying us and I shall never be able to save my child
from death. Cover my poor body, hurry me to the ships. I
go to a fine wedding, having lost my child.

LEADER. Hapless Troy, you have lost thousands of your
sons, thanks to one woman and her hateful bed.

TALTHYBIUS. Come, child. Leave your poor mother's loving
embraces. Come to the highest parapet of your ancestral
towers. There you must relinquish life, as the decree demands. Seize him. You want another sort of herald for jobs
like this, one who is merciless, one whose heart has more taste
for brutality than mine has.

[*Exit Talthybius with party.*]

HECUBA. O my child, son of my poor son, we are robbed of
you, unjustly robbed, your mother and I. What has come
over me? What can I do for you, luckless one? Here is my
offering to you; I smite my head, I rend my breasts. This is

all I am mistress of. I grieve for my city, I grieve for you. What sorrow is not ours? What more is wanting to complete our utter ruin?

[*She collapses.*]

CHORUS. *O Telamon, king of Salamis, haunt of the bees, you established your abode on the sea-girt isle that nestles under the sacred hills where Athena revealed the first green shoots of olive, shining Athens' heavenly crown of glory. Then you went away, away to the field of valor, with Alcmena's archer son, to sack Ilium, our city of Ilium [yes, ours even in that far-off time when you came from Greece].*

*In his fury at the loss of the mares, he brought with him the flower of Greece's chivalry. Over the sea came his ships and in the lovely estuary of Simois he hove to and made fast his cables to the sterns. Then he took from his ship his sure arrows, that meant death for Laomedon. The walls that the chisel of Phoebus had made square and plumb he destroyed with the red breath of fire and he pillaged the land of Troy. Thus twice has the blow fallen; twice has the bloody spear overthrown the defences round Dardania.*

*Then it is of no avail, it seems, O son of Laomedon, that you walk delicately with goblets of gold and have the filling of Zeus's cups, a most honorable service. And the land that gave you birth is devastated by fire. On the shore by the sea there is wailing, like the scream of a bird over her brood; wailing for husbands, for children, for aged mothers. Gone are the baths that refreshed you, gone are the gymnasiums and the race tracks. Yet you, beside the throne of Zeus, compose your lovely young face in untroubled serenity, while the Greek spear destroys the land of Priam.*

*Love, Love, you came of old to the halls of Dardanus, troubling the hearts of the Heavenly Ones. How greatly you exalted Troy in those days when she made connections in heaven. Of Zeus and his shame I shall say no more. But this very day Dawn with her white wings, the light that mortals love, saw the havoc of our land, saw the destruction of our towers. Yet in this land she got the husband of her bridal bower, the father of her children (Tithonus) carried off to Heaven on a golden car drawn by four stars. High ran the hopes in his native land. But Troy has lost the charm that held the gods.*

[*Enter Menelaus, with soldiers.*]

MENELAUS. How beautiful is the brilliance of the sun to-
day, this day in which I shall get possession of my wife
[Helen. I am Menelaus and I have labored much for her, I
and the Achaean army]. I came to Troy not so much to get
my wife (that's what men are thinking) but rather to meet
the man who deceived his host and carried off my wife from
my house. That man, thanks to heaven, has paid the penalty;
the Greek spear has destroyed him and his country. Now
I am come to take away the Woman of Sparta—I hate to
say the name of my wife, my wife that was. She is within
these prisoners' tents, reckoned amongst the other Trojan
women. They that fought this weary war to get her have
given her to me to kill—or, if I do not choose to kill her, to
have her taken back to the land of Argos. For my part I
have decided to postpone her fate while I am in Troy and to
take her back on my ship to the land of Greece and *then*
hand her over to the vengeance of those whose friends have
died at Ilium; they will kill her.

Well then, my men, enter the tents and fetch her here.
Drag her by her cursed hair. Whenever favorable breezes
come, we shall escort her to Greece.

HECUBA [*rising.*] O you who are the support of the earth
and are by earth supported, whatever you are, you who
defy the guess of our knowledge, O Zeus, whether you are
the Law of Necessity in nature, or the Law of Reason in
man, hear my prayers. You are everywhere, pursuing your
noiseless path, ordering the affairs of mortals according to
justice.

MENELAUS. What's this? You are starting a new fashion in
prayer.

HECUBA. I commend you, Menelaus, for your intention to
kill your wife. But flee the sight of her, lest she captivate
you with longing. She captivates the eyes of men, she destroys cities, she sets homes aflame. Such are her witcheries.
I know her; so do you and all her victims.

[*Enter Helen, beautifully dressed, and her guards.*]

HELEN. Menelaus, this is a prelude well calculated to
terrify me; your servants lay rude hands on me and hustle
me out of these tents. I can well imagine, of course, that

you may hate me, but still I want to ask: what is the mind of the Greeks and you concerning my life?

MENELAUS. Your case was not specifically discussed, but the whole host has given you to me, whom you wronged, to be put to death.

HELEN. Have I permission to reply, to prove that my death, if I am killed, will be unjust?

MENELAUS. I did not come here to argue; I came to kill you.

HECUBA. Give her a hearing, Menelaus; you don't want to kill her without a hearing. But allow me to handle the prosecution's case against her. You do not know the evils she did in Troy; the indictment, compact and comprehensive, will justify her death and leave her no loophole of escape.

MENELAUS. I must have little to do to grant this favor. But if she wants to speak, she may. But I hope she realizes that I am making this concession on *your* urging, not as a favor to her.

HELEN [*to Menelaus*]. Since you regard me as your enemy, I don't suppose you will try to meet my points, however sound or unsound you may think them. But I think I know what charges you would make against me if it came to a debate, and I shall arrange my answers correspondingly [, your charges against mine, mine against yours].

In the first place, it was this woman here who gave birth to the whole bad business when she gave birth to Paris. Secondly, it was old Priam who ruined both Troy and me, when he did not kill the infant, the dream of the firebrand come true, too true, the future Alexander. That was the start of it; hear now the sequel. This Alexander was made the judge of the three goddesses. The offer of Pallas was the leadership of a Phrygian army that would overthrow Greece. Hera promised him empire over Asia and the furthest limits of Europe, if he would decide in her favor. Cypris told of my marvellous beauty and promised it to him, if she surpassed the other goddesses in beauty. Consider what follows logically from that. Cypris prevails, and see what a boon my nuptials conferred on Greece: she was not conquered by the barbarians, you had neither to meet them in battle nor submit to their empire. Greece's good fortune was my ruin. I was bought and sold for my beauty. And now I am reproached for what ought to have earned me a crown of honor for my head. You will say that I have not yet come to the point at issue, the explanation of my secret flight from your

house. The evil genius that was this woman's son, whether
you wish to call him Alexander or Paris, brought an ally
along with him, a most powerful goddess. Yet you, my unworthy husband, left him in your halls and sailed off to Crete
on a Spartan ship. So be it. The next question I shall put to
myself, not to you. Was I in my right mind when I ran away
from home with a stranger and left my country and my
house? Chastise the goddess, be stronger than Zeus who
bears rule over the other divinities but is the slave of Love.
I am not to blame.

There is another point which might afford you a specious
argument against me. When Alexander was dead and gone
below the earth, that ended divine interference in my love
affairs; I ought then to have left my home and returned to the
ships of the Argives. That is the very thing I sought to do.
My witnesses are the guards of the towers, the sentinels
on the walls, who time and again discovered me stealthily
letting myself down by ropes from the battlements. [More-
over it was by force that that new husband of mine, Deipho-
bus, took me and kept me as his wife, in defiance of the
Trojans.] What justification then would you have, my
husband, if you put me to an undeserved death? On the
one hand I was married against my will. On the other hand
my services to my own people have earned me bitter servitude, instead of a victor's prize. So be stronger than the gods
if you want to, but it's a silly thing to want.

LEADER. O queen, defend your children and your country.
Destroy the cogency of her pleadings. Eloquence allied to
wickedness, it is a fearful combination.

HECUBA. First of all I shall come to the defense of the
goddesses and show that her charges against them are unjust. For my part I do not believe that Hera and virgin
Pallas were ever so silly that the one was ready to barter
away Argos to the barbarian, and the other to make her
Athens the slave of Phrygia, and all for a childish whim that
took them to Ida to quarrel about their beauty. For why
should goddess Hera have conceived such a passion for
beauty? Did she hope to get a better husband than Zeus?
Was Athena laying her lines for a match with one of the
gods, Athena who shuns wedlock and begged the Father to
let her remain virgin? Don't make the gods silly to cover up
your own wickedness. You'll find you cannot convince the
wise. And Cypris—this is very funny—you say she came
with my son to the home of Menelaus. Could she not have

stayed quietly in heaven and brought you, Amyclae and all, to Ilium?

My son was of surpassing beauty; at the sight of him your heart transformed itself into Cypris. Every lewd impulse in man passes for Aphrodite. Rightly does her name begin like the word Aphrosyne—lewdness. So when you saw my son in the splendor of gold and barbaric raiment, mad desire took possession of your heart. In Argos you were used to a small retinue; having got rid of the Spartan city, you looked forward to a deluge of extravagance in Phrygia with its rivers of gold. The halls of Menelaus weren't large enough for your luxury to wanton in.

And so to your next point. You say you were *forced* to go with my son. Did anybody in Sparta hear anything? What sort of outcry did you make? Yet Castor was there, a strong young man, and his brother, not yet translated to the stars. Then when you had come to Troy with the Argives at your heels and the deadly jousting of spears had started, whenever a success of Menelaus was announced to you, you would praise him, just to torment my son with the reminder that he had a formidable rival in the lists of love. But if ever the Trojans were successful, Menelaus here was nobody. You kept an eye on Fortune and made it your practice to stick to her side. You had no taste for Virtue's side. Furthermore, you speak of trying to escape by stealth, of letting ropes down from the towers, as if you were there against your will. When, tell me, were you ever caught fixing a noose for your neck or whetting a sword? Yet that's what a noble woman would do who yearned for her former husband. In any case, I was constantly at you, remonstrating with you. "Go away, my daughter. My sons will find other brides, and I will have you conveyed out secretly to the Achaean ships. Stop this fighting between the Greeks and us." But you didn't like that. Why? Because you gloried and revelled in the palace of Alexander, because it gave you pleasure to receive the adoration of barbarians. [That, to you, was greatness.] And after all this you titivate yourself and come out here and brave the light of day beside your husband. O you abomination! You should have come crawling out in rags and tatters, in fear and trembling, your hair cropped to the scalp; modesty would become your guilty past better than impudence.

Menelaus, here is the culmination of my argument: crown Greece with honor, and do yourself justice, by killing this woman. And make this law for all other women: the woman who betrays her husband dies.

LEADER. Menelaus, be worthy of your ancestors and your house. Punish your wife. You have proved your quality to the Trojans; save yourself from the tongues of Greece, from the reproach of uxoriousness.

MENELAUS. You have come to the same conclusion as I, that she willingly left my home for a foreign bed; Cypris has been injected into her argument to make it sound well. [*To Helen.*] March, to the stoning party; die, and in an instant atone for the Achaeans' years of labor. You will learn not to dishonor me.

HELEN. Do not kill me, by your knees I ask you, do not blame me for the trouble that came from heaven. Forgive me.

HECUBA. There are also your allies whom she slew; do not betray them. On behalf of them and their children I entreat you.

MENELAUS. Say no more, old woman; I do not give her a thought. I command my servants to lead her away to the ships on which she is to sail.

HECUBA. Do not let her on board the same ship with you.

MENELAUS. What do you mean? Is she heavier than she was?

HECUBA. No lover ever loses all his liking.

MENELAUS. That depends on what comes of the disposition of the loved one. But your wish will be granted. She will not embark on the same ship as I. And when she comes to Argos she will get her deserts, a vile death for a vile woman, and she will teach all women to be chaste. No easy task, to be sure, but her death will put a godly fear in their lewd hearts, even if they are more detestable than she is.

[*Exit Menelaus with Helen. Hecuba lies down.*]

CHORUS. *So you have betrayed us to the Achaeans, O Zeus, you have deserted the temple in Ilium with its altars and incense, the burning wafers and the air filled with the fumes of burnt myrrh; you have forsaken holy Pergamum and the ivy-clad glens of Ida, where the torrents run swollen with snow, Ida where the sky ends, the holy ground that catches the radiance of the first shafts of the sun.*

*Gone are the sacrifices and the cheerful songs of the dancers; gone are the festivals of the gods in the darkness of night, gone are the graven images of gold. The moons of Phrygia look down no more on the Feasts of the Twelve Cakes. I wonder, O Lord, I wonder if you take thought of these things, mounted on your ethereal throne in heaven, while my city perishes, destroyed by the blazing rush of fire.*

*O my beloved, O husband mine, in the world of the dead you wander, unburied, unpurified, while I must cross the seas on the wings of a swift ship to Argos, land of horses, where men inhabit the soaring walls of stone that the Cyclopes built. At the gates a multitude of children cling to their mothers' skirts, weeping and wailing. A young girl cries: "Mother, ah me! The Achaeans are taking me away from you, away to the dark ship; over the sea the oars will carry me, either to sacred Salamis or to the peak at the Isthmus looking down on the two seas, the gates to the stronghold of Pelops."*

*When the ship of Menelaus is half way over the sea, may a blazing Aegean thunderbolt, hurled by Jove's holy hands, come crashing down into the midst of his fleet; for he is carrying me away from Ilium's land to exile and tearful servitude in Greece, while the daughter of Zeus takes up in her hands her golden mirrors that maidens love. May he never reach the Laconian land and the hearth and home of his fathers; may he never see the city of Pitana or the temple of the Bronze Gates; for he has taken his evil wife who brought shame on great Hellas and sorrow and suffering to the streams of Simois.*

[*Talthybius and his men arrive with the body of Astyanax.*]

*Oh! Oh! Here are fresh sorrows, succeeding sorrows still fresh, for our land. Hapless wives of the Trojans, you see here the body of Astyanax, whom the Danaans have slain, hurling him (O cruel throw!) from the battlements.*

TALTHYBIUS. Hecuba, one ship is left; its oars are about to take the rest of the booty of Neoptolemus to the shores of Phthia. He has already put to sea on hearing of fresh disasters that have befallen Peleus. They say that Acastus, son of Pelias, has driven him out of his land. This moved Neoptolemus more than any pleasure in staying here. So he is gone, and Andromache with him. When she left she brought tears aplenty to my eyes, as she wept for her native land and bade farewell to Hector's tomb. She asked Neoptolemus to grant burial to this body, your Hector's child, who lost his life when he was thrown from the walls. She begged him also not to take with him to Phthia this brazen shield, the terror of the Achaeans, with which the boy's father used to cover his sides, not to install it (a sorry sight to see) in the same chamber in which she herself, this dead child's mother, would receive her new bridegroom; but to let it serve as a cedar or stone coffin for her son's burial. The body was to be put into your arms, to be wrapped in its cerements and crowned with flowers, and everything done for it that your strength and your circumstances would allow. For she has gone and her master's urgency has prevented her from burying her own boy. So whenever you have dressed the corpse, we will cover it with earth and set sail.

You must lose no time in fulfilling your appointed task. There is one labor I have spared you. When I came across the streams of Scamander here I took the body and washed out the wounds. Well, I'll be off to break up the ground for his grave. You and I sharing the work together, will save time and get our ship launched for home all the sooner.

HECUBA. Lay Hector's shield on the ground. Its trim lines are a sorry sight, and a dear one, for my eyes.

O you Achaeans, with whom prowess in war bulks larger than wisdom, why did you fear this child and add slaughter to slaughter? Were you afraid he might some day raise fallen Troy? Then you are cowards after all. Our city is taken, Phrygia is destroyed, yet you were afraid of a child, a little child, though even Hector's victories and thousands of brave men besides could not prevent our doom. I do not admire a fear that has no basis of reason.

O dearest child, what a sorry death has overtaken you! If you had died in your city's defence, if you had enjoyed youth and wedlock and the royal power that makes men gods, then you would have been happy, if there is any happiness in these. As it was, my child, your life did know these joys, but knew them only by sight; you got no use of the kingship which was your heritage. Poor boy, what a tragic death! Your own ancestral walls, the battlements of Loxias, have shorn off the curls on which your mother lavished her care and her kisses. From the crushed skull (forgive me!) Death grins forth. O arms so sweet, to me so like your father's, you hang now loose and lifeless from the sockets.

O dear mouth, you are gone, with all your pretty prattle. It was not true, what you used to say to me, climbing on to my bed: "Mother, I'll cut off from my hair a great big curl for you and I'll bring crowds of my friends to your grave and give you fond farewells." But it was the other way round; it is I, the old crone, landless, childless, who bury your poor young corpse. Ah me! All my kisses, all my care, all our nights asleep together, all have been wasted. What will be the verse inscribed on your tomb? "Within this grave a little child is laid, slain by the Greeks because they were afraid." An inscription to make Greece blush. At any rate though you have lost your patrimony you will still have your father's bronze shield to be buried in.

O shield that kept safe my Hector's strong arms, you have lost the hero that kept you safe. How sweet it is to see in your loop the mark of Hector's arm, and on the skilful fashioning of the rim the sweat which dripped from Hector's face as, chin on shield, he bore the brunt of many a fight. Come, let such stores as we have afford a decent burial to this poor corpse. As god has shaped our circumstances, we cannot aim at splendor. But all I have is yours to take.

The mortal is mad who rests his happiness on the expectation of lasting welfare. Fortune is a whirling dervish that twists and turns and leaps now this way, now that. Success is not of a man's own making.

LEADER. Look, here are your women bringing in their arms from the spoils of Troy adornments to wrap the corpse in.

HECUBA. O my child, not for a triumph won over your fellows with chariot or bow in the honored exercises of Phrygia does your father's mother bring you these poor adornments; better she cannot hope for, from the wealth that was once yours. Now accursed Helen has robbed you of it, robbed you and destroyed your life, and ruined utterly your whole house.

CHORUS. *Ah! you move me, Ah! you touch my heart. O the mighty one I have lost, the prince of my land no more!*

HECUBA. The robes, the pride of Phrygia, which you were to wear on your wedding day, when you would wed the proudest princess in Asia, I now put on your body. And you, dear shield of Hector, mother of triumphs innumerable, for the glory of victories past receive this garland. Immortal shield, you will die with the dead. Yet you are much more to be honored than the armor of Odysseus, wise only in wickedness.

FIRST PART OF CHORUS. *Alas! What a bitter sorrow——*

SECOND PART OF CHORUS. *O child, the earth will receive you.*

FIRST PART. *—for you to bewail, mother.*

HECUBA. *Alas!*

SECOND PART. *'Tis the Song of the Dead.*

HECUBA. *My grief!*

FIRST PART. *Ah grief indeed! Ghastly are your afflictions.*

HECUBA. With bandages I shall play the doctor to your wounds, a sorry doctor, doctor in name with no skill to heal. For the rest, your father will take care of you, amongst the dead.

CHORUS. *Strike, strike your head. Sound the measured beat of hands. Ah me! Ah me!*

HECUBA [*gazing fixedly at the sky*]. Oh dearest women——

[*She breaks off, rapt, intense.*]

CHORUS [*alarmed*]. *Hecuba, we are with you, tell us, what means that cry?*

HECUBA [*as if coming out of a trance*]. In Heaven—there is nothing there for us—only my miseries—only hate for Troy, most hated of cities. We have been slaughtering our hecatombs for nothing. If only god had taken us—sunk beneath the earth—disappeared—unknown to fame. . . .

Go then, bury the body in its wretched grave. It has received such tendance as Hell requires. I imagine it makes little difference to the dead to honor them with rich ritual. It is the living who attach importance to such vanities.

[*Cortege departs.*]

CHORUS. *Oh! Oh! Your unhappy mother! Your death has torn to shreds and tatters her high hopes for the future. Greatly envied you were for your noble birth, but horrible was the death by which you perished.*

*Ah! Ah! What do I see yonder on the heights of Ilium, arms waving wildly in the blaze of firebrands? Some fresh sorrow threatens to fall on Troy.*

[*Enter Talthybius and soldiers.*]

TALTHYBIUS. You captains who have been assigned to set fire to this city of Priam, I give you the word. No longer keep the torches idle in your hands; apply the fire. Let us demolish the city of Ilium and then sail away happy to our homes.

As for you, daughters of Troy, I have two commands in one. The rest of you, march to the ships of the Achaeans whenever the commanders of the army sound the shrill note of the echoing trumpet, and you, old Hecuba, unhappiest of women, go with these men whom Odysseus has sent to fetch you. The lot made you his slave; he will take you away from Troy.

HECUBA. Ah wretched me! It has come at last, the culmination and crown of all my sorrows. I leave my country; the torch is put to my city. Old legs, press on, try hard; let me bid farewell to my hapless city. O Troy, that once held your head so high amongst barbarians, soon you will be robbed of your name and fame. They are burning you and leading us out of the land to slavery. O ye gods! Yet why should I call upon the gods? In the past they did not hear when they were called. Come, let us rush to the pyre; our greatest glory will be to perish in the flames in which our country perishes.

TALTHYBIUS. Poor thing, your sorrows are driving you frantic. [To the soldiers.] Come there, lead her away. Don't stand on ceremony. We must take Odysseus his prize and put her into his hands.

HECUBA. Alas! Alas! Alas! Son of Cronus, Lord of Phrygia, Father of our folk, do you see how they treat us, how they outrage the seed of Dardanus?

CHORUS. He sees, but the city, the great city, is a city no longer, it is fallen. Troy is dead.

HECUBA. Alas! Alas! Alas! Ilium is ablaze; the fire consumes the citadel, the roofs of the city, the tops of the walls!

CHORUS. Like smoke blown to heaven on the wings of the wind, our country, our conquered country, perishes. Its palaces are overrun by the fierce flames and the murderous spear.

HECUBA. O land that reared my children!

CHORUS. Ah! Ah!

HECUBA. Hear me, my children, listen to the voice of your mother.

CHORUS. You call on the dead with lamentation.

HECUBA. *Yes, I call on them, as I lay my old limbs on the ground and knock on the earth with my two hands.*

CHORUS. *We too in turn kneel on the earth and call on our husbands in the world of the dead.*

HECUBA. *We are driven off, we are haled away——*

CHORUS. *Grievous, grievous is your cry.*

HECUBA. *——to the halls where we must slave.*

CHORUS. *Ay, far from our fatherland.*

HECUBA. *Oh! Priam, Priam, dead, unburied, unbefriended, yet you are unconscious of my doom.*

CHORUS. *Yes, for darkness has enveloped his eyes, the darkness of blessed death, though cursed be his murderers.*

HECUBA. *O temples of the gods, O city of my love——*

CHORUS. *Ah! Ah!*

HECUBA. *——the deadly flames got you, and the spear of battle.*

CHORUS. *Soon you will fall, our dear land will cover you, and your name will be no more.*

HECUBA. *And the dust, like smoke, with wing outspread to heaven, will rob me of the sight of my home.*

CHORUS. *The name of the land will pass into oblivion. One thing after another, everything disappears. Hapless Troy is finished.*

[*The citadel collapses.*]

HECUBA. *Did you notice, did you hear?*

CHORUS. *The crash of the falling citadel.*

HECUBA. *Ruin, everywhere ruin——*

CHORUS. *It will engulf the city.*

[*Trumpets sound.*]

HECUBA. *Ah! My trembling limbs, lead me on my path. On with you, poor limbs, to lifelong slavery.*

CHORUS. *Ah hapless city! But still—forward, feet, to the waiting ships of the Achaeans.*

[*Exeunt.*]

# Electra

—◆—

THE differences between this *Electra* and the plays of Aeschylus and Sophocles on the same theme are an easy index to Euripides' dramaturgy. The scene is not a palace but a peasant's hut, and the personages are heroic only in name. They are not abstract types but carefully studied individuals whose conduct is referable to contemporary standards. Electra's language is full of nurses and babies and sex; she is motivated rather by envy of her mother than loyalty to her father. Orestes is a frightened vagabond who talks grandiloquently of nobility. The murders are merely repulsive, and the perpetrators are crushed when they see the results of behavior expected of an Orestes and an Electra.

The ridicule of the tokens by which Aeschylus effects Orestes' recognition is an expression of Euripides' wit; but his more sophisticated identification by means of a scar is significant of the verisimilitude his more realistic drama required. The hearty and homely sea-god out of the machine openly criticizes Apollo for instigating the horror, but we have seen enough to understand that it was not necessarily Apollo but false beliefs concerning him that caused the tragedy.

# ELECTRA

## CHARACTERS

PEASANT, *a poor but honorable Mycenaean wedded in name to Electra*

ELECTRA, *daughter of Agamemnon*

ORESTES, *son of Agamemnon*

PYLADES, *prince of Phocis, friend of Orestes*

CHORUS, *of Argive women*

TUTOR, *once servant of Agamemnon*

MESSENGER, *servant of Orestes*

CLYTEMNESTRA, *wife of Agamemnon*

THE DIOSCURI (CASTOR AND POLLUX), *sons of Zeus and Leda, and so brothers of Clytemnestra and Helen*

ATTENDANTS

The scene represents the Peasant's cottage at the borders of Argolis.

Electra was acted approximately 413 B.C.

———————◆———————

[*Enter the peasant from the cottage.*]

PEASANT. Ah, ancient Argos, streams of Inachus! From you King Agamemnon once carried War in a thousand ships and sailed to the Trojan land. When he had killed Priam, ruler of the Ilian country, and had taken the famous city of Dardanus he came back here to Argos and in its high temples he deposited much plunder from the foreigners. In Troy he was lucky. But in his own house he perished by a trick of his wife, Clytemnestra, and the hand of Thyestes' son, Aegisthus.

And so he died and left behind him the ancient scepter of Tantalus. Now Aegisthus is king of the land and has to wife the daughter of Tyndareus who was Agamemnon's wife. When King Agamemnon sailed to Troy he left his children at home, a boy, Orestes, and a girl, Electra. Of these his father's old tutor stole Orestes away, for Aegisthus was going to kill him, and he gave him to Strophius to be brought up in the land of the Phocians. The girl, Electra, stayed on in her father's house. When she was in the tender bloom of youth, suitors from all Hellas, the principal people in the country, sought her hand. But Aegisthus was afraid she might bear one of these noblemen a child who would become Agamemnon's avenger, and so he kept her at home, and did not mate her with any bridegroom. But even this situation was fraught with danger—she might bear children surreptitiously to some nobleman—so he decided to kill her; but her mother, although she was cruel-hearted, saved her from Aegisthus' hand. She had had an excuse for killing her husband, but she was afraid that the murder of children would arouse odium.

Upon this Aegisthus then contrived this scheme. He announced a reward of gold to anyone who would kill the son of Agamemnon that had departed in exile; and Electra he gave to *me* to have for a wife. Now I am sprung of Mycenaean parentage and I cannot be reproached on that account; but though I am of excellent descent I am poor in substance, and nobility does not survive poverty. So Aegisthus gave her to a weakling, that his fear might be weakened. If some man that had position had her to wife, Agamemnon's murder would have been roused from its sleep, and retribution would then have fallen on Aegisthus. But I declare that I have never shamed her bed—Cypris is my witness; she is still a virgin. I think it shame to take the child of a lordly house and outrage her; my position is not worthy of her. I sigh for poor Orestes, my kinsman in name, if ever he should come to Argos and see his sister's unhappy marriage.

Some one might call me a fool for taking a young maiden into my house and then not touching her; such a man measures temperance by the naughty yard-stick of his own character. He must know that he is himself what he calls me.

[*Enter Electra with a water-jug on her head.*]

ELECTRA. Black night, nurse of the golden stars! At night I place this vessel upon my head and go to fetch the fountain's flood. I have not indeed been reduced to such a necessity, but I wish to demonstrate to the gods the iniquity of Aegisthus. I utter wails for my father to the great ether. That accursed Tyndarid, my mother, has thrown me out of the house to oblige her husband. She has borne Aegisthus other children, and so regards Orestes and me as incidentals in her household.

PEASANT. Why is it, poor girl, that you labor and toil for my sake, when you have been brought up delicately? Why don't you give it up, when I tell you to?

ELECTRA. I count you a friend, equal to the gods; for in my tribulations you have not outraged me. It is a blessing for mortals when things go wrong to find a man like you to mend them. It is my duty to lighten your toil as far as I can, even though I am not bidden to; to share your labors so that your burden will be lighter. You have enough work outdoors; it behooves me to attend to the house. When a laborer comes in from the field it is pleasant to find things at home in good order.

PEASANT. If that is your mind go ahead. As a matter of fact, the fountain is not far from the house. Day is dawning; I will drive the cattle to pasture and plant the fields. No lazy man can gather a livelihood without toil even if the gods are always on his lips.

[*Exeunt, severally; enter Orestes and Pylades.*]

ORESTES. Pylades, above all men I consider you my faithful friend and comrade. Alone of my friends you have shown regard for Orestes, in the sorry plight in which you see him, wronged by Aegisthus. He killed my father—he and my accursed mother. I have come to Argive soil straight from the god's oracle. No one knows I am here. I shall requite my father's murderer with murder. During this night I have gone to his tomb and I gave him my tears and offered a lock of hair, and poured upon his pyre the blood of a slaughtered sheep—unknown to the masters that bear rule over this land. I do not set foot within the walls; I stop here on the border. And that for two reasons: I can shift quickly to another land if any of the watchers discover me, and I seek my sister— they say she lives united in matrimony and no longer bides a maid—to get in touch with her and get her as an accomplice for the murder. I want to find out precisely what is going on inside the walls.

But now Dawn is raising her pale face; let us step aside from this path. Some plowman or some slave woman will appear, and we can inquire whether my sister lives in these parts. Ah, I see there a servant girl carrying on her shaved head a heavy jug of water. Let us crouch down and learn from this slave woman. Perhaps we shall gather some news about the things for which we have come to this land.

*[Orestes and Pylades retire to the rear; re-enter Electra.]*

ELECTRA. *Speed your foot's motion, for it is time; keep on, ah, keep on, with bitter weeping; alas for me, alas. I was sprung of Agamemnon, and Clytemnestra bore me, Tyndareus' hateful daughter; the townsfolk call me hapless Electra. Alas and alack for my wretched toils, for my hateful life! Ah, father, you are lying in Hades, slaughtered by your wife and Aegisthus, ah, Agamemnon!*

*On, awake the self-same lamentation. Weep and wail; there is pleasure in that.*

*Speed your foot's motion, for it is time; keep on, ah, keep on, with bitter weeping, alas, for me, alas. In what city, in what house, O my poor brother, are you a wanderer, far from the pitiful sister you left behind to most grievous distress in your ancestral halls? Come and redeem me from these woeful sorrows—Zeus, ah, Zeus! Avenge our father for his blood foully shed, draw your wandering foot to Argos.*

*I will raise this pitcher. I will put it from off my head. Let me greet the dawn, as I greeted the night, with lamentations for my father, with dirges of Death, of Death. My father, beneath the earth, I pour out for you my lamentations; they are ever my pursuit day by day. My dear neck I furrow with my nails, and I lay heavy hands upon my shorn head for your death.*

*Alas! Alas! Rend the hair! Like some tuneful swan by a river's flood that calls for its dear sire that has perished in the guileful meshes of a net, so my poor dear father, do I bewail you,*

*How you poured over your body the water of that last bath, how you lay down in the most pitiful couch of death. Woe is me, woe is me, for that axe's bitter blade, for the bitter plot to which you came back from Troy. Not with garlands did your wife receive you, not with crowns; with a sword, the two-edged sword of Aegisthus, she did that foul crime and won her treacherous lover.*

*[Enter Chorus.]*

CHORUS. *Agamemnon's daughter Electra, I have come to your rustic home. A man came by, a milk-drinking, mountain-*

*ranging Mycenaean came by, bringing word that the Argives have proclaimed a festival for the day after to-morrow. All the maidens are to go in procession to Hera's temple.*

ELECTRA. *Brilliant raiment does not set my heart a-flutter, friends, nor golden necklaces, poor wretch that I am; nor shall I stand in the dance with the Argive girls and trip it with a whirling foot. With tears I pass the night, tears are my sorrowful charge by day. Look at my tangled hair, at these rags of clothes. Are they becoming to Agamemnon's royal maid, becoming to Troy which remembers that my father sacked it?*

CHORUS. *Great is the goddess. Come, borrow of me a close-woven mantle to put on, and shining golden ornaments—do oblige us. Do you think tears will prevail over your enemies, if you do not honor the gods? You must revere the gods, not with groans, but with prayers to obtain happy days, my child.*

ELECTRA. *No god gives ear to this wretched girl's cries, nor regard to my father's sacrifices of old. I grieve for him that is perished, and for him that is alive and a wanderer. Some-where, in some strange land he lingers, a wretched vagabond at some slave-hearth—he that was sprung of a noble father. I myself dwell in a poor house and my soul pines away; I am banished from my ancestral home to the cliffs of the mountains. And my mother dwells united to another upon a bed stained with murder.*

LEADER. The blame for many troubles to the Hellenes and to your house belongs to your mother's sister, Helen.

[*Orestes and Pylades approach.*]

ELECTRA. Oh, Oh! Women, I must leave my sorrowing. Some strangers who have been hiding near the house have risen from their ambush. You flee down the road and I'll run into the house to escape these rogues.

ORESTES [*intercepting her*]. Stay, poor girl. Do not tremble at my hand.

ELECTRA. Phoebus Apollo, I implore you, don't let me be killed!

ORESTES. May I kill others, less dear than you.

ELECTRA. Go away. Do not touch what you must not touch.

ORESTES. There is no one I may touch with better right.

ELECTRA. Then why do you lie in wait at my house sword in hand?

ORESTES. Stay and hear me. Soon you will not gainsay me.

ELECTRA. I do stay. I am in your power; you are the stronger.

ORESTES. I bring you word from your brother.

ELECTRA. Ah, dear friend! Is he alive or dead?

ORESTES. He lives. First I wish to give you this good news.

ELECTRA. Bless you!—my reward for your very sweet words.

ORESTES. Your blessing on us both, to share in common.

ELECTRA. Where in the world is the wretched man passing his wretched exile?

ORESTES. He is a vagabond that observes no single city's law.

ELECTRA. He is not in want for his daily livelihood?

ORESTES. That he has, but a man in exile is without resources.

ELECTRA. What message do you bring from him?

ORESTES. He asks whether you are alive, and if so what are your circumstances.

ELECTRA. You see, first of all, how withered my body is.

ORESTES. Yes, so wasted with grief that I could groan.

ELECTRA. My head, my curls—shorn short with a razor.

ORESTES. The thought of your brother gnaws at your heart —perhaps, your father that is dead?

ELECTRA. Ah me! What can be dearer to me than they?

ORESTES. Alas, alas. But how do you suppose your brother regards you?

ELECTRA. He is my friend, but a distant friend, when he should be close.

ORESTES. Why do you live here, so far from the city?

ELECTRA. I am married, stranger; a marriage that is like death.

ORESTES. I groan for your brother's sake. To some Mycenaean?

ELECTRA. Not the sort of man to whom my father once expected to give me.

ORESTES. Tell me, so that I can carry the word to your brother.

ELECTRA. This is my husband's house, far from the city.

ORESTES. Some ditcher or cowherd would suit such a house.

ELECTRA. He is a poor man, but generous, and respectful to me.

ORESTES. What sort of respect is this that your husband shows?

ELECTRA. He has never presumed to touch my couch.

ORESTES. Is it some religious chastity he practices or does he scorn you?

ELECTRA. He does not think it right to outrage my parents.

ORESTES. How was he not delighted to attain to such a match?

ELECTRA. He did not recognize the authority of him who gave me in marriage.

ORESTES. I understand. He is afraid he may sometime have to give satisfaction to Orestes.

ELECTRA. He is afraid of that. But also, he is naturally good.

ORESTES. Ah, it is a generous spirit you describe. He must be rewarded.

ELECTRA. Yes, if the absent ever returns.

ORESTES. Did your own mother suffer you to be so treated?

ELECTRA. Women are their husbands' friends, stranger, not their children's.

ORESTES. Why did Aegisthus treat you so outrageously?

ELECTRA. He wanted me to bear insignificant children, so he gave me to this sort of man.

ORESTES. So that you should not bear children, I suppose, who would exact vengeance?

ELECTRA. That was his plan. May he render me full requital for it!

ORESTES. Does your mother's husband know that you are still virgin?

ELECTRA. He does not. I have concealed it from him, kept it quiet.

ORESTES. Are these your friends that overhear this conversation?

ELECTRA. Yes, they will keep your words and mine well hidden.

ORESTES. What could Orestes do about this if he should come to Argos?

ELECTRA. Do you ask? Your suggestion is disgraceful. Is it not high time?

ORESTES. If he came how could he kill your father's murderers?

ELECTRA. By daring what his enemies dared against our father.

ORESTES. And would you dare to kill your mother along with him?

ELECTRA. Yes, with the very same axe with which my father was destroyed.

ORESTES. Shall I tell him this? Are you firmly resolved?

ELECTRA. Let me shed my mother's blood, and die!

ORESTES. Ah, would Orestes were near to hear this.

ELECTRA. But stranger, I should not know him if I saw him.

ORESTES. No wonder, you were both children when you were separated.

ELECTRA. Only one of my friends would know him.

ORESTES. The man they say stole him away from death?

ELECTRA. Yes, an old man, my father's old tutor.

ORESTES. When your father died, did he obtain burial?

ELECTRA. If you can call it burial. He was thrown out of his house.

ORESTES. Ah, what a tale you tell—the sight of even stranger's troubles distresses human beings. But speak on, so that I may know and bring to your brother words, not joyful to be sure, but such as demand attention. The educated are capable of compassion, which the uncouth know not. To have an understanding heart is not without its price to men of feeling.

LEADER. My heart's desire is as this man's. I live far from town and do not know what wrongs are done in the city; now I, too, wish to learn.

ELECTRA. I shall speak out if I must—and I must speak out to a friend—of the grievous fortunes which are mine and my father's. Since you have prompted this tale, I beseech you, stranger, tell Orestes of the insults heaped on me and him. Tell him of my clothes, like a farm-hand's. Tell him of the filth with which I am laden. Tell him the sort of house I live in—I that come from royal halls. I work at my own clothes with my shuttle, or I should have none to cover my naked body. I carry water from the spring with my own hands. I have no part in the holy festivals. I am deprived of a share in the dances. I am ashamed to mix with women, for I am a maid; I am ashamed to think of Castor, my kinsman, to whom they betrothed me before he went to the gods. But my mother sits on a throne amidst the spoils of Phrygia, and about her seat are stationed Asiatic captive women whom my father won; they wear Idaean robes clasped with brooches of gold. Yet my father's blood is still black and rotten in the house, while he that killed him mounts and rides forth on the same chariot my father rode, and he gloats as he holds in his murder-defiled hands the scepter with which my father marshalled the Hellenes. And Agamemnon's tomb is dishonored; it has never received drink offerings or branches of myrtle; the pyre is bare of all adornment. And that glorious husband of my mother, as they call him, is soaked in wine and leaps on the grave and pelts my father's stone monument with rocks, and has the effrontery to say such a word as this to us: "Where is the lad Orestes? Isn't he here, fine fellow, to defend this tomb?" So is he mocked in his absence.

I beseech you, stranger, tell him all this. I am but the spokesman for the many that summon him: my hands, my tongue, my stricken heart, my shaven head, and the father that begot him. It is disgraceful if the man whose father annihilated the Phrygians cannot kill his enemy in single combat, man against man; he is younger and sprung of a better sire.

LEADER. I see that man—your husband I mean—coming toward the house, his work over.

[*Enter Peasant.*]

PEASANT. Ha! Who are these strangers I see at my house? Why have they come to these rustic doors? Do they want me? For a woman it is disgraceful to stand around with young men.

ELECTRA. Ah, dear friend, do not become suspicious of me. You shall know the truth of the story. These strangers have come to me from Orestes and bring me tidings of him. [*To Orestes and Pylades.*] Strangers, you must forgive what was said.

PEASANT. What do they say? Is the man alive? Does he look upon the light?

ELECTRA. Yes, according to their story; and I believe what they say.

PEASANT. And is he mindful of his father's troubles and of yours?

ELECTRA. These are matters for hope. A man in exile is weak.

PEASANT. What word do they bring you from Orestes?

ELECTRA. He sent them to investigate my troubles.

PEASANT. Well, they can see some of them, and I suppose you are telling them the rest.

ELECTRA. They know. There is nothing they have still to learn.

PEASANT. But shouldn't you have opened your doors to them long ago? [*To Orestes and Pylades.*] Come into the house. For your good news accept such hospitality as my house affords. [*To Orestes' and Pylades' henchmen.*] Take this baggage into the house, men. [*To Orestes and Pylades as they hesitate.*] Do not say me nay. You are friends come from a man that is a friend. Even though I am poor I shall not show a mean disposition.

[*Retires to the rear.*]

ORESTES. By heaven, is this the man that helps you to frustrate your marriage, is this the man who refuses to shame Orestes?

ELECTRA. He it is who is called hapless Electra's husband.

ORESTES. Ah, there is no sure mark of a manly spirit. Men's natures are full of confusion. I have seen the son of a noble father who was a cipher, and I have seen goodly children of lowly parents. I have seen dearth in the heart of a rich man and a great spirit in a humble body.

How can a man distinguish them, judge between them truly? By wealth? He would use a sorry gauge. Is poverty a better pointer? No. It suffers from this ailment: it teaches a man to be evil because of his need. Shall I take prowess? But who can look at a spear and testify which is the good man? It is best to disregard these things and let them go as they will.

Here is a man who is not great among the Argives, who is not puffed up with the pride of a great house; he is one of the many, and he is discovered a true gentleman. Will you not learn wisdom, you whom vain guesswork fills with error? Judge men as you find them, measure nobility by character.

Such men as these manage states well, manage their homes well. But hulks of flesh, empty of sense, are statues in the market place. Nor does the strong arm better abide the spear's onset than the weak; this depends rather on nature and on greatness of spirit.

So let us accept the entertainment of this house; present or absent, Agamemnon's son, for whose sake we have come, merits it. We must pass inside, slaves. I would rather have a host that is poor but glad to have me than a rich one. I accept with thanks my reception into this house. I could wish that your brother were now prospering and could lead me into a home that was prospering. And perhaps he may come, for Loxias' oracles stand firm; as for human divination, I let that go.

LEADER. More than ever, Electra, my heart is warmed with

gladness. Things are mending slowly; perhaps happiness is ahead.

ELECTRA [to Peasant]. Poor man, you know the want in your own house: why do you receive these guests that are too great for you?

PEASANT. Why? If they are as noble as they seem, will they not still be content whether the provision is scant or not?

ELECTRA. Since you have made this error, you who are so poor, go to my father's dear old tutor who follows his flocks near the Tanais river, which is the boundary that cuts the Argive land off from Spartan country; he has been banished from the city. Bid him come and provide some repast for these guests that have come to me. He will be overjoyed and will thank heaven when he hears that the boy he once saved is still alive. We could not get anything out of my father's house from my mother. Bitter news we should be bringing if that wretched woman should learn that Orestes is yet alive.

PEASANT. Well, if it pleases you so, I will go and take your message to the old man. But go into the house as quickly as you can and prepare the things there. A woman can find plenty to eke a meal out if she wants to. Indeed there is enough in the house now to satisfy these men with food for one day.

[Exit Electra into the house.]

At times like this, when I come to think of it, I realize what great power wealth possesses. One can give to guests, and by spending money, save one's body when it falls into disease. Food day by day comes to but little. When a man is filled it amounts to the same thing whether he is rich or poor.

[Exit Peasant.]

CHORUS. Ships renowned that once came to Troy with countless oars, dancing over the waters with the Nereids, where the music-loving dolphin bounded and whirled about the dark blue prows, escorting Thetis' son, so light-footed in leaping, along with Agamemnon to the banks of Simois at Troy!

It was the same Nereids that fetched the armor and the shield, wrought on the golden anvils of Hephaestus. The headlands of Euboea they left behind them; on past Pelion they went and the sacred glens beneath Mount Ossa, where *the Nymphs keep sentinel. They were searching for a young man and for that home where a gentle father reared the son of the sea-nymph Thetis to be a light to Hellas and give fleet-footed service to the sons of Atreus.*

*From one who had returned from Ilium, in the Nauplian harbor I heard, child of Thetis, of your famous shield. Upon its circle were symbols graven to cast dread into the Phrygians. On the rim that ran round the edge Perseus, hovering over the sea with his winged sandals was holding the Gorgon's head, severed at the throat; and with him was Zeus' messenger Hermes, Maia's youth, deity of the fields.*

*In the center of the shield the brilliant disk of the sun blazed forth, drawn along by flying steeds. And there too were the dancing stars of Heaven, the Pleiades and the Hyades, to tell Hector his star was setting. On the gold of the helmet were Sphinxes, carrying off in their talons the victims of the riddle. On the breast-plate a charging lioness, breathing fire, launched herself with eager claws on a colt of Pirene.*

*Upon his death-dealing sword a four-horse team hurtled on and a dark dust-cloud rolled up about their backs. Such were the valiant heroes that your husband, O Tyndarid, commanded, the husband whom you slew, woman blackhearted. Therefore will the heavenly powers one day send you to slaughter, and I shall yet see your blood spilt by the steel; I shall yet see the gore shed from your neck.*

*[Enter Tutor.]*

TUTOR. Where, where is the young lady, where is my mistress, the child of Agamemnon whom I once reared? What a steep approach her house has for this wrinkled old man to climb on foot. Still, to meet my friends I must drag on my spine that is doubled over and my tottering knees.

Ah, daughter—I see you there, at the house—here I come with a new-born suckling from my folds which I took from the ewe, and garlands, and cheese taken from the baskets, and this old treasure of Dionysus with a delicious bouquet; there is only a little, but it is excellent to mix a cup of it with a drink that is weaker. Someone go and take these things to the guests in the house. I want to wipe my eyeballs dry with this rag of my clothes; I have wet them with my tears.

ELECTRA. Why, old man, are your eyes so flooded with tears? Have my troubles roused your memory of long ago? Is it for Orestes' unhappy exile you sigh, for my father whom you once held in your hands and nurtured? Little delight it brought you and your friends.

TUTOR. Aye, little indeed. Still, it was for this that I could not refrain my tears: I came here by way of the tomb and, in passing, I knelt and I wept for I found it deserted; then I loosened the skin-bottle that I brought your guests and poured a drink offering, and I placed myrtle branches about the tomb. But there on the pyre I saw a sheep with a black fleece that had been sacrificed, the blood but lately poured, and ringlets of golden hair that had been shorn, and I wondered, child, who in the world dared come near that tomb; it was certainly no Argive.

But perhaps your brother has somehow come here in secret, and on his coming paid his respects to your father's poor tomb. Look at this lock of hair and compare it with your own; see whether the color of the shorn clipping is the same. It often happens that people who have the same blood, of one father, have a natural resemblance in many parts of the body.

ELECTRA. Your talk is not worthy of a clever man, old friend, if you think that my brave brother has come to this land surreptitiously, out of fear of Aegisthus. Then, how can a lock of his hair match with mine; the hair of a man reared in noble sports with the hair of a woman, combed soft? It is impossible. Besides, old man, you will find that many people have similar hair, when they are not sprung of the same blood.

TUTOR. Then step into his track and see whether the print of his boot is of a size with your foot, child.

ELECTRA. How could feet make any impression on a rocky surface? And if they could, the feet of brother and sister, of man and woman would not be equal, but the foot of the male is larger.

TUTOR. If your brother did come to this land is there no work of your shuttle by which you could recognize him, the clothes in which I stole him away from death?

ELECTRA. Don't you know that I was only a child when Orestes was exiled from the country? And if I had woven garments how could he have now the same clothes he once had as a child—unless his clothes grew along with his body?

Either some stranger took pity on the tomb and offered a lock of his hair, or he himself sent it here by his spies——

TUTOR. The strangers—where are they? I want to see them to inquire about your brother.

ELECTRA. Here they come briskly out of the house.

[*Enter Orestes and Pylades.*]

TUTOR [*aside*]. They are noble, indeed, but that is deceptive. Many that are noble are knaves. And yet— [*aloud*] I give greetings to the strangers.

ORESTES. Greetings, old man. Electra, to which of your friends does this ancient remnant belong?

ELECTRA. It was he that nurtured my father, stranger.

ORESTES. What do you say? Is this the man that stole away your brother?

ELECTRA. He it is that saved him, if he is still alive.

ORESTES. Ah! Why does he stare at me as if he were examining the stamp on a new coin? Is he likening me to anyone?

ELECTRA. Perhaps it gives him pleasure to see a comrade of Orestes.

ORESTES. Yes, a dear friend's comrade. But why does he walk round me?

ELECTRA. I, too, am surprised at that, stranger.

TUTOR. My lady, my daughter Electra, pray to the gods——

ELECTRA. For what? Something not here? Something here?

TUTOR. To win a dear treasure, which heaven is revealing.

ELECTRA. See, I do call upon the gods. But what is your meaning, old man?

TUTOR. Look now at this man, child, this precious man.

ELECTRA. I have been looking at him for a long while. I am afraid you are gone out of your senses.

TUTOR. I, out of my senses, when I see your own brother?

ELECTRA. What's that you say? Incredible!

TUTOR. I say I see here Orestes, son of Agamemnon.

ELECTRA. How am I to believe you? Have you seen some mark?

TUTOR. The scar by his eyebrow which was gashed once in your father's house when he fell while chasing a fawn with you.

ELECTRA. What do you say? I see the mark of a fall!

TUTOR. Then do you hesitate to rush into his loving arms?

ELECTRA. Ah, no longer, old man. My heart is persuaded by your tokens. At long last you appear! I hold you, beyond all hope.

ORESTES. And are held by me, at long last.

ELECTRA. I had never imagined it.

ORESTES. And I had never expected it.

ELECTRA. Are you really he?

ORESTES. Yes, your only ally. If only I may draw the net which I have come to cast! I am sure I will. Or else we must believe in the gods no longer if injustice is to prevail over justice.

CHORUS. *You have come, you have come, day long awaited; you have shone forth, you have revealed to the city its brilliant torch. Long has been his exile; far from his ancestral home he has travelled, in homeless misery. A god, yes, some great god is now bringing us victory, my friend. Lift up your hands, lift up your voice; send forth your prayers to the gods, that luck, good luck, may attend your brother's steps in his own country.*

ORESTES. So be it. Your welcome is very kind, and I appreciate it. In time I shall make some return.

But you, old man—you have come most opportunely—tell me what I must do to avenge my father's murder? Are there any friends in Argos well-disposed toward me, or am I altogether a broken man, like my fortunes? Whom shall I make my ally? Shall I act by night or by day? What path shall I take against my foes?

TUTOR. My son, no one is your friend in misfortune. This thing is a rarity indeed, a friend that shares good and evil alike. Since you are totally bereft of friends, and have no hope left, hear me and know that the recovery of your ancestral house and city depends altogether on yourself— and chance.

ORESTES. What must I do to achieve this end?

TUTOR. You must kill Thyestes' son and your own mother.

ORESTES. That is the prize I have come to win. How shall I get it?

TUTOR. Never by going inside the walls, even if you were willing to.

ORESTES. Are they patrolled and guarded by armed men?

TUTOR. That is it. He is afraid of you and he does not sleep sound.

ORESTES. Well! Advise the next step, old man.

TUTOR. And *you* listen. I have just had an idea.

ORESTES. May your advice be good, and good for me to hear.

TUTOR. I saw Aegisthus as I crept this way.

ORESTES. I understand the hint. Where was it?

TUTOR. Near these fields, by the horse pastures.

ORESTES. What was he doing? I see hope out of despair.

TUTOR. He seemed to be preparing a feast for the Nymphs.

ORESTES. For nurture of children, or in anticipation of a birth?

TUTOR. I know only one thing. He was getting ready to slaughter an ox.

ORESTES. With how many men? Or was he alone with slaves?

TUTOR. There was no Argive there, only a handful of domestics.

ORESTES. Is there anyone who could recognize me if he saw me, old man?

TUTOR. They are slaves, they have never seen you.

ORESTES. Would they be friendly to me if I won?

TUTOR. Yes, it is slaves' nature, and to your advantage.

ORESTES. How could I manage to approach him?

TUTOR. Go where he will see you when he is offering sacrifice.

ORESTES. His fields are near the road?

TUTOR. Yes, he will see you and invite you to join in the feast.

ORESTES. And a bitter guest I shall be, god willing.

TUTOR. After that watch for the chance.

ORESTES. You are right. But my mother—where is she?

TUTOR. In Argos. She will attend the feast presently.

ORESTES. Why does not my mother start alone with her husband?

TUTOR. She was afraid of the citizens' reproach, and stayed behind.

ORESTES. I understand. She knows she is suspect to the city.

TUTOR. Just so. A wicked woman is an object of hate.

ORESTES. How then can I kill him and her at the same time?

ELECTRA. *I* shall manage our mother's death.

ORESTES. Then fortune will manage the rest.

ELECTRA. This man [*pointing to the Tutor*] can be of service to both of us.

TUTOR. So he shall. How will you contrive your mother's death?

ELECTRA. Go to Clytemnestra, old man, and tell her. . . . Say that I have given birth to a boy.

TUTOR. Born some time ago or recently?

ELECTRA. Within ten suns, the period of a mother's purification.

TUTOR. And how can this bring death upon your mother?

ELECTRA. She will come when she hears I am ill with a baby.

TUTOR. Why? What makes you think she cares for you, child?

ELECTRA. She will come all right; and she will cry over my child's degradation.

TUTOR. Perhaps. But bring your story back to the point.

ELECTRA. It's plain enough! When she comes, she dies.

TUTOR. Yes, I see. Let her just enter the doors of your house . . .

ELECTRA. And it's only a step from there to Hades.

TUTOR. I should die happy, if only I could see it.

ELECTRA. First of all then, old man, be *his* [*pointing to Orestes*] guide——

TUTOR. To where Aegisthus is offering sacrifice to the gods?

ELECTRA. Then find my mother and give her my message.

TUTOR. I shall. She will think she hears it from your own lips.

ELECTRA [*to Orestes*]. Now to *your* task. Luck has given you the first blood to spill.

ORESTES. I will go if I have a guide for the way.

TUTOR. Here am I to escort you, very willingly.

[*All lift their hands in prayer.*]

ORESTES. O Zeus, God of Fathers, be also Avenger of Enemies——

ELECTRA. Pity us; pitiful are the wrongs we suffered.

TUTOR. Yea, pity the children sprung of you.

ELECTRA. Hera, Queen of Mycenae's altars——

ORESTES. Grant us victory if our claims are just——

TUTOR. Yea, grant them just vengeance for their father.

[*All fall prostrate.*]

ORESTES. And you, father, who dwell beneath the Earth by a foul wrong——

ELECTRA. And Queen Earth, to whom I stretch my hands——

TUTOR. Fend, yea, fend for these precious children.

ORESTES. Come *now;* and bring as your ally all the dead——

ELECTRA. Those whose spears vanquished the Phrygians with you——

TUTOR. Yea, and all that hate wickedness and sin.

*[All rise.]*

ELECTRA. Do you hear, you that were foully dealt with by my mother?

TUTOR. All these things your father hears, I know. It is high time we went.

ELECTRA. One further word. Aegisthus must die. If you lose the bout and meet your death, I, too, am dead; speak of me no longer as living. I shall pierce my liver with the two-edged sword.

I shall go into the house and make ready. If good news of you comes, the whole house shall shout for joy. But if you die, there will be the contrary. This I tell you.

ORESTES. I understand entirely.

ELECTRA. And so it behooves you to play the man.

*[Exeunt Orestes and Tutor.]*

And you, women, blaze out the proclamation of this contest. I will keep watch and have a weapon ready to my hand. I may lose, but I shall never give my enemies the satisfaction of outraging my person.

*[Exit into house.]*

CHORUS. *Among hoary traditions the tale abides that Pan, the guardian of the fields, conducted a lamb with a comely fleece all golden ·from its tender mother on the Argive hills by breathing a sweetly trilling melody upon his harmonious reeds. Upon steps of stone the herald took his stand and proclaimed: "To the public square, to the public square, Mycenaeans, and see the wonder that foreshows a blessed reign to him that owns it". And it was the house of* Atreus *they honored with dances.*

*The gold-decked temples were opened, and through the city fire blazed upon the altars of the Argives. The lotus-flute, the Muses' minister, uttered forth a beautiful strain, and lovely songs were multiplied, in praise of the golden lamb . . . of* Thyestes. *For he had seduced Atreus' dear wife to his clandestine couch, and to his own house had borne off the prodigy. He returns· to the assembly and declares he possesses in his own house the horned creature with the golden fleece.*

*Then, ah then, did Zeus change the gleaming stars in their courses, and the sun's splendor and dawn's silvery face. The westerly regions he vexes with the hot flame of divine fire; and the water-laden clouds flee to the North, and the dry seats of Ammon wither for want of dew and are robbed of Zeus' fair showers.*

*There is a tradition—which has but little credit with me— that the sun turned his golden countenance and removed from his warm station because of human unhappiness, for the sake of mortal justice. These tales that make men fear are to the advantage of religion. But you remembered them not, mother of the glorious pair, when you slew your husband.*

LEADER. Ha! Friends, did you hear a shout—or is it only an illusion of mine—as of Zeus' rumbling under the earth? Look, the breeze wafted here is not without meaning. Lady, Electra, come out of the house!

[*Enter Electra.*]

ELECTRA. Friends, what is the matter? How do we stand in the contest?

LEADER. I know only one thing. I hear a death cry.

ELECTRA. I hear it too. It is far off, still I hear it.

LEADER. The sound comes a long way, but it is audible.

ELECTRA. Is it an Argive shriek? Is it my friends'?

LEADER. I do not know. The tone of the cry is all confused.

ELECTRA. It is my death sentence you utter. Why do I hesitate?

LEADER. Wait; learn exactly how your fortune stands.

ELECTRA. It's no use. We are beaten. Where are his messengers?

LEADER. They will come. It is no simple task to kill a king.

[*Enter Messenger.*]

MESSENGER. Victory, maids of Mycenae! I announce to all his friends that Orestes has won the victory. Agamemnon's murderer, Aegisthus, lies upon the field. It is fitting for us to adore the gods.

ELECTRA. Who are you? How can you assure me these things are true?

MESSENGER. Don't you remember I am your brother's attendant that you saw?

ELECTRA. Ah, dear friend. I was so afraid; I could not

recognize your face. But I know you now. What do you say? The loathed murderer of my father is dead?

MESSENGER. He is dead. I give you the same word twice, since you wish it.

ELECTRA. Ye gods! Justice that sees all, you have come at last.

But in what way did he kill Thyestes' son? Give me the details. I want to know.

MESSENGER. When we had marched off from this house we found ourselves in a two-lane wagon road, and there was the famous king of the Mycenaeans. It happened that he was walking in his well-watered gardens and plucking tender sprigs of myrtle for his head. When he saw us he called out: "Hail, strangers! Who may you be and whence do you come? To what land do you belong?" Orestes answered: "We are Thessalians. We are on our way to the Alpheus to sacrifice to Olympian Zeus." When Aegisthus heard this he spoke as follows: "But now you must be my guests and share the feast with me. It happens that I am offering sacrifice to the Nymphs. At dawn you can rise from your beds and be as far on your way. Do let us go into the house." As he said this he took hold of our hands and led us in: "You must not say me nay," he said, "let someone bring water for our guests with all speed, so that they may stand about the altar near the lustral bowls."

But Orestes spoke: "We have but lately been cleansed with the pure ablutions of running streams. If it is proper for strangers to join in sacrifice with townspeople, Aegisthus, we are ready, and will not say you nay, sire."

Such was the speech they uttered in plain hearing. Then the slaves laid down their spears, with which they protected their master, and one and all set their hands to the work. Some brought the blood-bowl, others raised the sacrificial baskets, still others kindled the fire and arranged the caul- drons around the hearth. The whole house was in a din. Then your mother's bed-fellow took the meal-cakes and cast them upon the altar, and pronounced these words: "Nymphs of the rocks, grant that I may offer many a bull in sacrifice, and that I and my Tyndarid wife at home may fare well, as we do now, and that our enemies may fare ill"—he meant Orestes and you. My master prayed to the opposite effect, not pronouncing his words distinctly, that he should regain his ancestral home.

Then Aegisthus took a straight knife from the basket, cut

hair from the bullock's head, and placed it on the sacred fire with his right hand. When the slaves had heaved the bullock upon their shoulders, he slaughtered it, and spoke to your brother as follows: "The Thessalians boast that it is among their accomplishments to quarter a bull skilfully and to break horses. Take the steel, stranger, and prove the Thessalian reputation true". Orestes grasped a well-wrought Dorian blade in his hands, and flung off from his shoulders his handsome cloak with its brooch and chose Pylades his helper in the task; the slaves he thrust away. Then he took hold of the bullock's foot, and with outstretched hand laid the white flesh bare. He flayed the hide off quicker than a runner in the horse course could finish two laps; then he opened the flanks.

Aegisthus took the sacred inward parts in his hands and gazed at them. There was no liver-lobe in the entrails; the valves and the gall-bladder hard by indicated evil issues for the examiner. Aegisthus frowned but my master inquired, "Why are you dispirited?" "Stranger", said he, "I fear some outsider's cunning; most hateful of mortals to me, and most hostile to my house is the son of Agamemnon." Orestes said: "You fear the cunning of an exile, you that rule over the city? Let us get on to the enjoyment of the feast; will not someone bring us a Phthian cleaver instead of this Dorian? I will cleave through the thorax." He received it and cut through. Aegisthus grasped the entrails and gazed at them as he drew them apart. As he bent down your brother rose upon tiptoe and smote on his spine and crashed through the joints of his back. His whole body jerked up and down in convulsions, and he cried out, in the agony of bloody death.

When the slaves saw, they rushed for their spears at once, many men ready to fight against two. But Pylades and Orestes confronted them like men and brandished their weapons. Said Orestes: "I come with no hostile intent against this city or against my servants; I have avenged the murder of my father, I am hapless Orestes. Do not kill me; you were my father's servants long ago." When they heard these words they held back their spears. He was recognized by an old man who had long been in the house. Straightway they crowned your brother with garlands, and rejoiced, and shouted. He is coming and bringing you the head to show, not a Gorgon's, but Aegisthus' whom you hate. To him that is now dead blood for blood has come with bitter interest.

[*Exit Messenger.*]

CHORUS. *Set your pace for a dance, dear friend, like a fawn who lightly leaps into the air for joy. Your brother has conquered, he has won a wreath of victory far better than those of Alpheus' streams. Raise the glorious chant of victory as we dance.*

ELECTRA. How brilliant is the splendor of the chariot of the sun! O earth! O night! On you alone did I gaze aforetime, but now I may lift up my eyes in freedom, for Aegisthus has fallen, my father's murderer! Come, friends, such adornment as I possess, as my house contains, I will bring out for my hair, and I will crown the head of my brother, the bringer of victory.

[*Goes into the house for a moment.*]

CHORUS. *Bring forth ornaments for the head, while our dance that is dear to the Muses goes forward. Now our beloved kings of old rule over the land and justly; those that were unjust have they removed. Let the shout go forth, attune it with joy!*

[*Enter Orestes and Pylades with Aegisthus' body; and Electra from house.*]

ELECTRA. Glorious victor, sprung of a father that brought victory from the war at Ilium! Receive, Orestes, this diadem for the clusters of your hair. You return from no profitless six-lap race that you have won, but from killing your enemy, Aegisthus, who destroyed your father and mine. And you, Pylades, his comrade in arms, fosterling of a man most pious, accept this crown at my hand. You, too, bear an equal share with him in this contest. May you always appear prosperous in my eyes.

ORESTES. Think first of the gods, Electra, the authors of this happy event; then praise me also, who have but served the gods and fortune. [*Pause.*]

I am come from a battle of deeds not words. I have killed Aegisthus. To set this forth clearly for all to know I bring you the dead man himself. If you like, expose him for the wild beasts to devour, or impale him on a high stake to be plunder for the birds, the children of the sky. He is now yours.

ELECTRA. I am ashamed, yet I should like to speak——

ORESTES. What? Say it. You have nothing now to fear.

ELECTRA. I am ashamed to insult the dead for fear some ill will may strike me.

ORESTES. There is not anyone who would blame you.

ELECTRA. Our city is hard to please and quick to find fault.

ORESTES. Say whatever you will, sister. The enmity we have entered on with this man is without conditions or truce.

ELECTRA. So be it. What beginning shall I make of my reproaches against you? What shall be the end? What shall occupy the middle place in my argument? Indeed, morning by morning, I have never left off rehearsing what I wished to say to your face if ever I should be free of the fear I once felt. Well, now I am free, and I shall pay you out with hard words which I wished to say to you when you were alive.

You ruined me; you orphaned me of my dear father, me and Orestes, though we had done you no wrong. You married my mother, shamefully, and you slew her husband; though you never marched to Troy, you slew the commander of the Greek army. To such a depth of folly did you sink that you expected my mother, my father's wife whom you seduced, to be a true wife to you. If a man corrupts another's wife with secret dalliance and then is forced to marry her, let him know that he is a poor fool if he thinks she will possess chastity in his house when she did not with her first husband. Your life was most wretched, though you thought it quite happy. You knew you had made an unholy marriage; my mother knew she had a scoundrel to husband. Both of you were wicked, and each was infected with the other's evil; she took your lot and you took her sin. Among all the Argives it was said, "Clytemnestra's husband," not "Aegisthus' wife."

It is disgraceful when the woman and not the man rules the household. I loathe it too when children are called in the city not by the name of their father, the man, but of their mother. When a man makes a match with a woman of distinguished station, higher than his own, no one takes any account of the husband, but only of the wife.

In this especially you were deceived and did not realize it: you boasted you were somebody, relying on your wealth. But wealth does nothing more than keep you company for a short time. Character, not money, is the stable thing. For character abides forever, and banishes evil. But wealth is unjust and keeps company with boors, and it flits out of the house when it has bloomed for a short while.

As to your women, I say nothing, for it is not a nice subject for a maiden; but I shall hint, not darkly. You were conceited because you possessed a royal house and because you were endued with beauty. But my wish would be not for a girl-faced husband, but for one of a more manly sort. The children of such men cleave to Ares, but comeliness is only an ornament for the dance.

Be damned, unsuspecting fool; for your sins, which time has discovered, you have paid the penalty. Let no evil-doer think, if he has run the first lap well, that he has out-run justice; let him first come to the final mark and round the goal of life.

LEADER. Horrible deeds has he done and horrible is his retribution to you and to Orestes. Great is the might of justice.

ELECTRA. Very well. We must take this man's body in and put it out of sight, slaves; when my mother comes, she must not see it before she dies.

[*The body is carried in; a carriage appears in the distance.*]

ORESTES. Hold! We must revise our plan.

ELECTRA. What is it? Do you see reinforcements from Mycenae?

ORESTES. No, but the mother, the woman that gave me birth.

ELECTRA. Splendid! She is coming right into the net. Look how grand she is with her chariot and her robes!

ORESTES. What on earth shall we do? Our mother—shall we murder her?

ELECTRA. You aren't seized with pity at sight of your mother?

ORESTES. Ah, how can I kill her? She nursed me, bore me.

ELECTRA. Even as she destroyed your father and mine.

ORESTES. O Phoebus, a great folly did your oracle bid——

ELECTRA. Where Apollo is foolish, who are the wise?

ORESTES. —when you pronounced my mother's death. It cannot be right.

ELECTRA. Where is the harm in avenging your own father?

ORESTES. I have always been pure. Now I shall be charged with matricide.

ELECTRA. Yes, but if you do not fend for your father, you will be impious.

ORESTES. I shall have to account to my mother for her blood.

ELECTRA. And to whom, if you neglect vengeance for your father?

ORESTES. Was it not some fiend that bade it, assuming the god's likeness?

ELECTRA. Sitting at the holy tripod? I should think not!

ORESTES. Nobody will ever persuade me that this oracle is good.

ELECTRA. Do not turn craven, do not fall into cowardice.

ORESTES. Then I must lay the same snare for her?

ELECTRA. The same with which you caught and slew her husband, Aegisthus.

ORESTES. I will go in. It is a dreadful trial I enter upon, yes, and I shall do a dreadful thing—so be it, if the gods will have it so. Bitter for me and sweet too is this contest.

[*Orestes and Pylades go into the house; Clytemnestra enters in a carriage with captive Trojan women for attendants.*]

CHORUS. *Lady, queen of the Argive land, child of Tyndareus, sister of the goodly twin sons of Zeus, who dwell in fiery ether among the stars, whose function is the saving of mortals in the surge of the sea, hail! I revere you even as the gods for your great wealth's sake and your blessedness. It is right that your fortune receive tendance. Hail, Queen!*

CLYTEMNESTRA. Descend from the carriage, women of Troy, take hold of my hand, so that I can set my foot down from this car. The temples of the gods are decked with Phrygian spoils; these women brought from the Trojan country I possess for my own household, a small reward but a nice one for my lost daughter (Iphigenia).

ELECTRA. May I, mother—for I too am a slave cast out of my father's home and living here in misery—may I take hold of your blessed hand?

CLYTEMNESTRA. There are slave women here, don't you trouble.

ELECTRA. But why? Am I not a slave, carried off from my home? When my house was taken captive I was taken captive, like these women, and orphaned and left fatherless.

CLYTEMNESTRA. That was because of the schemes your father devised against those near to him, whom it least behooved him to treat so. I shall tell you. . . . Of course, when a bad reputation lays its hold on a woman, tongues are bitter against her. In my case it is unjust. When you have understood the situation, if you have good reason to hate

me, hate me you may; but if not, why should you loathe
me?

Tyndareus gave me to your father, but not that I should
die, nor that my children should. But Agamemnon took my
child off from home to the naval station at Aulis, on the plea
of marriage with Achilles; there he stretched my Iphigenia
over the fire and cut through her white throat. Now if he had
been seeking a remedy against the capture of his city, if he
were acting for the advantage of his house and preserving
the lives of his other children by killing one to save many, it
would have been pardonable. But what were the facts? Just
because Helen was a wanton and the man that had her did
not understand how to discipline an erring wife, *my* child
was destroyed! Even so, although I was wronged in this I
would not have grown furious. I would not have killed my
husband. But he came and brought that raving madwoman to
his bed, and there we were with two brides in the very same
house!

Women are silly, of course, I do not deny it. That being
the case, when the husband strays and neglects his bed at
home, the wife is apt to imitate her husband and to acquire
another friend. Then people fairly glow with indignation at
*our* conduct; but the husbands, who are really responsible, are
not criticized at all.

If *Menelaus* had secretly been kidnaped from home, would
I have had to kill *Orestes* to save my sister's husband? Would
your father have tolerated such a thing? If *he* did not deserve to die after killing my daughter, did *I* deserve this
wrong at his hands? I killed him. I took the only path that
was open to me; I turned to his enemies. Who of your father's *friends* would have taken part in his murder with me?

Speak if you wish and set forth freely why it was not just
for your father to die.

ELECTRA. You plead justice, but your plea is shameful. It
behooves a woman of sense to yield to her husband in all
things. Women who think otherwise, I maintain, just do not
count. Don't forget, mother, the last words you spoke, when
you gave me leave to speak my mind to you.

CLYTEMNESTRA. I say it again, daughter, I do not deny it.

ELECTRA. But after you have heard me, mother, will you
hurt me?

CLYTEMNESTRA. No. I shall humor your mood.

ELECTRA. Then I will speak, and my preface will be this: I
wish you had a better heart, my mother. Your *beauty* deserves

praise, yours and Helen's, two true sisters, both wantons, both unworthy of Castor. *She* was kidnaped and lost her virtue *gladly*. Then you destroyed the bravest man of Hellas; and you hold out the pretense that you killed your husband for the sake of your child! People do not know you as well as I. Why, even before your daughter's sacrifice had been determined, when your husband had but newly left home, you were already training the golden clusters of your hair before a mirror. Any woman that cultivates her beauty when her husband is far from home can be written down as a wanton. There is no need for her to display a face made fair unless she is looking for some mischief. You were the only Hellene woman, I know you were, who was happy when the Trojan side prospered, and when they were getting the worse of it your eyes were all clouded. You did not want Agamemnon to come back from Troy. And yet it was so easy for you to be chaste. You had a husband who was at least as good as Aegisthus; Hellas chose him to be her general. After your sister Helen had done what she did, you had a chance to win great glory. Evil deeds afford precept and example to the good.

And even if, as you say, my father killed your daughter, how did I or my brother injure you? Why, when you killed your husband, did you not give us our ancestral home? You brought an outsider into it; you bought his love at that price. Your lover was not exiled, though your son was. Your lover was not slain. I was. Yes, though I am alive, he has inflicted on me double my sister's death. If blood for blood is the law, then must I and your son, Orestes, kill you to avenge our father. If your conduct was right then this must be right. [The man who marries a bad woman, unable to see beyond wealth or noble birth, is a fool. A humble and chaste wife is better than a high and mighty one.

LEADER. Chance directs the marriage of women. I observe that the marriages of some mortals fall out well and some badly.]

CLYTEMNESTRA. My girl, it has always been your nature to love your father. So it goes; some are fond of their male parent, others love their mothers more than their fathers. I pardon you. Indeed, I am not so very happy about the things I have done, my child.

But you—why are you unwashed and badly dressed, you the mother of a new baby? Ah me! I am sorry for my schemes. I have incited my husband to anger more than was right.

ELECTRA. You sigh too late, when you have no cure. My father is dead. Why don't you bring back your son who is wandering in exile from this land?

CLYTEMNESTRA. I am afraid. I have myself to consider, not him. He is angry, they say, about the death of his father.

ELECTRA. Why do you keep your husband so savage against me?

CLYTEMNESTRA. That is his way; you, too, are very stubborn.

ELECTRA. Because I am hurt. But I shall give over my anger.

CLYTEMNESTRA. Well, then he will not be hard on you any more.

ELECTRA. He is proud, because he lives in my house.

CLYTEMNESTRA. You see? There you go kindling the quarrel anew.

ELECTRA. I say no more; I fear him as I fear him.

CLYTEMNESTRA. Stop this talk. Why did you call me, child?

ELECTRA. You heard, I suppose, of my baby. Make the offering for him on my behalf—I don't know how—whatever is customary for the child's tenth day. I have had no experience, for I have had no children before.

CLYTEMNESTRA. This is a case for another woman, the one who helped you in your travail.

ELECTRA. I travailed myself, and I bore my infant alone.

CLYTEMNESTRA. Do you live away from all friends and neighbors?

ELECTRA. No one wants the poor for friends.

CLYTEMNESTRA. Well, I will go and make the offering for the fulfilment of the child's days. When I have done you this kindness I shall go to the fields where my husband is offering sacrifice to the Nymphs. Take my horses, servants, and put them in stalls. When you think I have done with this offering to the gods, be on hand. I must humor my husband also.

ELECTRA. Enter my humble house; but take care that my sooty room does not spot your dress. You will offer such an offering to the deities as behooves you.

[Clytemnestra enters the house; Electra remains outside.]

The sacrificial basket is in proper order, the knife is whet-

ted with which he slew the bull; by his side you shall be struck
down. In the house of Hades you will be the bride of the man
with whom you slept in this world's light. So much kindness
I will give to you; do you give me vengeance for my father.

[*Enters the house.*]

CHORUS. *Evil for evil! Changed are the breezes that blow
for this house. Once in the bath my king, my own king, was
slain. The roof resounded and the stone coping of the house
when he cried: "Woman, wretched woman, why do you kill
me when I am returning to my dear country after ten harvests?"*

*And now revolving time brings punishment upon this
woman, this sinful woman who betrayed her bed; with her
own hand, with a sharp-whetted weapon, she slew her husband, with an axe that she grasped in her hands, when he returned after a long absence to his home, to the Cyclopean
walls that soared to heaven. Ah, miserable husband, what a
wretched woman he had for his bane!*

*Like some lioness of the mountains that ranges the oak
forests did she perpetrate this deed.*

CLYTEMNESTRA [*within*]. Children, by the gods, do not
kill your mother!

LEADER. Do you hear the shriek under the roof?

CLYTEMNESTRA [*within*]. Ah me, Ah!

LEADER. I too groan for her, slaughtered by her children.

CHORUS. *God gives each his due at the time allotted. Cruel
deeds were done to you; but unholy deeds have you perpetrated, poor woman, upon your husband.*

LEADER. Ah, they return, all stained with the newly shed
blood of their mother, a sign that they have triumphed in the
horrible slaughter. There is no house, there never has been
a house more wretched than the House of Tantalus.

[*Orestes and Pylades come out of house; a stage device
reveals the dead bodies of Aegisthus and Clytemnestra.*]

ORESTES. *O Earth and Zeus that beholds all things human,
look upon these bloody and detestable deeds, two bodies
lying on the ground by the stroke of my hand, retribution for
my woes . . .*

ELECTRA. *Matter enough for tears, my brother, and I am to*

*blame. My anger burned furiously against this my mother, who gave me birth, her daughter.*

CHORUS. *Alas for fortune, your fortune, mother! You have brought into the world the avengers of your own sins, grievous things and more than grievous have you suffered at your children's hands. But righteous was your atonement for their father's murder.*

ORESTES. *Ah, Phoebus! You ordained the vengeance. To the light of day you have wakened the griefs that were sleeping. A murderer's doom you have brought on me, far from the land of Hellas. To what other city shall I go? What host, what pious man will look upon the face of the matricide?*

ELECTRA. *Woe is me, woe! What dance can I join? What marriage? What husband will receive me in his marriage bed?*

CHORUS. *Again your heart has changed, again it has veered with the gale. Now your thoughts are pious; but then your thoughts were not, and a horrible deed, dear friend, you worked upon your brother who desired it not.*

ORESTES. *Did you see how the poor thing threw her dress aside, how she bared her breasts as she was being murdered— ah me—how those limbs, our mother's limbs, lay on the ground? And her hair I——*

ELECTRA. *I know very well the anguish you felt when you heard the pitiful groan of the mother that bore you.*

ORESTES. *This was her cry, when she put her hand upon my chin: "My child, I implore you." Her hands clung to my cheeks, so that my weapon nigh fell from my hands.*

CHORUS [to Electra]. *Poor girl, how could you endure to look upon your mother's murder, to see her gasping her life out?*

ORESTES. *I threw my mantle over my eyes, and I began the slaughter with my sword; into my mother's neck I kept thrusting it.*

ELECTRA. *And I urged you on and I grasped the sword along with you.*

CHORUS. *Most horrible is the deed you have wrought.*

ORESTES. *Take her up, cover my mother's limbs with robes, close up her wounds. The children you bore have become your murderers.*

ELECTRA. *See, we cast these mantles about her, that we hated—and love.*

CHORUS. *This is the end of great tribulations for this house.*

[Castor and Pollux appear aloft.]

*But who are these beings that appear over the house-top—*
*spirits or gods from heaven? Their path is not for mortals.*
*Why have they come into the plain sight of men?*

CASTOR. Child of Agamemnon, we that call you are the
twin Dioscuri, your mother's brothers. I am Castor and this
is my brother, Polydeuces. We have just put an end to a
storm at sea which was a terror to ships; and we came to
Argos when we saw the killing of this our sister, your mother.
For her part, she has received justice, but what you have
done is not just. And Phoebus, Phoebus—but he is my king
and so I am dumb. Clever he is, but what he required of
you was not clever. But we must accept these things. Hence-
forth, you must do what Zeus and Fate have decreed for
you.

Let Pylades take Electra to wife in his house. But you
must leave Argos. It is not for you to tread its streets, for
you have slain your mother. The dread Furies, those dog-
faced goddesses, will trundle you about, a lunatic and a vagabond. Go to Athens and clasp Pallas' sacred image. She will
frighten them with her awful dragons and keep them away
so they will not touch you; she will stretch her shield with
the Gorgon face over your head. There is a hill of Ares
where the gods first sat to vote on a question of bloodshed,
when fierce-tempered Ares, because of anger at the unholy
bridals of his daughter, slew the son of the ruler of the sea,
Halirrothius. Thence derives a very holy and firm tribunal
of the gods. There you too must face trial for murder. Equal
votes shall save you from the penalty of death. Loxias will
take the blame upon himself, for he prescribed the murder of
your mother. And in future this law shall be established: the
defendant shall always win if the votes are equal. The
dread goddesses in anguish at this defeat, will sink into a
chasm in the earth near that same hill, which shall be a
sacred oracle revered by men. You must settle in a city of
the Arcadians upon the streams of Alpheus hard by the
Lycaean shrine; the city shall be called after your name.

So much I say to you. As for this corpse of Aegisthus, the
citizens of Argos will cover it in a tomb. Your mother, Menelaus and Helen will bury. He has lately come to Nauplia
from sacking the land of Troy. Helen has come from Pro-
teus' house, from Egypt; she never went to Phrygia. It was
Zeus that sent a phantom of Helen to Ilium, that there
might be strife and slaughter of mortals.

Let Pylades take this maiden to wife and go home from the Achaean land; let him take your nominal brother-in-law to the land of the Phocians and load him with wealth. Do you go by way of the neck of the Isthmian land to the blessed hill of Cecrops. When you have fulfilled the destiny decreed for this murder, you shall be freed from these toils and live happy.

CHORUS. *O children of Zeus, is it lawful for us to approach you in speech?*

CASTOR. *It is, for you are not defiled with this slaughter.*

ELECTRA. *And may I, too, share this speech, sons of Tyndareus?*

CASTOR. *You too. Upon Phoebus I lay the bloody deed.*

CHORUS. *How was it that you, who are gods and brothers of this woman that is destroyed, did not keep the powers of death from her house?*

CASTOR. *Fate and destiny drew her to her doom, and the unwise utterance of Phoebus' tongue.*

ELECTRA. *But no Apollo, no oracles, drove me to become my mother's murderess.*

CASTOR. *Shared were the deeds, shared the doom; a single ancestral curse has ruined you both.*

ORESTES. *O sister mine, after a long time I have seen you, and now I am at once bereft of your dear presence; I part from you, you part from me.*

CASTOR. *She has a husband and a house; she has suffered nothing that must be pitied, except that she must leave the Argive city.*

ELECTRA. *But what greater cause for groans can there be than to leave one's fatherland behind?*

ORESTES. *But I shall depart from the house of my father and be tried for my mother's murder by an alien court.*

CASTOR. *Courage! You will come to the holy city of Pallas. Bear up!*

ELECTRA. *Clasp me, breast to breast, dearest brother; a murdered mother's curse has cut us off from the home of our fathers.*

ORESTES. *Fling your arms about me, hold me close; lament as at the tomb of the dead.*

CASTOR. *Alas, alas! Sad is your plaint to hear, even for gods. For in me, too, as in all the children of heaven, there is pity for the many hardships of mortals.*

ORESTES. *I shall see you no more.*

ELECTRA. *Nor shall I come near your eyes.*

ORESTES. *This is our last speech together.*

ELECTRA. *Farewell, my city; farewell, my city's women, a long farewell.*

ORESTES. *Truest sister, are you already going?*

ELECTRA. *I am going. My tender eyelids are wet.*

ORESTES. *Pylades, go in joy; be a true husband to Electra.*

CASTOR. *The wedding shall be their care. But escape those hell-hounds, on toward Athens! They are on your track, fearfully they come rushing at you; they are dragon-handed, their flesh is black, and they bring a harvest of fearful woes.*

[*Exit Orestes.*]

*But we must hurry to the Sicilian waters to save the prows of ships of the sea. We go through the spaces of ether; we bear no assistance to those that are polluted, but those to whom piety and justice are dear in life we free from their heavy toils and preserve. So let no one will to do wrong, let none voyage with men perjured. I am a god that publish this to mortals.*

CHORUS. *Farewell! The mortal that can fare well, and meets no hard calamity, will have happy days.*

[*Exeunt.*]

# Iphigenia Among the Taurians

IPHIGENIA AMONG THE TAURIANS is excellent theater by any standard. Its plot is carefully conceived, its characters are clearly defined and behave plausibly and interestingly in crises that are credible; there is the thrill of danger, the romance of far places and strange ways, the sentimentality of old memories and mixed loyalties and nostalgic yearnings. The relationship of Orestes and Pylades (who has at last found his tongue) adds a new dimension of poignancy. The tense and credible recognition scene evoked even Aristotle's admiration. Here if anywhere it is clear that Euripides is dramatist, not pamphleteer. Yet when he is most unmistakably the poet, Euripides is still the teacher. The introduction of a barbarian serves to bring certain unlovely Greek characteristics into relief. The account of Orestes' hallucination at the time of his mad seizure suggests a rational interpretation of the accepted story of the Avenging Furies. Apollo's wisdom and honesty are again impugned.

As always in Euripides, the god out of the machine which ensures the happy ending is an equivocation; but here a mind not resolutely sceptical can entertain both alternatives simultaneously. Without Athena's intervention, it is clear, the Greek party would never escape, and their inevitable doom would underscore the tragic meaning of their antecedent history. But the atmosphere of the remote and wonderful which surrounds the whole makes it easy to accept a final miracle without compromising the total effect.

# IPHIGENIA AMONG THE TAURIANS

## CHARACTERS

IPHIGENIA, *daughter of Aga-memnon, and Priestess of Artemis*

ORESTES, *brother of Iphi-genia.*

PYLADES, *friend of Orestes*

CHORUS, *captive Greek maidens, attendants of Iphigenia*

HERDSMAN, *a Thracian*

THOAS, *King of Thrace*

MESSENGER, *servant of Thoas*

ATHENA

The scene represents the front of the temple of Artemis in the land of the Taurians (modern Crimea). The altar is in the center.

Iphigenia Among the Taurians was acted approximately 414-412 B.C.

———◆———

[*Iphigenia enters from the temple.*]

IPHIGENIA. Pelops the son of Tantalus came to Pisa with swift horses and married the daughter of Oenomaus. Of her Atreus was born, who had children, Menelaus and Agamemnon; I am Agamemnon's daughter Iphigenia, the child of the daughter of Tyndareus. By the banks of the Euripus, where the frequent gusts churn the dark waters of the rolling river in eddies unceasing, my father slaughtered me, as he thought, for Helen's sake, a victim to Artemis, in the famous glens of Aulis.

There had Lord Agamemnon assembled a Hellenic armada of a thousand ships; for he desired to win for Hellas a glorious crown of victory over Ilium and to avenge the outrage done to Helen's marriage bond, this to do grace to Menelaus. But when he met with dire difficulty in sailing and wanted a breeze, he resorted to divination by fire; and Calchas said: "Captain, who hold sway over this Hellene host, Lord

Agamemnon, never will you launch your vessels from this
shore until Artemis receives as victim your maiden daughter,
Iphigenia; for you did vow you would sacrifice to the Goddess of Light the fairest thing that a year would bring
forth. Your wife, Clytemnestra has borne you a child in your
house" (this sorry prize of beauty he conferred on me),
"and her you must offer as sacrifice." By Odysseus' con-
trivances they took me from my mother, as if to wed me
to Achilles. I came to Aulis, poor girl; I was seized and
raised aloft over a pyre; they sought to kill me with the
sword. But Artemis stole me away and gave the Achaeans a
deer in my place, and conducted me through the bright
ether to this land of the Taurians, where she gave me a
home.

Here among his barbarians, the barbarian Thoas rules the
land. (He won his name because of his swiftness of foot: he
runs with the swiftness of wings.) She made me priestess in
this temple. From that time, I have conducted the sacrifices
according to the rites of the Festival in which Goddess
Artemis takes pleasure. Its name alone is festive; for the rest
I am silent, for I fear the goddess. It is a usage in this city
of old, carried out whenever any Hellene comes to this
land. I perform the consecration only; the slaughter is the
charge of others: unspeakable things—done in the darkness
of the goddess' shrine.

The strange visions which the night has brought I shall
utter to the air, if there is any help in that. In my dream I
seemed to have departed from this land and to dwell in Argos,
and I slept in the recesses of my girlhood chamber. The
earth's surface heaved and shook; I fled, stood outside, saw
the cornice of the house fall. The whole structure crashed
down in ruins, from the tops of the pillars down to the
pavement. A single column seemed to me to be left, alone of
all my father's house. From its capital it sprouted forth gold-
en hair, and was endued with a human voice. Then I, ob-
serving this ministry which is mine, to slay strangers, be-
sprinkled him as for death, and I wept. The dream I interpret
thus: Orestes is dead, for he it was whom I consigned to
slaughter; for the pillars of a house are its man-children,
and those die upon whom my sprinklings fall. I have no
other friends to fit into my dream: Strophius had no child
when I 'died'. Now therefore I wish to bestow his funeral
libations upon my brother, though he is far, far away—
that at least I can do. And my attendants will help me,

Greek women whom the king has given me. But what is the reason that they are not yet here? I shall withdraw into the rooms in which I dwell, within the precincts of the goddess.

[*Exit; enter guardedly Pylades, then Orestes.*]

ORESTES. Look, take care that no one is in our path.

PYLADES. I am looking, I am turning my eyes and spying in every direction.

ORESTES. Pylades, do you think this is the goddess' temple for which we sailed our ship over the sea from Argos?

PYLADES. I do, Orestes, and you must think so too.

ORESTES. And the altar where Hellene blood drips?

PYLADES. At any rate its top is brown with blood stains.

ORESTES. And do you see the spoils hung from the coping?

PYLADES. I see the trophies taken from bodies of slain guests. But I must look around and examine things more closely.

[*Pylades leaves Orestes and examines the Temple.*]

ORESTES. Ah, Phoebus, why have you again led me into a net with your oracles? After I avenged the blood of my father by slaying my mother, I was pursued by troops upon troops of Furies, far from my own land, and I covered many a course doubling to and fro. Then I came to you and asked how I might escape from this wheel of madness and end the sufferings, the agonies, that drove me up and down Hellas. You told me to come to the confines of the Tauric land, where your sister Artemis possessed altars, and to take from there the goddess' image which men say fell into this temple here from heaven. When I had got it, either by trickery or good luck, and the adventure was over, I was to present it to the land of the Athenians—no further commands were given—and so doing I should have rest from my labors. In obedience to your words I am come here to this unknown, this inhospitable land.

[*Pylades rejoins Orestes.*]

I ask you, Pylades, you are my helper in this labor, what shall we do? You see the height of these encircling walls. Shall we make our way through the entrance of the building? But how could we, unobserved? Shall we loosen the brazen bolts with crowbars? But we know nothing about them. If we are caught opening the gates or devising some entry, we die.

But before we die let us flee toward the ship on which we voyaged here.

PYLADES. To flee is intolerable; it is not our way. We must not fail the god's oracle through cowardice. Let us withdraw from the temple and hide ourselves in the cave which the dark sea sluices with its waters—far from the ship, in case someone sees its hull and tells the authorities. Then we would be overpowered. But when the dark eye of night is come we must make the attempt and use all our wits to get the graven image from the temple. See, there is an empty space between the triglyphs, where a man could let himself down. Good men are not afraid of hardships; cowards never get anywhere.

ORESTES. No, we have not come this distance on our ship only to take our journey homeward again from the very goal. Your advice is good, it must be obeyed. We must retreat to a spot where we can hide ourselves safely. At least it will not be my fault if the oracle ends in frustration. We must dare. Young men have no excuse for shirking hard work.

[*Exeunt; enter chorus of Greek captive women.*]

SOME OF CHORUS. *Keep reverent silence, you who dwell about the twin rocks that clash together in the Unfriendly Sea.*

OTHERS. *Child of Leto, Dictynna, mountain maid: toward your courts, your pillared temple with its golden cornice, I attend the holy steps of the holy virgin who keeps the keys of your temple. From the towers of Hellas, land of fine horses, from its walls, I am banished in slavery; I am banished from Europe's pastures and goodly trees, from the seat of my ancestral home.*

OTHERS. *I am come. What has happened? What is your anxiety? Why have you brought me here, brought me before the temple, child of Atreus' son, child of him who came to Troy's towers with a glorious fleet, with a thousand ships and ten thousand armed men?*

[*Iphigenia enters with attendants bearing libations.*]

IPHIGENIA. *Ah, my maidens, I am busy with lamentations most lamentable, with dreary dirges in a key the Muses love not, alas! alas!—in a great grief for a kinsman. Sore is the grief which has befallen me, for I bewail the life of my brother; such a vision, such a vision of dreams I saw in the night whose darkness is just departed. I am ruined, ruined, the house of my fathers is no more. Woe is me, woe, vanished is my race. Alas, alas, for the sorrows of Argos. Ah destiny, you have robbed me of my only brother, you have sent him to Hades! For him I shall sprinkle upon the earth's surface these libations, the cup of the dead: milk from the mountain kine, wine draughts of Bacchus, and the labor of the tawny bees, the offerings established for soothing the departed.*

*Hand me the vessel of gold, Hades' libation.*

*Scion of Argos, you who are beneath the earth, we bring these offerings as for the dead: accept them. To your tomb I cannot bring my yellow hair, my tears. Far from your country and mine I dwell apart; there they think I lie dead, cruelly slaughtered.*

CHORUS. *I will utter a responsive strain to you, my mistress, a barbaric chant of Asiatic melodies, the music of dirges dear to the dead, songs which Hades chants, dirges of defeat. Woe is me for the house of the Atreids. The light of its scepter is departed, woe is me: departed the glory of its ancestral halls. Gone is its prosperity, gone is the rule of the kings at Argos. Sorrow rains sorrow upon the house.*

*The sun's flying chariot wheeled round; the holy eye of day was driven from its accustomed place. Such was the affliction on affliction that the Golden Lamb brought on these halls, and death on death, woe on woe. Retribution for the Tantalids that died of old works itself out against the house. Fate rushes against you, on evil bent.*

IPHIGENIA. *From the beginning my life has been cursed, from my mother's bridal night, from the night I was conceived. From the beginning the goddesses of Life and Fate have conspired against me: hard has been my schooling. I was born of her that was wooed by the noblest of the Hellenes, the first-begotten fruit in the chamber of Leda's hapless daughter; born and reared to be slaughtered for a father's crime, the sorry victim of a father's prayer.*

*In a chariot with horses they brought me to the sands of Aulis, a bride (oh! the mockery of it!) for the son of Nereus' daughter, alas! alas! To-day I live an alien in the cheerless abodes of the Unfriendly Sea, husbandless, childless, homeless, loveless. I do not chant of Hera of Argos; my shuttle does not embroider on a sweetly humming loom the picture of Attic Pallas and the Titans. With hideous blood-*

*shed I embrue these altars, with the blood of doomed stran-*
*gers; and piteous is the voice of their agony, and piteous the*
*tears they shed.*

*But even such things I can now forget, as I bewail him that*
*is dead in Argos, my brother, whom I left a suckling, a*
*babe, a youngling, an infant, in his mother's arms, at his*
*mother's breast, in Argos, royal Orestes.*

[*Iphigenia remains sunk in sorrow, then as the Herds-*
*man approaches, the Leader speaks.*]

LEADER. Ah, here comes a herdsman from the shores of
the sea with some message for you.

HERDSMAN. Child of Agamemnon and Clytemnestra, hear
the strange news I bring.

IPHIGENIA. What is there so alarming in your news? ·

HERDSMAN. There have come to this land, safe on a boat,
through the Symplegades, a pair of young men, a pleasing
sacrifice and offering to Goddess Artemis. There's no time to
waste. Make ready the lustral water and the rites of consecration.

IPHIGENIA. Whence? What country's fashion do the strangers wear?

HERDSMAN. Hellenes; so much I know and nothing more. ·

IPHIGENIA. Did you not even hear their names, so you
could tell them?

HERDSMAN. The one was called Pylades by the other.

IPHIGENIA. And what was the name of his comrade?

HERDSMAN. No one knows; we did not manage to hear it.

IPHIGENIA. Where did you see them, how did you catch
them?

HERDSMAN. Just where the waves of the Unfriendly Sea
break——

IPHIGENIA. What have cowherds to do with the sea?

HERDSMAN. We came to wash our cattle in sea brine.

IPHIGENIA. Go back to that point, tell me where you
caught them, and how. I wish to know. They've been a long
time coming; the goddess' altar has waited long for the red
streams of Hellenic blood.

HERDSMAN. When we had brought our woodland cattle
down to the sea that flows through the Symplegades we
found a cave in the cliff, hollowed out by the constant
dashing of the sea waves, a haunt of fishermen for purple.
There one of our cattlemen saw the two young men, and he

retreated back, directing his steps on tip-toe. Then he said: "Do you not see? They are gods that sit there!" One of our number that was god-fearing raised his hands and looked toward them and prayed; "Child of Sea-Goddess Leucothea, guardian of ships, Lord Palaemon, be gracious unto us; or if you are the Dioscuri that sit upon that shore, or darlings of Nereus, who begot the noble choir of fifty Nereids—." Another fellow, an irreverent, brazen sinner, scoffed at their prayers. He declared they were castaway sailors that sat in the cave, out of fear of our law, because they had heard that we sacrifice strangers here. To most of us he seemed to speak well, and we determined to hunt the customary victims for the goddess.

In the meanwhile one of the strangers left the rock and stood forth, and shook his head up and down, and groaned and trembled to the tips of his hands. His wits wandered in a frenzy and he shouted like a hunter: "Pylades, do you see her? Don't you see this dragon of Hades, how she wants to kill me, how she fronts me with a horrible row of vipers? She is breathing fire and murder out of her garments; she hovers on her wings; she has my mother in her arms; that mass of rock—she will throw it at me! Ah, me! She will kill me! Where shall I fly?" There were no such forms and shapes to be seen; he mistook the bellowing of the cows and the dogs' barking. They do say the Erinyes utter cries like that. We huddled together, expecting the worst, silent, waiting. He drew his sword and rushed into the midst of our cattle like a lion. He thrust at their flanks with the steel; he pierced their ribs, fancying that he was in this way beating back the divine Erinyes, until the sea grew bloody blossoms.

In the meanwhile, when we saw our herds being slain and pillaged, each of us armed himself, and blew on conch-shells, and gathered the countryside. We reckoned that herdsmen were feeble opposition to strangers young and athletic. In a while we made up a good number, whereas the stranger checked his mad career and collapsed; froth dripped down his chin. Seeing our opportunity in his downfall, every man of us did his best, pelting and beating him. But the second stranger wiped the foam away, and nursed him, and shielded him with the fine web of his cloak, guarding him against the rain of blows. He ministered to his friend with loving care.

The stranger came to his senses and leapt to his feet. He saw the threatening cloud of enemies and realized that present fate was at hand for him and his comrade. He groaned, but we did not stop hurling our stones as we pressed upon them from this side and from that. Then did we hear that terrible exhortation: "To our death, Pylades, but see that we die like heroes! Draw your sword and follow me."

When we saw the two swords waving in the hands of our enemies, we filled the forest glens with our flight. But if some fled others pressed on and kept pelting the strangers, and if they thrust these away, those that had given ground came back with a barrage of stones. But it was unbelievable. Though stones were flung from countless hands none succeeded in hitting the goddess' victims. After much trouble we got the better of them, but it wasn't thanks to our courage; we hemmed them in and with stones knocked the swords out of their hands, and from weariness they sank to the ground on their knees. Then we brought them to the ruler of this land. He looked at them and sent them to you with all speed, to the lustral water and the blood-bowls.

Pray, maiden, that other strangers, as fine as these, be sent as victims to your altar. A few more like these to slaughter, and Hellas will pay in full for slaughtering you, will pay the penalty for the sacrifice at Aulis.

LEADER. This is a strange tale of madness, whoever this man is, that has come to the Unfriendly Sea from Hellene land.

IPHIGENIA. So be it. Go and bring those strangers. I shall arrange for the due rites here.

*[Exit Herdsman.]*

Ah, poor heart of mine. Once you were gentle to strangers and merciful always, paying kindred race its due meed of tears when you received Hellene men into your hands. But now my dreams have made me savage; they tell me that Orestes no longer looks upon the light. Therefore you will find me hard of heart, whoever you are that come. True is that saying, friends, I perceive it now: the unfortunate, who once enjoyed prosperity, are not kindly minded to those more fortunate than themselves. Ah, but never at all has any breeze come from Zeus, never any ship making its way through the Clashing Rocks, to bring me that Helen who ruined me, or Menelaus; then might I have had my revenge and paid them back—another Aulis here for that one far away, where the Danaans laid hold of me like a calf and tried to slaughter me—and the father that begot me was the priest! Ah, me! I cannot banish that hour's misery from my memory. How many times I stretched my hands to his beard, how many times to my father's knees, and clung to them, and said: "O father, the shame of it, to give your daughter away like this! My mother and the Argive women are chanting marriage hymns, while you are killing me; all the house is tuneful with flutes, and I am dying, at your hands. He is Hades then, this Achilles, and not Peleus' son whom you lured me here to marry; in a chariot car you guided me to this bloody bridal. O treachery!" I had my eyes covered with a fine-spun veil, and I did not take my brother in my arms—that brother who has now perished. From modesty, I did not join my lips to my sister's, for I was going to the halls of Peleus. I stored up for another time all those fond greetings, thinking I would soon be back again in Argos.

Poor boy, if you have died, what a splendid fortune, what an enviable patrimony you have lost, Orestes. [*Pauses thoughtfully.*] The goddess equivocates. I like it not. If any mortal stain his hand with blood-shed, if any hand touch a woman in child-bed or a dead body, she keeps him from her altars and counts him unclean. But *she* takes pleasure in sacrificial murder. Leto, the wife of Zeus, could not be the mother of such depravity. For my part I do not believe that Tantalus spread a banquet for the gods at which they enjoyed a child for victuals! It is the men of this land, I believe, being themselves murderers, who lay their own guilt on the gods. No god, I am sure, can be evil.

[*Exit into temple.*]

CHORUS. *Dark, dark crossways of the sea, by which the Gadfly winged its way from Argos over the Inhospitable Surge, crossing from Europe into Asia's land! What men are these, come from lovely Eurotas, green with rushes, or from Dirce's holy stream, come to this forbidding land, where the daughter of Zeus bedews altars and colonnaded temples with the blood of mortals?*

*Over the waves of the sea their naval craft has been brought by the double propulsion of their splashing oars of pine, their sails swelling in the breezes. Were they racing after wealth and still more wealth for their houses? Hope is precious, but it works mischief for mortals through their insatiable greed. To win for themselves a load of prosperity they become wanderers over the surging seas and in foreign lands pass from city to city in vain expectation. For some*

men even good judgment cannot win wealth; other men it
rushes to meet.

How did they pass between the Clashing Rocks, how did
they pass the unresting capes of Phineus, as over the surge
of Amphitrite, where the fifty daughters of Nereus dance in
a ring and sing, they raced along the coast before the breezes
that filled their sails, while at the stern the rudder creaked
in its groove, the breezes from the South or the breath of
Zephyrus bringing them to the land of many birds, to White
Beach, where Achilles ran his glorious courses, beside the
Unfriendly Sea?

Would that the prayers of my mistress could bring Helen
here, Leda's darling child, bring her from the city of Troy to
die at my lady's hand, the blood from her gashed throat
streaming round the curls of her hair! Then the score would
be evened. Most joyfully too would we receive the tidings
if it were some mariner come from the Hellene land to put
an end to the toils and miseries of our slavery. Would that,
even in dreams, I were again in my home, in the city of my
fathers, to enjoy the delight of sleep, to share the joys of the
fortunate.

LEADER. But here they come, the latest victims for the goddess, their hands roped together with coupling chains. Silence,
my friends. These are first-fruits of Hellas that approach the
temple. The herdsman spoke no false tidings.

Holy One, if these rites of this people are pleasing to you,
accept the sacrifices, unholy in Hellene eyes, which the
custom of this place publicly offers.

[Enter Iphigenia from the Temple. Orestes and Pylades
in bonds are brought in.]

IPHIGENIA. So be it. My first thought must be to see that
what pertains to the goddess is done properly. Loosen the
strangers' hands; they are hallowed and may therefore no
longer be bound. Go into the temple and make ready what
is requisite and customary for circumstances like the present.

[Exeunt attendants.]

[Aside.] Ah, who was the mother that bore you, who
was your father? Who was your sister, if you have a sister.
. . . What a pair of young men for her to lose, all brotherless.
Who knows upon whom such fates shall fall? Always the gods

move mysteriously and no one knows the evil ahead. Fate leads us on into dark places.

Where are you from, unhappy strangers? A long way have you sailed to this land, a long while will you be from home, for ever—dead.

ORESTES. Why are you so sorrowful? Why add your grief to the troubles that threaten us, lady, whoever you are? I do not count him wise who, condemned to death, seeks by lamentation to blunt the horror of extinction, or, when Death is at hand and all hope of rescue is gone, tries to move pity. He contrives two evils out of one; he proves himself a fool and dies just the same. We must let things take their course. You need make no moan for us. We *know;* we realize the sacrificial rites here current.

IPHIGENIA. Which of you was called by the name Pylades? This I wish to know first.

ORESTES. This man, if knowing it gives you pleasure.

IPHIGENIA. Of what Hellene country is he a citizen?

ORESTES. How would it profit you to know this, lady?

IPHIGENIA. You are two brothers, born of one mother?

ORESTES. Brothers in love, yes; by birth we are not brothers.

IPHIGENIA. What name did the father that begot you call you?

ORESTES. I might rightly be called Unfortunate.

IPHIGENIA. It is not that I ask. Attribute that to fortune.

ORESTES. If I die nameless, I shall not be triumphed over.

IPHIGENIA. Why do you begrudge me this? Are you so proud?

ORESTES. You shall sacrifice my body, not my name.

IPHIGENIA. Will you not even tell me what city is yours?

ORESTES. There is no use in asking that of a man about to die.

IPHIGENIA. But a favor—what prevents your granting it to me?

ORESTES. Famous Argos I claim for my country.

IPHIGENIA. By the gods, stranger, truly, are you sprung from there?

ORESTES. Yes, from Mycenae, once so prosperous.

IPHIGENIA. Did you leave your country an exile, or what happened?

ORESTES. I am an exile after a fashion, involuntary and voluntary too.

IPHIGENIA. Welcome was your coming from Argos.

ORESTES. Not on my side. If you desired it, that is your affair.

IPHIGENIA. Would you tell me something I long to know?

ORESTES. It is but a trifle in my situation.

IPHIGENIA. Perhaps you know of Troy; everybody talks of it.

ORESTES. Would I did not, would I had not even seen it in a dream.

IPHIGENIA. They say it is no more, that it has fallen to the spear.

ORESTES. That is so. You have not heard empty words.

IPHIGENIA. Has Helen returned to the house of Menelaus?

ORESTES. She has and with evil for someone belonging to me.

IPHIGENIA. Where is she? She owes me an older debt of evil.

ORESTES. She is living at Sparta with her former husband.

IPHIGENIA. Ah, creature hateful to all Hellenes, not to me alone.

ORESTES. I, too, have had some taste of her bridals.

IPHIGENIA. Did the Achaeans get back home, as is announced?

ORESTES. You are asking me all your questions at once.

IPHIGENIA. I wish to have this favor of you before you die.

ORESTES. Ask on, if it pleases you so; I shall answer.

IPHIGENIA. Has a certain Calchas, a prophet, come home again from Troy?

ORESTES. He is dead; so was the story in Mycenae.

IPHIGENIA. Holy One, how excellent!—What of Laertes' son?

ORESTES. He has not yet reached home, but he is alive, they say.

IPHIGENIA. Ruin take him! May he never return to his native land!

ORESTES. Do not curse him; his whole world is blighted.

IPHIGENIA. Nereid Thetis' son—is he yet alive?

ORESTES. He is not. He had no profit of his bridal at Aulis.

IPHIGENIA. A treacherous bridal it was, according to those who came through it.

ORESTES. Who are you anyway? How apt are your questions about the affairs of Hellas!

IPHIGENIA. I come from there. When I was yet a child I was lost.

ORESTES. Then you may well long to know what is happening there, lady.

IPHIGENIA. What of the general whom they call 'prosperous.'

ORESTES. Who? Not prosperous is he that I know.

IPHIGENIA. Atreus' son he was called, one Agamemnon, the king.

ORESTES. I do not know. Desist from this talk, lady.

IPHIGENIA. Nay, by the gods, but tell me, stranger, give me this pleasure.

ORESTES. He is dead, poor man, and has ruined another also.

IPHIGENIA. Dead? How did that happen? Ah, woe is me!

ORESTES. Why do you groan at this? Was he anything to you?

IPHIGENIA. It was for his happiness in time past that I groaned.

ORESTES. Horrible was his going, murdered by his wife.

IPHIGENIA. Altogether pitiable is she that killed . . . and he that was killed.

ORESTES. Cease now, ask no further.

IPHIGENIA. Only this. Is the poor man's wife alive?

ORESTES. She is not. The son whom she bore—he killed her.

IPHIGENIA. Ah, house confounded! What was his motive?

ORESTES. He avenged his father's death upon her.

IPHIGENIA. Alas! How well he executed justice that was evil!

ORESTES. But the gods have not given him the happiness he earned.

IPHIGENIA. Did Agamemnon leave another child in his house?

ORESTES. One daughter, Electra.

IPHIGENIA. I see. Do they ever speak of the daughter that was sacrificed?

ORESTES. Never, except to say that she is dead and gone from the world.

IPHIGENIA. Poor girl! Poor father that slew her!

ORESTES. She was destroyed to gain (but where was the gain?) an evil woman.

IPHIGENIA. The dead king's son—does he yet live in Argos?

ORESTES. He lives, in misery, nowhere, everywhere.

IPHIGENIA. Lying dreams, farewell! You were nothing after all.

ORESTES. Neither are the deities, whom men call wise, any less deceitful than winged dreams. In the affairs of the gods, as in the world of mortals, there is much confusion. One thing alone can cause a man sorrow: when he is ruined, not by his folly, but . because he has trusted words of prophecy—as one man was ruined, whom those that know know.

LEADER. Alas, alas! What of us? What of our parents? Are they alive? Are they not alive? Who can tell?

IPHIGENIA. Listen. I have thought of a certain plan, strangers, by which I can further your interests and my own at once. Success can be best attained if the same proposition is satisfactory to all parties. Would you be willing, if I save you, to take a message for me to Argos? Would you go to my friends there and carry a letter? It was written by a captive who took pity on me and did not regard my hand as murderous but held that he died by the law of the goddess who deems such things right. I have had no one who would go and take my message to Argos, none who could be saved to take my letter to one of my friends. But you —you are of gentle birth, and you know Mycenae and the people I mean—be saved, accept this reward, no dishonorable one, your safety, for the sake of some mere writing. But this man must be an offering for the goddess since the state so compels; he must be separated from you.

ORESTES. You say well in all respects but one, stranger lady. For this man to be sacrificed is a heavy grief to me. I am the one that piloted him to this disaster. He sailed with me out of pity for my troubles. It would not be fair, then, that I should do you a kindness at the cost of this man's destruction while I myself escape from trouble. But let it be this way. Give him the letter. He will take it to Argos, and carry out your wishes. Let who will slay me. It is most disgraceful for a man to get his friend into trouble, and then himself be saved. This man is a real friend; his life means as much to me as my own.

IPHIGENIA. O excellent spirit! From some noble shoot are you sprung, a true friend to your friends. May my surviving brother be a man like you. You must know, strangers, I am not brotherless; it is only that I do not see him. Since you will have it so, I shall send this man with my letter, and you shall die. Some great desire for death appears to possess you.

ORESTES. Who will offer me up? Who will brave the horrible act?

IPHIGENIA. I. I hold this office of the goddess.

ORESTES. An unenviable office, girl, and not a happy one.

IPHIGENIA. I am under a necessity, which must be observed.

ORESTES. A woman, herself, with a sword, sacrificing men?

IPHIGENIA. No, I only sprinkle the lustral water about your hair.

ORESTES. And who is the slaughterer, if I may ask?

IPHIGENIA. There are those within, whose charge that is.

ORESTES. What sort of tomb will receive me when I am dead?

IPHIGENIA. A sacred fire within, and a broad chasm of rock.

ORESTES. Ah, would that a sister's hand might dress my limbs!

IPHIGENIA. It is a vain prayer, poor man, whoever you are. She lives far away from this barbarian country. Yet because you happen to be an Argive I shall spare no service that is possible. I shall set out much adornment for your burial, and I shall quench your body with yellow oil, and I shall cast upon your pyre the bright labor of the tawny mountain bee, gathered from the flowers.

But I shall go and bring the letter from the goddess' shrine. [*Iphigenia turns toward the temple, addresses a word to Orestes, another to the attendants, and the remainder to herself as she enters the temple.*] Do not take this hard-heartedness as from *me*. Guard them, attendants, but without chains. Perhaps I shall send tidings unhoped for to Argos, to the friend whom I love most; this letter shall say to him that one is alive whom he thinks dead; it will bring him a joy he can trust.

SOME OF THE CHORUS [*to Orestes*]. *I pity you; yours is the doom of the lustral bowls and the rain of blood.*

ORESTES. Here is no cause for pity; but fare you well, stranger women.

OTHERS OF THE CHORUS [*to Pylades*]. *But you we count blessed for your happy fortune, young man; your foot will tread your native land again.*

PYLADES. Unenviable is such fortune for friends, when their friends die.

SOME OF THE CHORUS. *Ah, a sad homecoming.*

OTHERS. *Alas, alack, you are ruined utterly.*

OTHERS. *Ah me! ah me! whose is the better lot?*

OTHERS. *Even yet my mind wavers in doubtful indecision, whether for you first, or for you, I should sigh and lament.*

ORESTES. Pylades, by the gods, did the same thought strike you?

PYLADES. I don't know. You are asking me what I cannot tell.

ORESTES. Who is this young woman? How like a Hellene to ask us all about the labors of Troy, the home-coming of the Achaeans; about Calchas, the expert in augury, and Achilles, by name. How she pitied poor Agamemnon, and asked me about his wife and children. Surely this stranger is from those parts, an Argive by birth. Otherwise, she would never be sending her letter, nor be inquiring into these things as if she had a real interest in the welfare of Argos.

PYLADES. You got in a little ahead of me. You have stolen my own thoughts. Except for one thing: the disasters of royalty are common knowledge wherever folk foregather. But another thought has occurred to me.

ORESTES. What is it? Share it with me, and it will become clearer.

PYLADES. I cannot honorably look upon the light if you are killed. Together with you I sailed, together with you I must die. I shall pass for a knave and a coward in Argos and in all the glens of Phocis. Most people, being knaves themselves, will believe that I betrayed you to win my own way home alone. They may even think I murdered you, taking advantage of your stricken fortunes to plot your death for the sake of the throne, which would come to me, presumably, as your sister's husband. I am afraid to face the shame of that. Nothing else is possible: I must breathe my last with you, with you be slaughtered, and with your body mine must be burned. I am your friend, and I shrink from reproach.

ORESTES. Hush, for god's sake! My own doom I must bear. But a single grief is enough; I will not have it doubled. This talk of yours about the agonies of shame applies to me too, if you are to die for sharing my labors. For all I care, it is no bad thing for me to die, when the gods treat me like this. But *you* are happy. Your halls are pure and untainted; mine are luckless and godless. If you are saved you will beget sons of my sister whom I gave you to wife; my name shall live, my father's line shall not be blotted out for lack of heirs. Go your way, live; dwell in my father's house. When you come to Hellas and to Argos, land of horses, by this right hand I charge you, raise a cairn, and set upon it a memorial of me. Let my sister lavish her tears and her hair for my burial. Tell how I died at the hands of an Argive woman, in consecrated slaughter at an altar. And do not forsake my sister, when you see the desolation and friendlessness of our father's house. Farewell. I have found you the dearest of the dear, comrade in the chase, comrade in the home: full many of my heavy troubles have you borne.

Me, Phoebus has deceived, prophet though he is. This was a trick of his concoction to drive me as far as possible from Hellas; he is ashamed of his earlier oracles. To him I gave my all: I obeyed his words and slew my mother. Now it is my turn to be destroyed.

PYLADES. You shall have a burial; your sister's bed I shall never betray, poor fellow; in death I shall hold your love dearer even than in life. But still, the god's oracle has not yet destroyed you, though you are in the jaws of death. There is the chance, the odd chance, of extreme misfortune swinging to the other extreme.

ORESTES. Hush. Phoebus' words cannot help me. Here is the woman coming out of the house.

*[Enter Iphigenia.]*

IPHIGENIA *[to guards]*. Away you, go and get things ready within for the ministers of sacrifice. *[Exeunt guards.]* Here, strangers, are the folded tablets of my letter. Listen to the rest of my wishes. A man under duress becomes another being when the danger is past and he feels safe again. I am afraid that whoever offers to take this tablet to Argos will think my letter of no consequence the moment he is safely out of the country.

ORESTES. What is your desire then? Where is your difficulty?

IPHIGENIA. Let him give me an oath that he will convey this writing to Argos, to the friends I wish it to reach.

ORESTES. Will you give him as good an oath in turn?

IPHIGENIA. To do, or not do, what? Tell me.

ORESTES. To let him leave this barbarian land alive.

IPHIGENIA. A just demand. How else could he deliver my message?

ORESTES. But will the king allow this?

IPHIGENIA. Yes. I shall persuade him. And I myself shall put him on board ship.

ORESTES *[to Pylades]*. Swear. *[To Iphigenia.]* And you, propose an oath that will be sacred.

IPHIGENIA. "I shall deliver this letter to your friends." Say it.

PYLADES. I shall deliver this letter to your friends.

IPHIGENIA. And I shall send you safe beyond the Dark Rocks.

PYLADES. Which of the gods do you invoke to watch over this oath?

IPHIGENIA. Artemis, in whose house I hold office.

PYLADES. And I call upon the lord of Heaven, hallowed Zeus.

IPHIGENIA. If you scamp your oath and do me wrong?

PYLADES. May I never reach home. And what of you, if you do not save me?

IPHIGENIA. May I never live to set foot in Argos.

PYLADES. But listen, we forget something.

IPHIGENIA. We can still change the oath, if desirable.

PYLADES. Grant me this exception. If anything happens to the boat, if the letter is lost in the sea along with my belongings, and I save only my person, let the oath no longer be binding.

IPHIGENIA. Do you know what I shall do? The more resources the better success. The contents written in the folds of this letter I shall recite to you orally so that you may report it all to my friends. This is the safe way. If then you save my letter it will declare what is written in it without speech, but if the letter is lost at sea, then if you preserve your person you will also preserve my message.

PYLADES. You provide well both for your interests and mine. Tell me then to whom I am to take this letter in Argos, and what I am to say you told me.

IPHIGENIA [*hands the letter to Pylades and recites from memory*]. Take this word to Orestes, Agamemnon's son. "She that was sacrificed in Aulis sends this message, Iphigenia, still alive, though dead to those at Argos . . .

ORESTES. Where is she? Has the dead returned?

IPHIGENIA [*impatiently, her attention fixed on her recitation*]. You are looking at her. Do not interrupt with questions—"Fetch me back to Argos, my brother, before I die. Rescue me from this barbarian land, free me from this slaughterous priesthood, in which it is my office to kill strangers . . .

ORESTES. Pylades, what shall I say? Where have we found ourselves?

IPHIGENIA. "Else I shall become a curse upon your house,

Orestes." [*To Pylades.*] Hear the name again, you will remember it better.

ORESTES. Ye gods!

IPHIGENIA. Why do you call on the gods? This is my concern.

ORESTES. It is nothing. Go on. My thoughts wandered. [*Aside.*] If I question you, I might easily find—no, it is incredible.

IPHIGENIA. Say: "Goddess Artemis saved me and substituted a deer, which my father sacrificed believing he was thrusting the sharp blade into me. Then she brought me to stay in this land." Here is the letter, that is what is written in the tablets.

PYLADES. Ah, it is an easy oath you lay upon me, an excellent oath for me. I shall not take long to make good my pledged word. [*To Orestes.*] Look, I bring you a letter which I now deliver, from your sister here.

ORESTES. I accept it. The opening of it can wait, while first I snatch a pleasure no words can give.

Dearest sister, I am overwhelmed, I rush to the delight of your embrace, with arms all incredulous. This news is marvellous.

LEADER. Stranger, this is not lawful, you defile the handmaid of the goddess, the robes you clasp may not be touched.

ORESTES. O sister, my sister, daughter of Agamemnon my own father, do not repulse me. You have the brother you never thought to have.

IPHIGENIA. I? You my brother? Do not say such things. It is Argos his presence fills, or Nauplia.

ORESTES. Your brother is not there, poor girl.

IPHIGENIA. Do you mean that the Spartan woman, the daughter of Tyndareus, is your mother?

ORESTES. Yes, and Pelops' grandson is my father.

IPHIGENIA. What do you say? Have you any proof of this for me?

ORESTES. I have. Ask about anything in our father's house.

IPHIGENIA. No, it is you must speak, and I must judge.

ORESTES. Speak I will, and first the thing I heard from Electra. You have heard of the strife between Atreus and Thyestes?

IPHIGENIA. I have. It was when they quarreled about a golden lamb.

ORESTES. Do you recall embroidering the scene on a fine web?

IPHIGENIA. Dearest! How close you take the turn of my thoughts!

ORESTES. You made a design in the cloth, the sun turning back?

IPHIGENIA. I did indeed weave that design, with fine threads.

ORESTES. Did you receive the lustral water your mother sent to Aulis?

IPHIGENIA. Well I remember. Was it not a splendid marriage that took me away——

ORESTES. Yes, and how you gave your hair to be taken to your mother.

IPHIGENIA. As a memorial for my cenotaph.

ORESTES. And now, for proof, I shall tell the things I saw myself. In our father's house was Pelops' ancient spear, which he brandished in his hands when he killed Oenomaus and won Hippodamia, the maid of Pisa; in your maiden chamber the spear was hidden away.

IPHIGENIA. *Dearest! Surely my dearest, nothing else. I clasp you, Orestes, my darling, far from our native Argos, my dear one.*

ORESTES. And I clasp you whom we thought dead. Streaming tears, streams of sorrow, but of gladness too, wet your eyes, and wet mine also.

IPHIGENIA. *You were still an infant then, a little baby in the house, in your nurse's arms, when I left you. O, too great for words is the happiness in my heart! What can I say? More than marvellous, beyond telling, is this thing that has come to me.*

ORESTES. May our future be as happy together.

IPHIGENIA. *A joy unheard of is this I have got, dear friends. I fear it will take wings and flutter out of my hands, off into the sky. O Cyclopean hearth, O fatherland, beloved Mycenae, I thank you for giving life, I thank you for giving nurture to this brother of mine, for raising him to be the light of our house.*

ORESTES. Our birth was blessed, my sister, but our luckless lives were made for sorrow.

IPHIGENIA. *I remember, ah me, I remember when my poor father put the blade to my throat.*

ORESTES. Ah me! Though I was far away I think I see you there.

IPHIGENIA. *It was for no bridal, my brother, that I was*

*led by treachery to the couch of Achilles. By the altar were
tears and lamentation. Alas, alas, for the lustrations there.*

ORESTES. I too groan for the starkness of my father's deed.

IPHIGENIA. *Unfatherly, unfatherly has life been for me, an
unbroken chain of sorrow, by the act of some god.*

ORESTES. What if you had killed your own brother, poor
girl!

IPHIGENIA. *Ah, miserable am I for my horrible boldness! I
brought myself to do horrible things, my brother, horrible
things, woe is me. You narrowly escaped a shocking death,
slain at my hands.*

*But the sequel, how will it end? What friendly chance will
come my way? What way can I devise to get you out of the
country, away from death, back home to Argos, before the
sword comes near your blood? Here, here, poor heart, is your
problem to solve. Will you go overland? Not by ship, but on
swift feet? Then death will be near as you pass amongst barbarian tribes and by paths that are no paths. But the road
through the straits of the Dark Rocks is a long one for escape
by boat. Ah me! Ah me! What god, what man, what unfore-
seen chance will succeed in finding a way out of these
troubles? Who will show deliverance to the two lone survivors
of the house of Atreus?*

LEADER. Marvellous and stranger than any tale are these
things. And I have seen them with my own eyes; I shall not
be speaking from hearsay.

PYLADES. When friends see their friends again it is natural,
Orestes, to embrace. But now we must leave off commisera-
tion and turn to the task of winning glorious safety and getting out of this barbarian country. Wise men ride their luck;
they seize the chance to win other delights.

ORESTES. You are quite right. And I think fortune will take
care of our rescue, with our assistance. If a man is acting and
eager, the divine power is more effective, one may presume.

IPHIGENIA. You cannot hold me back, you will not turn me
from my questions. First I ask what Electra's lot in life has
been. You are all precious to me.

ORESTES. She is married to this man and has a happy life.

IPHIGENIA. Where is he from? Who is his father?

ORESTES. Strophius, the Phocian, is his father.

IPHIGENIA. And his mother is Atreus' daughter? He is a
blood relation of mine?

ORESTES. Your cousin, and my one true friend.

IPHIGENIA. This man was not alive when my father 'killed' me.

ORESTES. No. Strophius was childless for some time.

IPHIGENIA. Hail to you, husband of my own sister!

ORESTES. And my savior too, not only my kinsman.

IPHIGENIA. That horrible thing about mother—how could you dare?

ORESTES. Let us not speak of that. I was avenging my father.

IPHIGENIA. But what was her reason for killing her husband?

ORESTES. Let mother's affair be. It is not seemly for you to hear.

IPHIGENIA. I say nothing. And does Argos now look to you?

ORESTES. Menelaus reigns there; I am an exile from my father's land.

IPHIGENIA. Surely he, your uncle, did not insult our fallen fortunes?

ORESTES. No, dread of the Erinyes has cast me out of the land.

IPHIGENIA. This was the madness that was reported of you on the sea-shore?

ORESTES. Yes, that was it, and that is not the first time people have seen me its victim.

IPHIGENIA. I see. It is for mother's sake the goddesses haunt you.

ORESTES. Ay, and thrust a bloody bridle in my mouth.

IPHIGENIA. Why did your feet drift to this country?

ORESTES. I came here by the bidding of Phoebus' oracle.

IPHIGENIA. To do what? Can you tell or must it be kept quiet?

ORESTES. I will tell you. These are the beginnings of my many tribulations. When my mother's—when that evil thing of which we speak not had devolved on me, I was driven forth into exile, haunted by the Erinyes. Then Loxias directed my steps to Athens, to give satisfaction to the Nameless Goddesses. There is a holy tribunal, which Zeus once instituted for Ares for some pollution of his hands. I went there—at first no host was willing to receive me because I was hated by the gods. Some, however, had pity and offered me hospitality, but though I was under the same roof, I sat at a table alone; their silence excluded me from their conversation, so that I partook of their food and their drink, but apart from them.

The wine they served in individual cups, filled with an equal measure for all, and so they took their pleasure. Not thinking it right to question my hosts, I grieved in silence and pretended not to notice, but I groaned deeply because I was my mother's murderer. I hear that my misfortunes have become a religious rite for the Athenians, and that the usage still obtains for the folk of Pallas to honor the Little Cups.

Then I came to Mars' Hill to stand my trial; I took the defendant's seat and the eldest of the Erinyes took the other. Arguments about my mother's bloodshed were given and heard. Phoebus saved me by his testimony; the hand of Pallas evened the votes for me at the counting, and I came off winner in the trial for murder. The Erinyes that acquiesced in the sentence determined to have their sanctuary near the tribunal itself. Those that did not agree to the ruling kept hounding me with homeless wanderings, until I came again to Phoebus' sacred plain. I threw myself down in front of the shrine and abstained from food, and I swore that I would die there and dash out my life if Phoebus who had ruined me refused to save me. Then Phoebus uttered some sound from his golden tripod and sent me here to seize the image that fell from the sky and set it up in the land of the Athenians. Now help me achieve my appointed salvation. If we can lay hold of the goddess' idol I shall be cured of my madness and I shall put you on a ship with many oars and settle you in Mycenae back home.

Ah, dearly beloved, O dearest sister, preserve our father's house, help me to safety. My own fortunes are ruined, and all the house of Pelops unless we capture the idol that came from the heavens.

LEADER. The anger of heaven, strange and terrible, seethes up and drives the seed of Tantalus through tribulations.

IPHIGENIA. I was all eager, before you came here, to be in Argos and to see you, my brother. My desire is as yours, to set you free from your tribulations and to restore the ailing house of our father—I bear no grudge for his 'killing' me. That is my desire; thus I would keep my hands clean of your slaughter, and preserve our house. But I fear the goddess (she will see me) and the king, when he finds the stone pedestal empty and the image gone. I shall surely die. What excuse have I? But if we can secure both ends at once—if you carry off the image and take me too on your good ship, the risk is worth venturing. If the image goes and I stay, I perish, it is true, but you will secure your end and obtain a

safe return home. However, I will not shrink, even if I must
die to save you. There is no doubt about it: a man's death
is a sore loss to a house, a woman's is of little account.

ORESTES. I will not be *your* murderer as well as my mother's. Her blood is enough. With hearts at one I wish to live
with you, or to die and share your lot. I shall take you home,
if I can myself get out of here, or I shall stay and die with
you. This is what I think. If this deed were disagreeable to
Artemis, how could Loxias have ordained me to bring the
goddess' statue to Pallas' town? How would he have granted
me to see your face? When I put all these considerations
together, I have good hopes of winning my way home.

IPHIGENIA. How is it possible, not merely for us to escape,
but also to carry off the thing we want? There's what balks
our return home for all our yearning.

ORESTES. Couldn't we manage to kill the king?

IPHIGENIA. O horrible! Visitors kill their host?

ORESTES. But if it will save you and me we must venture it.

IPHIGENIA. I could not. But I admire your thoroughness.

ORESTES. What if you were to hide me in this temple?

IPHIGENIA. That we may take advantage of the dark to
smuggle it out?

ORESTES. Yes, night is the time for thieves; for truth
the light of day.

IPHIGENIA. There are sacred watchmen within; we could
not elude them.

ORESTES. Ah me, we are ruined! How can we be saved?

IPHIGENIA. I think I have it, a novel device.

ORESTES. What kind? Share your mind, let me also know.

IPHIGENIA. Your misfortunes will supply my persuasions.

ORESTES. Women are clever at concocting schemes.

IPHIGENIA. I shall say you are a matricide from Argos.

ORESTES. Make use of my troubles if you can profit by
them.

IPHIGENIA. I shall say it is not lawful to offer you to the
goddess——

ORESTES. What reason will you offer? I am beginning to
see.

IPHIGENIA. Because you are not pure. Only that which is
holy will I offer for slaughter.

ORESTES. How will that help us to get the goddess' image?

IPHIGENIA. I shall desire to sanctify you in streams of
sea-water——

ORESTES. But the statue for which we sailed still stays in the temple.

IPHIGENIA. I shall say that it too must be taken to be cleaned because you touched it.

ORESTES. Where? Is it some watery inlet of the sea you mean?

IPHIGENIA. I mean where your vessel rides at anchor on hempen hawsers.

ORESTES. Will you or some other person carry the idol?

IPHIGENIA. I will. I am the only one whom the ritual law permits to touch it.

ORESTES. What part in this task shall we assign Pylades here?

IPHIGENIA. I shall say his hands have the same pollution as yours.

ORESTES. Will you act in secret? Or is the king to know?

IPHIGENIA. I shall tell him a plausible story. I couldn't keep it secret.

ORESTES. This is where the thrashing oars of my good ship come in.

IPHIGENIA. It is for you to manage the rest successfully.

ORESTES. Only one thing we need: these women must keep this secret. Beg them, find words to sway them. A woman has power to awake pity. And for the rest, doubtless it will be all right.

IPHIGENIA. Dearest women, I count on you. In your hands are my fortunes, either to find happiness or to be reduced to nothing, to be deprived of my country, my dear brother, my precious sister. Let me put this thought in the forefront of my plea: we are women, we naturally befriend our sex, we can be relied on to guard our common interests. Please keep silence. Help us to work out our escape. It is an excellent thing to have a faithful tongue. See three dear friends in one predicament: to win home or die. [Addressing individuals in Chorus.] If I am saved I shall see that you too share my fortune. I shall save you and bring you to Hellas. You I beseech by your right hand, and you: you by your dear cheeks, by your knees, by your dear ones at home, your father and mother, by your children, those of you who have them. What will you say? Who says yes? Who refuses—speak up—to do it? If my words do not win you, I am ruined, I and my poor brother.

LEADER. Courage, dear mistress, do but save yourself. As

far as I am concerned, the silence you impose on us—
great Zeus be my witness—will be kept intact.

IPHIGENIA. Bless you for these words! May you be happy!
[*To Orestes and Pylades.*] It is your part and yours to enter
into the temple. The lord of this land will soon come to inquire whether the sacrifice of the strangers has been com-
pleted.

[*Exeunt Orestes and Pylades to temple.*]

Revered Lady, who amidst the glens of Aulis did save me
from the horror of a father's slaughterous hand, save me now
again, save these men! Or no more, thanks to you, will mortals see truth on the lips of Loxias. Graciously consent to
leave this barbarian land and go to Athens. This land is no fit
home for you, whom a blessed city awaits.

CHORUS. *Winged halcyon, on rocky reefs of the sea, in accents that touch the feeling heart, you chant the dirge of
your unhappy life, of that lost mate whom you lament in
song for ever. I too have lamentations to rival yours, I a
wingless bird, yearning for the assemblies of the Hellenes,
yearning for Artemis, goddess of mothers, in her dwelling by
the Cynthian hill, by the delicate palm tree and the lovely
laurel and the sacred shoots of the pale olive, sweet shelter
of Leto's travail, by the swirling waters of the circular
lake where the swans pay melodious service to the Muses.*

*O the deep fountains of tears, that gushed down my cheeks
when our towers were destroyed and I was carried to the
ships, among the oars and the spears of our enemies, to be
bartered for gold in a barbarian land. Here I serve the daughter of Agamemnon, herself the handmaid of the huntress
goddess, at altars where Hellenes are sacrificed. I envy the
man who has known no happiness. Hardships do not distress
him; they are his familiar companions. Misery lies in reversal
of bliss; to meet outrageous fortune after knowing joy is a
wearisome existence for mortals.*

*You, my lady, an Argive ship of fifty oars, will bring to
your home. The piping of the wax-bound reed, mountain
Pan's instrument, will put mettle in the oarsmen; seer Apollo,
singing to the accompaniment of the music of his seven-
stringed lyre, will escort you fairly to the Athenian's shining
land. Me you will leave here as the oars splash in the water
and you depart. The halyards will hoist the sails to the breeze,
bellying finely forward out over the beak, as the ship speeds
on its way.*

*O that I might follow the bright course of the Sun's chariot, where the air is a fine fire, and over the chambers of my own home stay the fluttering of the wings on my shoulders. O to take my stand in the dances, where long ago I stood at brilliant nuptials, whirling around in sweet competition of grace with merry bands of friends, eagerly vying with them in richness of adornment, matching against theirs the gorgeous veils and the curls which clustered darkly round my cheeks.*

[*Thoas enters. He meets Iphigenia as she emerges from the temple with the image.*]

THOAS [*to the Chorus*]. Where is the Hellene woman who guards this temple? Has she already performed the first rites over the strangers? Are their bodies already brightly burning within the holy shrine?

LEADER. Here she is, lord; she will declare all to you plainly.

[*Enter Iphigenia carrying the image in her arms.*]

THOAS. Why have you taken in your arms the goddess' image, child of Agamemnon, why are you shifting it from its inviolable pedestal?

IPHIGENIA. Lord, stay where you are, at the entrance.

THOAS. What is it, Iphigenia, what strange thing is in the temple?

IPHIGENIA. Blot the thing out! I bestow the word on Holiness.

THOAS. To what news is this a preface? Speak plainly.

IPHIGENIA. Not pure were the offerings you hunted down for me, king.

THOAS. What proof have you? Or is it a guess?

IPHIGENIA. The statue of the goddess turned backwards on its base.

THOAS. Of its own accord, or did some earthquake move it?

IPHIGENIA. Of its own accord. And it shut its eyes tight.

THOAS. What is the cause? Is it the taint of the strangers?

IPHIGENIA. That and nothing else. They have done a horrible thing.

THOAS. Did they kill some of our barbarians on the shore?

IPHIGENIA. They arrived here with blood on their hands, the blood of kin.

THOAS. How? I am eager to know.

IPHIGENIA. Together they did their mother to death with a sword.

THOAS. Apollo! No barbarian could have been so hard.

IPHIGENIA. They were hunted and driven from all Hellas.

THOAS. Because of them then you are carrying the image outdoors?

IPHIGENIA. Yes, underneath the holy sky, to banish the taint of murder.

THOAS. How did you discover the strangers' pollution?

IPHIGENIA. I questioned them when the goddess' image turned.

THOAS. Hellas raised you a clever child, to see so sharply.

IPHIGENIA. Yes, and just now they dropped a seductive bait for my heart.

THOAS. Did they bring you some pleasing news from Argos to charm you?

IPHIGENIA. They told me that my only brother, Orestes, was well and happy.

THOAS. So you would spare them for the pleasant news they brought?

IPHIGENIA. And that my father was alive and prospering.

THOAS. But you took the side of the goddess, of course.

IPHIGENIA. Yes, I hate all Hellas; it destroyed me.

THOAS. What must we do now, tell me, about the strangers?

IPHIGENIA. The established law must be reverently observed.

THOAS. Are not your lustral bowl and knife ready for action?

IPHIGENIA. I wish to cleanse them first with pure ablutions.

THOAS. In spring or sea water?

IPHIGENIA. The sea washes away all the sins of men.

THOAS. At any rate they will make a purer sacrifice.

IPHIGENIA. And so my designs shall speed better.

[*Starts away.*]

THOAS. But do not the waves break right beside the temple?

IPHIGENIA. I need solitude. There are other things for me to do.

THOAS. Take them where you will. I have no desire to look upon mystic rites.

IPHIGENIA. I must purify the image too.

THOAS. Yes, the taint of matricide is on it.

IPHIGENIA. Otherwise I should never have taken it up from its pedestal.

THOAS. True piety and prudence!

IPHIGENIA. Do you know what you must do for me?

THOAS. It is for you to say.

IPHIGENIA. Lay fetters upon the strangers.

THOAS. Where could they escape to?

IPHIGENIA. Hellas knows no faith.

THOAS. Go, servants, attend to the fetters.

IPHIGENIA. Let them bring the strangers out here——

THOAS. It shall be done.

IPHIGENIA. When they have covered their heads with their robes.

THOAS. To keep the sun's beam from the taint.

IPHIGENIA. Send some of your henchmen with me.

THOAS. These men shall attend you.

IPHIGENIA. And send someone to warn the city——

THOAS. Against what?

IPHIGENIA. To remain indoors, every man.

THOAS. To avoid contact with murder?

IPHIGENIA. Such things are an abomination.

THOAS. Go, you, and make proclamation——

IPHIGENIA. That none shall come within sight.

THOAS. How well you care for the city!

IPHIGENIA. Ay, and for the friends to whom I owe most——

THOAS. You speak of me. How rightly does the whole city admire you!

IPHIGENIA. You remain here before the temple and serve the goddess——

THOAS. What am I to do?

IPHIGENIA. —by cleansing her hall with torches.

THOAS. So that it will be clean for you to return to.

IPHIGENIA. When the strangers pass out of the temple——

THOAS. How must I act?

IPHIGENIA. Draw your cloak over your eyes.

THOAS. Yes, to avoid the contagion of murder.

IPHIGENIA. If I seem to tarry over long——

THOAS. What shall be my limit?

IPHIGENIA. Do not be surprised.

THOAS. Do what the goddess requires, take your time, do it well.

IPHIGENIA. May this cleansing turn out as I desire!

THOAS. I join that prayer.

[*Thoas' attendants with Orestes and Pylades appear at the temple door and descend the steps, followed by servants bearing vessels for the purification and leading animals for sacrifice. The procession moves off.*]

IPHIGENIA. The strangers are leaving the temple I see, with the robes of the goddess and newborn lambs whose slaughter will wash away the taint of slaughter. Here too are the gleaming torches and the other instruments of purification which I prescribed for the strangers and for the goddess.

[*She joins the procession, walking in the rear.*]

I warn all citizens to avoid this pollution. All temple servants who keep clean hands for the service of the gods, and all who are about to enter wedlock, and all who are heavy with child, flee away, stand off, contract not this pollution.

Maiden queen, Zeus' daughter and Leto's, if I wash away the blood guilt of these men, if I reach the proper place for sacrifices, you will dwell in a house that is pure, and we shall be happy. Of the rest I speak not, but my will I show to the gods whose knowledge is abundant, and to you, Goddess Artemis.

[*The procession moves off; Thoas enters the temple.*]

CHORUS. *A comely child was Leto's babe whom once she bore in the fruitful vales of Delos; a golden-haired boy, clever with the harp did she bear, and a girl whose joy is in true archery. From the rock by the sea did she carry him, forsaking the scene of her glorious travail, and brought him to Parnassus, mother of gushing waters, the peak where Dionysus holds his revels. There the ruddy-faced serpent with the spotted back, his mail of bronze gleaming amidst the thick shade of the leafy laurel, a monstrous prodigy of the earth, frequented the infernal oracle. That monster you slew, Phoebus, though you were yet a babe, still leaping in your mother's arms, and you entered the sacred oracle. You sit at the golden tripod, on the throne of truth; from the depths of the holy place you dispense oracular commands to mortals. Hard by Castalia's stream you dwell in your temple at earth's center.*

*But his coming dispossessed Themis, Earth's child, from Pytho's sacred oracle; wherefore Earth begot nocturnal phantoms, dreams which declared unto many among mortals during sleep, upon darkened couches of the Earth, the things which had been and all the things which were hereafter to be. Thus did Earth rob Phoebus of his oracular privileges, being jealous for her daughter. Swiftly then did the king rush to Olympus and twined his baby fingers about the throne of Zeus and begged him to deliver his Pythian home from the fury of Earth. Zeus smiled when he saw that the child had lost no time in coming to claim a worship so productive of wealth. He shook his locks in consent and agreed to put a stop to the nocturnal voices. He took away from mortals the truth of the night and Loxias had his privileges restored to him. Mortals were given confidence again in the oracles he chanted, and visitors flocked to his seat.*

[*Enter Messenger, who begins shouting at the temple doors.*]

MESSENGER. Ho temple guards, altar attendants, where is Thoas, king of this country? Open the sturdy doors and call the ruler of this land out of these halls.

LEADER. What is it, if I may speak without being bidden?

MESSENGER. Clean gone are the two young men by the contrivance of Agamemnon's child. They have escaped out of this land and they have taken the sacred image in the hold of a Hellene ship.

LEADER. Your story is incredible. But the man you wish to see, the king of the land, has just left the temple.

MESSENGER. Where? He must know what is happening.

LEADER. We do not know. But go and hurry after him and report your tale to him where you find him.

MESSENGER. Look you, how faithless is womankind! You, too, have some share in this affair.

LEADER. You are mad. What have we to do with the strangers' flight? Why don't you hurry off to the royal gates?

MESSENGER. Not until this interpreter [*seizes knocker*] tells me whether the ruler of this land is or is not within.

[*Knocks.*] Ho, there, throw open the bars, you inside, I mean; tell our master that I am here at the gates, carrying a load of bad news.

[*Enter Thoas.*]

THOAS. Who is it that sets up such a shout at the goddess' house, hammering at the doors and hurling such confusion within?

MESSENGER. Ah, those women tried to tell me you were out, and so make me leave the temple, and you were in the house after all.

THOAS. What advantage did they expect? What were they angling for?

MESSENGER. I'll tell you about them another time. But hear the business now in hand. The young woman whose place was beside the altar here, Iphigenia, has gone out of the country with those strangers and has taken with her the sacred image of the goddess. The cleansing was only a trick.

THOAS. What's that? So that is how the wind lay?

MESSENGER. To save Orestes; there is a surprise for you.

THOAS. Orestes, you say? You mean the son of the Tyndarid?

MESSENGER. The man the goddess had us dedicate to these altars.

THOAS. It is a miracle. What stronger word can I find for it?

MESSENGER. Forget that and listen to me. Attend closely to what I say and think out some method of pursuit to overtake the strangers.

THOAS. Speak on, your advice is good. They have far to sail, before they escape my power.

MESSENGER. When we had come to the shore of the sea where Orestes' vessel was hidden at anchor, the child of Agamemnon motioned to us whom you had sent along with the strangers' fetters to stand off at a distance and leave her to perform the rites of fire and purification for which she had come; she walked behind alone, holding the fetters in her hands. This was suspicious to be sure, but your servants were satisfied, O king.

After a time she uttered a solemn cry, to make us think she was about some great business, and she chanted unintelligible strains as part of her magic rites as if she were washing away the stain of murder.

When we had been sitting there for a long while it occurred to us that the strangers (who had been set free) might kill her and run away. On the other hand, fear of seeing what we should not see kept us sitting in silence.

Finally we all had the same idea, to go where they were even though we had been forbidden.

And there we see the hull of a Hellene ship, winged with a fine broadside of blades, and fifty seamen sitting at the tholes, oars in hand. The young men freed of their fetters were standing at the ship's stern. Some of the crew were steadying the prow with poles, others were raising the anchor to the catheads, others hastily ran the stern-cables through their hands and let a ladder down to the sea for our strangers.

When we perceived the cunning trickery we threw aside all scruples and laid hold of the woman and the cables and tried to wrest the rudder blades from their portholes at the stern of the good ship. Words, too, passed between us: "On what plea do you raid our country and steal images and priestesses? Who are you and whose son, to kidnap this woman out of our land?" Then he replied: "Orestes, this woman's brother, let me tell you, Agamemnon's son. It is my own sister that I seize; I am taking her to my home, from which I lost her."

But we did not slacken our hold on the woman, as we tried to make her come with us to you. That was where I got these fearful blows on my cheeks. They had no steel to their hands, nor did we. Their fists came crashing upon us, and the feet of both the young men shot at our ribs and stomachs; the concussion knocked the strength out of our limbs. They stamped their fearful signatures upon us, till we ran to the cliff, some with bloody wounds on the head, others in the eyes. On the hill we made a stand and defended ourselves more prudently with a barrage of stones. But their bowmen stood on the stern and kept us back with their shafts, driving us further and further back. Meanwhile a frightful wave swung the ship toward the beach but the maiden was afraid of stepping into the surf. Orestes took his sister upon his left shoulder, stepped into the sea, leapt upon the ladder, and put her down inside the heroic ship, along with the image of Zeus' Maid which had fallen from heaven. From the waist of the boat a shout rang out: "Sailors of Hellas, grip your oars and churn the foam into white swirls. We have got that for which we sailed past the Symplegades into the Unfriendly Sea."

They then roared out a yell of joy and smote the brine. As long as the ship was within the harbor it made way, but when she cleared its mouth she met with a heavy sea and began to labor: a frightful gale had come up suddenly and thrust the ship back, stern first. They labored valiantly, struggling vainly against the waves; still the surging backflow drove the vessel to land again. Then did Agamemnon's child stand forth and offer prayer: "Maid of Leto, save me, thy priestess, help me unto Hellas from this barbaric land, forgive my theft. You, too, goddess, love your brother. Remember that I also love my kin."

The sailors chanted the paean in response to the maiden's prayer, and with arms bare to the shoulders they leaned to their oars at the word of command. Nearer and nearer the rocks the vessel rushed. Some of us waded out into the sea, others made loops of rope fast on land. I came straight here to you to report to you, lord, what has taken place there.

Hurry, take chains and ropes with you. If the sea does not sink to a calm, the strangers have no hope of safety. Revered Poseidon, ruler of the sea, watches over Ilium in his enmity to the children of Pelops. So now he will deliver Agamemnon's son, I doubt not, into your hands, and the hands of your citizens, and also his sister who has manifestly betrayed the goddess, forgetting the slaughter at Aulis.

LEADER. Ah, hapless Iphigenia, you will die, along with your brother; again you have fallen into the power of your masters.

THOAS. Ho all citizens of this barbaric land, throw bridles upon your horses! Run along the shore and seize the stranded ship; with the help of the goddess make haste to hunt down those impious men. Others of you drag my swift ships down to the sea. With ships by sea and cavalry by land, we shall catch them and fling them from some rough rock or impale their bodies on stakes.

You women, accomplices of this scheme, we shall punish another time at our leisure. But now we have this business before us; we shall not sit idle.

*[Athena appears aloft.]*

ATHENA. Whither, whither do you lead this chase, King Thoas? Listen to my words, Athena's words. Stop your men from streaming in pursuit. It was the oracles of Loxias that sent Orestes here to escape the angry Erinyes and bring his fair sister back to Argos, and the sacred image to my land. Thus he would gain respite from his present troubles. This is my word to you. As for Orestes whom you think to take in the stormy sea and kill—Poseidon in kindness to me is already calming the ruffled waters, so that he may sail in his ship.

And you, Orestes, learn my bidding—you hear my voice, the voice of a goddess, though you are not present—fare on with the image and your sister. When you come to god-built Athens, there is a place in the furthest confines of Attica, near the Carystian rock, a holy place, which my people call Halae. Build a temple there and set up the image, to be named after the Taurian land and your agonized toilsome wanderings up and down Greece, goaded on by the Furies. For the future mortals shall hymn her as Artemis the Taurian Goddess. Establish too this usage: whenever the folk keep this festival as compensation for your life spared at the altar, let the priest apply the knife to the neck of some man and let him let blood, for religion's sake, that the goddess may have her honors.

You, Iphigenia, must be key-warden to this goddess at the sacred terraces of Brauron. There you shall die and be buried. Garments of fine-spun web—which women leave in their homes who give up the ghost in childbirth—will they consecrate to you as an offering.

These Hellene women I bid you send forth from this land for their loyalty's sake.

[LACUNA IN TEXT]

Orestes, I saved you once before on Mars' Hill when I decreed the votes equal. The custom shall abide: whoever receives equal votes shall prevail. Take your sister from this land, son of Agamemnon, and you, Thoas, be not angry.

THOAS. Queen Athena, whoever hears the words of the gods and heeds them not is out of his mind. I am not angry with Orestes for carrying off the goddess' image, nor with his sister. What good can there be in strife with the gods who are strong? Let them go to your land with the statue of the goddess, and let them set the image up with good luck. These women I shall send to blessed Hellas, as your mandate enjoins. I shall withhold the spear which I raised against the strangers, and the crews of my ships, for such is your pleasure, goddess.

ATHENA. I commend you. Necessity is stronger than you, it is stronger than the gods. Onward, breezes, speed Aga-

memnon's child to Athens. I shall journey in company with
them, to guard my sister's sacred image.

*[Athena disappears.]*

CHORUS. *Onward with good fortune, rejoice in your deliverance.*

*Pallas Athena, revered among the immortal gods and
mortal men, we shall do even as you bid. Altogether delightful and unhoped for is the message my ears have received.*

*Great and revered Victory, abide with me through life.
Cease to crown me never.*

*[Exeunt.]*

# The Bacchants

———◆———

BECAUSE of its theme *Bacchants* has often been regarded as a tract. At one extreme it has been described as the aged Euripides' recantation of his earlier rationalism; at the other, as his severest indictment of religion. But to justify these and intermediate positions, commentators have had to fix upon isolated passages and ignore others that do not fit the favored theory. If nothing else, the variety in interpretation shows that *Bacchants* is not a tract but a drama which illuminates a particularly rich cast of characters by their interactions upon one another. Pentheus and Dionysus are not merely spokesmen for different theologies but a pair of passionate young cousins whose likeness is as important as their differences.

But the catalyst for the interactions is religion, and we must understand the religious issue to understand the drama. Pentheus' Apolline opposition to the new cult cannot be the approved position, for Pentheus' own righteousness is superficial as well as headstrong; it is he that brings naughtiness with him when he goes to spy on the women's frolics. Nor, surely, can Euripides be upholding a Dionysiac fanaticism which makes Agave, who accepted the new cult, murder her own son. The rationalism of the Apolline and the enrichment of the Dionysiac are both good things. If there is a lesson it is that it is irrational not to recognize the irrational, and impoverishing and dangerous as well.

Dionysus can be heartless as well as beneficent, and men cannot choose to keep him out of their lives. The ancient Greeks and later Mediterranean peoples have understood that a few days of Dionysiac carnival might help preserve rationalism during the rest of the year.

# THE BACCHANTS

### CHARACTERS

DIONYSUS, *also called Bac-*
*chus, Bromius, Evius*
CHORUS, *Asiatic women,*
*devotees of Dionysus*
TIRESIAS, *the Theban proph-*
*et, old and blind*
CADMUS, *founder and for-*
*merly king of Thebes*
PENTHEUS, *king of Thebes,*
*grandson of Cadmus*

THE STRANGER, *a missionary*
*prophet of Dionysus*
SERVANT *of Pentheus*
FIRST MESSENGER, *herds-*
*man from Cithaeron*
SECOND MESSENGER, *servant*
*of Pentheus*
AGAVE, *mother of Pentheus,*
*daughter of Cadmus*
Guards, *attendants, others*

The scene represents the front of the royal palace at
Thebes.

*The Bacchants* was written in Macedon, where Euripides
spent the last years of his life (408-406) in virtual exile. It
was played in Athens after its author's death.

———◆———

*[Enter Dionysus.]*

DIONYSUS. Zeus' child has come back to the land of the
Thebans. I am Dionysus whom Cadmus' daughter, Semele,
bore long ago by the flaming thunderbolt's midwifery. My
form I have changed from divine to human, as I come now to
Dirce's streams, to the water of Ismenus. Close by the
palace here I mark the monument of my mother, the thunder-
blasted. The ruins of her home, I see, are smouldering
still; the divine fire is still alive—Hera's undying insult to
my mother. All praise to Cadmus; he has made this spot
holy ground, his daughter's chapel. But it was I who
wreathed it in the greenery of the clustering vine.
I come from Lydia's fields that teem with gold, and Phrygia's. I have conquered the Persians' sun-smitten steppes
and the walled towns of Bactria, the wintry land of Media
and Arabia the Blest. All Asia is mine, all that lies by the salt

sea and possesses fair-towered cities filled with mingled Hellenes and barbarians together. This is the first city I have come to in Hellas. Everywhere else I have instituted my dances and my mysteries, that my godhead might be manifest to mortals.

First of this Hellene land I have filled Thebes with the cries of exultant women; I have fitted the fawn-skin to their bodies and have put into their hands the militant thyrsus, entwined with ivy. For my mother's own sisters—*they* at least should have known better—said that Dionysus was no son of Zeus; that Semele had given her love to some mortal; that, schooled by Cadmus, she was fathering on Zeus her own sinful passion. That was why Zeus killed her, they vaunted aloud; because she had lied about her lover. These same sisters, therefore, I have driven in mad frenzy from their homes; they are living in the mountain, out of their minds. I have made them wear the habit of my orgies. And all the womenfolk of Thebes, every woman in the city, I have driven from home distraught, to join the daughters of Cadmus; together they sit beneath the silver firs, on the open rocks. This city must learn, whether it likes it or not, that it still wants initiation into my Bacchic rites. The cause of my mother Semele I must defend by proving to mortals that I *am* a god, borne by her to Zeus.

Now Cadmus has bestowed the kingship and its rights upon his grandson Pentheus, who opposes my worship. He thrusts me away from his offerings, and in his prayers nowhere makes mention of me. Therefore I mean to reveal myself to him and to all the Thebans as a god indeed. When I have settled things here to my satisfaction I shall direct my steps to another land and manifest myself. If the city of the Thebans becomes enraged and tries to drive the bacchants from the mountain by force of arms, I shall lead my Maenads into battle against them. That is why I have assumed this mortal form, changing myself to look like a natural man.

Ho, women that have come from Tmolus, Lydia's bulwark, my own revel band! I have brought you from among barbarians to be my companions, wherever I stay, wherever I go. Raise the native music of your Phrygian homeland, the timbrels which mother Rhea and I invented. Come to this royal palace of Pentheus, sound them loud, for the whole city to come and see. I shall go to the glens of Cithaeron where the bacchants are, and there I shall join in their dances.

*[Exit Dionysus before the Chorus enters bearing thyrsi and timbrels*

CHORUS *[The mark at the beginning of a line indicates a change of speaker].* From the land of Asia I come, leaving sacred Tmolus behind me. In Bromius' honor I eagerly ply my pleasant task, my toil of ease, crying glory to the Bacchic god.

—Is any profane man in the street? Is any within? Let him withdraw. Hushed be every lip to holy silence. Ever shall I hymn Dionysus in the old, old way.

—Ah, blessed is he whom the gods love, who understands the secret rites of the gods, whose life is consecrated, whose very soul dances with holy joy. In the mountains he knows the bacchic thrill, the holy purifications; he observes the orgies of Cybele, the Great Mother; he brandishes the thyrsus on high, and crowns himself with ivy in the service of Dionysus.

—On ye bacchants, on ye bacchants; bring home Bromius the god, the son of the god, bring Dionysus from the Phrygian mountains, bring Bromius to the open squares of Hellas, spacious for dances.

—Him on a time his pregnant mother with painful travail brought forth, blasted from her womb by the flying thunderbolt of Zeus. In the stroke of the lightning she lost her own life, but straightway, in the very chamber where the mother lay, Cronian Zeus received him and concealed him in his thigh, fastening him in with golden buckles, hidden from Hera.

And when the fates had formed the babe perfect, the father brought forth the bull-horned god; and he wreathed him with the coils of serpents. That is why the Maenads catch wild serpents to twine in their hair.

—O Thebes, Semele's nurse, crown yourself with ivy, burgeon forth, burgeon forth with verdant smilax with its bright berries. Make yourself a very bacchant with branches of oak or fir. On with the fawn-skins, dapple the hems with fleecy tufts of silvery goat's hair. Riot with the fennel-stalk, but devoutly. Soon all the land will dance—he is Bromius, whoever leads the revel-band—dance off to the mountains, to the mountains where the throng of women await, driven from loom and shuttle by the frenzy of Dionysus.

—O chamber of the Curetes, O holy haunts of Crete, which saw the birth of Zeus! In your caves the corybants,

with helmets of triple rim, contrived this my timbrel's circle
of stretched hide. For our fierce bacchic-revelry they blended
its note with the sweet voice of the Phrygian flute, and they
placed it in the hand of Mother Rhea. To its booming the
bacchants would one day utter their revel-shouts. For from
the divine Mother the raving satyrs appropriated it and wedded
it to the dances of the biennial festivals in which Dionysus
delights.

—My love is in the mountains. He sinks to the ground
from the racing revel-band. He wears the holy habit of fawn-
skin; he hunts the goat and kills it and delights in the raw
flesh. He rushes to the mountains of Phrygia, of Lydia. He
is Bromius, the leader of our dance. Evoe! The ground
flows with milk, flows with wine, flows with the nectar of
bees. Fragrant as Syrian frankincense is the fume of the
pine-torch which our bacchic leader holds aloft. Its ruddy
flame shoots from the end of the fennel-stalk as he runs
and dances, his delicate tresses streaming in the air, as he
rouses the scattered band and shouts them to their feet.
"Evoe" he cries, then loudly: "On, ye bacchants, on bright
glory of Tmolus and its golden streams, hymn Dionysus to
the deep booming of the timbrels; in bacchic fashion, with
Phrygian cries and call, glorify the bacchic god, while the
flute, sweet-toned and holy, plays happy anthems for the
wild bands trooping to the mountains, to the mountains".
Then indeed the bacchant maid rejoices and gambols, light-
footed, like a foal by its mother's side in the pasture.

[Enter Tiresias.]

TIRESIAS. Who is at the gate? Call Cadmus from the
house, Agenor's son, who left the Sidonian city and built the
towers of this Theban town.

Go someone, tell him that Tiresias is seeking him. He
knows himself why I have come. He knows the arrangement
I have made, with a man even older than myself, to dress
the thyrsus and put on skins of fawns and wreathe our heads
with shoots of ivy.

[Enter Cadmus.]

CADMUS. Ah, my wise old friend!—I knew it was you
the moment I heard your wise old voice. Here I am, all ready,
in this livery of the god. For he is my own daughter's child
[this Dionysus who has proved his godhead to men]; and

we must do all we can to glorify his might. Where do we dance? Where do we plant our feet and toss our old, grey heads? Expound it to me, Tiresias, as one old man to another. You are the expert, I shall never weary, night or day, beating the earth with the thyrsus. In my happiness I have forgotten how old I am.

TIRESIAS. Then you feel as I do. I, too, feel young again. I, too, shall attempt the dance.

CADMUS. Well then, shall we get a carriage to carry us to the mountain?

TIRESIAS. That would not be the same tribute to the god.

CADMUS. My aged arm, then, will guide your aged feet.

TIRESIAS. The god will lead us there with no trouble.

CADMUS. Shall we be the only ones in the city to dance for Bacchus?

TIRESIAS. We alone are right. The others are wrong.

CADMUS. We delay too long. Take hold of my hand.

TIRESIAS. There you are, clasp hands, link yours with mine.

CADMUS. I am a mere mortal. I do not feel superior to the gods.

TIRESIAS. We do not rationalize about the gods. We have the traditions of our fathers, old as time itself. No argument can knock *them* down, however clever the sophistry, however keen the wit. People may say that I have no shame, at *my* age, going dancing and binding my head with ivy. Let them. The god has not specified that only the young must dance or only the old. He is pleased to receive honor from all alike. He wishes to be extolled; he does not count up a person's years.

CADMUS. Since you cannot see, Tiresias, I shall speak for you. Here is Pentheus hurrying towards the house, Echion's son, to whom I gave the rule of this land. How excited he is! What news will he tell?

*[Enter Pentheus.]*

PENTHEUS. I happened to be out of the country, but a tale of strange mischief in the city here has brought me back. Our women have left home, they tell me, in sham ecstasies. They are frisking about on the shadowy hills, honoring with dances this new-fashioned divinity, this Dionysus of theirs. In the midst of each rowdy group a brimming wine-bowl stands. Then they slink off separately to lonely corners to serve the beds of men. Of course they pretend they are priestesses, inspired priestesses; but they make more of Aphrodite than of Bacchus.

I have caught a number of them. Jailers have them safely manacled in the public prison. Those that are missing I'll chase off the mountain [—Ino and Agave, who bore me to Echion, and Autonoe, the mother of Actaeon]. I'll catch them in iron traps and put a quick stop to this immoral revelry.

They say that a stranger has arrived, a wizard, a sorcerer from Lydia, with fragrant golden curls and ruddy face and spells of love in his eyes. He spends his days and nights in the company of young women, pretending to initiate them in the bacchic mysteries. If I catch him in this house I'll stop him from beating his thyrsus and tossing his curls. I'll cut his neck from his body.

It is he that says Dionysus is a god (yes, *he* says so) and was once sewn up in the thigh of Zeus—the child that was burnt up by the flaming thunderbolt along with his mother, because she falsely named Zeus as her lover. Is it not enough to make a man hang himself in agony—this insolent effrontery, this mysterious stranger?

But look! Here's a new phenomenon. The seer Tiresias in dappled fawn-skins! And my own grandfather—how ridiculous—playing the bacchant with a fennel wand! Sir, this is not my mother's father. So old and so foolish! Please throw that ivy away. Let go that thyrsus, rid your hand of it.

This is *your* instigation, Tiresias. This is another device of yours to make money out of your bird-gazing and burnt sacrifices—introducing a *new* god to men. It is only your grey hairs that save you from sitting in chains among the bacchants for introducing these unholy rites. When the sparkle of wine finds a place at women's feasts, there is something rotten about such celebrations, I tell you.

LEADER. What blasphemy! Stranger, have you no respect for the gods, no respect for Cadmus who sowed the crop of dragon's teeth? Will the son of Echion disgrace his family?

TIRESIAS. Give a clever man a good theme to talk on, and it is easy enough to speak well. Your tongue, indeed, runs smoothly, as if you had wit, but there is no wit in what you say. The man whose strength is his impudence, whose ability is all in his tongue, makes a bad citizen—and a stupid one.

This new divinity whom you ridicule—words cannot describe how great will be his power throughout Hellas. Mankind, young man, has two chief blessings: goddess De-

meter—the earth, that is; call her whichever name you will
—who sustains men with solid food, and this son of Semele,
who came later and matched her gift. He invented the liquid
draught of the grape and introduced it to mortals. When they
get their fill of the flowing grape, it stops their grief. It gives
them sleep and forgetfulness of daily sorrows. There is no
other medicine for trouble. The libations we pour are the
god himself making *our* peace with the gods, so that through
him mankind may obtain blessings.

You sneer at the story that he was stitched inside the thigh
of Zeus. I will teach you the true interpretation of that. When
Zeus snatched him from the thunderbolt's flame and brought
the infant god to Olympus, Hera wanted to cast him out of
heaven. But Zeus contrived a counter device, as a god might.
He broke off a piece of the earth-enveloping sky and gave
jealous Hera an *incorporeal* Dionysus. But in time mortals
got the word changed and said the child had been *in-
corporated* in Zeus. So they made up the story that he had
been stitched inside the thigh of the god.

He is a prophetic god. Those whom his spirit fills, like people possessed, have no small prophetic power. Whenever the
god enters the body in full strength, he takes possession of
men and makes them tell the future. He also has taken
over a part of Ares' functions. A host under arms, ay already
drawn up in line, is often scattered in *panic* before raising a
spear. This also is a sort of madness sent by Dionysus (and
his follower *Pan*). A time will come when you will see him
even on Delphi's rock, bounding over the double peak of
Parnassus with his pine-torches, brandishing and tossing his
bacchic wand. He shall be great throughout Hellas. Listen to
*me*, Pentheus. Do not presume that mere power has influence with men. Do not be wise in your own diseased imagination. Welcome the god to the land, pour libations, wreathe
your head, revel.

Not even Dionysus can compel women to be chaste. For
that you must look to the women's own nature [for a chastity proof against all shocks]. Even in bacchic revels the
good woman, at least, will not be corrupted.

You see, *you* take pleasure when a multitude stands at your
gates and the city magnifies the name of Pentheus. He, too,
I judge, takes delight in being honored. I then, and Cadmus,
whom you laugh at, shall crown ourselves with ivy and dance.
A hoary old pair, but dance we must. I shall not be persuaded by your logic to combat gods. You are mad, most

distressingly mad. No spells can cure a disease which is itself a spell.

LEADER. Old man, your words do honor to Phoebus and you are wise in honoring Bromius; he is a mighty god.

CADMUS. My boy, Tiresias has advised you well. Dwell with us, do not break with our old ways. You are flighty at the moment. Your wisdom is unwise. Even if this is no god, as you say, pretend to yourself that he is. It is a most honorable falsehood. It makes Semele seem to be the mother of a god and it will redound to the credit of our whole family.

You are familiar with the sorry fate of Actaeon. The flesh-devouring dogs that he himself had raised tore him to pieces in the fields because he boasted that he was better at the hunt than Artemis. Don't let anything like that happen to you. Come, let me crown your head with ivy. Join us in honoring the god.

PENTHEUS. Do not lay your hand upon me. Go play the bacchant. Do not wipe off your folly on me! This teacher of your foolishness will get what he deserves. Let someone go with all speed—go to this man's seat where he examines his birds. Heave it up with crowbars, turn it upside down. Make a general havoc of the whole place. Throw his fillets to the winds and storms. That will gall him more than anything.

Let others of you scour the city and track out this foreign epicene who has brought this strange madness upon the women and is defiling our beds. If you catch him bring him here in chains to die the death he deserves—by stoning. He will live to rue his revelry in Thebes.

*[Exit Pentheus.]*

TIRESIAS. Poor wretch, how little you know what you are saying. Now you are really mad. You did go off your head once before.

Let us go, Cadmus, and entreat the god, on this man's behalf, savage though he is, and for the city's sake, to bring no evil to pass. Come, follow me with your ivy staff. Try to hold my body up, as I do yours. It would be disgraceful for two old men to fall. However, never mind. We must serve Bacchus, son of Zeus. But beware, Cadmus, lest Pentheus bring into your house his namesake Penthos—Sorrow. That is no prophecy, but plain fact. A fool speaks folly.

*[The two old men totter off.]*

CHORUS. *Holiness, Holiness, queen of Heaven, as you turn your golden wings earthwards, do you hear these words of Pentheus? Do you hear this unholy defiance of Bromius, Semele's son, the god of lovely garlands and good cheer, the prince of the Blessed Ones? This is his realm: revelry and dancing, flute-playing and laughter and the banishing of care, whether the presence of the grape brightens the banquets of the gods, or on earth the wine bowl casts the mantle of sleep around the ivy-wreathed merrymakers.*

*Of unbridled lips and lawless folly the only end is disaster; but the quiet life of wisdom abides unshaken and sustains the home. For though they dwell remote in the sky, the sons of heaven regard the affairs of men. Knowledge is not wisdom. Thoughts too long make life short. If man, in his brief moment, goes after things too great for him, he may lose the joys within his reach. To my mind, that is the way of madness and perversity.*

*Oh that I might come to Cyprus, Aphrodite's isle, where dwell the Loves that soothe the hearts of men; to Paphos where the hundred-mouthed streams of the barbarian river bring fruits without rain. Where stands Pieria, queen of beauty, seat of the Muses, where the holy hill of Olympus stands—thither take me, Bromius, divine Bromius, leading your bacchic rout. There the Graces dwell, there dwells Desire, there it is lawful for the bacchants to celebrate their orgies.*

*The deity, Zeus' son, rejoices in festivals. He loves goddess Peace, who brings prosperity and cherishes youth. To rich and poor he gives in equal measure the blessed joy of wine. But he hates the man who has no taste for such things— to live a life of happy days and sweet and happy nights, in wisdom to keep his mind and heart aloof from over-busy men. Whatever the majority, the simple folk, believe and follow, that way I will accept.*

[*Pentheus enters and is met by a Servant, leading attendants with the Lydian Stranger, bound.*]

SERVANT. Pentheus, here we are. We have caught the prey you sent us to catch; our expedition was not in vain. Our quarry—here he is—is a tame creature. He did not take cover or run away. No pallor of fear chased the blood from his cheek. Of his own free will he surrendered. He even smiled as he consented to be arrested and bound. He waited for me to do my duty—he even helped me. I was touched and said to him: "Stranger, not of my will do I take you, but by the orders of Pentheus who sent me".

On the other hand, those bacchants you caught and shut up in the public jail are gone. They slipped the bonds that bound them and gambolled off to the meadows, calling upon Bromius as their god. The fetters of their feet burst asunder of their own accord, and the gates were unbarred by no human hand. This man who has come to our Thebes is full of miracles. The rest is your affair.

PENTHEUS. Free this man's hands. Trapped as he is, he cannot have the speed to escape me.

Well! You are quite handsome, stranger, for women's taste —and that is what brings you to Thebes. Your hair is long —apparently you never wrestle. It flows over your cheeks, full of appeal. And your complexion is so clear, studiously so. The sun never gets at it; it is in the shade you go hunting, hunting Aphrodite with your beauty. Tell me first who you are, of what race?

THE STRANGER. There is nothing to boast of, it is easy to tell. You have doubtless heard of flowery Tmolus.

PENTHEUS. I know. The circle of its hills surrounds the city of Sardis.

THE STRANGER. I am from there, Lydia is my country.

PENTHEUS. How come you to bring these rites to Hellas?

THE STRANGER. Dionysus initiated me, Zeus' son.

PENTHEUS. Is there a Zeus over there who begets new gods?

THE STRANGER. No, he is the same Zeus who joined in wedlock here with Semele.

PENTHEUS. Was it in a dream, or face to face, that he pressed you into his service?

THE STRANGER. He saw me and I saw him. For proof he gave me sacred rites.

PENTHEUS. These orgies of yours, what form do they take?

THE STRANGER. It is unlawful for profane mortals to know them.

PENTHEUS. What profit do they afford to the votaries?

THE STRANGER. It is not right for you to hear, but they are worth knowing.

PENTHEUS. You gild the tale well, to make me curious.

THE STRANGER. The god's orgies loathe the man who practises impiety.

PENTHEUS. You say you saw the god clearly. What like was he?

THE STRANGER. What like he pleased; it was not for me to dictate.

PENTHEUS. Again you side-step nimbly, and avoid the point.

THE STRANGER. Talk wisdom to the stupid and they will think *you* foolish.

PENTHEUS. And is this the first place to which you bring your god?

THE STRANGER. All the barbarians celebrate his rites and dances.

PENTHEUS. They have far less sense than Hellenes.

THE STRANGER. In this, at least, they have more. Customs differ.

PENTHEUS. These rites—do you perform them at night or by day?

THE STRANGER. At night, for the most part; darkness gives solemnity.

PENTHEUS. It betrays women and undermines their morals.

THE STRANGER. By day, too, shameful things may be contrived.

PENTHEUS. You ought to be punished for your vile sophistries.

THE STRANGER. And you for your coarse blasphemies against the god.

PENTHEUS. How bold our bacchant, a pretty fencer—with words!

THE STRANGER. Tell me my fate. What is the awful thing you are going to do to me?

PENTHEUS. First I will cut off your pretty curls.

THE STRANGER. I dedicate them to the god. It is for him I keep them.

PENTHEUS. Next hand over this thyrsus.

THE STRANGER. Take it from me yourself. It is Dionysus' thyrsus I carry.

PENTHEUS. And I will shut you up safe in prison.

THE STRANGER. The god himself will free me, whenever I desire.

PENTHEUS. Perhaps so, when you stand among your bacchants and call upon him.

THE STRANGER. Even now he is near and sees what I undergo.

PENTHEUS. Then where is he? He is not apparent to *my* eyes.

THE STRANGER. He is with me, but your impiety will not let you see him.

PENTHEUS [*to guards*]. Seize him. The fellow mocks me and Thebes.

THE STRANGER. I give you sober warning: do not bind me, you fools.

PENTHEUS. But I have more authority than you. I say 'Bind'.

THE STRANGER. You do not know your station. You do not realize what you are doing. You forget who you are.

PENTHEUS. I am Pentheus, Agave's son and Echion's.

THE STRANGER. An apt name to be unlucky in.

PENTHEUS. Begone! Imprison him near the palace, in the horses' stables. Let him see glooms and darkness. Dance away *there*. These women here, whom you have brought with you, your accomplices in mischief, I shall either sell off, or keep them at the loom as my slaves. That will stop their hands from this thudding and beating of hides.

THE STRANGER. I shall go. I can but fulfil my destiny. But remember: Dionysus, whom you deny, will exact full payment for this outrage. When you assault me you are putting *him* in bonds.

[*Exeunt Pentheus and the Stranger, guarded.*]

CHORUS. *Daughter of Achelous, holy Dirce, blessed maiden! Once you received Zeus' babe in your fountains, when Zeus that begot him snatched him from the undying flame and placed him in his thigh and called aloud: "Come, Dithyrambus, enter this my male womb. By this name, my Bacchus, I proclaim you to Thebes, that they may so call you." And yet, blessed Dirce, you thrust me away when I hold my begarlanded revels in your land. Why do you disown me? Why do you avoid me? The time will come, I swear by the lovely clusters of Dionysus' vine, the time will come when you too shall take thought of Bromius.*

[*What passion, what passion.*] *Pentheus publishes abroad his earth-born lineage, his descent from the Dragon of old, Pentheus earth-born Echion's son. A savage monster he is; no mortal man he, but a bloody earth-born giant battling the gods. Soon he will throw chains upon me, who belong to Bromius. Already he holds my fellow-reveller within his house, hidden away in a dark prison. Do you see these things,*

*Dionysus, son of Zeus? Do you see your prophets amid trials
and tribulations? Come, king, come down Olympus, brandishing your golden thyrsus. Quell the presumption of this
bloody man.*

*Where, I wonder, on Nysa, the lair of wild beasts, are you
holding your revels, thyrsus in hand? Or are you upon the
Corycian peaks? Or perhaps you are on Olympus, embowered
in thick forests, where once upon a time the music of the
harp of Orpheus marshalled the trees to him, marshalled the
beasts of the wildwood. You are blessed, Pieria; Evius rever-
ences you and will come to hold his revels upon you with
bacchic dances. He will cross the racing stream of Axius. He
will lead his whirling maenads over Lydias, father of waters,
the giver of wealth and blessing to man. Loveliest of waters
are his streams, they tell me, enriching a land of noble
horses.*

      *[There is a roar of thunder. Lightning flashes over the
         tomb of Semele. The earth trembles. The Chorus
         dashes about shrieking. Then a voice is heard.]*

VOICE [*within*]. *Ho, hear me, hear my voice! Ho, bacchants,
Ho, bacchants!*

SOME OF CHORUS. *What cry, what cry is that? Whence
came the call, the bacchic call, to summon me?*

VOICE [*within*]. *Ho! ho! Again I call. Semele's child,
the son of Zeus.*

OTHERS. *Ho! ho! our lord, our lord! Come to our revel
rout, O Bromius, Bromius.*

VOICE [*within*]. *Shake the earth's floor, awful Earthquake.*

SOME OF CHORUS. *Aha! aha! Soon the house of Pentheus
will be shaken to ruins.*

OTHERS. *Dionysus is in the palace! Adore him!*

OTHERS. *O, we adore him!*

OTHERS. *Did you mark how the stone capitals yonder on
the pillars parted asunder? Bromius chants his own triumph
within the halls.*

VOICE [*within*]. *Kindle the thunderbolt's lurid torch.
Burn, burn down, the palace of Pentheus.*

      *[Lightning blazes over the palace and the monument
        of Semele.]*

SOME OF CHORUS. *Aha! aha! Look, see Semele's holy tomb.*
*How it blazes! It is the flame the thunder-god left there*
*long ago, the flame of Zeus' thunderbolt. Hurl to the*
*ground your shuddering limbs, Maenads. Our king comes,*
*the son of Zeus, confounding utterly these halls.*

[*Enter the stranger.*]

THE STRANGER. Foreign women, are you so astounded
with fear that you have fallen to the ground? You have
perceived, it seems, how Bacchus shook the house of
Pentheus. But raise yourselves and take courage. Still your
shuddering limbs.

LEADER. O brightest light of our bacchant revel, how glad
I am to see you. We were alone, forsaken

THE STRANGER. Did you despair when they led me in
and were about to hurl me into Pentheus' dark dungeons?

LEADER. Despair indeed. Who was there to be my protector
if any mischance were to befall you? But how did you
escape from the clutches of that godless man?

THE STRANGER. With effortless ease I saved myself un-
aided.

LEADER. Did he not bind your hands with chains and fetters?

THE STRANGER. There too I mocked him. He thought he
was binding me but he never so much as laid a finger on me.
He fed on fancy. In the stable where he took me to imprison
me he found a bull, and he threw his nooses around its knees
and the hooves of its feet. He panted furiously and dripped
sweat from his body and dug his teeth into his lips. There
I was, sitting nearby at my ease and looking on. At this
moment Bacchus came and shook the building and kindled a
fire on his mother's tomb. Seeing the glare, Pentheus thought
the place was on fire and rushed back and forth ordering the
servants to bring buckets of water. Every slave was busy at
the task, but they had their trouble for nothing. Then he
thought I had escaped. So he suspended these labors and
rushed into the house with his dark sword drawn. But Bromius, as it seems to me—I give you my conjecture—created a
phantom in the court. Pentheus attacked it with a rush
and stabbed at the bright ether as if he were butchering
me. Besides this, Bacchus brings these other afflictions on
him: the prison he razed to the ground, everything lies in
ruin. Most bitterly he must rue my imprisonment. Fatigue

has made him drop his sword, and he lies exhausted. A mere
man, he had the effrontery to join battle with a god. I slipped
quietly out of the house and have come to you. I care
nothing for Pentheus.

It seems to me—a boot is clattering in the house—he will
soon come to the front. What will he say after this? Let him
come in all his bluster; I shall bear it easily. A modest nonchalance—that is the mark of wisdom.

[*Enter Pentheus.*]

PENTHEUS. This is an outrage. The stranger has escaped,
the one that was lately bound fast with chains. Ha! Here is
the man! What is this? How is it you appear in front of my
house? How did you come out?

THE STRANGER. Stay your foot! Teach your anger to walk
quietly.

PENTHEUS. How did you escape from your chains and
get out here?

THE STRANGER. Did I not say—or did you not hear me—
that someone would free me?

PENTHEUS. Who? With you it is one strange saying after
another.

THE STRANGER. He who raises the clustering vine for man.

PENTHEUS. [A sorry gift—to make men forget themselves.]

THE STRANGER. What you sneer at does him honor.

PENTHEUS. I will have every gate in the walls barred.

THE STRANGER. Why? Can gods not overleap your walls?

PENTHEUS. Clever you are, very clever—but not clever
enough.

THE STRANGER. In the most important thing I am clever
enough. But first hear and mark the words of this man who
is coming from the mountain with some message for you. I
shall await your pleasure, I shall not flee.

[*Enter Herdsman.*]

HERDSMAN. Pentheus, ruler of this Theban land, I come
from Cithaeron, where . . . [the bright flakes of white snow
never cease].

PENTHEUS [*interrupting*]. What tidings do you bring in
such haste?

HERDSMAN. I have seen the raving bacchants, who rushed
barefooted from their homes in frenzy. I am here all eager to
tell you and the city, king, the fearsome things they do,

things surpassing wonder. Am I to speak of these events freely or abridge my story? I want you to say, O king. I am afraid of your hasty temper, so passionate, so imperious.

PENTHEUS. Speak on. You are quite safe from punishment on my part. To grow angry with just men is not right. The more awful your story about the bacchants, the greater the punishment I shall inflict upon this man who taught the women these arts.

HERDSMAN. Our herds of pasturing kine had just begun to ascend the steep to the ridge, at the hour when the sun shoots forth his rays to warm the earth. I saw three bands of women dancers; Autonoe was leader of the first choir, your mother Agave of the second, and Ino of the third. They all lay in the sleep of exhaustion. Some were reclining with their backs against branches of fir, others had flung themselves at random on the ground on leaves of oak [modestly, not, as you charge, intoxicated with the wine-bowl and the sound of the flute and hunting Cypris in the lonely forest].

Then your mother rose up in the midst of the bacchants and called upon them to bestir their limbs from sleep when she heard the lowing of the horned kine. The women then cast the heavy sleep from their eyes and sprang upright, a sight of wondrous comeliness. There were young women and old women and maids yet unmarried. First they let their hair fly loose about their shoulders and tucked up their fawnskins, those whose fastenings had become unloosed, and girt the speckled skins about them with serpents that licked their cheek. Others held gazelles in their arms, or the untamed whelps of wolves, feeding them with white milk. These were young mothers who had left their infants behind and still had their breasts swollen with milk. Then they put on ivy wreaths and crowns of oak and flowery smilax. One took her thyrsus and struck it against a rock, and there sprang from it a dewy stream of water. Another struck her fennel wand upon the ground, and the god sent up a fountain of wine for her. Those that had a desire for the white drink scraped the earth with the tips of their fingers, and had rich store of milk. From the wands of ivy there dripped sweet streams of honey. If you had been there to see, you would have approached with prayers the god whom you now revile.

We cowherds and shepherds came together to argue and debate with one another on the fearful and wonderful things they did. One fellow who was fond of loafing about town, an experienced talker, spoke out to all and sundry:

"You who dwell upon the holy terraces of the mountains, do you vote that we chase Pentheus' mother, Agave, from her bacchic revels and do our king a kindness?" He seemed to us to speak well, and so we set an ambush amidst the leafy thickets and hid ourselves. At the set time they waved the thyrsus for their revelling and all together, with one voice, invoked Bacchus, Zeus' offspring Bromius. The whole mountain cried "Bacchus" with them. The animals joined in the revelry. Everywhere there was a stirring as they raced along.

Now Agave happened to come racing by me and I jumped out and made to seize her, evacuating the ambush where I was hiding. But she raised a cry: "Ah, my fleet hounds, we are being hunted by these men! But follow me, follow with your wands in your hands for weapons."

We fled and escaped a rending at the bacchants' hands. But, with naked, unarmed, hands, the women attacked the heifers that were grazing on the grass. You could see one holding wide the legs of a well-fed calf which bellowed and bellowed. Others rent heifers apart. You could see ribs or cloven hooves tossed here and there, and pieces smeared with gore hanging from the firs, dripping blood. The wanton bulls—forgotten the menace of their levelled horns—were tripped and dragged to the ground by the hands of countless young women. Quicker were their coverings of flesh torn asunder than you could close the lids of your royal eyes. Like birds they soared off the ground in their flight as they scoured the spreading plains by the streams of Asopus which grow the fine harvests of Thebes. Like an invading army they fell upon Hysiae and Erythrae, which nestle under Cithaeron's slopes, and everywhere they wrought confusion and havoc. They pillaged homes at random. Their loot they put upon their shoulders, and though it was not tied on, it held fast; nothing fell to the dark earth, neither brass nor iron. They carried fire in their curls and it did not burn them. Some of us, angered by the depradations of the bacchants, resorted to arms. And *there* was a terrible sight to see, O king. Pointed spears drew no blood, whereas the women flung wands from their hands and wounded their assailants till they turned tail and ran. Women defeating men! There was a god with them. Then they went back whence they had started, to the fountains which the god had shot up for them. They washed off the blood, while the serpents licked clean the clots from their cheeks.

This deity then, whoever he is, O king, receive into the

city. In many things he is powerful. This also they say of him,
I hear, that he gave mortals the wine which ends sorrow. If *he*
exists not, then neither does Cypris, nor any other joy for
men at all.

[LEADER.] I am fearful of speaking out freely to one
who is my master, but I shall have my say: there is no god
greater than Dionysus.

*[Exit Herdsman.]*

PENTHEUS. This brings it close, like a spreading fire—
this bacchic menace. We are disgraced in the eyes of Hellas.
There must be no delay. Go to the Electran gates; order all
the hoplites and all the riders of swift horses to muster, all
those who brandish targes and those whose hands twang the
bow-string. We shall march against the bacchants. This is
truly going too far—to be treated like this at the hands of
women.

THE STRANGER. My words, no doubt, will fail to persuade
you, Pentheus; but despite the wrong you have done me
I advise you not to take up arms against a god. Keep calm.
Bromius will not allow you to drive his bacchants from
their hills of revelry.

PENTHEUS. Do not lecture me. You have escaped from
bonds; keep that in mind. Or shall I call back justice upon
you?

THE STRANGER. If I were you, I would sacrifice to him
rather than rage and kick against the pricks—a man against
a god.

PENTHEUS. I shall sacrifice indeed—these women. I shall
make great and deserved slaughter in the glens of Cithaeron.

THE STRANGER. You will all be put to flight. And that will
be a disgrace—when they with their bacchic wands turn back
your brazen shields.

PENTHEUS. There's no dealing with this stranger we are at
grips with. Both going and coming he will have his say.

THE STRANGER. Friend, it is still possible to mend the
situation.

PENTHEUS. By doing what? Being a slave to my own
slaves?

THE STRANGER. I shall bring the women here without
using weapons.

PENTHEUS. Ah me, this is a cunning plot against me.

THE STRANGER. How a plot, if I want to *save* you by my
devices?

PENTHEUS. You are in conspiracy with them, to establish your revels for all time.

THE STRANGER. In conspiracy indeed—that is true—but with the god.

PENTHEUS [to Servants]. Bring me my armor here. [To the Stranger.] And you stop your talk!

THE STRANGER [after thought]. Ah! Would you like to see them in their gatherings upon the mountain?

PENTHEUS. Very much. Ay, and pay uncounted gold for the pleasure.

THE STRANGER. Why have you conceived so strong a desire?

PENTHEUS. Though it would pain me to see them drunk with wine——

THE STRANGER. Yet you would like to see them, pain and all.

PENTHEUS. Be sure I would, if I could sit quietly under the firs.

THE STRANGER. But they will track you out, even if you come unseen.

PENTHEUS. Then it shall be openly; your point is quite right.

THE STRANGER. Do we go then? Will you undertake the journey?

PENTHEUS. Lead me with all speed. I grudge you every minute.

THE STRANGER. Put upon your body clothes of fine linen.

PENTHEUS. Why so? Am I, a man, to enroll in the other sex?

THE STRANGER. They may kill you, if you are seen there as a man.

PENTHEUS. Again your point is quite right. You are something of a veteran in guile.

THE STRANGER. It was Dionysus taught me this lore.

PENTHEUS. How then shall your advice be properly carried out?

THE STRANGER. I shall come inside and dress you.

PENTHEUS. What sort of dress? A woman's? I am ashamed.

THE STRANGER. You are no longer eager to see the spectacle of maenads.

PENTHEUS. What dress will you put on my body?

THE STRANGER. I shall spread your hair out long over your head.

PENTHEUS. What is the next item in my outfit?

THE STRANGER. Robes that reach to the feet, and on your head a snood.

PENTHEUS. Is there anything else you want to add?

THE STRANGER. A thyrsus for your hand, and the dappled skin of a fawn.

PENTHEUS. I could not possibly put on a woman's dress.

THE STRANGER. Then you will have to fight the bacchants and cause bloodshed.

PENTHEUS. Right. We must first go and reconnoitre.

THE STRANGER. If you *will* seek evil ends, it is at least wise to eschew evil means.

PENTHEUS. But how can I go through the city unseen by the citizens?

THE STRANGER. We will go by deserted ways. I will lead you.

PENTHEUS. Anything is better than to have the bacchants jeer at me. Let us go inside—I shall consider what is best.

THE STRANGER. By all means. In any event, *I* am prepared.

PENTHEUS. I will come. I shall either go under arms or take your advice.

[*Exit Pentheus into palace.*]

THE STRANGER. Women, our fish is ready for the strike. He will go to the bacchants and there he will forfeit his life.

Dionysus, the task is now yours. You are not far off. Let us punish this man. First drive him from his wits, make him a little mad. If he is in his right mind, there is no chance of his ever consenting to put on a woman's dress. But if he is driven out of his mind he will put it on. After those truculent threats of his, I want him to become a laughing-stock to the Thebans as he is led through the city looking like a woman. I shall go and dress Pentheus in the apparel which he will take with him to Hades, slaughtered by his mother's hands. He shall come to know Dionysus, son of Zeus, who is every bit a god, terrible in power, but to mankind most gentle.

[*Exit into palace.*]

CHORUS. *Shall I ever again in the night-long dances plant my white foot in bacchic revelry, tossing back my head in the dewy air, like a sportive fawn rejoicing in green pastures, delivered from the terror of the chase, from the watching eyes and the well-meshed nets, from the huntsman cheering on his eager, racing pack? Sorely pressed, she flies over the river-flats, swift as a storm-wind, and re-joices in the leafy shade of forest trees, in solitudes un-broken by man.*

*What is wisdom? What boon from the gods is fairer among men than to hold a victorious hand over the head of one's enemies? What is fair is ever dear.*

*Slowly, yet surely withal, the power divine advances. It chastises those mortals who honor brutality, who in mad delusion do not give glory to the gods. The gods are cunning: they lie in wait a long march of time to trap the impious. Above the established doctrines neither knowledge nor practice should seek to go. It costs but little to believe in the power and mystery of the gods, to accept what is grounded in nature and accepted by the usage of long ages.*

*What is wisdom? What boon from the gods is fairer among men than to hold a victorious hand over the head of one's enemies? What is fair is ever dear.*

*Happy is he who has escaped the tempest at sea and found harbor. Happy is he who has risen triumphant over his toils. In one way or another one man outstrips another in the race for wealth and power. And a thousand others are cherishing a thousand hopes; some result in happiness for mortals and some fail. But I call blessed the man whose life is happy day by day.*

*[The Stranger enters and calls upon Pentheus, whom he has been dressing, to come out.]*

THE STRANGER. Pentheus! If you are so eager to pry into secret things, so bent on evil, come out in front of the house; let us see how you look dressed like a woman, a bacchic maenad, off to spy on your mother and her company.

*[Enter Pentheus in bacchic attire; he moves and speaks as if under some strange influence.]*

You *do* look like one of Cadmus' daughters.

PENTHEUS. I seem to see two suns, and a double Thebes, ay, two seven-gated cities. And a bull is leading me on—you seem to be a bull, with horns growing on your head. *Were* you ever an animal? Certainly you have the look of a bull.

THE STRANGER. The god is our escort. He was hostile before, but now he has made his peace with us. Now you see as you should.

PENTHEUS. What *do* I look like? Have I not the pose of Ino? Or Agave, yes, my own mother Agave?

THE STRANGER. When I look at you I seem to see their very selves. But here's one of your tresses out of place. It is not as I fixed it, under your snood.

PENTHEUS. I must have dislodged it inside, while I was tossing my locks up and down in bacchic ecstasy.

THE STRANGER. I will arrange it again, I am your maid. Come, hold your head up.

PENTHEUS. There, you dress it. I depend on you.

THE STRANGER. Your girdle has come undone. And the tucks of your dress are all uneven at the ankles.

PENTHEUS. I think so too, at least by the right foot. The rest hangs straight enough, by the left.

THE STRANGER. I am sure you will think me your best friend when I surprise you and show you the bacchants sober.

PENTHEUS. Do I hold the thyrsus in my right hand or in this one to be more like a bacchant?

THE STRANGER. Hold it in your right hand, and advance it when you advance your right foot. I am glad your mind is changed.

PENTHEUS. Do you think I could carry the crags of Cithaeron, bacchants and all, upon my shoulders?

THE STRANGER. You could, if you wished. The mind you had before was not sound, but now you are in a proper state.

PENTHEUS. Shall we take crowbars? Or shall I tear the crags up with my hands, putting a shoulder or an arm to the peaks?

THE STRANGER. O please! Don't destroy the shrines of the Nymphs and the haunts of Pan and his pipings.

PENTHEUS. Right you are. One does not overcome women by force. I shall conceal myself in the firs.

THE STRANGER. You will get all the concealment I think you need—creeping up to spy on the maenads.

PENTHEUS. Besides, I expect they won't leave their couches in the thickets, caught like birds—and loving it.

THE STRANGER. That is the very thing you are going to watch. Perhaps you will surprise them—if you are not surprised first yourself.

PENTHEUS. Take me through the middle of Thebes. I am the only man of them that would make this venture.

THE STRANGER. You are the only one that troubles about

your city, the only one. Therefore, trials await you, fitting trials. Follow me. I shall guide you in safety; another will bring you back——

PENTHEUS. Yes, my mother.

THE STRANGER. A shining example to all.

PENTHEUS. It is for that I come.

THE STRANGER. You will be carried back——

PENTHEUS. You promise me luxury.

THE STRANGER. In your mother's hands.

PENTHEUS. You will make an elegant of me.

THE STRANGER. Elegant indeed!

PENTHEUS. My enterprise will earn it.

THE STRANGER. You are a remarkable man, remarkable indeed; and it is to a remarkable experience that you are going. You will attain renown towering to heaven. Open your arms, Agave, and you her sisters, daughters of Cadmus. I bring this bold youth to a famous contest. The victor will be I, and Bromius. The rest the event will show.

*[Exit with Pentheus.]*

CHORUS. *On, swift hounds of Madness, on to where the daughters of Cadmus hold their revels. Goad them to fury against him who masquerades in woman's attire, the maniac who spies on the maenads. His mother will see him first, as he peers from behind a smooth rock or tree-stump. She will cry out to the maenads: "Who is this sleuth who has come to the mountain, come to spy on us Thebans where we revel on the mountain? Who was the mother that bore him? Not of the blood of women is this man's birth, of some lioness, some Gorgon of Libya".*

*Let Justice advance in plain sight, advance sword in hand, to strike through the throat, to slaughter the godless, the lawless, the ruthless man, the earth-born son of Echion.*

*With ruthless temper and lawless rage he visits your orgies, Bacchus, yours and your mother's. In the madness of his heart, in the delusion of his wits, he thinks his violence can master the Invincible. But there is One ready and willing to correct his heresies—Death. To know the limits of mortality is a life without sorrow. False knowledge I do not envy; I rejoice to hunt it down. The other things, the greater things, are not abstruse. Ah, let my life flow quietly; let me seek the good, in purity and piety from morn till night, honoring the gods and eschewing all unrighteous practices.*

*Let Justice advance in plain sight, advance sword in hand,
to strike through the throat, to slaughter the godless, the
lawless, the ruthless man, the earth-born son of Echion.*

*Appear as a bull, as a many-headed dragon to the view, as
a fiery glaring lion to the sight. Up, Bacchus, with smiling
face cast your noose around the hunter of the bacchants,
fallen among the deadly band of maenads.*

[*Enter Messenger.*]

MESSENGER. Ah, house once prosperous throughout Hellas,
house of the old man of Sidon who in the land of the
Serpent sowed the dragon's earth-born crop, how I groan for
you! I am just a slave, but still—— [good slaves are
touched by their masters' calamities.]

LEADER. What is it? Have you news to tell of the bacchants?

MESSENGER. Pentheus is dead, the son of Echion.

CHORUS. *Lord Bromius, you show yourself a mighty god!*

MESSENGER. What do you say? What was that? Do you rejoice at the misfortunes of my master, woman?

CHORUS. *An alien I am, and in barbaric strains I hail my
god. No longer do I cower in fear of chains.*

MESSENGER. Do you think Thebes is so wanting in men——

CHORUS. *It is Dionysus, Dionysus and not Thebes, who has
power over me.*

MESSENGER. I can understand; but it is not fair, women, to
rejoice over afflictions past cure.

LEADER. *Tell me, say, what death did he die, the wicked
man, the worker of wickedness?*

MESSENGER. When we had put behind us the homesteads
of this Theban land and crossed over the streams of Asopus
we came to the heights of Cithaeron, Pentheus and I—I was
attending my master—and the stranger who headed our pilgrimage.

First, we halted in a grassy glade. We kept silence, of
tread and tongue alike, in order to see without being seen.
And there, across a precipitous ravine, where the pines stood
dark over the waters of a stream, the maenads were sitting,
their hands busy with pleasant tasks. Some of them were
wreathing afresh their worn-out wands with new tresses of
ivy. Others, like colts freed from the gaudy yoke, were singing lustily their bacchic antiphons. Pentheus, poor man, did
not see the crowd of women, and said: "Stranger, where

we stand my eyes cannot reach these bastard maenads. If I stood at the edge and climbed a tall fir, I would get a perfect view of their wild obscenities."

Then came the miracle—I saw the stranger seize the topmost branches of a soaring fir and force it down, down, down to the black earth, till it was arched like a bow, or like an arc described by the peg-and-string in drawing the circumference of a rounded wheel. So the stranger tugged at that mountain branch with his hands, and bent it down to earth: it was no mortal deed he wrought. When he had set Pentheus on the branches of the fir, he slipped his hands along the trunk, letting it straighten again; but gently, for fear the mount should throw the rider. Aloft into the lofty air rose the sturdy fir, with my master sitting on top. And now he saw the maenads—but not so well as they saw him. They had scarcely spied him on his lofty seat, when the stranger disappeared from sight, and a voice out of the sky, I guess it was Dionysus, cried aloud: "Young women, I bring the man who has cast ridicule upon you and upon me and upon our holy rites. Take vengeance on him." Even as he spoke, he caused a mysterious pillar of fire to rise from earth to heaven.

The air was hushed, hushed were the leaves of the trees in the glen—not a cry to be heard of any creature. But the bacchants had not heard the shout distinctly. They leapt to their feet and swept the scene with their eyes. And again he exhorted them. Then the daughters of Cadmus recognized the clear command of Bacchus. They shot forth, swift as a flock of doves, speeding along on eager, straining feet, his mother Agave and her sisters and all the bacchants. Through the glen, over torrents and boulders, they leapt, maddened with the inspiration of the god. When they saw my master sitting upon the fir, they first took their stand on a towering rock opposite him and began to pelt him hard with stones. Some shot branches of fir at him, others sent their wands flying through the air. But their aim was wretched and they had no success. He sat high above their eager reach, a pitiful and helpless captive. Finally they violently rived off branches of oak and set about prying up the roots of his tree with their improvised crowbars. When they failed to achieve the end of their toils Agave spoke: "Come, stand about in a circle and take hold of the trunk. We must capture the treed beast [or he will publish the secrets of the god's dances]." Then they applied countless hands to the fir and wrenched it from the ground. Down from his lofty perch, down whirling to the earth, falls Pentheus. Many and many were his moans; for he knew his hour was near. His mother attacked him—the priestess commencing the sacrifice. He flung off his head-dress, in order that poor Agave might recognize him and not kill him. He touched her cheek and said: "I am your child, mother, Pentheus, whom you bore in Echion's house. Pity me, mother; do not, because of *my* sins, kill *your* child."

But she was foaming at the mouth and rolling distorted eyeballs, out of her right mind, possessed by Bacchus. His pleadings were of no avail. She seized the hand of his left arm and set her foot against the poor wretch's side and tore off his arm at the shoulder—not of her own strength; it was the god who made easy the work of her hands. Ino wrought havoc on the other side, rending the flesh, while Autonoe and the whole bacchic horde pressed on. All was one wild din—he groaning with the little breath that was left him, and they shrieking in triumph. One carried off an arm, another a foot, shoe and all. They stripped the flesh from his ribs with their tearing. One and all, with blood-bespattered hands, they played ball with the flesh of Pentheus.

His body lies in pieces, part under the jagged rocks, part in the green depths of the forest; no easy thing to find. His mother has his poor head. She seized it in her hands and fixed it on the top of a thyrsus. She thinks' it is the head of a mountain lion that she carries through the midst of Cithaeron. She has left her sisters at the dances of the maenads and is returning within these walls gloating over her hapless prey. She is calling upon Bacchus, her "fellow-huntsman", her "comrade in the chase", her "conquering hero". Bitter for her are the fruits of victory she brings him.

I shall get out of the way of this calamity before Agave comes home. It is the loveliest thing to be virtuous and god-fearing. And I imagine it is also the *wisest* course for mortals to follow.

[*Exit Messenger.*]

CHORUS. *Let us dance to the glory of Bacchus, let us shout for the calamity of Pentheus, the spawn of the ancient serpent. He took woman's attire, he took a fair shaft of fennel: the uniform of the god—of death. And a bull showed him the way to destruction. Bacchants of Thebes,*

*glorious is the paean you have achieved, ending in wailing
and tears. It is a goodly sport to fling about one's child an
arm dripping with his own blood.*

LEADER. But stay. I see Pentheus' mother, Agave, rushing
wild-eyed towards the house. Welcome you the revel of the
bacchic god.

[*Enter Agave, frenzied, blood-stained, with Pentheus'
head on her thyrsus.*]

AGAVE. *Bacchants of Asia——*

CHORUS. *To what will you urge me? Oh!*

AGAVE. *I bring to our halls from the mountains a tendril
newly cut. Happy was the hunting.*

CHORUS. *I see; and I welcome you to join our revel.*

AGAVE. *Without a noose I snared it—the young whelp of a
savage lion. Look and see.*

CHORUS. *From where in the wilds?*

AGAVE. *Cithaeron——*

CHORUS. *Cithaeron?*

AGAVE. *—Slew him.*

CHORUS. *Who was she who smote him?*

AGAVE. *Mine was the first honor. "Happy Agave" they call
me in the revel.*

CHORUS. *And who else?*

AGAVE. *Cadmus' own——*

CHORUS. *Cadmus' what?*

AGAVE. *His own children. They reached the prey, but after
me, after me. Happy with this hunting.*

CHORUS. [LACUNA]

AGAVE. *Then share in the feast.*

CHORUS. *What? Shall I share it? Poor woman!*

AGAVE. *The whelp is yet young; the down of his cheek is
just blooming beneath his crest of delicate hair.*

CHORUS. *By its mane it might be a beast of the field.*

AGAVE. *Bacchus, the skilful hunter, skilfully roused the
maenads against this beast.*

CHORUS. *Our king is a hunter.*

AGAVE. *Do you praise me?*

CHORUS. *I do praise you.*

AGAVE. *Soon the Thebans——*

CHORUS. *Yes, and your son Pentheus——*

AGAVE. *Will praise his mother for catching this quarry, this
lion cub.*

CHORUS. *Remarkable quarry!*

AGAVE. *Remarkably caught!*

CHORUS. *Are you proud?*

AGAVE. *Overjoyed. Greatness, manifest greatness, I have achieved in this capture.*

LEADER. Show the townspeople, poor woman, your victory's booty, which you brought with you.

AGAVE. O you that dwell in this fair-towered town of the Theban land, come and see this prey, the beast which we daughters of Cadmus hunted down, not by the looped darts of the Thessalians, not with nets, but with our white arms and hands. Why then must men boast and get instruments from the armorers in vain? With our bare hands we took this animal and tore the beast's joints asunder.

Where is my old father? Let him come near. And Pentheus, my son, where is he? Let him bring a strong stepladder and set it against the house, so that he can nail to the triglyphs this lion's head I have brought from the hunt.

[*Enter Cadmus slowly with servants carrying the remains of Pentheus on a bier.*]

CADMUS. Follow me and bring your sad burden—the corpse of Pentheus. Follow me, servants, to the house where I am taking this body. After endless wearisome searching I found it in the trackless wood, torn to pieces in the glens of Cithaeron. No two parts were in the same spot.

I had come back from among the bacchants with the old man Tiresias, and I was already within the city's walls, when some one told me of my daughter's desperate deeds. I returned again to the mountain to fetch home her child, killed by the maenads. There I saw her that once bore Actaeon to Aristaeus, Autonoe I mean, her and Ino, still frenzy-stung, poor women, in the oak forest. But Agave, they told me, was coming back here with frenzied pace. And what I heard was not untrue; for there I see her, no happy sight.

AGAVE. Father, the proudest boast is yours to make: you have begotten daughters by far the best in all the world—all your daughters, I say, but me above all. I have left my shuttle by the loom; I have gone to greater things, to hunting animals with my hands. I bring in my arms, as you see, this prize of my courage, to hang on your walls. Take it father, in your hands. Exult in my hunting and invite your friends to a feast. You are blessed, yes blessed, in the achievement I have wrought.

CADMUS. Ah grief beyond measure—I cannot look upon it. Murder it is that you have wrought with your wretched hands. A noble victim it is that you have laid low for the gods; and now you invite this Thebes and me to the feast! Ah me for these woes, yours first and then mine. What ruin the god, king Bromius, has dealt us; with justice indeed, but not mercy, though he is born of our house.

AGAVE. What a crabbed thing old age is in men, how morose of aspect! I wish my son might take after his mother's ways, and be as lucky in the chase when he goes hunting wild beasts with the young men of Thebes. But that fellow is only good for quarreling with gods. He ought to be admonished, father; and you are the one to do it. Somebody call him here into my sight, to see me in my happiness.

CADMUS. Alas, alas! If you ever realize what you have done you will grieve with a bitter grief. But if you remain to the end in your present state, your affliction will be a blessing in disguise.

AGAVE. What is there in this that is not right? What is there to grieve for?

CADMUS. Turn your eyes first to yonder sky.

AGAVE. There. Why do you tell me to look at it?

CADMUS. Is it still the same, or does it seem different to you?

AGAVE. It is brighter than before, more pellucid.

CADMUS. Is there the same unrest in your soul?

AGAVE. Unrest? I do not know. I am becoming—somehow —[sensible. The thoughts I had have gone.]

CADMUS. Can you hear? Can you answer clearly?

AGAVE. I have forgotten what we were saying, father.

CADMUS. To whose house did you come as a bride?

AGAVE. You gave me to Echion—Echion of the Dragon race, they say.

CADMUS. What child was born to your husband in your house?

AGAVE. Pentheus, to me and his father together.

CADMUS. Whose is the face you have in your arms?

AGAVE. A lion's, at least those who hunted it said so.

CADMUS. Look right at it. It is small effort to see it.

AGAVE. Ha! What do I see? What is this I bring home in my hands?

CADMUS. Gaze at it, study it more truly.

AGAVE. I see a mighty grief. Ah, miserable am I!

CADMUS. It doesn't seem to you to resemble a lion?

AGAVE. No, it is Pentheus' head I hold, O misery!

CADMUS. Yes, bewailed by me before *you* recognized him.

AGAVE. Who killed him? How did he come into my hands?

CADMUS. Unhappy truth, how unseasonably you dawn!

AGAVE. Speak, my heart leaps in dread of what's to come.

CADMUS. You killed him, you and your sisters.

AGAVE. Where did he die? Was it at home? Somewhere outside?

CADMUS. Where the dogs once tore Actaeon to pieces.

AGAVE. Why did the unhappy creature go to Cithaeron?

CADMUS. He went to mock the god and your bacchic revels.

AGAVE. But we—how did we get out there?

CADMUS. You were mad, the whole city was in the frenzy of Bacchus.

AGAVE. Dionysus has undone us. Too late I see it.

CADMUS. Yes, for affronts put on him; you did not count him a god.

AGAVE. My son's dear body, father—where is it?

CADMUS. Here I bring it—retrieved with difficulty.

AGAVE. Is it all decently composed? [*Cadmus is silent.*] What part had my madness in Pentheus' fate?

CADMUS. He was like you—blaspheming against the god. So the god joined all of you in a single destruction, you and this unfortunate. The house is undone and I too; for I am without male children, and I have seen this shoot from your womb, poor woman, foully and horribly slain. [*To the body of Pentheus.*] To you the house looked up; you were the stay of my halls, child. Son of my own daughter, you had the city in awe of you. No one that looked upon your presence dared outrage the old man; for you would exact due penalty. But now I shall be cast out of my house dishonored—I, the great Cadmus, who sowed the race of Thebans and harvested a most excellent crop. Ah, dearest of men—yes, even in death I shall count you with the dearest, my child—never more will you touch this chin of mine with your hand and call me "mother's father" and embrace me, child, and say: "Is anyone wronging you? Is anyone dishonoring you, old man? Is anyone annoying you and vexing your heart? Tell me, and I shall punish whoever does you wrong, father."

But now it is sorrow for me and misery for you, grief for your mother and for her sisters misery. If there is anyone who disdains the deities, let him look at the death of this man and believe in the gods.

LEADER. I grieve for your sorrow, Cadmus. Your grandson has his deserts, his just deserts, but grievous for you.

AGAVE. Father, you see how all is changed for me——

[A LONG LAMENT OF AGAVE, A FEW LINES OF THE CHORUS
ANNOUNCING THE APPEARANCE OF DIONYSUS, AND
THE BEGINNING OF THE GOD'S SPEECH ARE LOST.]

DIONYSUS. * * * You will change and become a serpent; and your wife Harmonia, Ares' daughter, whom you got to wife though you were a mortal, will take a brutish form and be changed into a snake. A chariot drawn by bullocks, Zeus' oracle says, you will drive, your wife by your side, at the head of barbarians. You will sack many cities with an unnumbered host. But when they plunder the oracle of Loxias, they will receive a sorry homecoming. But Ares shall save you and Harmonia and establish your life in the land of the blessed.

These things say I, Dionysus, born of no mortal father but of Zeus. If you had learned wisdom then, when you would not, you would have been happy now, with the son of Zeus for your ally.

CADMUS. Dionysus, we beseech you, we have sinned.

DIONYSUS. Too late you have learned to know me. When the knowledge was wanted, you had it not.

CADMUS. We realize it. But you go too far against us.

DIONYSUS. Because you outraged my divinity.

CADMUS. It ill beseems gods to imitate the passions of mortals.

DIONYSUS. My father, Zeus, ordained these things of old.

AGAVE. Alas, it is decreed, old man—the misery of banishment.

DIONYSUS. Why then do you delay when necessity constrains?

[Dionysus disappears.]

CADMUS. Ah child, to what a fearful pass we have all come, you and your unhappy sisters, and I the sorrowful. In my old age I go to an alien land to dwell among barbarians. And there is also the prophecy—that I must lead a mingled barbarian host against Hellas. Myself a serpent, with my wife Harmonia, Ares' child, a wild and savage serpent too, I shall lead an army of spearsmen against altars and tombs of Hellas. Cadmus the Sorrowful! My sufferings will never end.

Not even when I go down the chasm of Acheron river shall I have rest.

AGAVE. Ah, father, I shall lose you, I shall live in exile.

CADMUS. Why do you fling your arms about me, poor child —a white swan embracing its old decrepit sire?

AGAVE. Where then shall I turn when I am cast out of my land?

CADMUS. I do not know, child; your father is small help.

AGAVE. *Farewell, my home; farewell my native city. I leave you for misery, for exile, far from home and love.*

CADMUS. *Go, my child, to Aristaeus (your sister's husband); he——*

AGAVE. *I groan for you father.*

CADMUS. *And I for you, child; and I weep for your sisters.*

AGAVE. *In dreadful wise has king Dionysus brought this confusion upon your house.*

CADMUS. *Dreadful was his treatment at your hands. His name was without honor in Thebes.*

AGAVE. *Farewell, my father.*

CADMUS. *Farewell, my poor child. It will not be easy—if you ever do find welfare.*

AGAVE. *Take me, my guides, where I shall find my unhappy sisters, my companions in exile. Let me go where foul Cithaeron may never see me, nor my eyes see Cithaeron, to some place where stands no memorial of the thyrsus! Let others be bacchants and care for these things.*

CHORUS. *Many are the forms of divine intervention; many things beyond expectation do the gods fulfil. That which was expected has not been accomplished; for that which was unexpected has god found the way. Such was the end of this story.*

[Exeunt.]

# Iphigenia at Aulis

————◆————

IPHIGENIA AT AULIS marks the end of Euripides' dramaturgy in several senses. It was the last play he wrote and was produced after his death—which may explain why it has more than its share of interpolations and dislocations, especially at the beginning and end. But it also carries Euripidean techniques and viewpoints to an extreme. No shred of heroic dignity is left to the great names of the Trojan War, and hence the war itself becomes foolish as well as wicked. Not only the Atreidae and Odysseus but even Achilles, who had always been above criticism, is shown to be arrogant and incompetent and lacking in physical as in moral courage. Never again could the familiar cast and story be used for authentic heroic tragedy.

But *Iphigenia at Aulis* is not only the most manifest end of the old; it is also the most manifest beginning of the new. If we look away from the traditionally tragic elements, which the readily-foreseen happy ending makes it easy to do, we find that the substance of the action has to do with preparations for the marriage of an ambitious matron's daughter with a highly eligible young man. The key is now so far reduced that we are no longer angry at abuses, but actually sympathize with the little people caught in roles too big for them. If we look away from the traditional story, as we look away from the miracle at its end, we can see that Agamemnon and Menelaus are a decent father and uncle and that even Achilles may grow wiser and firmer. But the clearest evidence that our play is more than parody of the old is the new and authentic heroism achieved by the simple Iphigenia.

# IPHIGENIA AT AULIS

## CHARACTERS

AGAMEMNON, *leader of the Greek host*

OLD SERVANT *of Agamemnon*

CHORUS, *women of Chalcis in Euboea who have crossed over to Aulis to see the fleet*

MENELAUS, *brother of Agamemnon, husband of Helen*

FIRST MESSENGER

CLYTEMNESTRA, *wife of Agamemnon*

IPHIGENIA, *daughter of Agamemnon*

ACHILLES, *son of the sea-goddess Thetis, prince of the Myrmidons*

SECOND MESSENGER

*The infant* Orestes, *attendants, guards*

The scene represents the front of the tent of Agamemnon in the Greek camp at Aulis. The action begins just before dawn.

Iphigenia at Aulis was acted shortly after 406 B. C.

The text of this play appears to be seriously mutilated in several places. Some editors, for example, hold that the prologue as we have it is made up of fragments of two separate prologues. The ending of the play is obviously spurious. An apparently authentic fragment cited as from this play seems to come from a speech of Artemis (as *deus ex machina*) consoling Clytemnestra for the loss of her child.

———◆———

[THE SPEECH THAT FOLLOWS IS APPARENTLY A PROLOGUE IN ITSELF, THOUGH IN THE MANUSCRIPTS IT IS EMBEDDED IN THE MIDDLE OF THE LYRICAL PROLOGUE WITH WHICH THE PLAY OPENS. IT CONSTITUTES VERSES 49-114.]

AGAMEMNON. To Leda, daughter of Thestius, three girls were born: Phoebe; Clytemnestra, my wife; and Helen. For Helen's hand the noblest and wealthiest young men of

Hellas came as suitors. Fierce threats were bandied about: death for the chosen one at the hands of his defeated rivals. This situation perplexed her father Tyndareus. Should he give her in marriage or not? What was the best way to handle the situation? Then this idea occurred to him. Let the suitors take a mutual pledge, giving their right hands to it and sealing it with burnt sacrifices and solemn oaths, that they would each and all defend the man who won to wife the daughter of Tyndareus, if anyone ever carried her off from her home and dispossessed the husband of her bed; that they would war upon his city and destroy it, whether Hellene or barbarian, by force of arms.

When they had all so pledged themselves—for old Tyndareus was much too cunning for them—he left the choice to his daughter, according to the promptings of her heart's love. She chose—in an evil moment—Menelaus. Then that judge of divine beauties, as the Argive story has it, came from Phrygia to Lacedaemon; the habit of his dress was flowery, he glittered with gold—barbaric finery. Helen fell in love with him, and he with her; and so, with Menelaus abroad at the time, off he went with his plunder to the ranches of Ida. Menelaus, goaded to frenzy, dashed up and down Hellas invoking the old pledge of mutual assistance against aggression.

Then Hellas rushed to arms. They brought their armaments to these narrow straits of Aulis, their ships and their shields, their cavalry and their chariots. They chose me to be general. I suppose it was a favor to Menelaus, since I was his brother; but I wish some other man had won this honor instead of me. When the army had been brought together and mustered, we were kept idle at Aulis, for want of sailing weather. In our difficulty, the seer Calchas pronounced that Iphigenia, my own daughter, must be sacrificed to Artemis whose soil this is; thus, and not otherwise, we could sail away and sack Phrygia.

When I heard this I told Talthybius to let the trumpet blare forth and disband the whole army, for I would never bring myself to kill my own daughter. Thereupon my brother pleaded with me and pleaded with me, till he persuaded me to do the awful deed. In the folds of a letter I wrote and told my wife to send our daughter here to become the bride of Achilles. I enlarged upon Achilles' distinction and said he refused to sail with the Achaeans unless a bride of our house should go to his Phthia. I used this pretext as a means of per-

suading my wife [, concocting a sham marriage in order to
get the girl. Of the Achaeans only we four know the true situation: Calchas, Odysseus, Menelaus, and I. Now I am trying to retrieve my error by writing another letter, this one
you saw me opening and sealing again under cloud of night,
old man. Here, take it and make your way to Argos. I shall
tell you in words the secret message written within the letter's folds, for you are loyal to my wife and to my house].

*　　*　　*　　*　　*　　*　　*

[*The old servant can be seen by the light of a lamp
which burns before Agamemnon's tent; Agamemnon
appears at the entrance.*]

AGAMEMNON. *Old man, come here in front of my tent.*

OLD SERVANT. *I am coming. What new purpose have you in
mind, King Agamemnon?*

AGAMEMNON. *Won't you hurry?*

OLD SERVANT. *I will. This old age of mine is wakeful and is
an alert watcher over my eyes.*

AGAMEMNON. *What star is that in its course?*

OLD SERVANT. *Sirius. He is still high in heaven sailing near
the seven Pleiads.*

AGAMEMNON. *There is no sound, neither of birds nor of
the sea. Windless silence holds this Euripus fast.*

OLD SERVANT. *But why are you astir outside your tent, King
Agamemnon? It is yet quiet here in Aulis. The watch along
the walls is not stirring. Let us go in.*

AGAMEMNON. *I envy you, old man. I envy any man that has
lived a life of quiet days, unknown to fame. Less envy have I
for power and office.*

OLD SERVANT. *And yet there is glory in the latter kind of
life.*

AGAMEMNON. *Yes, but this glory is perilous; honor is
sweet, but it is the near neighbor of grief. Sometimes incor-
rect service of the gods overturns a man's life; sometimes
the opinions of men, diverse and intractable, shatter it.*

OLD SERVANT. *I do not admire this attitude in a chief.
Atreus did not beget you to enjoy unmixed happiness, Agamemnon. You must have joy, and grief too; for you are a
mortal man. Whether you like it or not, such will be the will
of the gods.
But you have kindled your lamp's light; you have written*

*upon this tablet which you carry about in your hands, then
you scrape off your own writing; you seal your letter then
open it again, you throw it upon the ground and you pour a
flood of tears from your eyes; you want none of the symp-
toms of despair to prove you mad. What is your difficulty?
What is new with you, Agamemnon? Come, share the story
with me. You are talking to a good and faithful man. Long
ago Tyndareus sent me to you as an honest bridal attendant
for your wife, part of her dowry.*

[VERSES 49-114 REMOVED FROM HERE.]

[*Agamemnon maintains silence for a few moments.*]

OLD SERVANT. *Speak, tell me. Then my tongue can corrobo-
rate your writing.*

AGAMEMNON. "*I send you this letter to supplement my former one, seed of Leda. Do not send your child to the open
bosom of Euboea, waveless Aulis. Our child's wedding celebrations are postponed indefinitely.*"

OLD SERVANT. *How will you cheat Achilles of his bride
without fanning his fury into a mighty blaze against you and
your wife? That is a danger indeed. Tell me what you have
to say.*

AGAMEMNON. *Achilles provides the name, nothing else. He
knows nothing about a marriage, or about our plot either, or
about my professed willingness to give my child to the nuptial
embraces of his loving arms.*

OLD SERVANT. *A bold and fearful deed, King Agamemnon.
To bring your daughter here for the Argives to slay, you
have held out the prospect of marriage with divine Achilles.*

AGAMEMNON. *Ah me, I am out of my mind. I am heading
for ruin. But go, speed your foot, yield nothing to old age.*

OLD SERVANT. *I hasten, King.*

AGAMEMNON. *Do not sit down by shady fountains, or seek
the comfort of sleep.*

OLD SERVANT. *How can you suggest such a thing?*

AGAMEMNON. *When you pass a fork in the road look in
every direction and take care you let no carriage roll past
you, bringing my daughter here to the Argive ships.*

OLD SERVANT. *It shall be done.*

AGAMEMNON. *If she has left the haven of her rooms and
you meet her escort on the way, pilot her back home; whip up
speed, and race for the Cyclopean shrines.*

OLD SERVANT. *But tell me, how will they believe me when I tell this to your daughter [and to your wife]?*

AGAMEMNON. *Take care of this seal on the letter. Be on your way. Look, already the light of the sun's fiery car is growing bright in the east. Help me in my trouble.*

[*Exit Old Servant.*]

*No mortal knows real prosperity or happiness; never has one been born free from sorrow.*

[*Exit Agamemnon into tent; enter Chorus.*]

CHORUS. *I came to the sandy shore of Aulis by the sea. Through the pouring waters of Euripus' narrow channel I plied my boat, leaving behind me my own city Chalcis, nurse of famous Arethusa whose waters join the sea. To see the Achaean host I came, and the sea-faring ships of the Achaean heroes. These heroes, our husbands tell us, with a fleet of a thousand vessels, are led by fair-haired Menelaus and noble Agamemnon in quest of Helen. Cowherd Paris took her from reedy Eurotas, a gift of Aphrodite when at the fountain dews the Cyprian held contest of beauty with Hera and with Pallas.*

*Through Artemis' grove of many sacrifices I came in haste, and my cheeks were dyed with blushes of youthful shyness, for I wished to see the army's stronghold and the tents of the Danaan warriors, and the crowd of horses. I saw the two Ajaxes sitting talking together, Oeleus' son, and Telamon's, the pride of Salamis. Protesilaus I saw and Palamedes whom Poseidon's daughter bore, sitting on seats and taking their pleasure in the complicated moves of the draught-board; and Diomede delighting in the joy of the discus; and near him Merion, scion of Ares, a marvel to mortals; and Laertes' son from the island hills; and Nireus too, handsomest of the Achaeans.*

*And swift-running Achilles I saw, whose feet are like the wind, him that Thetis bore and Chiron trained; he was running a race in full armor on the shingle by the sea-shore. He ran hard, racing a four-horse chariot, lap after lap, straining for victory. The charioteer kept shouting; he was Eumelus of Pheres' race, and I saw his beautiful horses, and their elaborate bridles of gold. He was urging them on with a goad. The middle horses at the yoke were dappled with white-flecked*

*hairs, while the trace-horses on the outside were bays, and at
the ankles of their whole hooves their fetlocks were dappled.
They ran close to the turns of the course, and beside them
sprinted Peleus' son, fully armed, keeping alongside the
chariot rail by the wheels of the car.*

*I came to the host of ships; it was a marvellous spectacle to
satisfy the sight of a woman's eyes, a pleasure honey-sweet.
The right wing of the fleet was held by the Myrmidon armament from Phthia, fifty dashing vessels. In golden images the
Nereid goddesses stood at the sterns, the insignia of the forces
of Achilles.*

*A like number of oared ships of the Argive stood hard by.
The commander of these was Mecisteus' son whose foster-
father was Talaus, and with him was Sthenelus, son of Capa-
neus. The next station Theseus' son held, leading sixty Attic
ships. Their ensign was Pallas riding on winged steeds, a
sight to cheer the sailors.*

*I saw the Boeotian naval armament of fifty vessels,
equipped with their ensigns; this was Cadmus holding a gold-
en dragon at the curved sterns. Earth-born Leitus commanded
their naval host. And there were vessels from the land of
Phocis and also ships of Locris equal to them in number, led
by Oeleus' son, who came from the famous city of Thro-
nium.*

*From Cyclopean Mycenae Atreus' son sent a hundred ves-
sels and their men. With him was the chieftain Adrastus,
standing by his friend, in order that Hellas might take righteous vengeance on the one who forsook her home for the
sake of barbarian bridals. I saw the ensign of the prows of
Gerenian Nestor of Pylos: the river Alpheus, his neighbor,
represented with bulls' feet.*

*Of the Aenians there were twelve ships, which King Gou-
neus commanded. Not far from these were the chiefs of Elis,
whom all the folk called Epeians. Eurytus commanded these,
and also led the armament of the Taphians with white oars,
whose King was Meges; he was the son of Phyleus and came
from the islands of Echinae which sailors avoid.*

[1] *We had passed along the line from right to left, and
there at the end, close beside the neighboring ships, was the
fleet of Ajax, nurseling of Salamis, twelve of the trimmest
ships, completing the line. Thus much I have seen, or been*

---

[1] Text corrupt. We give what seems to be the approximate sense.

*told, of the fleet. If any foreign hulks come to grips with these, they will not get off easily, so formidable is the armada I saw there! I keep in mind too the things about the gathered host which I heard at home.*

[*Enter the Old Servant grasping at the letter, which Menelaus has snatched from him.*]

OLD SERVANT. Menelaus, this is an outrage, an unjustified outrage.

MENELAUS. Stand back! You are too loyal to your master.

OLD SERVANT. Your reproach does me honor.

MENELAUS. You'll be sorry, if you go too far.

OLD SERVANT. *You* go too far in opening the letter I was carrying.

MENELAUS. And you in carrying mischief for all the Greeks.

OLD SERVANT. Argue that with another, let me have this letter.

MENELAUS. I will not yield it up.

OLD SERVANT. And I will not let go of it.

MENELAUS. I will soon bloody your head with my scepter.

OLD SERVANT. It is glorious to die on behalf of one's master.

MENELAUS. Let go. You talk too much for a slave.

OLD SERVANT. Ho, master! We are being assaulted.

[*Enter Agamemnon.*]

This man snatched your letter from my hands by violence, Agamemnon. He has no regard for justice.

AGAMEMNON. Ha! What is this disturbance at my gates, what is this brawl?

MENELAUS. My story has a better right to be told than his.

AGAMEMNON. How have you come to quarrel with this man, Menelaus, why do you use violence?

[*Exit Old Servant.*]

MENELAUS. Look at me. I shall preface my argument with this.

AGAMEMNON. Shall I dread to show my eyes, who am sprung from Atreus the undreading?

MENELAUS. Do you see this letter, this villainous go-between?

AGAMEMNON. I see it. First of all, hand it over to me.

MENELAUS. Not till I have revealed its contents to all the Danaans.

AGAMEMNON. Have you learned what is no business of yours? Did you break the seal?

MENELAUS. Yes, I opened it, and you will be sorry. I know your guilty secret.

AGAMEMNON. Where did you catch him? Gods, what impudent effrontery!

MENELAUS. I was watching for your child to come to the camp from Argos.

AGAMEMNON. What need have you to watch for my affairs? Isn't this impudence?

MENELAUS. Because the fancy took me; I am not your slave.

AGAMEMNON. Isn't this outrageous? Shall I not be allowed to be master in my own house?

MENELAUS. No, you steer a crooked course, here, there, and everywhere.

AGAMEMNON. You make out a clever case—for dishonesty. I hate a smart tongue.

MENELAUS. And *I* hate a shifty mind that knows neither justice nor frankness. I will prove your guilt. Don't *you* bluster false denials, and *I*, for my part, won't press too hard.

Do you remember when it was your ambition to be the leader of the Danaans against Ilium? You made an appearance of reluctance, but in your heart you were eager enough. How low you sank! You touched every man's right hand. You kept your doors unbolted for any of the citizens that wished to come in. You accosted every single one whether they wished it or not. By complaisance you sought to bid for popularity against all comers. And then, when you had got the command, you changed your tune. You were no longer the friend of all your old friends. You were difficult to get to, you lived behind barred doors, you scarcely ever appeared. A good man ought not to change his disposition when he gets up in the world. That is just the time when his friends ought to be able to count on him, when his prosperity enables him to do more for them than ever.

This is the first point in which I reprove you, the first in which I find you wanting. Then when you and the army of all the Hellenes came to Aulis, and we were denied a favoring wind, you touched bottom; the divine dispensation filled you with fear, when the Danaans were loudly demanding that the ships be sent home and an end put to their fruitless toil at Aulis. What an unhappy face you showed, what distress at the thought of not filling the fields of Priam with war at the head of your thousand ships! And you sought my help: "What shall I do? What way out can I find? Where?" All to keep you from being deprived of your command and losing the great glory. When Calchas said you were to sacrifice your daughter at the altar and then the Danaans would be able to sail, you were glad at heart, and readily promised. You sent to your wife of your own will and not under duress—do not say that—to have your child brought here on the pretext of marrying Achilles. Then you face about and are caught sending a different message: you would no longer be your daughter's murderer. Just so. This is the same sky that witnessed your conduct then. Innumerable men have gone through the same experience. They work constantly to win to power—and then they lose it shamefully. In some cases it is the citizens who cannot appreciate brains; but often it is the men themselves who are just incompetent to guard the city's interests. As for me, I groan chiefly for unhappy Hellas. Hellas planned a glorious deed; now she must let those barbarian nobodies go scorning her, because of you and your girl.

Not for his courage, would I make a man chief of his country or commander of its armies. A general must have a head; any man with shrewdness may be governor of a state.

LEADER. It is dreadful when brothers fall into discord and quarrelsome words pass between them.

AGAMEMNON. Now it is my turn to criticize you. I will not be merciless or too supercilious, but considerate, like a brother. Good men tend to be merciful.

Tell me, why this angry panting, why this flushed face? Who has wronged you? What do you want? Do you yearn to win a good wife? I cannot help you there. The one you got you managed badly. Must I pay the penalty for your mistakes? *I* am not the cuckold. It is not *my* ambition that torments you. No, you long to hold a beautiful woman in your arms; discretion and decency you cast to the winds. A wicked man's pleasures are low. If I have the wit to repair a previous mistake—am I then mad? You are the madman, rather. You got rid of a wicked wife and now you want to get her back, when Heaven gives you the chance. Those misguided suitors gave their oath to Tyndareus in their zeal to win the bride; but it was a goddess, I imagine—to wit Hope—who brought it to pass rather than you and your strength. Take them and be their leader; they are ready enough in the folly of their hearts. The gods are not fools. They can discern evil compacts and oaths made under duress. I shall not slay *my* children. Why shall your fortunes prosper, in despite of justice, by vengeance on a worthless wife, while my days and nights are consumed with tears for my crimes, my unjust crimes against my own children?

These are my words to you, brief and clear and intelligible. If you won't see sense, don't. But I shall manage my own affairs to my own liking.

LEADER. This is a change of talk, but a change for the better—to refuse to harm your children.

MENELAUS. Ah me! I find, alas, that I have no friends.

AGAMEMNON. Yes, you have, when you do not seek your friends' destruction.

MENELAUS. How will you show you are my own father's son?

AGAMEMNON. I will share your virtues, but not your vices.

MENELAUS. You should share my misfortunes, like a friend.

AGAMEMNON. Do *good* if you will admonish me, but not when you are causing me pain.

MENELAUS. Are you not ready to endure this labor with Hellas?

AGAMEMNON. Hellas, like you, is afflicted by some god.

MENELAUS. Glory in your scepter! Betray your brother! I shall have recourse to other plans, to other friends——

*[Enter Messenger.]*

MESSENGER. King of all the Hellenes, Agamemnon, I bring you your daughter, whom you called Iphigenia in your palace. Her mother accompanies her, your noble Clytemnestra, and also the child Orestes. She knows you will rejoice to see him, after your long absence from home.

They have had a long journey and are now easing their delicate feet by a fountain's gracious stream, ladies and steeds alike. The horses we turned loose to browse upon the grass of the meadows. I come on in advance to warn you to make ready. The army has learned—so quickly does rumor spread abroad—that your child has arrived. The whole crowd is hurrying to the spectacle with all speed, to catch sight of the girl. Persons of position are well known to all and objects of attention to people. They are saying: "Is there to be a marriage or something? Did King Agamemnon so miss his daughter that he had her fetched?" From others I may hear this: "They are making the young woman's bridal offerings to Artemis, Queen of Aulis. Who is to be the groom?"

Come, attend to the next step, begin the rites with the sacrificial baskets; crown your heads. You too, King Menelaus, order the hymeneals; let the flute ring out in the hall, let there be the sound of dancing feet. This is a blessed day that dawns for the maid.

AGAMEMNON. You have done well. Go within the house; the rest, in the course of events, will be well.

[*Exit Messenger.*]

Ah me, what shall I say, poor wretch? Where shall I begin? The heavy yoke of circumstance is on my neck. Destiny has circumvented me and shown itself much cleverer than my clever devices. Humble birth has its advantages. It is easy for such folk to weep and tell all their unhappiness. To the man of noble birth come miseries no less; but we have decorum to rule our lives and are in bondage to the mob. So I am ashamed to shed a tear. On the other hand, if I do not weep, it is shameful. What lot could be harder than mine?

Ah, well. What shall I say to my wife? How shall I receive her? With what face shall I greet her? She has undone me, coming like this unbidden. I had troubles enough already. But I might have known she would come with her daughter, to do a mother's office for the bride, to surrender her precious—where she will discover me a villain. The poor maid—but why 'maid'? Hades, it seems, will soon wed her—how I pity her! I can imagine her imploring me: "Father, will you kill me? May you find such a marriage yourself, and anyone that is dear to you." And Orestes will be there and wail, meaningless cries that all will understand. He is yet a babe. Alas, alas! How Priam's Paris has ruined me by winning Helen's hand; *he* has done this mischief.

LEADER. I, too, am moved with pity, if a stranger woman may sigh for her masters' misfortunes.

MENELAUS. Brother, give me your right hand to touch.

AGAMEMNON. I give it. Yours is the victory, and mine the sorrow.

MENELAUS. By Pelops I swear, called father to your father

and mine, and by Atreus that begot us, that I shall say to you plainly what is in my heart, no special pleading, but my whole mind.

When I see you shedding tears from your eyes, I take pity and shed a tear in turn for your sake. I withdraw my previous arguments; you have nothing to fear from me. I will go your way. Take my advice: do not kill your child; do not prefer my interests to your own. It is not in justice that *you* should groan while my lot is sweet, that *your* dear ones should die while mine look upon the light.

What is it I want? Can I not make other choice matches if it is marriage I crave? Should I ruin my brother—what wrong could be greater?—just to win Helen, an ill gift for a good? I was wrong and hasty. I did not stop to look at the thing closely and see what it means to kill one's children. Above all, I feel compassion for the poor girl, when I recall our relationship. She was to be sacrificed for the sake of my marriage! What has your maid to do with Helen?

Let the army be dismissed and leave Aulis. Stop flooding your eyes with tears, brother, and moving me to tears too. Whatever is *your* concern in the oracles about your daughter, let me have no concern in them; I make over my interest to you.

Have I suddenly changed my terrible tone? Well, it's only natural. It is love, love for my own mother's son, that has changed me. It is no bad turn for a man to take—to make the best of every situation.

LEADER. Noble are your words, worthy of Tantalus, Zeus' son. You do not shame your forebears.

AGAMEMNON. I commend you, Menelaus. I did not expect this; but what you suggest now is honorable and worthy of yourself. Discord of brothers arises because of love or family ambition. It is mutually painful; I loathe it.

But things leave me no choice: the bloody murder of my daughter must be accomplished.

MENELAUS. How? Who will force you to kill your own?

AGAMEMNON. The whole assembly of the Achaean host.

MENELAUS. Not if you send her back to Argos.

AGAMEMNON. *That* I might manage to keep secret, but not the other thing.

MENELAUS. What other? One ought not to be too timid with the mob.

AGAMEMNON. Calchas will declare his oracles to the army.

MENELAUS. Not if he dies first. That is easy.

AGAMEMNON. The whole breed of prophets is rotten with ambition.

MENELAUS. Ay, good or bad, they are no help.

AGAMEMNON. Do you not fear a possibility that has occurred to me?

MENELAUS. If you do not tell me, how can I guess your meaning?

AGAMEMNON. The seed of Sisyphus knows all this.

MENELAUS. Odysseus is nothing for you or me to fear.

AGAMEMNON. He is subtle, always with the crowd.

MENELAUS. He is indeed a slave to ambition, a terrible disease.

AGAMEMNON. Can't you imagine him standing up in the midst of the Argives to tell the oracles that Calchas interpreted, to tell how I promised the sacrifice to Artemis and then played false? Will he not carry the army with him, and bid the Argives kill you and me and then sacrifice the girl? Even if I escape to Argos, they will come and raze the city to the ground, immemorial walls and all.

Such are my afflictions. Ah, poor devil that I am, there's nothing I can do, plagued by the gods like this! Take care of one thing for me, Menelaus, as you go through the army: see that Clytemnestra learns nothing of this till I have seized my child and offered her to Hades. Let me accomplish my woe with the fewest tears possible.

Do you too keep silence, stranger women.

[*Exeunt Agamemnon and Menelaus severally.*]

CHORUS. *Blessed are they who in measure due have their share in marriage bliss, to whom Aphrodite's sway is mild, who enjoy a calm free from stinging passions. When golden-haired Eros bends his two-fold bow of charm, one is for a fate of happy days, and the other for life's confounding. This other, I pray, fairest Cyprian, keep far away from my chamber. Let love's charm rest upon me in due measure; may pure desires be mine. May Aphrodite come to me in measure; I wish not her fury.*

*Diverse are the natures of mortals, diverse their manners. True goodness is ever clear. Nurture and education are a great aid to virtue. True modesty is itself wisdom; it has a charm which compels the mind to see the right. Where it is present, fame brings ageless renown to life. It is a great thing to pursue virtue. Among women it is a cloistered thing, touching their love, whereas the honor of men has countless forms; it makes cities great.*

*There you came, Paris, to the place where you were reared, a herdsman among the white heifers on Ida's mount; a barbaric melody you piped, breathing upon reeds an imitation of the Phrygian pipes of Olympus. One day, as your fat cattle were browsing, the goddesses came for trial. And mad hopes stirred in your heart, that sent you to Hellas. By the ivory palace of Helen you stood, and you darted love into her eyes that looked into yours, and by love you were yourself distracted. Thence arose the strife that drives Hellas in strife of men and ships against the battlements of Troy.*

[*Enter Clytemnestra, Iphigenia, Orestes, in a carriage, with attendants.*]

CHORUS OF ARGIVE MEN. *Lo, lo, great is the blessedness of the great. Behold the King's daughter, Iphigenia my queen, and Tyndareus' daughter Clytemnestra. Of what great houses are they sprung, to what exalted fortune have they attained! The powerful and the wealthy are gods in the eyes of meaner mortals.*

CHORUS. *Let us stand by, foster daughters of Chalcis; let us receive the queen from her carriage to the earth, steadily, with tender hands and gentle strength. Let not Agamemnon's glorious child know fear on her first arrival. Let us stranger women occasion neither disturbance nor dismay to the stranger woman from Argos.*

CLYTEMNESTRA. An omen of good I count your kindness and your gracious greeting. My hope is that I am come to be bride's matron for a happy marriage. From the carriages take the dower gifts, which I bring for the maid, and carry them into the house carefully. You, my child, leave the horse-drawn carriage, set down your tender and delicate feet. And you, young women, receive her in your arms, and escort her from the carriage. Someone lend me the support of her arm so that I may leave this car-seat gracefully. Some of you stand before the horses' yoke; the horse's eye is timorous when none is by to soothe. This boy, this son of Agamemnon, Orestes, take him; he is only a babe.

Child, are you sleeping? Have you been overcome by the carriage's motion? Awake for your sister's wedding, happily. A goodly man will you get for kinsman, my noble boy, the son of the Nereid of divine descent.

*[Clytemnestra is escorted to a seat, the infant Orestes
is in his nurse's arms at her feet.]*

Take your place here at my foot, child; stand next to your
mother, Iphigenia, and show these stranger women how
happy I am. Your dear father—here he comes, greet him.

IPHIGENIA [*running into Agamemnon's arms*]. Mother,
I run from you, but don't be angry. I will press my breast
against my father's breast.

CLYTEMNESTRA. My most revered king, Agamemnon, we
have come. We have not disobeyed your behests.

IPHIGENIA. I so longed to see your face. Don't be angry.

- CLYTEMNESTRA. Quite right, my child. You have always
loved your father most, of all the children I bore him.

IPHIGENIA. Father, I am so glad to see you. It has been so
long.

AGAMEMNON. And your father to see you. You speak for
us both.

IPHIGENIA. Greetings! Thank you, father, for bringing me
to you.

AGAMEMNON. Perhaps, my child, and perhaps not. I do
not know.

IPHIGENIA. Ah! How uneasy you look, for one who is so
glad to see me.

AGAMEMNON. A king and general has much to think
about.

IPHIGENIA. Attend to me now. Forget your worries.

AGAMEMNON. I am altogether with you now, my thoughts
are nowhere else.

IPHIGENIA. Then away with your frown, smooth your brow
and make it friendly.

AGAMEMNON. There! I am as happy as I can be, to see you.

IPHIGENIA. And yet tears are pouring from your eyes?

AGAMEMNON. The separation to come is long.

IPHIGENIA. I do not understand what you say, dearest
father, I do not understand.

AGAMEMNON. Your sensible remarks move me the more
to pity.

IPHIGENIA. Then I will talk nonsense, if I can make you
happy so.

AGAMEMNON [*aside*]. Damnation! I have not the strength
to keep silent. [*Aloud.*] That's a good child.

IPHIGENIA. Stay, father, stay at home for your children.

AGAMEMNON. I want to. It is because I cannot have the wish that I grieve.

IPHIGENIA. Perish wars and the grievances of Menelaus!

AGAMEMNON. It will first make others perish, the thing that is ruining me.

IPHIGENIA. You have been hidden away so long in Aulis!

AGAMEMNON. And even yet something hinders the army from starting.

IPHIGENIA. Where do they say the Phrygians live, father?

AGAMEMNON. Where I would that Priam's Paris never lived!

IPHIGENIA. You are going on a long voyage, father, and leaving me behind.

AGAMEMNON. You are in the same case, my daughter, as your father.

IPHIGENIA. Ah, I wish my position and yours would permit you to take me along on your voyage.

AGAMEMNON. You, too, have a voyage to make and you will think of your father.

IPHIGENIA. Shall I go sailing with mother or alone?

AGAMEMNON. Alone, where your father and your mother cannot be with you.

IPHIGENIA. Do you mean that you have found me a new home, father?

AGAMEMNON. Enough. Girls ought not to know such things.

IPHIGENIA. Hurry back to me from Phrygia, father, when you have finished your business there.

AGAMEMNON. I must first offer a certain sacrifice here.

IPHIGENIA. Yes, religion requires holy rites.

AGAMEMNON. You shall see. You will stand near the lavers.

IPHIGENIA. Shall we have dances round the altar, father?

AGAMEMNON [aside]. I envy your blissful ignorance. [Aloud.] Go into the house: it hurts girls to be seen. Kiss me, give me your hand. You are going to be long away from your father's home.

Ah, bosom and cheeks, ah, yellow hair, a heavy burden has the Phrygian city and Helen laid upon you. But I shall stop; a sudden moisture wells up from my eyes when I touch you. Go into the house.

[Exit Iphigenia.]

I entreat you, child of Leda, bear with me if I grieve too much over giving my daughter to Achilles. Such partings may be happy, but they gnaw at the heart of parents, when a father surrenders to another house the children he has painstakingly reared.

CLYTEMNESTRA. I am not so insensible; know that I too will feel the same pang when I lead the girl out to the marriage songs—so I do not admonish you. But marriage is a common thing, and time dries all tears.

I know the name of the favored bridegroom, but I should like to know what his lineage is and whence he comes.

AGAMEMNON. Aegina was the daughter of Asopus.

CLYTEMNESTRA. And did a mortal or some god marry her?

AGAMEMNON. Zeus; and he begot Aeacus, Oenone's lord.

CLYTEMNESTRA. Which child of Aeacus possessed his house?

AGAMEMNON. Peleus, who married a daughter of Nereus.

CLYTEMNESTRA. Did the god give her to him, or did he take her in spite of the gods?

AGAMEMNON. Zeus betrothed her and gave her in marriage; he was her guardian.

CLYTEMNESTRA. Where did he marry her? Was it under the sea waves?

AGAMEMNON. Where Chiron dwells under holy Pelion.

CLYTEMNESTRA. Where they say the race of Centaurs lives?

AGAMEMNON. There the gods celebrated Peleus' marriage.

CLYTEMNESTRA. Did Thetis or his father rear Achilles?

AGAMEMNON. Chiron did, so that he should not learn wickedness from men.

CLYTEMNESTRA. Ah, wise was the teacher, and he that so entrusted him even wiser.

AGAMEMNON. Such is the man who will be your child's husband.

CLYTEMNESTRA. No fault is to be found with him. In what city of Hellas does he live?

AGAMEMNON. In Phthia, by the river Apidanus.

CLYTEMNESTRA. Is it there he will take your girl and mine?

AGAMEMNON. He will see to that, the one who gets her.

CLYTEMNESTRA. Blessings on them! What day is the wedding?

AGAMEMNON. When the full moon comes round. That is lucky.

CLYTEMNESTRA. Have you already offered the preliminary sacrifices to the gods?

AGAMEMNON. I am going to. It is this duty I am now busy with.

CLYTEMNESTRA. Then afterwards you will celebrate the marriage feast?

AGAMEMNON. Yes, when I have sacrificed to the gods the offerings they require.

CLYTEMNESTRA. Where shall I make the feast for the women?

AGAMEMNON. Here, by the Argive vessels with their fine prows.

CLYTEMNESTRA. It is well, since it must be. May it be for the best.

AGAMEMNON. Do you know what you must do, lady? Do as I say——

CLYTEMNESTRA. Do what? I am used to doing as you say.

AGAMEMNON. Here, where the bride-groom is *I* shall——

CLYTEMNESTRA. What will you do in the mother's absence which it is my office to do?

AGAMEMNON. I shall give your child in marriage amidst the Danaans.

CLYTEMNESTRA. And where am *I* to be meanwhile?

AGAMEMNON. Go to Argos, take care of your girls.

CLYTEMNESTRA. And leave my child here? Who will raise the bridal torch?

AGAMEMNON. I shall provide the bridal fires.

CLYTEMNESTRA. But that is not the usual style; these things must not be looked on as trifles.

AGAMEMNON. It is not proper for you to mingle with the mob of soldiery——

CLYTEMNESTRA. But it is proper for me as mother to give my own child in marriage.

AGAMEMNON. Nor for the girls at home to be all alone.

CLYTEMNESTRA. They are well taken care of in the protection of their chambers.

AGAMEMNON. Do obey.

CLYTEMNESTRA. No, by the Argive goddess Queen. Go and attend to things abroad, I shall see to things at home [, especially the girls and their weddings].

[*Exit Clytemnestra.*]

AGAMEMNON. Ah me. It was an idle move. My plan to get my wife away has been frustrated. I make clever plans and contrive schemes against those I love best, and I am baffled on all fronts. But I will go with priest Calchas to arrange for the gods' pleasure—for me disaster. I bear the burdens of Hellas. It behooves a wise man to keep in his house a helpful and good wife or not to keep one at all.

[*Exit.*]

CHORUS. *Now to Simois and the whirl of silvery waters will come the gathered host of Hellas on ship-board and in arms. To Ilium they will come, to the plains of Troy, the Troy of Phoebus, where Cassandra, as I hear, decked with a garland of green-leaved bay, tosses her yellow tresses, whenever the throes of inspired prophecy grip her.*

*Upon the battlements of Troy and around its walls the Trojans will stand; from over the sea Ares of the brazen shield draws near with the oarage of his goodly ships to the channels of Simois; he is seeking to bring back Helen, the sister of the twin Dioscuri that dwell in heaven, back from Priam's land to Hellas, by Achaean war toil with shield and spear.*

*When the son of Atreus has girdled Pergamum, the Phrygians' city, and its stone bulwarks with the slaughter of war, when he has cut the head of Paris from off its neck and has overturned the city from its foundations, then will he bring many tears to the maidens and to Priam's consort. And Helen, Zeus' daughter, will sit bathed in tears for the husband she has lost. Never upon me or upon my children's children may such boding come as the Lydian ladies rich in gold and the wives of the Phrygians conceive, as they converse with one another at the loom: "What man will tighten his grasp on my abundant tresses, and pluck me, weeping, as a flower is plucked, from my perishing country?"—all because of you, child of the long-necked swan, if the story they tell is true, that Zeus changed his form to a winged bird. Or are these things just stories, without point or truth, brought to mankind from the pages of poets?*

[*Enter Achilles.*]

ACHILLES. Whereabouts is the general of the Achaeans? Will some man of his tell him that Peleus' son, Achilles, is seeking him at his door? Not all of us that are waiting by the Euripus are in the same condition. Some of us who [left our homes to come and] sit here on the shore are unmarried, others have wives and children. A violent passion for this expedition, a supernatural passion, has fallen upon Hellas. Let me then state my own case. Anyone else that wishes can speak for himself. I left Peleus behind in the land of Pharsalus, and here I am waiting for a breath of wind on the Euripus, and holding my Myrmidons in check. They are forever urging me and saying: "Achilles, why are we lingering? How long the measure of our waiting for the voyage to Ilium? Do something, if you are going to; or lead your army back home and wait no more for the dallying of the sons of Atreus."

[Enter Clytemnestra.]

CLYTEMNESTRA. Child of the Nereid goddess, I heard your words indoors, and I have come out in front of the house.

ACHILLES. In the name of Modesty, what woman is this I see that possesses so lovely a form?

CLYTEMNESTRA. No wonder you do not recognize me. You have not hitherto been anything to me. I like your respect for modesty.

ACHILLES. Who are you? Why have you come to the gathering of the Danaans, a woman to men fenced with shields?

CLYTEMNESTRA. I am the child of Leda, Clytemnestra is my name. My husband is King Agamemnon.

ACHILLES. You have given me the essentials briefly and fairly. But it is improper for me to have words with women.

CLYTEMNESTRA. Stay, why do you run away? Join your right hand with mine, as a happy omen for the bridals.

ACHILLES. What is it you say? I touch your hand? I could not face Agamemnon if I touched what I have no right to.

CLYTEMNESTRA. What better right do you want? You are to marry my daughter, son of the Nereid Goddess of the sea.

ACHILLES. Marriage? What do you mean? I am struck dumb, lady—unless it is some delusion that makes you talk so strangely?

CLYTEMNESTRA. It is natural for any man to be shy when he sees his new kin and thinks of his wedlock.

ACHILLES. I have never courted your daughter, lady; and no talk of marriage has reached me from the sons of Atreus.

CLYTEMNESTRA. What can this be? You may well wonder at *my* words. What *you* say fills me with wonder.

ACHILLES. Think. We must think this out together. Both of us are not likely to be mistaken in what we say.

CLYTEMNESTRA. Have I been abused? Have I been matchmaking when there is, it seems, no match? I am mortified!

ACHILLES. Perhaps someone has been joking with me and with you. Pay no attention to it; take it lightly.

CLYTEMNESTRA. Farewell. I can no longer look you in the face. I have been made a liar. I am humiliated. Goodbye.

ACHILLES. Farewell to you. I shall go to find your husband in the house here.

[*The Old Servant is heard calling through the open door.*]

OLD SERVANT. Stranger, seed of Aeacus, stay! It is you I mean, the child sprung of the gods; and you, daughter of Leda.

ACHILLES. Who is it that calls from behind these half-opened doors? How nervously he calls.

OLD SERVANT. A slave; I am not fastidious about it; fortune does not allow me to be.

ACHILLES. Whose? Not mine; my property and Agamemnon's are apart.

OLD SERVANT. Hers that is in front of the house. Her father, Tyndareus, gave me to her.

ACHILLES. I am staying. Tell me why you kept me back. What is it you want?

OLD SERVANT. Are you two quite alone here at the gates?

ACHILLES. Speak, we are alone; come out of the royal house.

[*Enter Old Servant.*]

OLD SERVANT. Ah Fortune and my own foresight, save those I want saved!

ACHILLES. This speech will do for another time, it is somewhat turgid.

CLYTEMNESTRA [*as the Old Servant is about to kneel to her*]. Do not mind touching my hand if you wish to say something to me.

OLD SERVANT. You know my character, how devoted I've been to you and your children.

CLYTEMNESTRA. I know that you are an old servant of my house.

OLD SERVANT. And that King Agamemnon received me as part of your dowry?

CLYTEMNESTRA. You came to Argos with me and have been mine for many a day.

OLD SERVANT. So it is. I seek *your* interests—less so your husband's.

CLYTEMNESTRA. Well now, disclose whatever secret you have for me.

OLD SERVANT. The father that begot her is going to kill your child with his own hand.

CLYTEMNESTRA. How? Out upon your story, old man! You are not sane!

OLD SERVANT. He will slash the poor girl's white neck with a sword.

CLYTEMNESTRA. Ah, poor me! Has my husband gone mad?

OLD SERVANT. He is in his senses, except toward you and your child; there he is not sane.

CLYTEMNESTRA. For what reason? What demon is driving him to this.

OLD SERVANT. Oracles, so at least Calchas says, if the army is to proceed.

CLYTEMNESTRA. Where? Poor me, and poor girl, whose father will kill her!

OLD SERVANT. To the home of Dardanus, to recover Menelaus' Helen.

CLYTEMNESTRA. Was Helen's homecoming a doom against Iphigenia?

OLD SERVANT. You have the whole story. Her father is going to sacrifice your child to Artemis.

CLYTEMNESTRA. So he made the marriage a pretext. And then the marriage brought *me* here.

OLD SERVANT. Yes, happy to bring your child to be Achilles' bride.

CLYTEMNESTRA. Ah daughter, you have come to meet destruction, you and your mother.

OLD SERVANT. Both you and she are suffering a pitiful outrage. It is a horrible deed that Agamemnon is contriving.

CLYTEMNESTRA. I am undone, ah me; my eyes no longer can hold their tears.

OLD SERVANT. If it is sorrow to be bereft of children, let the tears flow.

CLYTEMNESTRA. But where do you say you learned this, old man? How did you find it out?

OLD SERVANT. I was sent off with a letter to you, a letter about the earlier one.

CLYTEMESTRA. Did it forbid me to bring my child to die or urge it like the first?

OLD SERVANT. It said not to bring her. Your husband was sane at that moment.

CLYTEMNESTRA. Then how was it, if you had such a letter, that you did not deliver it to me?

OLD SERVANT. Menelaus took it away from me. He is the cause of all this trouble.

CLYTEMNESTRA. O child of the Nereid, O son of Peleus, do you hear this?

ACHILLES. I hear it. I realize your sorrow. But what of my part? I cannot ignore that.

CLYTEMNESTRA. They will kill my child. Your marriage was the snare.

[ACHILLES. I, too, blame your husband. I am *doubly* enraged.]

CLYTEMNESTRA. I shall feel no shame to clasp your knees, I a mortal and you born of a goddess. Why should I make a show of pride? Where should I rather spend my zeal than in my child's interest?

Child of the goddess, champion my distress and hers that was called your wife—falsely so called, but help her for all that. For you I garlanded her and I brought her here to be your bride. Now it is to slaughter I bring her. Upon you reproach will fall, for not defending her. Even though you were not joined in wedlock, still you were called the poor girl's dear husband.

By your beard, by your right hand, by your mother—it is your prestige that ruined me; your prestige ought now to protect me. I have no altar other than your knees for a refuge. No friend has a smile for me. Of Agamemnon you have heard, how cruel he is, how utterly unscrupulous. And here I am, as you see, a woman in an army of sailors, undisciplined sailors, bold for any mischief. Even so they can be helpful if they will. If you will venture to stretch your hand over me we are saved; if not, we are not.

LEADER. Motherhood is a wonderful thing. It possesses a magic power all mothers feel, which makes them undergo any toil for their children's sake.

ACHILLES. My pride runs high and far. But I have learned

to temper my grief in trouble and my joy in prosperity. Such mortals have calculated things to a nicety; they live intelligently. There are times when it is pleasant not to be over wise, there are times when it is useful to possess good sense. Now I was brought up in the house of Chiron, a most godfearing man, and I learned the habit of straightforwardness. And in the case of the sons of Atreus, if their leadership is good, I shall obey them; when it is not good, I shall not obey. Here and in Troy I will keep my nature free, and I shall glorify Ares with my spear, as far as in me lies.

You have been treated wretchedly by your nearest and dearest; all the compassion a soldier can feel I bestow on you. Never shall your daughter that was spoken of as mine be slaughtered by her father. I shall not yield my person to your husband to play tricks with. My very name, a murderer though it never lifted sword, will have killed your child. And your husband is the cause. My very body is no longer pure if this girl must suffer unendurable horrors and incredible outrage, if she must die because of me and my marriage.

I am, it seems, the greatest coward in the army, the veriest cipher, and Menelaus a man; I am no son of Peleus but some fiend's son, if my name commits murder for your husband. By Nereus that was nurtured in the watery waves, by the begetter of Thetis that gave me birth, King Agamemnon shall not lay hands on your daughter. He shall not so much as touch her dress with his finger. Else Sipylus, that barbarian camp, whence the generals' race derives, shall be called a city, and the name of Phthia shall never be mentioned. To his cost will prophet Calchas raise his meal-cakes and lustral waters. Who is your seer? A man who tells one truth for ten lies when he is in luck. When his luck ends, so does he.

It is not for a bride's sake that I say this—ten thousand girls are hunting for marriage with me. But King Agamemnon has insulted me. He ought to have asked me for the use of my name to snare his child. It was my name and fame that persuaded Clytemnestra to surrender her daughter to her husband. I would have *lent* the Hellenes my name, if that were the hitch in the voyage to Ilium. I would not have refused to advance the common interest of my companions in war. But now I am of no account; it is a matter of indifference to the generals whether they treat me well or treat me ill. My sword may have something to say. Before I go to

Phrygia I shall tarnish it with the stain of someone's life-blood, if he tries to wrest your daughter from me.

Keep calm. You see in me a god powerful to save you. If I am not one, I shall become one.

LEADER. Your speech, son of Peleus, is worthy of you and of that revered goddess of the sea.

CLYTEMNESTRA. Ah, how can I praise you with words not too fulsome, [aside] yet not so sparing as to lose his favor? [Aloud.] When good men are praised they get a sort of distaste for those that praise them, if the praise is excessive. I am ashamed to intrude the sorrowful story of my private affliction: you are not suffering from my trouble. But it shows well for a good man to succor the unfortunate, far removed though he be from their trouble. Pity me: my sufferings are pitiful. First I thought I would have you for a son-in-law, and I found that hope empty. Furthermore my child's death might be ominous for your marriage, when you come to marry. It is well to guard against this. But you were right in what you said, first and last: if you decide so, my child shall be saved.

Do you wish her to embrace your knees in supplication? It is not a maiden's part, but if it please you she shall come, with modesty in her frank regard. If my prayer shall prevail without her presence, let her remain at home. She is shy, too shy. But still we must respect her modesty as much as possible.

ACHILLES. Do not bring your child into my sight, lady. Let us not incur the reproach of the vulgar. An army gathered from everywhere and free from home cares loves dirty gossip and slander. In any case you will get no further with supplications than without. My one main task is to deliver you from danger. Hear one thing and be assured: I will not speak falsehood. If I lie, if I delude you to no purpose, let me die. As I live, I shall save the girl.

CLYTEMNESTRA. Bless you again and again for helping the unhappy!

ACHILLES. Hear me now, so that the business may prosper.

CLYTEMNESTRA. What do you mean? You must be heard.

ACHILLES. Let us persuade the father to come to a better mind.

CLYTEMNESTRA. He is a coward who is too afraid of the army.

ACHILLES. Some arguments can overthrow others.

CLYTEMNESTRA. It is a chilly hope. But tell me what I must do.

ACHILLES. First beseech him not to kill the child. If he denies you, then you must come to me. If you persuade him to grant your desire, there is no need for me to intercede; for your salvation will be won. I shall remain on better terms with my friend, nor can the army find fault with me if I accomplish our ends by discretion rather than by force. If this goes well, everything will turn out as you and your friends desire even without my intervention.

CLYTEMNESTRA. These are wise words. I must do as seems best to you. But if, on the other hand, my plans do not prosper, where shall I see you again, where? Must I come and find you, poor wretch that I am, to protect me from evil?

ACHILLES. I shall watch for you in a suitable place, so that no one may see you dashing through the crowd of Danaans in consternation. Do not put the house of your ancestors to shame. Tyndareus must be saved from scandal; his name is great among the Hellenes.

CLYTEMNESTRA. So it is. You give orders, I must be your slave. If there are gods, you, being a righteous man, will obtain their blessing; if not, what need for toil?

[*Exeunt Achilles and Clytemnestra severally.*]

CHORUS. *What was the song Hymenaeus raised on the Libyan flute, to the strains of the dance-loving harp and the piping of reeds, when over Pelion the fair-tressed Pierides came to the feast of the gods, beating the earth with the print of their golden sandals? To Peleus' wedding they came; and their tuneful melodies in the Centaurs' mountain haunts and in the woodlands of Pelion celebrated Thetis and the son of Aeacus. And he of the Dardan line, Phrygian Ganymede, the darling of Zeus' couch, was there to draw libations from wine mixed in the depths of golden bowls. Upon the white gleaming sand Nereus' fifty maidens wove their circling mazes and celebrated the nuptials with their dance.*

*Among the firs with their green crowns came the rout of mounted Centaurs; to the feast of the gods they came, to the bowl of Bacchus. And loud did they cry: "O daughter of Nereus, the seer that is skilled in the lore of Phoebus, even Chiron, has proclaimed that you will bear a son that shall be a great light for Thessaly. He shall come to the Trojan land with the spears and shields of his Myrmidons, and shall set the land of Priam ablaze. He shall be furnished with a suit of mail for his body, golden armor which Hephaestus shall make; he shall have it as the gift of his mother, of Thetis that bore him." On that day the deities blessed the marriage of the first of the noble Nereids, the wedding of Peleus.*

*But your head, Iphigenia, with its clustering tresses, the Argives shall wreathe like a brindled heifer, undefiled, from a rocky cave in the mountains; they will stain a human throat with blood. Not with the shepherds' pipe were you brought up, not with the whistling of the herdsman; but you were reared by your mother's side to be one day decked as a bride for some son of Inachus. How can Shame's face or Virtue's be of avail, when Impiety is enthroned and mortals put Virtue behind them and heed her not, when Lawlessness prevails over laws and it is no longer the common problem of mortals to avoid the displeasure of the gods?*

*[Enter Clytemnestra.]*

CLYTEMNESTRA. I have come out of the house while waiting for my husband; he has been away for a long while from his rooms. My poor child is in tears; she is sounding all the notes of sorrow. For she has heard of the death which her father plans.

I mentioned the man and here he comes. Here is Agamemnon. His guilt will soon be disclosed, his wicked scheming against his own child.

*[Enter Agamemnon.]*

AGAMEMNON. Child of Leda, opportunely I find you outside the house. I may speak to you, apart from the girl, of things which it is improper for brides to hear.

CLYTEMNESTRA. What is it for which you find the occasion so apt?

AGAMEMNON [*abruptly*]. Fetch the child from the house to join her father. The lustral waters are prepared and ready, as are the meal-cakes to throw in the cleansing fire and the victims which must be slain before the marriage ceremony [victims whose dark blood must gush forth for Artemis].

CLYTEMNESTRA. [*aside, as she goes over to the door and speaks inside*]. Fine words you speak, but your deeds—I have no fine words for them. Come, daughter, come out. You know your father's purpose, in any case. Take your brother, Orestes, under your mantle, child, and come. [*Aloud to Agamemnon as Iphigenia enters with Orestes.*] Look, she is here, obedient to your will. For the rest, I shall speak on her behalf and on mine.

AGAMEMNON. Child, why are you crying? Where have those smiles gone? Why do you keep your face to the ground and hold your mantle before your eyes?

CLYTEMNESTRA [to herself]. Where am I to begin the tale of my woes? I can use them all, beginning, end, middle, anywhere.

AGAMEMNON. What is it? How you all conspire to show me faces full of consternation and alarm.

CLYTEMNESTRA. Answer what I shall ask like a man, husband.

AGAMEMNON. No encouragement is necessary. I am willing to be questioned.

CLYTEMNESTRA. This child, yours and mine—are you going to kill her?

AGAMEMNON. Ha! What cruel words! What unjust suspicions!

CLYTEMNESTRA. Keep calm; answer me my first question.

AGAMEMNON. Ask reasonable questions and you will get reasonable answers.

CLYTEMNESTRA. I ask only one question. Answer me that and nothing else.

AGAMEMNON. Holy heavens! My wretched fate!

CLYTEMNESTRA. And mine and hers; one wretched fate for three.

AGAMEMNON. Who has wronged you?

CLYTEMNESTRA. Are you asking me that? This cleverness of yours is not at all clever.

AGAMEMNON. I am ruined. My secrets are betrayed.

CLYTEMNESTRA. I know everything. I have discovered what you intend to do to me; your very silence is a confession, all those groans. Don't tire yourself with much talk.

AGAMEMNON. See, I am silent. What need is there for me to lie and add effrontery to my misfortunes?

CLYTEMNESTRA. Hear me now. I shall make my words plain. We shall use no more twists and riddles.

The first of my reproaches to you is this. You married me against my will, you seized me by force and killed my former husband, Tantalus (son of Thyestes). My babe you wrenched rudely from my breast and crushed him to the ground beneath your tread. The twin sons of Zeus, my brothers, made war upon you on their shining horses, but my aged father, Tyndareus, defended you, when you became his suppliant. And so *you* got me for your wife.

I became reconciled to you, and you will bear me witness that I was a blameless wife toward you and your house. I was temperate in Aphrodite's realm, and I increased your house so that your coming in was joyful and your going out happy. It is a rare catch for a man to win such a consort; to have a bad wife is no rarity at all. I bore you this son after three daughters. Of one of them you will cruelly bereave me. If anyone should ask you why you will kill her, tell me, what will you say? Or must I say it for you? So that Menelaus may have Helen. One's own child is a fine price to pay for a harlot! We buy what we loathe with what we love.

Come, if you go off to war and leave me at home, and are absent a long time, how do you think my heart will feel? As I go through the rooms and see the chairs all empty of her presence, and empty maiden-chambers, I shall sit down with nothing to occupy my mind but tears and continual lamentations [: "He destroyed you, my child, the father that begot you himself killed you, no other, with no other hand. Such is the homecoming he left"]. Already it needs only some slight pretext for me and your daughters left at home to receive you with the welcome you deserve. Do not force me, by heaven, to forget my duty toward you: do not yourself forget your duty. Ah, well. When you sacrifice the child what prayers will you utter? What is the blessing that you will pray for as you butcher your child? Will it be for a woeful homecoming to match your shameful departure? Is it right for *me* to pray for any good for you? Must we not believe the gods are witless if we keep kind thoughts for murderers? When you come to Argos will you embrace your children? Heaven forbids it. Which of your children will look at you, in order to be clasped to your bosom—and put to death?

Did you stay to consider this, or is your only thought to parade your scepter and play the general? This is a fair word you should have spoken to the Argives: "Do you wish, Achaeans, to sail to the land of the Phrygians? Determine by lot whose child must die." That would have been an equitable arrangement, but not that you should make a special offer of your own child as a victim for the Danaans; or that Menelaus should kill Hermione for her mother's sake. Yet it *is* his quarrel. But now I who have been loyal to your bed am to lose my child, while that wanton will keep her young woman safe in Sparta and have all the luck.

Answer me if anything that I say is not correct. But if I
have spoken truly, then do not kill your child and mine, and
you will be sensible.

LEADER. Be persuaded. It is proper for you to join in
saving your child; no man will deny it.

IPHIGENIA. If I had Orpheus' eloquence, father, the power
to charm the rocks and persuade them to follow me, so that
I could bewitch with words whomever I would, I would
have recourse to that art. But now my only art is tears, and
those I offer; *that* I can do. Like a suppliant bough I press
against your knees this body of mine which this woman
bore to you; do not destroy me before my time. It is sweet to
look upon the light: do not force me to see the things below.
I was the first to call you father, the first you called child; I
was the first to relax my body upon your knees, to bestow
loving caresses and to receive them in turn. Then your word
used to be: "Child, shall I see you happy in a husband's house,
alive and flourishing to do me credit?" Then my hand would
cleave to your beard even as it now clings to you, and I
would say: "And how shall I find you, father? Shall I welcome you in your old age into my house with loving
hospitality, and repay you for all the devoted care of my
upbringing?"

These talks I keep in memory, but you have forgotten.
You want to kill me. Ah, no, by Pelops, by your father
Atreus, by my mother here who travailed with me long ago
and is now undergoing this second travail! What have I to
do with Alexander's amours and Helen's? Why must his
coming result in my destruction, father? Look at me, give me
a glance, a kiss, that I may have this at least as a memory
of you when I die, if you will not heed my words.

Brother, little enough help can you be to your friends, but
weep with me; beseech your father that your sister may not
die. [*Orestes wails.*] There is perception of sorrow even
in babes. Look, he has no words, but he implores you, father.

Have mercy upon me, pity my youth. Yes, by your
beard we implore you, devoted both, one a fledgling, the other
a grown girl.

With one brief plea I win my case entirely. Passing sweet
it is for mortals to look upon the light; the nether world is
nothing. A man who prays for death is mad. A poor life is
better than a grand death.

LEADER. Ah, vile Helen! Because of you and your amours a
great trial has come upon the Atreidae and their children.

AGAMEMNON. I am sensible of what is pitiful and what is not, and I love my own children; otherwise I should be mad. It is horrible for me to do this dreadful thing, it is horrible for me not to. It is the same for me either way. You see this huge armada, this multitude of Hellene warriors—for them there can be no voyage against the towers of Ilium unless I sacrifice you as prophet Calchas says; Troy's famous citadel cannot be taken. There rages a passion in the Hellene host to sail with all speed to the barbarian land and to put an end to the rape of Hellene wives. They will kill my daughters in Argos, they will kill you, and me, if I break the gods' oracles. It is not Menelaus that holds me enslaved, child; it is not by his desire that I am guided. It is Hellas for whom I must, whether I wish or not, offer you as sacrifice. I cannot resist the claim of country. Free must she be, as far as you or I can make her. We are Hellenes; we must not allow our women to be violated and carried off by barbarians.

[*Exit*]

CLYTEMNESTRA. *O strangers—and O my child! Woe is me for your death! Your father is running away and leaving you to die.*

IPHIGENIA. *Alas for me, my mother, the same strain of sorrow befits us both. No longer is the light mine, no longer the rays of the sun. Alas, alas! In a snow-clad glen of Phrygia, in a mountain haunt of Ida, Priam once cast forth for the doom of death the tender infant which he tore from its mother, the infant Paris. He was called the child of Ida, the child of Ida was he called when he returned to the city of the Phrygians. Would that he had never been nurtured a herdsman among the kine, never found a home, that Alexander, about the bright waters where the fountains of the Nymphs are, and meadows blooming with verdant flowers, and roses and hyacinths for the goddesses to pluck. There on a time did Pallas come, and crafty Cypris, and Hera, and Hermes, messenger of Zeus. Cypris was vain of the love which she inspires, Pallas of her spear, and Hera of her royal union with Lord Zeus. So they came to that hateful judgment, that strife of beauty, a deadly strife for me. But to the Danaans, O maidens, comes glory thereby; for Artemis accepts the sacrifice for the expedition to Ilium. But he that begot me, ah mother, my mother, he has gone and left me forsaken. Ah the sorry day for me when I first saw Helen,*

*evil Helen, to my cost, to my cost! I am slain, I perish, foully
slaughtered by a godless father. I wish that Aulis had never
received into these havens the sterns of the bronze-beaked
ships, the fleet that speeds the host to Troy. Why should Zeus
raise winds on the Euripus to bar our voyage? He
sends pleasant winds to other men, for happy sailing. Many
are his winds: [winds of sorrow and winds of hardship,]
winds to set sail in and winds to drop sail in, and winds of
waiting. Mortals are born to sorrow,·ay, creatures of a day
and born to sorrow; they fulfil their destiny in misery.*

*Alas, alas! Great is the suffering, great the pain, which the
Tyndarid brings upon the sons of the Danaans.*

LEADER. I pity you for the sorrow that has come to you; I
wish you could have been spared it.

IPHIGENIA. Mother, my mother, I see a crowd of men
draw near.

CLYTEMNESTRA. It is the goddess' son, my child, for whom
you came here.

IPHIGENIA. Open the house, servants, I will hide myself.

CLYTEMNESTRA. Why do you run away, child?

IPHIGENIA. I am ashamed to see this Achilles.

CLYTEMNESTRA. Why?

IPHIGENIA. This marriage, this unhappy marriage embar-
rasses me.

CLYTEMNESTRA. You cannot be fastidious in your plight.
Stay, I tell you. This is no time for shyness, if we can help
ourselves.

[*Enter Achilles hurriedly*]

ACHILLES. Ah, daughter of Leda, unhappy lady——

CLYTEMNESTRA. That is no lie.

ACHILLES. There are fearful clamors among the Argives——

CLYTEMNESTRA. What is the clamor? Tell me.

ACHILLES. About your child. They say——

CLYTEMNESTRA. There is an evil omen in your words.

ACHILLES. That she must be sacrificed.

CLYTEMNESTRA. Does no one uphold the other side?

ACHILLES. I myself got into some danger.

CLYTEMNESTRA. What danger, friend?

ACHILLES. Of being pelted with stones.

CLYTEMNESTRA. In trying to save my daughter?

ACHILLES. Exactly.

CLYTEMNESTRA. Who was so bold as to touch your person?

ACHILLES. All the Hellenes.

CLYTEMNESTRA. Wasn't your Myrmidon force there with you?

ACHILLES. It was the first to show hostility.

CLYTEMNESTRA. Child, it is the end for us.

ACHILLES. Why, they abused me, called me uxorious.

CLYTEMNESTRA. And what did you answer?

ACHILLES. That they should not kill the bride that was meant for me——

CLYTEMNESTRA. That was right.

ACHILLES. Whom her father had promised me.

CLYTEMNESTRA. He even fetched her from Argos.

ACHILLES. But I was beaten by the tumult.

CLYTEMNESTRA. The rabble is a curse.

ACHILLES. Even so I will protect you.

CLYTEMNESTRA. Will you fight against the crowd single-handed?

ACHILLES. You see my armor-bearers here?

CLYTEMNESTRA. May your generous temper be rewarded!

ACHILLES. I *shall* have my reward.

CLYTEMNESTRA. Then the child will not now be slaughtered?

ACHILLES. Never, with my consent.

CLYTEMNESTRA. Will some one come to lay hold of the girl?

ACHILLES. Yes, a host of them. Odysseus will lead them.

CLYTEMNESTRA. Sisyphus' seed, is it?

ACHILLES. The very man.

CLYTEMNESTRA. On his own account, or is he charged to do it by the army?

ACHILLES. Chosen—a willing servant.

CLYTEMNESTRA. A wicked choice—to perpetrate murder!

ACHILLES. But I shall stop him.

CLYTEMNESTRA. Will he seize her and drag her off even if she is unwilling?

ACHILLES. Of course, even by her golden hair.

CLYTEMNESTRA. What must I do then?

ACHILLES. Cling to your daughter.

CLYTEMNESTRA. If that is all, she shall not die.

ACHILLES. But it will come to that.

IPHIGENIA. Mother—hear you my words, both. I see you are angry at your husband to no purpose; where the odds are impossible it is hard to resist. It is only right that we commend this stranger for his zeal; but at the same time you must see that his name does not suffer with the army. We should be no better off, and for him it would be a misfortune.

But here, mother, the thought that occurred to me as I pondered the thing. I am resolved to die. And I will do it gloriously. I have put all mean thoughts out of my heart. Come, see it with me, mother, see how right I am. The whole might of Hellas depends on me. Upon me depends the passage of the ships over the sea, and the overthrow of the Phrygians. With me it rests to prevent the barbarians from carrying our women off from happy Hellas in the future, should they attempt such a thing. [They will pay for the bane of Helen whom Paris stole.] All these things I shall achieve by my death, and my name, as the liberator of Hellas, shall be blessed. Indeed, it behooves me not to be too fond of life; you bore me for the common good of all the Hellenes, not for yourself alone. Ten thousand men are armed with shields, ten thousand men have oars in their hands; their country has been wronged and they have the courage to do brave deeds against the foe and to die on behalf of Hellas. Shall my single life be a hindrance to all this? Where is the justice in it? What word have we for answer?

I come to another point. It is not right that this man come to blows with all the Argives and die for a woman's sake. One man is worthier to look upon the light than ten thousand women. If Artemis has willed to take my body, shall I, a mortal woman, thwart the goddess? It cannot be. I give my body to Hellas. Sacrifice me, sack Troy. That will be my monument for long ages, that will be my children, my marriage, my good name. It is natural for Hellenes to rule barbarians, and not, mother, for barbarians to rule Hellenes. They are a slave race, Hellenes are free.

LEADER. Your part, young woman, you carry nobly; it is fortune's part and the goddess' that is at fault.

ACHILLES. Child of Agamemnon, one of the gods meant to make me happy, if I won you for my wife. I count Hellas blessed in you, and you blessed in Hellas. Noble were your words, and a credit to your fatherland. You gave up battling with the gods who are stronger than you. You faced necessity and saw your duty. All the more does a yearning for your love come upon me when I look at your character; for you *are* noble. Look now, I am eager to do you a kindness, eager to win you for my house. It will be *my* sorrow—be

Thetis my witness—if I do not fight the Danaans and save your life. Consider; death is a fearful thing.

IPHIGENIA. I say this [without misgivings of any sort]. The Tyndarid woman has done enough by *her* beauty to cause quarrels and bloodshed among men. Do not die for me, stranger; and do not kill anyone. Let me save Hellas, if I may.

ACHILLES. Ah, noble soul! I have nothing further to say if that is your decision. Your sentiments are noble! Why should a man not confess the truth? And yet, in case you happen to change your mind [, I speak *my* mind for you to know,] I shall go and put my weapons near the altar, ready not to let you die but to prevent it. Perhaps you will make use of my offer when you see the sword near your throat.

No, I shall not let you die for a mad impulse. I shall go to the goddess' temple with these weapons and await your presence there.

[*Exit.*]

IPHIGENIA. Mother, why do you wet your eyes with tears? Speak to me.

CLYTEMNESTRA. I have reason, ah me, for my heart to ache.

IPHIGENIA. Do stop. Do not make me a coward. Humor me in this.

CLYTEMNESTRA. Speak, child; you will get justice from *me*.

IPHIGENIA. Do not cut your clustering hair, do not swathe yourself in black robes.

CLYTEMNESTRA. Why do you say this, child? When I have lost you?

IPHIGENIA. But you have not. I am saved and you will be famous through me.

CLYTEMNESTRA. What do you say? Must I not mourn for your life?

IPHIGENIA. Not at all, for no tomb will be heaped up for me.

CLYTEMNESTRA. What then? It is the dead, not the tomb, men mourn.

IPHIGENIA. The altar of the goddess, the daughter of Zeus, is my memorial——

CLYTEMNESTRA. Yes, child, I will do as you say, you are right.

IPHIGENIA. For I am blessed. I am a benefactress of Hellas.

CLYTEMNESTRA. What message shall I take to your sisters?

IPHIGENIA. Do not put black robes on them either.

CLYTEMNESTRA. Shall I give the girls some word of love from you?

IPHIGENIA. Bid them farewell. See that you raise Orestes here to be a man.

CLYTEMNESTRA. Embrace him; you see him for the last time.

IPHIGENIA [to Orestes]. Ah, dearest, you helped your friends all you could.

CLYTEMNESTRA. Is there anything I can do in Argos to please you?

IPHIGENIA. Do not hate my father, your husband.

CLYTEMNESTRA. A fearful race must he run because of you.

IPHIGENIA. He did not wish it. It was for Hellas that he destroyed me.

CLYTEMNESTRA. By treachery and cowardice unworthy of Atreus.

IPHIGENIA. Who will lead me there before they drag me by the hair?

CLYTEMNESTRA. I will go with you——

IPHIGENIA. Not you, that is wrong.

CLYTEMNESTRA. I will cling to your robes.

IPHIGENIA. Heed me, mother, stay. It is better so for me and for you. Let one of my father's henchmen here conduct me to the meadow of Artemis where I am to be slain.

CLYTEMNESTRA. Ah, child, are you going?

IPHIGENIA. And I shall never, never return.

CLYTEMNESTRA. Are you leaving your mother?

IPHIGENIA. As you see; with a brave heart.

CLYTEMNESTRA. Stop, do not leave me!

IPHIGENIA. I forbid you to shed tears. [Clytemnestra sinks to the ground.] Do you, young women, raise with good omen the paean for my lot, to Zeus' maid, Artemis. Let a solemn silence be proclaimed for the Danaans. Let someone initiate the rites with the sacred baskets; let the fire blaze with the cakes of purification and let my father circle the altar from the left toward the right. I come to bring the Hellenes salvation and victory.

*Lead me, a sacker of cities, of Troy and of Phrygia. Give me garlands to put on—here is my hair to crown. Bring me fountains of lustral water. Weave the dance about the temple, about the altar of Artemis, about Queen Artemis the blessed.*

*With my blood, if I must, with my sacrifice I shall wash away
her oracle's bidding. Ah, revered mother, mother revered, my
tears I shall not give you; at the sanctuary tears may not flow.
Ho, damsels, ho! Join with me in singing the praise of Artemis
who is worshipped over against Chalcis, where now in the
narrow haven of Aulis by reason of me the angry spearmen
are thirsting for the fight. Ho, Pelasgia my motherland, and
Mycenae my home!*

CHORUS. *Are you calling on the city of Perseus, which
the Cyclopes labored to build?*

IPHIGENIA. *For a light unto Hellas you nurtured me: I do
not shirk death.*

CHORUS. *Fame shall never forsake you.*

IPHIGENIA. *Ho, Day the Light-bringer, ho, radiance of
Zeus! Another life, another state will be mine. Farewell, beloved light.*

[*Iphigenia departs. Clytemnestra goes into the tent.*]

CHORUS. *Ho! Ho! Look upon the sacker of cities, of Troy
and of Phrygia, as she goes to have garlands put upon her
head and sprinklings of lustral water; she goes to stain with
the drops of flowing blood the altar of the divine goddess
and her own throat, her body's lovely throat. The dewy
sprinklings of your father await you, and the lustral bowls,
and the army of the Achaeans eager to proceed to Troy. But
let us celebrate Zeus' maid, let us celebrate Artemis, queen
of the gods. We hope for a happy destiny. O Lady, revered
Lady, by the sacrifice of a human victim made propitious,
send upon its way to the Phrygians' land and the treacherous
abodes of Troy the host of the Hellenes, and grant that
Agamemnon may wreathe the Hellene lances with a crown
of fame, and his own brows with imperishable glory.*

[FROM THIS POINT ON THE GREEK BECOMES MORE AND
MORE SUSPECT.]

[*Enter Second Messenger.*]

MESSENGER. Child of Tyndareus, Clytemnestra, come forth
that you may hear my words.

[*Enter Clytemnestra.*]

CLYTEMNESTRA. I come at the sound of your voice; I am

wretched with shock and distracted with fear. You are not bringing me a fresh calamity to add to what I have?

MESSENGER. Touching your child I wish to tell you wonderful and fearful things.

CLYTEMNESTRA. Then do not delay, but speak with all speed.

MESSENGER. Yes, dear mistress, you shall learn it all. I shall be clear and tell it from the beginning, unless my mind falters and disturbs my tongue in its telling.

When we arrived at the precinct of Zeus' maid Artemis, at her flower-laden meadow, and brought your child to the place where was the muster of the Achaean host, a crowd of Argives collected at once. When King Agamemnon saw the girl marching to the precinct for slaughter he heaved a sigh, and turned his head aside and wept, holding his robe before his eyes.

But the maiden took her stand next to him that begot her and she said: "Father, I am here, at your bidding. My body I freely give on behalf of my own country and on behalf of all the land of Hellas. Lead me to the altar to sacrifice, if so it is ordained. May you prosper as far as rests in me. May you attain the prize of victory, and win back to your native land. Therefore let no Argive lay hands on me; quietly, and with good courage, I will offer my throat."

So she spoke, and everyone was astonished on hearing the maiden's heroism and her virtue. Then Talthybius, whose charge it was, stood forth and proclaimed reverent silence and attention through the army. Then Calchas, the seer, put into the gold-studded basket a sharp knife which his hand drew out of its scabbard, and he crowned the maiden's head. The son of Peleus circled the goddess' altar holding the basket, and at the same time sprinkled the lustral water; and he said, "Child of Zeus, slayer of wild beasts, whirler of the gleaming light by night, receive this sacrifice which we offer you, the host of the Achaeans and King Agamemnon, the undefiled blood of a fair maiden's throat; grant an untroubled voyage for our ships, grant that our spears may sack the towers of Troy."

The priest grasped his knife and prayed and sought where he should strike the throat. No small anguish troubled my soul, and I stood with head downcast. Suddenly there was a marvel to behold. Every man clearly heard the sound of the stroke, but no one saw where in the world the maiden van-

ished. The priest cried out and the whole army echoed his
shout as they saw an amazing prodigy from some god, incredible even if they saw it. A deer was lying on the ground,
gasping: she was very large and handsome to see, and the
goddess' altar was thoroughly sprinkled with her blood. Then
Calchas said—with what joy do you suppose?—, "Chiefs of
this common host of Achaeans, do you see this victim which
the goddess has laid before her altar, this deer of the hills?
More acceptable than the maid by far she welcomes this offering, that she may not stain her altar with noble blood. Gladly has she received the sacrifice, and she grants us a favorable
voyage and a successful invasion of Ilium. Therefore, let
every mariner raise his courage and march to his ship, for on
this day we must leave the hollow bay of Aulis and sail over
the Aegean main." When the whole victim had been reduced
to ashes in Hephaestus' flame, he offered the suitable prayer,
that the army might attain to a homecoming. Agamemnon
has sent me to tell you these things and to say what fortune
he has received from the gods, what deathless fame he has
got throughout Hellas. I was there, and I tell you the thing
as I saw it. Clearly, your child has been wafted to the gods.

Away with your grief then. Put aside your anger against
your husband. Inscrutable to mortals are the ways of the
gods, but whom they love they preserve. This day has seen
your child dead and alive again.

LEADER. How rejoiced I am to hear the messenger's words.
He says your child lives and abides among the gods.

CLYTEMNESTRA. My child, what god has stolen you? How
shall I address you? What shall I say? Is this an idle story
to comfort me, to end my bitter grief for you?

LEADER. Here comes King Agamemnon, with the same
story to tell you.

[*Enter Agamemnon.*]

AGAMEMNON. Lady, on our daughter's account we may be
happy, for she truly possesses fellowship with the gods. You
must take this noble youngling and journey home. The army
is looking to the voyage. Farewell, it will be long before I address you again—after Troy. May things go well with you.

CHORUS. *With joy, son of Atreus, go to the Phrygian land,
and with joy return, when you have taken splendid spoils, I
pray, from Troy.*

[*Exeunt.*]

\*        \*        \*        \*        \*        \*        \*

The following occurs in Aelian, *Historia animalium* 7.39: "Euripides in his Iphigenia says, 'I shall put a horned deer into the Achaeans' dear hands, and they shall imagine, as they sacrifice it, that they are sacrificing your daughter.' "

Porson recognized that this fragment was from a speech of Artemis, speaking *ex machina,* consoling Clytemnestra. This item constitutes additional proof that the ending of the play as we have it is spurious.

# Glossary

This list is by no means a complete list of Proper Names. It is intended merely to afford the reader some assistance with mythological or topographical allusions.

ADRASTEIA, goddess of inevitable destiny, generally retributive

AEACUS, father of Peleus, father of Achilles; and also of Telamon, father of Ajax

AGENOR, father of Cadmus, Phoenix, Cilix, founders respectively of Thebes, Phoenicia, Cilicia

ALCATHOUS, son of Pelops, king of Megara

ALEXANDER, a name of Paris

ALPHEUS, river at Olympia

AMMON, Egyptian god identified with Zeus

AMPHION, son of Zeus and Antiope, moved the stones of Thebes into place by his music. His monument was a landmark near Thebes

AMYMONE, fountain at Argos, for which it stands

ASOPUS, river (and river-god) of Thebes

ATREUS, son of Pelops and Hippodamia, brother of Thyestes, father of Menelaus and Agamemnon. He had a golden lamb which was regarded as assuring sovereignty to its possessor

BROMIUS, a surname of Bacchus

CADMUS, son of Agenor of Phoenicia, founder of Thebes

CALLISTO, Arcadian nymph changed by Hera into a bear

CASSANDRA, daughter of Priam and Hecuba. She had the gift of prophecy from Apollo, but was doomed never to be trusted. Ajax dragged her from the altar of Athena at Troy. She was brought by Agamemnon to Mycenae, where she was killed by Clytemnestra

CASTALIA, spring near Delphi sacred to Apollo and the Muses

CECROPS, first king of Attica

CENTAURS, a savage and dissolute race of Thessaly conceived of as half man and half horse. As guests at the wedding of the Lapith king Pirithous they attempted to seize the women

CEPHALUS, faithful husband of Procris who was carried off for his beauty by the goddess Eos (Dawn)

CEPHISUS, river of Athens

CHIRON, Centaur teacher of Achilles

CITHAERON, mountain near Thebes

COLCHIS, Medea's original home, at the remote end of the Black Sea

CORA, ("the Maid") used for Persephone

CORYBANTS, priests of the orgiastic cult of Cybele

CYCLOPEAN, primitive masonry of large, irregular blocks, attributed to the Titans

CYPRIS, Aphrodite

DANAUS, father of fifty Danaids engaged to the fifty sons of his brother Aegyptus. Removing to Argos he became so powerful a king that later the Greeks were called Danaans

DARDANUS, founder of the royal family of Troy

DELOS, island, birthplace of Apollo and of Artemis

DICTYNNA, Artemis

DIONYSUS, god of the vine and of enthusiasm. He was prematurely born of his mother Semele, but Zeus sewed him into his own thigh and kept him there until he was mature for birth. He was reared by nymphs on Mount Nysa

DIOSCURI, Castor and Polydeuces, sons of Leda and Zeus (who visited her in the shape of a swan), brothers of Helen. They were regarded as helpers of men, particularly in distress at sea

DIRCE, wife of Lycus, king of Thebes; she was killed by being tied to a bull by her hair. Also, a fountain at Thebes

EINODIA, Hecate

ERECHTHEUS, early king of Athens, who introduced the worship of Athena and other elements of civilization

ERINYES, Furies

EUROTAS, river at Sparta

EURYSTHEUS, king of Mycenae, by the machination of Hera master over Heracles, whom he sent upon labors

GORGON, representation of a Medusa head, used as an emblem on shields for its horrific effect

HELENUS, son of Priam and Hecuba who possessed the gift of prophecy; ultimately he married Andromache, after both had been captives

IDA, mountain-range in Asia Minor which was the scene of the judgment of Paris, the rape of Ganymede, the worship of Cybele

INACHUS, river at Argos

IO, daughter of Inachus, changed by Zeus into a heifer to protect her from Hera. Hera set Argus to watch her, and, after Hermes killed Argus, a gad-fly whose sting drove her over Europe and Asia

ISMENUS, river of Thebes

LAOMEDON, king of Troy, father of Priam

LEDA, wife of Tyndareus, king of Sparta; mother of Castor, Polydeuces, Clytemnestra, Helen

LETO, mother of Apollo and Artemis, to whom she gave birth on Delos, which until that time had been a floating island

LOXIAS, Apollo

MINYAE, people of Orchomenus; frequently applied to Argonauts

MYRTILUS, Oenomaus' charioteer, by whose treachery Pelops won the race for the hand of Hippodamia. His dying curse when Pelops threw him into the sea brought woe upon the house of Pelops

NAUPLIUS, in revenge for an injury, by means of false beacons lured to their destruction the Greeks homeward bound from Troy. NAUPLIA was the Argive harbor

NEREUS, kindly, prophetic sea-divinity, father of the fifty Nereids, of whom the best known is Thetis, mother of Achilles by Peleus

OCEAN, the river that flowed in a circle round the edge of the earth

OENOMAUS, king of Pisa in Elis, who required his daughter Hippodamia's suitors to race with him. He was defeated by Pelops through the connivance of his charioteer Myrtilus

PARNASSUS, mountain at Delphi, sacred to Apollo and the Muses

PIRENE, fountain at Corinth

PELASGIA, Argos

PELOPS, son of Tantalus, won his bride Hippodamia by defeating her father Oenomaus in a chariot race; father of Atreus and Thyestes, and so grandfather of Menelaus, Agamemnon, Aegisthus

PERGAMUM, Troy

PERSEUS, son of Zeus and Danae, ruler of Argos and Tiryns

PROCNE, wife of Tereus of Thrace and mother of Itys: when Tereus violated her sister Philomela and cut out her tongue she killed Itys and served him to his father. Subsequently she and her sister and husband were turned into birds

SCAMANDER, river at Troy

SEMELE, daughter of Cadmus and Harmonia, mother of Dionysus. By the machination of Hera she was destroyed, but Zeus saved Dionysus, her son and his. Subsequently she became a goddess

Simois, river at Troy

Sown, The (Spartoi), warriors that sprang from the dragon's teeth sown by Cadmus at Thebes

Symplegades, clashing rocks that guarded the entrance to the Euxine

Thyestes, son of Pelops and Hippodamia, brother of Atreus, father of Aegisthus by his own daughter Pelopia. He seduced Aerope, wife of Atreus, and in punishment was made to eat the flesh of his own son

Zethus, builder of Thebes with his brother Amphion

Bantam Classics bring you the world's greatest literature—books that have stood the test of time—at specially low prices. These beautifully designed books
will be proud additions to your bookshelf. You'll
want all these time-tested classics for your own
reading pleasure.

### JANE AUSTEN

| | | | |
|---|---|---|---|
| ☐ | 21197 | **NORTHANGER ABBEY** | $2.50 |
| ☐ | 21159 | **EMMA** | $1.50 |
| ☐ | 21121 | **MANSFIELD PARK** | $3.50 |
| ☐ | 21137 | **PERSUASION** | $2.95 |
| ☐ | 21154 | **PRIDE & PREJUDICE** | $1.75 |
| ☐ | 21110 | **SENSE AND SENSIBILITY** | $2.50 |

| | | | |
|---|---|---|---|
| ☐ | 21148 | **DRACULA** Bram Stoker | $1.95 |
| ☐ | 21172 | **FRANKENSTEIN** Mary Shelley | $1.75 |
| ☐ | 21171 | **ANNA KARENINA** Leo Tolstoy | $2.95 |
| ☐ | 21035 | **THE DEATH OF IVAN ILYICH** Leo Tolstoy | $1.95 |
| ☐ | 21216 | **THE BROTHERS KARAMAZOV** Fyodor Dostoevsky | $3.95 |
| ☐ | 21175 | **CRIME AND PUNISHMENT** Fyodor Dostoevsky | $2.50 |
| ☐ | 21136 | **THE IDIOT** Fyodor Dostoevsky | $3.50 |
| ☐ | 21166 | **CANDIDE** Voltaire | $2.25 |
| ☐ | 21187 | **THE COUNT OF MONTE CRISTO** Alexandre Dumas | $3.50 |
| ☐ | 21118 | **CYRANO DE BERGERAC** Edmond Rostand | $1.75 |
| ☐ | 21032 | **THE HUNCHBACK OF NOTRE DAME** Victor Hugo | $1.95 |

---

### Prices and availability subject to change without notice.

**Buy them at your local bookstore or use this handy coupon for ordering:**

These books have been bestsellers for generations of readers. Bantam Classics now bring you the world's greatest literature in specially low-priced editions. From the American epic Moby Dick to Dostoevsky's towering works, you'll want all these time-tested classics for your own.

| | | | |
|---|---|---|---|
| ☐ | 21128 | THE ADVENTURES OF TOM SAWYER | $1.75 |
| ☐ | 21079 | THE ADVENTURES OF HUCKLEBERRY FINN | $1.75 |
| ☐ | 21143 | A CONNECTICUT YANKEE IN KING ARTHUR'S COURT | $1.95 |
| ☐ | 21142 | LIFE ON THE MISSISSIPPI | $1.95 |
| ☐ | 21150 | PRINCE AND THE PAUPER | $1.95 |
| ☐ | 21158 | PUDD'NHEAD WILSON | $1.95 |
| ☐ | 21185 | THE CALL OF THE WILD/WHITE FANG  Jack London | $1.95 |
| ☐ | 21103 | THE LAST OF THE MOHICANS  James Fenimore Cooper | $2.50 |
| ☐ | 21007 | MOBY DICK Herman Melville | $1.95 |
| ☐ | 21011 | THE RED BADGE OF COURAGE  Stephen Crane | $1.50 |
| ☐ | 21009 | THE SCARLET LETTER Nathaniel Hawthorne | $1.50 |
| ☐ | 21218 | UNCLE TOM'S CABIN  Harriet Beecher Stowe | $2.95 |
| ☐ | 21139 | WALDEN AND OTHER WRITINGS Thoreau | $1.95 |
| ☐ | 21094 | BILLY BUDD Herman Melville | $1.95 |
| ☐ | 21200 | DR. JEKYLL and MR. HYDE  Robert Louis Stevenson | $2.50 |
| ☐ | 21099 | TREASURE ISLAND Robert Louis Stevenson | $1.75 |
| ☐ | 21067 | KIDNAPPED Robert Louis Stevenson | $1.50 |

**Prices and availability subject to change without notice.**

Buy them at your local bookstore or use this handy coupon for ordering:

Bantam Books, Inc., Dept. CL2, 414 East Golf Road, Des Plaines, Ill. 60016

Please send me the books I have checked above. I am enclosing $_____ (please add $1.25 to cover postage and handling). Send check or money order —no cash or C.O.D.'s please.

Mr/Mrs/Miss _____

Address_____

City_____ State/Zip_____

CL2—11/85

Please allow four to six weeks for delivery. This offer expires 5/86.

Bantam Classics bring you the world's greatest literature—books that have stood the test of time—at specially low prices. These beautifully designed books will be proud additions to your bookshelf. You'll want all these time-tested classics for your own reading pleasure.

*Titles by Charles Dickens*

| | | |
|---|---|---|
| ☐ 21123 | **THE PICKWICK PAPERS** | $4.95 |
| ☐ 21193 | **BLEAK HOUSE** | $4.95 |
| ☐ 21086 | **NICHOLAS NICKLEBY** | $4.50 |
| ☐ 21189 | **DAVID COPPERFIELD** | $3.50 |
| ☐ 21113 | **GREAT EXPECTATIONS** | $2.50 |
| ☐ 21176 | **A TALE OF TWO CITIES** | $2.25 |
| ☐ 21016 | **HARD TIMES** | $1.95 |

*Titles by Thomas Hardy:*

| | | |
|---|---|---|
| ☐ 21191 | **JUDE THE OBSCURE** | $2.95 |
| ☐ 21024 | **THE MAYOR OF CASTERBRIDGE** | $1.95 |
| ☐ 21080 | **THE RETURN OF THE NATIVE** | $1.95 |
| ☐ 21168 | **TESS OF THE D'URBERVILLES** | $2.95 |
| ☐ 21131 | **FAR FROM THE MADDING CROWD** | $2.75 |

| | | |
|---|---|---|
| ☐ 21059 | **THE TURN OF THE SCREW AND OTHER SHORT FICTION** Henry James | $1.95 |
| ☐ 21141 | **WUTHERING HEIGHTS** Emily Brontë | $1.95 |
| ☐ 21149 | **LADY CHATTERLEY'S LOVER** D. H. Lawrence | $2.75 |
| ☐ 21159 | **EMMA** Jane Austen | $1.95 |

**Prices and availability subject to change without notice.**

Buy them at your local bookstore or use this handy coupon for ordering:

---

Bantam Books, Inc., Dept. CL3, 414 East Golf Road, Des Plaines, Ill. 60016

Please send me the books I have checked above. I am enclosing $_____ (please add $1.25 to cover postage and handling). Send check or money order —no cash or C.O.D.'s please.

Mr/Mrs/Miss _____

Address_____

City_____ State/Zip_____

CL3—12/85

Please allow four to six weeks for delivery. This offer expires 6/86.

# Special Offer
# Buy a Bantam Book
## *for only 50¢.*

Now you can have an up-to-date listing of Bantam's hundreds of titles plus take advantage of our unique and exciting bonus book offer. A special offer which gives you the opportunity to purchase a Bantam book for only 50¢. Here's how!

By ordering any five books at the regular price per order, you can also choose any other single book listed (up to a $4.95 value) for just 50¢. Some restrictions do apply, but for further details why not send for Bantam's listing of titles today!

Just send us your name and address and we will send you a catalog!